The
Relevance
of Reason

ALSO BY MACK W. BORGEN

The Relevance of Reason—Business and Politics

The
Relevance
of Reason

The **Hard Facts** and **Real Data** About the State of Current America

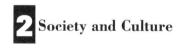

2 Society and Culture

MACK W. BORGEN

Brody
& Schmitt
Publishers

Santa Barbara, CA

© 2013 by Mack W. Borgen

 Brody & Schmitt Publishers
3905 State Street, Suite 7-294
Santa Barbara, California 93105
Brody and Schmitt Publishers is an Imprint of Summerland Publishing, CA.

First Edition

Brody & Schmitt books may be purchased for educational and business purposes. For information, please write, Brody & Schmitt Publishers—Special Markets, 3905 State Street, Suite 7-294, Santa Barbara, CA 93105.

Printed in the United States of America

Publisher's Cataloging-In-Publication
Borgen, Mack W.

The relevance of reason. 2. Society and culture : the hard facts and real data about the state of current America / Mack W. Borgen. -- 1st ed. -- Santa Barbara, CA : Brody & Schmitt Pub., c2013.

p. ; cm.

(The chance of a lifetime series)

ISBN: 978-0-9893996-3-0 (cloth) ; 978-0-9893996-4-7 (trade pbk) ; 978-0-9893996-5-4 (ebook)
Includes bibliographical references and index.
Summary: This book is written in response to one of the great paradoxes of modern life, the Age of Information-- that hard facts and real data are hard to find. The author's aim is to neutrally present a wealth of facts about American society and culture so that people of all political persuasions and economic levels can engage in thoughtful consideration of what's wrong and how we may make it right. The book is the companion book to the previously-published "The relevance of reason - business and politics."--Publisher.

1. United States--Politics and government--21st century. 2. Social values--United States. 3. United States--Social conditions--21st century. 4. United States--Environmental conditions--21st century. 5. United States--Civilization--21st century. 6. National characteristics, American--21st century. 7. Conduct of life. 8. Popular culture--United States. 9. United States--Social policy. 10. United States--Population. I. Title. II. Series.

JK275 .B672 2013   2013948321

973.93--dc23   1309

Book Consultant: Ellen Reid
Editing: Pamela Guerrieri and Gabriella West
Cover Design: George Foster
Interior Design: Ghislain Viau

To My Close Friends and Family Members,

Who over many years,
Have displayed to me their goodness,
Have offered to me their inspiration,
and
At times and when so needed,
Have shared with me their guidance.

NOTE TO READERS

This book, *The Relevance of Reason—Society and Culture,* is the companion book to the author's recently-published book *The Relevance of Reason—Business and Politics.* Both books seek to present the hard facts and real data about the state of Current America. The initial book focused upon facts and data relating to American business and politics. This book focuses upon facts and data relating to American society and culture.

Thus, the entire data sections, which discuss these various aspects of American society and culture and which are set forth in this book at Chapters 6 through 12, are entirely new. However, the genesis, purposes, assumptions, and underlying methodologies of both of these companion books are the same. Therefore, the Preface, Introduction, and Chapters 1 through 5 in this book, *The Relevance of Reason—Society and Culture,* are largely unchanged (excepting some minor corrections, modifications, and updates) from that previously presented in *The Relevance of Reason— Business and Politics.* Even though you may have read the prior companion book, you are invited, indeed encouraged, to re-read these sections in this book. However, you may wish to proceed directly to Chapter 6.

Table of Contents

PART IV

Housing, Education, and Health

PART V

American Life, Entertainment, Religion, and Culture

Appendices

It is not what you look at ...,
It is what you see.

Henry David Thoreau

and

It is not what you think,
It is what you know.

Preface
From Dutch Harbor to Key West

Dutch Harbor, Alaska is a tough and remote place. It is located 800 miles southwest of Anchorage. It is a small town built on two small islands on the edge of the Bering Sea. It is windy, cold, and usually foggy. And it is wet—225 rain days a year. It is one of the wettest places in the United States, and the dark of winter is never far away.

The town has only 927 households and 7 miles of paved roads, but it is home to the largest, by volume, fishing port in the country. There is one daily flight in and out of its small airport, but in the summer months, there's a ferry every other week from Kodiak.

The town has one hotel, the 112-room, Grand Aleutian Hotel, but it has several bars, One of them is dubiously-named the Cape Cheerful Lounge. The men drink their whiskey and down their beer. With deep laughs and tobacco-crusted voices, they exchange their stories; and, like the rest of us, they stretch their truths. Dutch Harbor's mayor says on the town's website that "(l)ife is good on our island," and I have no reason to doubt her. Indeed, Dutch Harbor has a long history and much of which to be proud. However, most of us have never been there, and most of us never will. We live elsewhere. We are warmly content to see Dutch Harbor through the lens of the *Deadliest Catch* camera crews who have been hanging around since 2005. We know of Dutch Harbor only as a distant audience. Without feeling the wind, the cold, the rain, and the isolation of that small town, we watch our TVs. Each week we root for our favorite ships—*The Time Bandit*, the *Northwestern*, and the *Cornelia Marie*. It is easy to forget that Dutch Harbor, even though distant, tough and remote, is part of America.

At the opposite corner of the country, on another island, at the end of another road, and also far removed, there is Key West, Florida. But unlike Dutch Harbor, Key West is not a tough place. It is neither cold nor rainy. Instead, it's hot and sunny—awash in nearly 285 hours of sunshine a month. It is not windy or foggy. Instead, it's balmy, clear and bright. It's not near Russia; it's near Cuba which is just 94 miles away. Unlike in Dutch Harbor, the beer in Key West is served with little limes. There is no Cape Cheerful Lounge. Instead, mai tais and pina coladas are served at places like the Rum Barrel and the Six-Toed Cat. And Key West has crowds. Nearly 860,000 tourists arrive annually and disembark off of their sweet-named cruise ships. There is fishing in Key West, but it's done for sport and not for income and survival. Key West, like Dutch Harbor, is remote, but the population in Key West lives in comfort, if not luxury. There is no *Time Bandit* or *Cornelia Marie*, but Key West has its own history. This is where Hemingway wrote *For Whom the Bell Tolls* and Tennessee Williams wrote *A Streetcar Named Desire*. The people of Key West are there more by choice than by the coincidence of the longitude and latitude of their birth. Even though likewise distant and remote, Key West is also a part of America, and in that sense there are strong bindings of commonality between the residents of Dutch Harbor and Key West.

The citizens of Dutch Harbor and Key West are governed by the same 4,543 words of the U.S. Constitution—the oldest and shortest written Constitution of any major government in the world.

They face the same electoral choices in the presidential election. They are subject to the same federal laws. They carry the same passports, and in many ways they share parallel, albeit probably different, dreams and aspirations. Since America's purchase of the former Russian colony of Alaska from the Russian Empire in 1867 nearly 150 years ago, Dutch Harbor and Key West have shared the same national history.

With enough patience, energy, and gas money, you can even drive from Dutch Harbor to Key West. But it's a long way. It is over 6,100 miles.

It takes Google Maps five pages to spit out the directions. You'll drive through fourteen states. You'll need to make 89 turns onto new highways. But you will see a lot of America. America is big.

You will cross the expanse of Alaska and through the deep green forests of Northwestern Montana. You will splice your way through the Rockies and drive through the Badlands of the Dakotas. You'll see the small towns and the big fields of the Great Plains. Depending on which way you go, you can see the oil derricks of Oklahoma or the lakes and streams of the Ozarks. You will see many different Americas—the large cities with freeways and skylines and the small towns with nothing more than grain elevators and a junction store. You can stop by Bourbon Street and measure the recovery of New Orleans. You can drive by the great plantation houses of Vicksburg and the Old South. You can rest up in Pensacola, and you can dry out or drink up in Fort Lauderdale. You can see the cruise ships in Miami and taste the cuisine of Little Havana before you head south on Highway 1. And when you run out of road, you'll be in Key West. Yes, you can make it from Dutch Harbor, Alaska to Key West, Florida. Driving like a maniac, you can do it in about six days. Time and money allowing, it can also take years. There is much to see.

Such a trip need not be merely to address some matter of curiosity, to satiate some interest, or to pass some time. Instead, such a trip could be more meaningful; more significant, more purposeful because there is, possibly now more than ever, a deep need for Americans to see our own country. There is, possibly now more than ever, a deep need for Americans to "feel" and "know" our own country for both that which it is and that which it isn't.

In an age when exaggeration is rampant, when refined misinformation is commonplace, and when falsities and half-truths are, with tired resignation, both tolerated and even expected, there comes a time when we Americans need to see America for ourselves. There is literally a need for more Americans to experience our country's wonders, to understand its resources, to sense its size, to grasp its potential, to feel its history; and, when necessary, to recognize its failings and shortcomings. There comes a time when we Americans need to know the facts about our own country— the good and the bad, the cold and the comforting.

Introduction

T his book, *The Relevance of Reason – Society and Culture,* together with the recently published companion book *The Relevance of Reason – Business and Politics,* present certain hard facts and data about the state of Current America—not early America at the time of its origin or as envisioned by our Founding Fathers; not nostalgia America as some Americans remember from their youth; not even the modern America of the late 20th Century, which most Americans have now lived through their own experiences. Instead, these books focus on *now*—the condition of our country, the current America as it exists *now.*

These books focus upon different components of American society (Society and Culture vis-à-vis Business and Politics). They are independent books. They stand on their own, and they may be read together or separately. However, the motivation for the writing of these books is the same. The motivation came from the widely shared observations that America is in trouble and that part of our country's problems result from the fact that Americans hold vastly different understandings about our society. We are in confusion or disagreement about the nature and extent of our problems and about the availability of alternative courses of action. Ignorance about the state of our country contributes greatly to the diminishment of our American conversation. The absence of any shared and common basis in the factual reality of our country's circumstance feeds our pervasive cynicism. Willful blindness leads to the argumentativeness of our discussions and contributes indirectly to the growing coarseness of our language. We know that the talk shows are too opinionated and the hosts are too heated. But we are becoming too opinionated and heated as well. Some people believe that the self-perceived purity of the culture wars and the rise of ideology have allowed both facts and reason to be dismissed too readily and too frequently.

Our American conversation has become terse and twisted. Too often we are approaching one another with preconceived ideas and with the simplistic, hair-trigger assumption that the opposite of truth is falsity. However, truth is more complex and more elusive than that. To the contrary, the opposite of truth may not be falsity at all—it may lie in ignorance or it may lie in our misunderstandings. The opposite of truth may be the result of our varying perceptions or our differing experiences. Amidst the resultant frustrations, facts get lost and data gets buried. Good theories are inadvertently dismissed. Clear conclusions become watered down or qualified. The answers remain hidden, and the waters stay muddy.

In defense, exhaustion, or anger, many Americans have chosen to withdraw. They have withdrawn to tight and ever-narrowing concepts and definitions of communities. Outside the perimeter of their carefully-chosen, small circle of friends, more and more Americans deflect uncomfortable intrusions. More and more Americans are starting to feel alone in the crowd. We are sharing less and less commonality with one another.

As America has become more divided, it seems as though every statement has a consequence. Every position is now wrapped in a risk and is carried with a price. Voluntarily or otherwise, we find ourselves divided into factions, camps, and allegiances—the rich and the poor; the concerned and the disgusted, the participatory and the apathetic, the delusional and the realists; the hopeful exceptionalists and the dark pessimists, the grumpy and the entitled; the bold and the assertive; the fearsome and the cautious; and on and on.

We agree less and less about whom we can believe; what we should do; and where we should go. Worse yet, there is less and less consensus about who we are and how we are. But an understanding of who and how we are is the only prudent place to begin.

However, knowing America is hard. The selection, the meaning, and the use of facts have themselves become a weaponized art form. The truth gets buried. Reason slowly becomes either negotiable or irrelevant. Part of our not knowing our own country is understandable since the first stubborn truth about America is that none of us have seen the same America. None of us have lived the same America. Younger Americans take for granted (and older Americans too often forget) the extraordinary achievements of this country in even the last half-century—the growth of affluence, the elevation of civil rights, the expansion of capitalism, the innovation of science, the wonders of technology, and the spread of democracy. For most Americans, these achievements came with a price—sometimes a societal price; sometimes a more personal price. At times, this country's challenges have seemed insurmountable. At times our country's progress has been slow. And just as Ernest Hemingway said, the dirty little secret for most of us is that "it all reads a lot better than it lived."

But *the facts* about America's achievements, its failings, and its current condition have somehow got lost in the mix. Not wanting to disturb us with details or burden us with precision, much of the media and most of our politicians present the world in a binary form—us or them, this way or that way, no prisoners and no middle ground. For a witch's brew of reasons—personal, monetary, ratings, and dispositions—some leaders and some groups are now more vested in the perpetuation of conflict rather than in the resolution of problems.

We no longer know whom to believe. All reporters are deemed to be too drive-by. All politicians are thought to be too compromised. The Pope is too Catholic, and Obama is too black. Cantor is too right, and Pelosi is too wrong. Reid is too mumbly, and Boehner is too tan. Cronkite is too dead, and Limbaugh is too self-infatuated. The networks can't be trusted, and Fox is too biased. The South is too conservative, and New England is too liberal. The Almanac's too ancient, and Wikipedia is too unreliable. And while we're at it, Kardashian is too everywhere and Charlie Sheen is too, well, Charlie. And thus, in one of the great paradoxes of modern life, in our Age of Information, facts are hard to find.[1]

---

1. For an interesting challenge to the concept that Americans are living in an "age of information," see Nolan, J., "Imagined Inventions," *The New Yorker*, May 20, 2013 ("We don't live in the information age. That would be an insult to information, which, on some level, is supposed to inform. We live in the communication age. Ten billion fingers fumbling away, unautocorrecting e-mails, texts and tweets....").

These books are a humble response. Their origin lies somewhere between a curiosity and a dare as to whether it was even possible to accurately describe the current state and condition of America in a manner which addresses those subjects of particular relevance, interest, and use to our country. The determination was (slowly) made that such description was possible; that the state of current America could be described by the organized presentation the facts and data—the good, the bad, the cold, the stubborn, the inconvenient, and the indisputable.

These two companion books, *The Relevance of Reason – Society and Culture* and its companion book, *The Relevance of Reason – Business and Politics,* argue that in addition to the assemblage of facts, reason must come to prevail over sheer hope and blind optimism. Reason must come to prevail over both greed and raw self-interest and over ideology and the many variant forms of supposed purism. While honest disagreements will continue, reason must remain relevant. Reason must be one of the themes by which we chart our course. Reason must be one of the tools by which we identify our shortcomings and assess our progress. And in turn, reason must be built upon a bedrock of shared facts as to the accurate reality of American life and to the realistic capacities of our society. Reason alone will not be enough, but it is important. And of late, reason has been too often lost in the fury and fire of our American conversation.

Part of the explanation for the repeated subjugation of reason lies simply in the first fact—that the world is complicated. Precision is easily and oftentimes lost. Facts can be hard to find. Their use can be especially risky since facts rarely alone can tell the story. Facts can rarely, by themselves, explain history. Facts can rarely, by themselves, point either with certainty or with clarity to any set of answers. To the contrary, facts can sometimes be almost chameleon in nature. They can have many characteristics, and any given fact can find itself subject to a litany of retorts; any litany of descriptions.

Facts can be raw, hard, powerful, and convincing. But they can also be the merely convenient tools of demagogues or, more constructively, they can be used to disarm those who attempt to distort the truth or persuade others to illogical action.

In this sense facts can be stubborn and uncompromising, but even if accurate and unqualified and stubborn and uncompromising, they can still be dismissed as petty or trivial. For example, amidst our practice of rigid team politics and us/them thinking, facts are routinely dismissed or wholly ignored due solely to the identity or the purpose of the speaker. By another line of attack, facts can also be discarded as dated, old, yesterday's news, and "oh, so 5-minutes ago." Facts can even be repudiated. The very power and persuasiveness of facts can be contained by the assertion that the subject has already been addressed or that they have been overtaken by intervening events and by new a new stream of facts—of which, in this accelerated age of Big Data, there are many.

In sum, facts can be overwhelming.

The sheer volume of facts and our ready google-wikipedia access to them encourages people to collect their own facts and to repeat their favorite facts of convenience. In our newly discovered age of scarcity, austerity, and economy, facts are almost unique if for no other reason than there are so many of them—indeed, too many of them. The sheer volume of data makes it hard to separate the important and useful data from the irrelevant or misleading data. It is hard to separate the "signal" from the "noise" in the parlance of Nate Silver, who even at the age of 34 is now one of the country's currently most famous and influential political forecasters. As he noted in a recent interview "(e)very day, three times per second, we produce the equivalent of the amount of data that the Library of Congress has in its entire print collection.... But most of it is cat videos on YouTube or 13-year-olds exchanging text messages about the next Twilight movie. Most of it is total f**ing irrelevant noise" and "unless you have a good technique for filtering and processing the information, (we're) going to get into trouble."[2]

Thus, the relentless truth about facts in the 21st Century is that there are plenty enough for everyone to have their own. And tomorrow there will be more.

---

2. See Silver, N., *The Signal and the Noise: Why So Many Predictions Fail—But Some Don't* (2012) and Heilpern, J., "Silver Streak," *Vanity Fair,* November, 2012, p. 70.

While it is beyond the scope of these books to analyze all of the multiple aspects of our society's response to our Age of Information, the sheer volume of data combined with our ready access to information are certainly two of the sideline wonders of our modern technology and our Age of Information. And yet for a myriad of reasons, especially in Current America, as that phrase is defined below, it is easier to parrot that which we have heard from others than to think for ourselves. Similarly, it is easier to rebut "your facts" with "my facts" rather than to do the heavier work of reasoning. This is due partly to the wired, info-laden nature of our society, but it also due to the zero-sum, Darwinistic view of our political and economic life and our escalation of healthy skepticism to rigid cynicism.

We live in a modern world of splintered and audience-focused media and says-who cynicism. Historically, there were persons to whom we looked for knowledge, for guidance, for leadership, and even for comfort. For our great grandparents, it was the reassuring, fireside voice of FDR. For our parents or grandparents, it was the velvet and calm voices of Walter Cronkite, Chet Huntley, David Brinkley, John Chancellor, and Eric Severeid. But now their successors—with the possible exception of Tom Brokaw and a few others—are harsher, more purpose-driven, and tightly categorized. Despite the wide-reach efforts of the major networks and despite (or because of) the availability of 24/7 news, the delivery of information has become highly managed and packaged, skillfully tailored, and carefully targeted for specific audiences, age groups, and other demographics. With obvious conflict, information is willy-nilly presented both as entertainment and news.

The public's cynicism also extends far beyond the media. It extends to the words of our political and social leaders as well. For some, the seeming logic and good-nature of President Reagan, the Great Communicator, forestalled the further erosion of our national community for a few years, but increasingly over especially the last several decades the press, the public, and our politicians have all become thickly encrusted with cynicism.

Many Americans are left to find their encouragement, solace, meaning, and what passes for reason from the voices on talk shows and from the banter of like-minded, talking heads. Increasingly, we are brought together only by events of national sorrow—9/11, Hurricane Katrina and Superstorm Sandy, and by the senseless killings at a political rally in Arizona, a college campus in Virginia, a shopping mall in Oregon, a Sikh temple in Wisconsin, a cafeteria in Texas, a movie theatre in Colorado and most recently by the shooting at an elementary school in Connecticut and a bombing at the Boston Marathon. The rest of the time we live amidst the turbulence and challenges of everyday life. But political elections, fiscal cliffs and financial sequestrations don't help. Our anger remains stirred; our frustrations elevated.

The correlation between the rise of public cynicism and the diminishment of reason is that cynicism allows, if not encourages, facts to be increasingly seen as matters of possession—"my facts" and "your facts"—to be hidden from enemies; traded like little gold nuggets among like-minded friends; used as tools, shields or weapons in the attack or defense of some supposed greater truth.

But, as noted above, facts also have their own inherent strengths as well. Facts have a certain stubborn independence. They can remain self-possessed in their accuracy, and they cannot be easily concealed or long buried. They can even achieve an almost unique power depending on when they are discovered, how they are used, and by whom they are revealed.

This book tries to be diligent in distinguishing between the concept of "facts," "opinions," and the far more elusive concept of "truth." Especially when talking about a subject as large as Current America, the distinctions between facts, opinions, and truth can be difficult. For example, it is certainly tempting to state that it is a "fact" that the *Honey Boo Boo* TV show is bad for the soul and that Anthony, aka "Carlos Danger," Weiner has problems. It is tempting to state that it is a "fact" that the darkest hour is just before dawn, that U.S. politics are overly partisan, and that the federal debt is too large. However, facts must be kept stubbornly immune from the touch of subjectivity. They must be rooted in more than consensus; even wide consensus.

This distinction between the presentation of facts and the assertions of truth also rests upon the belief that the American people are entirely competent, with reflection, to once again and over time reach those truths and make those decisions which are necessary for the betterment of this country and its citizens.[3]

But coming full circle, the place to begin is knowing who we are, what we are, what we have, what has been achieved, and what is left to address. These questions must all be addressed in the context of the many interwoven fibers of American—demographics, business and commerce, employment and wealth, government and governance, politics and elections, crime and punishment, housing and education, health and health care delivery, and society and culture.

Arguably, each of these subjects deserves its own book of facts, however any such series of thick tomes ignores the reality of the speed of American life, the impatience of the American reader, and the sometimes limited degree of interest which Americans have in these subjects. Furthermore, Americans are not in the mood to read long paragraphs. We are tired of minutiae detail. It is time for both our needs and our desires to align. We need to learn the actual facts about our country in as few words (and with as few facts) as possible.

---

3. Sometimes the clarity and even the meaning of the public's vote, the public's registered decisions about matters of the day and the electorally-spoken expression of the majority, are themselves the subject of debate and disagreement. Democracy in all of its glory is a clumsy process. It does not provide for, let alone assure, an easy and clarion means of public communication. This is especially true in the context of elections. Victors too often claim or overstate their mandate; losers too often minimize, refute or misstate the sometimes obvious meanings of their own or their party's loss. More recently in American political life, they litigate or otherwise dispute the outcomes, or they try to de-legitimize the elections themselves. The distinctions between facts, opinions, and truth arise again. It may be a fact that "the people have spoken," but it is also a fact that the people rarely speak clearly. In the 2012 presidential elections approximately 128,470,000 votes were cast. There was an outcome, but the votes reflected many motivations. They were cast for a multitude of varied reasons. There was not "one voice." Most of the country, happily or begrudgingly, accepted the winners of the election, but many citizens still dispute its meaning and its implied grant of mandate and authority. For a multitude of reasons—some sincere and honest and some heavily compromised with arrogance, belligerence, and stubborn self-interest—the message and the meaning of the election remain subjects of debate. This debate will continue until the next election. Then, the debate, literally as a part of the process, will begin anew.

In closing, one last observation is made. During the course of writing these books, I was consistently surprised and frequently pleased to learn the factual details about the state of Current America. I found that many aspects of Current America as presented in this book are at great deviance from the dark, gray, pessimistic, and even alarmist drone of many American politicians and commentators. While America's problems are many, in most cases, they are readily identifiable and, with patience and resolve, surmountable. It also became obvious that while some of our problems are serious and have been long neglected, America's successes (and in some cases its continued preeminence) have been too frequently lost in the mix and buried in the headlines. While much remains to be done, we *can* get there. We *can* get better. We *can* reclaim lost ground and re-direct our path. But the place to begin is to know America. We must come to know America *widely*. It is no longer enough to know our country only through the prism of our own perspective as dictated by our age, employment, level of income or wealth, race or ethnicity, geographic place or region of residence, hobbies and interests, religiosity, or level of education.

This is the subject of Part I of this book—the need and requisites for a renewed American conversation. It addresses the simultaneous realities: (1) that it is necessary to know our own country from Dutch Harbor[4] to Key West and (2) that America is both big and complex. Understanding composite America is hard, and our abilities to understand it have been impacted—and in some ways, adversely, by the Age of Big Data and the consequences of cascading data. However, the roadblocks cannot be allowed to redirect our course. The challenges do not alter the necessity.

---

4. Dutch Harbor technically is the name of the port facilities located in the city of Unalaska, the 12th largest city in Alaska and the westernmost city in the U.S. at 174 degrees 20 minutes West. The city of Unalaska is located off of mainland Alaska and consists of two, bridge-connected islands (Unalaska Island and the nearly adjacent Amaknak Island). Dutch Harbor, the port and the area where most of the population of the city lives, is far better known than the city's name, Unalaska, due to the national prominence as a fishing port and due to the Discovery Channel's popular television show, *Deadliest Catch,* which is seen by between 3.5 and 4.3MM viewers each week.

Part I also highlights the necessity for context and perspective. Two types or perspective are used: (1) the "horizontal" perspective which can be obtained by comparing data about Current America with other nations, and (2) the "vertical" perspective which can be obtained by comparing data about Current America with parallel data from our own most recent American history, the history of what is referred to as "modern America," 1957-2012. My assumptions, sources and the methodologies of fact selection, presentation, and citing are also summarized in this Part I.

In Parts II through V the facts about the current state and condition of our society and culture are organized into seven topical categories. At the beginning of each chapter, I have taken the liberty of presenting some exemplar facts about Current America which are striking and surprising, which are believed to be little known, or which may be of particular interest or curiosity to the reader.

These companion books, *The Relevance of Reason—Business and Politics* and *The Relevance of Reason—Society and Culture*, are the first books in a series of books entitled *The Chance of a Lifetime*. At Appendix A is an introduction to the other books in this series. Lastly, these books recognize the fast pace and near constant introduction of new words, meanings, phrases and colloquialisms into the American conversation. Thus, at Appendix B in each of these books is a list and explanatory definitions of such new words, meanings, phrases, and colloquialisms which may be helpful to the reader.

In closing, I believe that you will find that it is not the theories, opinions, exaggerations, or distortions about America which are most interesting. Instead, it is the facts about America which are most revealing and fascinating. They do not, of themselves, define where we must go and what we must do, but they do tell us where we are—and that's a good start. Read on.

PART I

The Need and Requisites for a
Renewed American Conversation
and The Concepts of Current
and Modern America

CHAPTER 1

The Need to Know
Our Own Country and Staring
Down the Face of Crazy

The Need to Know Our Own Country

There are many reasons why now, more than before, there is an escalating need to know our own country. Whether that need rises to the level of obligation or civic responsibility can be argued by others; on another day. The purposes of this book are rooted in a far simpler line of reasoning.

First, democracy by its very nature is built upon the concept of almost routinized change. Change is not just a campaign slogan and a politician's promise. Wholly apart from the change which has resulted from the forces of demographics and technological advancement, change is institutionalized by some of the very precepts of democracy. Change is inherent in the nature of representative voting, by the scheduled recurrence of our periodic elections, by our federalism and the reserved powers of our states to implement different approaches to even our common problems, by the powerful rights of constitutional amendment, and, more recently, by the use of the various forms of "direct democracy" powers such as impeachment, recall, initiative and referendum.

Since its inception America's democracy has gone further by its explicit recognition, encouragement, and enshrining of our people's individualism. However, for some Americans even that is not quite enough, which is why the American brand of individualism is so commonly referred to as our people's "rugged" individualism. This individualism, so distant from feudal arrangements and class and caste distinctions, allows many (but not yet all) Americans to select their own courses of study, to pursue their own careers and start their own businesses, to marry whom they wish and live as and where they choose, to travel and relocate themselves and their families, to reach and express their own conclusions, and to "change"—or, if seeking to make a slightly more dramatic, Hollywood statement, to even "reinvent" oneself.

But that same change, in turn and by its very nature, ensures a certain fragility in our politics, our economy, and in our culture. Both the availability and the frequency of change invite easy abuse. Change can be imposed upon us through mandate. Its source can be rooted in the graft of others or the abuse or corruption of our political or economic systems. Its arrival can come through the advancement of knowledge and understanding or, through the more subtle, hidden persuader tools which have come to dominate our economic and political systems. In the opinion of some, for example, the heavy tools of manipulation and demagoguery have been used of late to feed both our real and imagined fears. However, by and large and more and more, it is now the refined tools of sophisticated marketing, advertising, packaging, and narratives which are used to first present and then sell both American products and American politicians. In addition and over especially the last two decades, change has been delivered upon us by political interests and economic forces feeding our own greed or stoking our own sense of self-interest.

With the fluidity of change, with the powerful tools of creating change (or at least influencing the nature, direction or identity of that change), change is thus simultaneously both the blessing and the curse of democracy. Regardless of the documentary basis of our constitutional democracy and the good will and hard work of the intervening generations since our founding, democracy is (and as has been particularly evident of late) nothing more than "the recurrent suspicion" that 51% of the people are right 51% of the time. Democracy needs constant tending and deserves constant protection. However, by any measure 51%/49% are shaky odds. They allow for miserably thin margins of error.[1]

Thus, the first part of the reasoning which underlies this book is that change in American life is inevitable. It is institutionalized. Change can be delayed, and for some and for awhile, change can even be impeded or ignored by a wide range of emotions and defenses—by apathy, complacency, exhaustion, or resignation; by ignorance, denialism, willful blindness, or stubborn incalcitrance; and even by withdrawal for those who withdraw to the woods or try to live behind high gates and secure locks. But eventually the change will arrive. Eventually, it will be felt by all. It cannot, and sometimes should not, be denied.

The second part of the reasoning of this book is that in order to influence the nature and direction of our society's inevitable change, it is in each of our own self-interest to become not just informed, but, to the extent of our respective capacities, wise. When so written and when spoken out loud, such an encouragement "to become informed and wise" seems horrendously precocious and presumptuous. It has the stench of naïveté—a statement of near definitional absurdity. And yet this is what we ask in the course of every political and economic and social debate. We may be purely trying to persuade in order to win an argument, secure a vote, or get a job, but we are asking—admittedly without using the "*w*" word—for people to be

---

1. In the last decade there have been numerous assertions that a variation of this statement (i.e., that "(a) democracy is nothing more than mob rule, where 51% of the people may take away the rights of the other 49%") was made by Thomas Jefferson in the context of warning about the dangers of "mob rule," however there is no substantiation of this. The earliest known attribution of this statement to Jefferson in print was in 2004 (*monticello. org*), and it is far more likely that this attribution follows the continuing political trend in which all arguments eventually come to be based upon supposed quoted words of Thomas Jefferson or one of our nation's other Founding Fathers. There is, on the other hand, some consensus that this statement was made by E.B. White, (B: 1899, Mount Vernon, New York; D: 1985, North Brookline, Maine), the co-author of *The Elements of Style*, *Charlotte's Web*, and *Stuart Little*, and winner of the Pulitzer Prize (1978 for his entire body for work) and the Presidential Medal of Freedom (1963).

informed and *w*ise because it is America's collective wisdom which is our best hope. As if we need more challenge, it is our only hope.

But there is no short road home. The resurgence and assertion of the informed and wise individual in American life is the *only* way home. Decisions need to be made and the right paths needed to be selected. If we don't participate and decide the persons, policies, and paths we choose, they will be decided for us. Without our own caution, prudence, and effort, the technology of our age and the sophistication of its use (and especially the tools of marketing and communication) by those who aspire to control our political and economic systems will readily, and skillfully, fill the void. Be assured that the tools are normally used to sell persons, to provide answers, and to market products far more than they are used to promote reflection, understanding, and wisdom. Thus, the role of the individual remains—even amidst a nation of more than 311,600,000 people—important.

Ideally, knowledge and wisdom should be found as quickly and as easily as possible. But, instead, this is a difficult, foreboding, and relentless task. There are only so many hours in the day, and we all get tired. We live in the Era of the Internet and the Age of Big Data, but knowledge and truth are still hard to come by.[2]

Third, and as alluded to above, there is a certain immediacy at hand. There is a need for Americans to step up and step forward. *Now.* America cannot expect or await the arrival of a unifying force or a savior. For numerous reasons far beyond the humble scope of this book, the ages of the

---

2. It could be argued that the Internet and the availability (and deluge) of Big Data diminish both our inclinations and capacities to reason and to understand our world. This subject is generally beyond the scope of this book, and there is a certain counterintuity to the more-is-less argument as it relates to knowledge and information. Nevertheless, there are unquestionably powerful (and counter-productive) political, social and economic impacts associated with our age of information technology. Those impacts combined with the splintering of our media contribute to the ready availability of self-supporting opinions and myopic facts of convenience. In our current America, it is both possible and common for people to go through their entire day without having to be burdened by a contrary opinion or a fact which is troubling or inconsistent with their view on any given subject.

great presidents and the ages of the common (and identifiable) enemy (as was seen during World War II and the Cold War) have long since passed.

The reasons for this pressing immediacy for our "stepping up and stepping forward—now" can be easily found in the last decade alone. The last decade has been especially brutish and destructive to both the tone and the substance of our political and economic lives. But the last decade has also been usefully instructive.

In numerous contexts the last decade has reminded us, once again, of the imprudence in relying blindly upon the statements, the exhortations and the promises of others. We have all been reminded of the importance of considering the wisdom, the motives, and the actions of our leaders and advisors. It has reminded us all of the impact of incompetence, the power of greed, and the danger of entrusting our finances or our country to even the most well-meaning of our political or economic leaders. For some, but not all, it has reminded us of the irresponsible rage and misguided anger which can emanate from the talking (or shouting) heads of radio or television. For too many Americans, it has reminded us of the proximity of fear and the stubborn, constant presence of evil.

The last decade has also reminded us of the risks and boundaries of delegation. It has reminded us of the risks attendant to simply assigning our problems to the professionals or to the deep, but sometimes narrow, thinking of experts or academics. Some changes need to be made. Civility needs to be encouraged and must eventually be restored. Even in the context of deadly serious subjects, good will, graciousness, and sometimes even the lightness of humor, must be injected into our national conversation. They have all been too long sorely missed in our rushed, hectic, bottom-line, speed-driven, sober-faced, grumpy society. Above all, we must recognize the relevance of reason, and with purposeful commitment, we must individually reclaim our country—one informed vote at a time. One pay-it-forward, act of kindness at a time. One display of wisdom, at a time.

It is time to act. This must be done without panic or paranoia, but it must be done with resolve. America is in some trouble. It is not just that the power to change this country is in our hands. It is that the power to change this country is *only* in our hands. This statement is of little news. It is not intended to be either alarmist or declinist. It is merely observational.

And the good news is that we can do better. We can do much better. This is important for us, for our families, and for our communities. This is important for our children, with whom, in the end, our future resides. This is important because we owe it to others as well—for those who have fought and died for this country and for those who are still in harm's way doing so.

Staring Down the Face of Crazy

We are all heirs. This country was both built and preserved by the actions of our forefathers. Patriotism is at the core of many millions of Americans, and there is no claim by me of any special patriotism. Over the life of this country, it has been evidenced by every generation and by every family.

My uncle, possibly like yours, died in World War II protecting freedom and liberty and serving his nation. My best childhood friend, possibly like yours, died in Vietnam, serving the then-declared, if not accurate, needs of our country—again in the belief he was protecting freedom and liberty and serving his nation.[3]

My friend's son, possibly like yours, has now served honorably (and, with great fortune, safely) through two tours of duty in Afghanistan. My young son, still unawares, may eventually be called upon as well to serve this country in his own way. The service of all of these men and women and their families evidence how much they cared about this country. And millions of other Americans—farmers, workers, educators and entrepreneurs, single mothers and dedicated scientists, creative artists and store clerks, young and old, black, white and brown—share a great caring about this country. But over the last several decades, things have gotten muddled; very muddled.

---

3. For reasons even I do not fully understand, the Purple Heart of my uncle, a man whom I never got to meet, remains protected as a family treasure. For my childhood friend, a picture of The Vietnam Wall has for years been in my office hanging as my own small honor of my long-ago friend.

The tone of our conversation, the debasing of our rhetoric, and the frustration, if not anger, of our citizens serve as crude benchmark measures of the strained state of our nation. In the abbreviated parlance of today's speech, "it's complicated," but this book is offered to you, the reader, in the belief that neither the character nor the possibilities of America, as a people or a nation, have changed. That, you will find, is one of the core assumptions underlying this book.

The Relevance of Reason – Business and Politics and this book, *The Relevance of Reason – Society and Culture,* are the first two books in a series entitled, *The Chance of a Lifetime.* This series of seven books is about the need and the means for the patient remaking of American life. They all draw upon an analysis of the last fifty-five years from 1957 through 2012. They all include frequent references to America's history in order to remind us of both our nation's accomplishments and its failings. These books incorporate the perspectives of a wide array of contemporary writers, essayists, columnists, and critics holding vastly differing views. These books will collectively attempt to offer, with great humility, a number of proposals about what must be done to change the direction of our country and to improve the quality of American life.

The methodology of *The Chance of a Lifetime* series is direct. The first two books introduce facts and data about the state of Current America. Book Three (*Dead Serious and Light-Hearted, How to Get America ~~Right~~ Fixed*) introduces the multiple objectives of the series, the nature and importance of the national community, and the necessity for patience. Because we live in an age of deep cynicism and cluttered agendas, my personal background and the motivations behind these books are also presented. Then, based upon a more objective and accurate view of ourselves and the American condition (Book Four - *Grading on the Curve— Towards a More Objective Understanding of America*) and with a sense of optimism (Book Five - *A Reasoned Case for Optimism—America in the 21ˢᵗ Century*), ten specific changes are identified in Book Six (*No Dog in the Fight—The Ten Changes Necessary for the Remaking of American Life*) which we, as individuals, must make in order to patiently achieve the promise of American life. The final book (*The Brilliance of Many - 1,000 Ideas for*

Improving Life in America) is entirely different. This last book is a compilation of the many, sometimes brilliant, ideas about improving American life *which already exist.* These ideas have been assembled by the author, but they are presented without comment or recommendation. Some of them are already being implemented or tested either in America or elsewhere. However, due usually to under-funding and under-reporting, they are not well known and have not yet been widely considered.

These books address serious subjects, but they do so with a degree of humor and levity. They do not hesitate to draw upon the balloon-boy, Lady Gaga, Red Bull absurdities which have become a part of American life over the last decades.

The reasons for the inclusion of humor, levity and even the absurd are far more than mere matters of style. Americans have not taken a deep breath in two decades. We have forgotten how humor and levity can be humanizing. They can help us take the edge off our conversations. They may be the best means by which to slowly change the scowling, go-figure tone of our current American conversation. Americans have forgotten that we laugh better than we argue, but we have let the list of toxic subjects grow too long—guns and butter, war and peace, role of government, states' rights, church and state, and personal and civic responsibility. Each of these subjects brings forth a witch's brew of emotions as our frustrations, disillusionments, and anger surface too often and too readily.

In addition to the use of humor and levity, each of the books in this series will be kept short. Americans are tired of talking in paragraphs. We don't need another inch-thick book about defeatism and decline. Defeatism serves no purpose. Suggestions of declinism are misguided. The very words—*defeatism* and *declinism*—affront America's long traditions of ingenuity, self-reliance and success. While some would disagree, these books suggest that strains of denialism are too prevalent and that mere incantations of America's exceptionalism will not enough. As mentioned above and just like the tab on Facebook—"It's complicated."

But there are also areas of broadening consensus, and these books build upon them.

There is a broadening consensus that America's problems are numerous, compounding, and inter-related. Except in the one instance relating to poor generational conduct of us baby-boomers, none of these books expend energy or words in honing criticism or assigning blame. Those subjects have been well-covered by a hundred other writers.

There is a broadening consensus that our political system is dysfunctional. Americans know that our problems are not going to be corrected by the electoral arrival of unifying political leader, by a crop of new faces, by the improved behaviors of our leaders, or by the occurrence of some epiphanous enlightenment. Similarly, we can no longer await bursts of brilliance or moments of accidental honesty. Instead, we must adjust to the reality that without our action America's electoral and legislative processes are not going to readily change or quickly improve.

There is a broadening consensus that our economic system has become too Darwinian. Many now believe that the disparate allocations of income, wealth, and opportunity may be counter-productive to the long-run success and safety of our country. These are fair matters of honest debate, but it is unlikely that our economic system is going to correct itself by the free run of market forces or by the application of either more or less regulation. The American economy has not been hijacked, but as a matter of strategy, too many aspects of our economic system have become a mere part of the political grudge match currently in play.

There is a broadening consensus that our society has changed in many other ways as well. Many of our traditional behavioral restraints have been diminished. Many of our communities have been re-defined; others have been dangerously weakened. Anxiety, fear and pessimism have become pervasive forces. Good people fight for their jobs. Good parents fight for the good education of their children. Accurate information is terribly difficult to find despite the cascade of the Google-Wiki data which keeps coming. More and more, it seems as though we American can color within the lines, but we are having trouble connecting the dots.

There is a broadening consensus that our senses of personal and civic responsibilities have been affronted by the disappointing acts of some of our leaders and by the media's continuing obsession with ratings, celebrities, New

Jersey housewives, ice road truckers, and pawn shop owners. Half of America knows Lindsay Lohan's next prison release date. That itself is a problem.

For these and other reasons, enough is enough. The patience of many Americans has expired. We must act.

Defining the direction and achieving the changes which are necessary to improve the security and quality of American life are up to us. It is time for America to change. Once again. Through our words, our actions, and our example, it is now time *for us* to lead; to think; to restrain; and to encourage. We need to reign in our anxieties. We must contain our fears. We must stand together and stare down the face of crazy.

And there is a path home. Indeed, we may be in a period of peculiar opportunity. But "knowing" America is difficult; indeed, to a certain extent impossible. There are many reasons for this difficulty which are discussed in the next chapter—the size and complexity of our country; the onslaught abundance and unique characteristics of facts and the impact of Big Data; the acceleration of American life and our relentless demands for brevity and expectations of speed; and possibly above all, the stubborn elusiveness of truth.

CHAPTER 2

America Is Very Hard to See— The Data, Facts, and Truth

The Impact of Big Data; The Abundance of Facts and the Negotiability of Truth

America remains difficult to see. It is almost impossible to know. Our country is vast, and our society is complex, confusing, and at-times frustrating. For all of its wonders, technology has dangerously accelerated history itself. Technology has also accelerated our lives—what we do, what we read, what we "see," what we think about. As a people, we too often almost pride ourselves on our demand for to-the-point brevity and for our get-er-done impatience.

In this age of Big Data, speed is frequently more honored than accuracy. Nuance is seen as a wasteful, even nitpicking, enterprise. Details are left for the minions, and precision itself is thrown to the side for the clean-up crews. However, especially in an age of complexity, this may be dangerous. The same technology that has opened up our world is overwhelming us with data. Basically, we are getting more than we asked for. We are receiving more information than we can absorb.

Each day we are asked, in some cases even expected, to read, understand, assimilate, remember and apply a diffuse amount of news, data, statistics, estimates, projections, and warnings. Ever since Bill Gates left his garage, the volume of data and the speed of ready access to it have been accelerating. At times, it seems that information and knowledge is a zero-sum game—the more information there available, the less knowledge is assimilated.

In our prior lives, we were allowed some time to separate fact from fiction. Now, overwhelmed with data, we spend our time caged like hamsters on a wheel, trying to keep up, and trying, with a hint of near desperation, to not be *oh, so, 5-minutes ago*.

Reflection has become a lost art. Reflection is reserved as almost a luxury for the idle rich or the idle old. In the scramble of our lives and in the churning of America's political theatre, reason has become irrelevant; truth has become negotiable.

Initially, in defense and now by habit, facts (and especially numbers) are used to trump thought. And if a fact becomes inconvenient or stubborn, we feel like we can wait it out. Even if a fact may be fleetingly correct and accurately repeated, it can oftentimes be soon dismissed as irrelevant or outdated. By the mere passing of a few moments or with just a few keystrokes, I can replace your facts with mine. And the beauty of it all—there are enough facts for everybody to have their own.

There are enough facts to reinforce any position; to argue any theory; to advance any cause regardless of whether or not the position, the theory, or the cause is rooted in stupidity, paranoia, or narrow self-interest.

Most Americans endure lives that are more hectic and challenges that are more daunting and complicated than in earlier times. We still share music, enjoy our entertainment, and guiltily follow the lives and follies of celebrities. We can still root for our favorite teams and without grudge or disdain allow others to root for theirs, but the under-current is often one of separation and separateness. I know what I know. And you are wrong. I've got my news. And you are wrong. There is no need to debate. There is only the temptation to quote. There is a lightness in our thinking. Stand your ground has become the dominant ideology of American discourse.

But there is also, and possibly relatedly so, a certain lightness in the nature of our very identities and associations. There is a certain diminishment in our sense of and ties to the American community.

We unsurprisingly gravitate to like-minded folks with shared commonalities of interests, opinions, or beliefs. We associate with those of shared ethnicities, fears, religions, or political views Other Americans, whether as a matter of frustration, opportunism, or out of a mere sense of hip style, feel free and wholly unconstrained from constantly re-defining themselves. Without looking back, some Americans almost routinely change the identity and the very depth and nature of their associations with others. In the wired, hyper-mobile America of the 21st Century, these associations can be used to supplant what used to be called communities.

For some, chatrooms, the twitterverse, Facebook friends are the new boundaries of their new American communities. Internet cafes are the new front porches. Chatrooms are the new book clubs. Tweets and text messages are both the means and the depth of their conversations. For others, a new closedness has been erected. Doors are bolted and community gates are erected. Strangers are viewed with a certain restraint, if not caution, until more is known of their background; their beliefs; and their interests. Buzzwords are awaited; bumper stickers are read; judgments are withheld; and more must be known. Our time is deemed precious. Our family and assets are deemed at risk. For all of these reasons, it isn't surprising that our communities are weaker; that strangers are (and can remain) just that. For years.

But neither the technology nor the social restraints and in-bred fears of modern life can fully replace America. Begrudgingly or otherwise, we are still "in" America. This will not change. We are still a piece, our own piece, of this country. America. It remains ours. Except for a few survivalists back in the woods, we are still affected by the actions of our fellow Americans—even if we don't know their names; even if we don't have their email addresses. The commonality of Americans will always prevail and that guy in Dutch Harbor will always have the same power of vote as the guy in Key West. However, there is a constant tension between our individualism and desires for selfism and our needs for and obligations to community. Some, but not all, are separated by technology. Some, but not all, are isolated by technology. But there is far more.

In certain respects, we are unavoidably a separated nation, and this too will not change. We are definitionally separated by geography, by age, and by generational association. We are separated by the circumstances of our birth and by the strength or weakness or even presence of our families. From an early age we become further separated by what they have seen and by the sense of hope which may (or may not) have been instilled in us. We are separated by the quality and later the extent of our respective educations and by the availability of opportunities. We are separated by a wide array of ethnicities, heritage, race, creed, and color. We are separated by our height, weight, gender, and health. We are separated by our religious associations.

We are separated by our attitudes, by our dispositions and inclinations, and by our levels of empathy. We are separated by our senses of humor and by our capacity for laughter. By even early adulthood, we are separated by the whims of luck, by our accumulation of experiences, by our jobs or professions, by our finding of love and possibly by the blessing presence of children and close friends. Time and money allowing, we welcome, but are again separated, by our various hobbies, sports, affiliations, and interests.

And it is all of these disparate things, all of these disparate pieces which are Us. It is therefore not surprising that we do not "know" our own country. It is not as conveniently small as Andorra or Monaco. It is not as isolated and remote as Bhutan or Nepal. It is not as homogeneous as, until recently, the Scandinavian countries. And yet, too often and especially of late, we fail to understand or to remember that none of us has a clear or a shared perspective with the rest of the country. Instead, we vocalize impatience and express almost surprise that we Americans don't see the same thing; share the same dreams; and draw the same conclusions. Instead, we more and more often angrily disagree with one another. This is especially the case in the context of political and economic matters where such matters are rarely easy calls. Few things in our society are "obvious." This book addresses the problem that America is too often just lived but not studied.

America itself is neither well nor thoroughly taught in our schools. This must change so that we can each develop a better understanding of our own country—in all of its good and all of its bad. This must change so that we may be able to develop a better sense of patience with ourselves as we try to understand, if not agree with or assimilate, the thoughts and opinions of others.

It is not enough to know the score; we need to know the game.

Knowing America is not an easy task. But, it is a necessary task which has been too long ignored. It has always been important, but now it has become critical.

The Utility of Facts
and the Stubborn Elusiveness of Truth

This book presents a wide range of facts and data about America, but the topical selection of these facts and data is not just mine. Instead, they are drawn from the written pages of our American conversation as reflected in a wide and disparate array of newspapers, magazines and a myriad of other sources. Read together the reader may be able to form his or her own more accurate, more composite understanding of America. This book is not written for the scholar, the expert, the specialist, or the perfectionist. This book is written for that wide audience of Americans who want to *know* this country better by having a ready and organized access to an assemblage of balanced facts about the state of Modern and Current America.

As discussed above, knowing the realities about our country, our society, our economy, and our people will help us in understanding the nature and extent of both our problems and our successes. It is facts, as distinguished from hopes, dreams, and theories, that can help us evaluate alternative courses of actions.[1]

Facts cannot imbue the power of blind faith and the draw of ideologies, but they can assist us in selecting remedies and in allocating our limited and precious resources. They can help us in diminishing our fears and placing both our enemies and our problems in proper perspective. Facts

---

1. For purposes of this discussion in this book, no distinction is made between facts and data and the statistical compilations and presentations thereof. Few estimates and projections are included due to their prospective, anticipatory nature and because they inevitably remain subject to unforeseen circumstances or intervening events.

can improve our confidence and remind us of our accomplishments. Facts can show us the bad, but they can also show us the good.

But despite all of their allure and utility, it is not as simple as selecting facts over ignorance. To the contrary, facts also have troublesome characteristics, and the boundaries of their usefulness must be recognized.

First, there are just too many of them. Some of them may be interesting, but they are of little use. Some of them are more akin to finding isolated bits, near curiosities, of another age. For example, it is *fact* that Aristide, in 1873, was the first horse to win the Kentucky Derby. It is even more interesting that he was ridden by Calvin Borel, a black jockey riding before that all-white Kentucky crowd. "In fact," as they say, he went on to win three out of four of the next Kentucky Derbys. But, by themselves, these facts are more in the nature of trivia. Without thought and reflection, they tell us very little about horse racing in America or the limited rights of blacks in post-bellum Kentucky. Similarly, it is a *fact* that Ida May Fuller of Ludlow, Vermont was the first beneficiary of social security and that she got $650 per year for 35 years. But, by themselves, these facts about Ms. Fuller do nothing to guide us in evaluating the wisdom of our having expanded the social security benefits systems over the ensuing decades or the importance in our resolving the trajectory of financial insolvency which faces our 21st Century social security system.

Thus, the first troublesome nature of facts is their sheer volume and the variances of their respective importance. In our era of Big Data in which "2.5 quintillion bytes" of new information are generated each day, it is increasingly difficult to distinguish between, as Nate Silver has stated, "the signal and the noise."[2]

---

2. While it is beyond the scope of this book, some argue that in its own way and for its own, unique reasons the age of Big Data has become part of the problem; not part of the solution. Far too many Americans now surf in their chairs and spend hours in front of their computers. For too many Americans "wikipedia" is slowly becoming a verb, and reflection and reason are seen as antiquated, nostalgic characteristics of a prior age. The age of enlightenment gave way to the age of reason. Now, enlightened reason has been set aside, and we are living in an age where speed is the central theme and where technology and information delivery are merely the gateway tools thereof.

Second, facts are always vulnerable to subjectivities of selection and emphasis. My factual selection and emphasis will sometimes be different than yours. Furthermore, facts are not simply like stones lying in the ground. They can be bound together. They can be made to fit a pattern or serve a purpose.

Facts have even come to attract their own litany of descriptions and lexicon of adjectives—hard facts and cold facts. Facts can be omitted or distorted. Facts can be buried or concealed.. Facts can be out of context and contradictory. There are so many of them that one group of Americans can wrap themselves in one set of facts while another group blindly wraps itself around another set of facts. Aided by the age of technology, facts have become so readily available that they are far more tempting to use than the plodding, burdensome work of applying reason or thought. For some, facts, in their own willy-nilly way, are used to supplant useful conversation and respectable debate. Instead, they are exchanged in a chorus of "my facts" and "your facts," my "ya-buts" and your "what abouts."

Data, as an accumulation of assembled facts, can be similarly difficult to collect and measure. Data may be vulnerable to variances and exceptions. Data can be corroded by motivated reasoning or controlled, manipulated, or twisted by the slightest alteration of key definitions or by the inclusion or exclusion of aberrational information.

They can also be short-lived. They can become irrelevant or be deemed outdated. Facts can have a miserably short shelf life, and sometimes facts cannot make everything alright. They rarely can explain either the tragedies or the absurdities of life. They cannot explain Superstorm Sandy or Hurricane Katrina. They cannot make sense of Aurora, Colorado or Newtown, Connecticut or the hundreds of drive-by shootings which occur in this country every year. They usually cannot make rhyme or reason about who gets sick, who lives, and who dies. They cannot erase our memories, and they usually cannot contain our prejudices.

Worse yet, sometimes facts are of no use. Sometimes, facts themselves just do not make sense. Sometimes, facts can't provide answers to even our simpler, more insignificant concerns. They cannot begin to explain the sometimes whimsical outcomes in sports or why there are now fourteen collegiate teams in The Big Ten conference. They cannot shed light or logic upon the raw luck draws of the lottery or the absurdity of the PBS' filler music or Lady Gaga's hair. They don't help us understand how it is possible that the average age of The Rolling Stones is now less than the average age of the Justices on the current United States Supreme Court. Sometimes life just doesn't make sense, and facts won't help. That, too, is a fact.

But facts still count. Facts are still the only place to begin. Despite all of their problems and despite all of the necessary caveats and conditions, facts still matter. Inspiration can give us ideas. Dreams can give us hope. Hope can give us the courage. However, it is facts which provide us with the bedrock. Excepting only in the context of religious and spiritual faith, facts remain the only defensible place to begin.

As elusive as they may be, as a basis for reason and as a component of truth, facts surpass rumors and gossip. Facts are more useful than guessing and conjecture. Facts can adjust, indeed clarify, perspective. Facts can reveal options thought unachievable, and they can evidence successes not previously noted.

Lastly, facts can be inspiring and rewarding. As predictors of the probable consequences of our alternative courses of action, they are more useful than even our most noble dreams, hopes and aspirations. Properly assembled and considered, facts are a better basis for change than emotion; than eloquence; or even good intentions and honorable purpose.

As discussed above, part of the genesis of this book, however, is that despite their utility, "facts" are increasingly difficult to come by. This is reflected in (and compounded by) the focus of our media which has become more compromised as the result of its programming which is more and more often narrowly targeted to carefully defined audiences. But broad brush criticisms are too rampant because there are some—*even many*—talented, thoughtful, and informed writers and journalists in this country.

However, their stature has been unduly and dangerously diminished by the widely held perceptions that American journalism too readily pursues profits and too often abdicates its critical role in the accurate and full reporting of what is occurring in this country. There exists a constant frustration with the growth of advocacy journalism and with the banal reporting whereby all that occurs is treated with equal passion, with supposed equal import, and without objective evaluation and analysis. Lower standards of objectivity, investigation and analysis are now almost expected. But in a cautious defense of American journalism, we Americans need to assume some responsibility for the state of American journalism and reporting. The loss of objectivity has in many cases been simultaneously demanded and ridiculed by our bipolar nation.

But regardless of the state of American journalism and despite the difficulty in obtaining objective information, Americans still need to know their own country better. The facts about America remain both fascinating and instructive. The facts may not be the only place to begin, but they are a good place to begin in understanding both Modern America and current America.

CHAPTER 3

———•—•———

The Use of Context and the Necessity of Perspective

The "Horizontal" Context and the Use of Comparative Nations

S ome Americans possess a certain cynicism about the use of context and importance of perspective. They believe that context and perspective are merely tools of convenience and obfuscation which are used by politicians, the media, or others as cloud-cover. They believe that context and perspective are used solely to distract the attention of the reader, to bury the import of a story, or to conceal the full implications of facts which may be deemed uncomfortable, untimely, or inconvenient.

However, even though the potential for such cloud-cover abuses is acknowledged, the use of context and perspectives remains critical for other reasons.

The first reason is that only context and perspective—honestly presented and consistently applied—allow us to understand the full meaning of facts. They supply the measure of our successes and the back-drop of our failures. They allow us to better appreciate how far we have come or how far we have to go.

In a more ideal world, possibly the more pristine, untarnished, stan-dard of perfection itself could be used, but ideal worlds don't exist except in our dreams and in the movies. Furthermore, both the definition and the achievement of perfection with respect to almost any subject, would become, by itself, the subject of endless debate and folly. Perfection must remain aspirational. Even if it could be defined, it would serve poorly as a basis for comparison or measure of achievement because almost without exception, perfection is unobtainable.[1]

For example, the economy can always be better, the crime rate will never be zero, industrial accidents will always happen, and highway fatalities will always occur. In a perfect world—the world of perfection, there would be no illiteracy or poverty. However, except for the boundless optimist, the elimination of illiteracy and poverty must remain only a goal. The more reasonable and useful measures of our success or failure are found amidst defined, comparative contexts. For example, one contextual measure would be to compare our country's illiteracy and poverty rates to those of other nations. Another contextual measure would be to compare our country's illiteracy and poverty rates to those of prior years in order to determine whether they have increased or decreased. Thus, the better measure (and, truthfully, the only measure) is not the crisp absoluteness of perfection. The better measure is the honest application and consistent use of meaningful context and perspective.

The second reason for the use of context and the offering of perspective is due to the nature of most facts and data themselves. Without context or perspective, facts and data are, at best, frozen in time. They are only photographic in nature. They do not, by themselves, reveal what's over the horizon, around the corner, or behind the camera.

Because facts retain an almost isolated quality, they have limited value by themselves in revealing cycles, patterns, trending-lines, and long-term social or economic change. Some facts are not designed to suggest, let alone prove, causation. Without context and perspective, facts have little capacity

---

1. There are, admittedly, a few rare exceptions outside the arts and the world of sports where "perfection-level" achievement has been reached. The elimination of small pox and the near and foreseeable elimination of polio serve only as the reminder that the exceptions can prove the rule.

for incorporating the likelihood or the effect of unforeseen results or unintended consequences. Thus, they need to be placed in the context of a wider range of time so that we can perceive patterns, see trends, better understand our achievements and appreciate our progress, and better recognize our shortcomings and failings. Context and perspective also allow us to contain the impact of aberrational facts and data and to know when to ignore the misguided or alarmist rumblings of the media echo chambers.

Theoretically, when considering the meaning and import of any given fact or body of data, we could rely upon our shared perspective and our common history as a nation. But commonality is itself a difficult measure. For example, while nearly 80% of Americans speak English as their primary language, by definition, this means that 20%, or nearly 60,000,000 Americans, do not. In another context, many Americans may share a fondness for certain sports and certain interests, and many Americans see the same television shows and go to the same movies. Indeed, at times we tolerate and at even embrace some aggregations such as, in the political world, "conservative" or "liberal" or "progressive" or "libertarian" or "Republican" or "Democrat." But even in these instances, there is rarely a deeply shared, common or national perspective. Instead, each American is unique. Each American holds his or her own perspective. Each American draws upon his or her own experiences. Each American places varying weights upon both the meaning, relevance, and import of any interest, event, association, or fact.

As seen above in our comparisons of Dutch Harbor and Key West, personal histories and realities are very different. The only real commonality is that most of our perspectives are *not* shared; most of our histories are *not* the same. Instead, each of us draws from very different perspectives. We are differentiated by the latitude and longitude, by the circumstances of our birth, by our age, by our generational or community associations, by our gender, by our race and ethnicity, by our educational levels and our varying abilities of recall and reasoning, and by our interests, employment, and experience. Therefore, in most instances it is only the national context which allows a more widely shared and more collectively accurate understanding of our country. Almost by default, it is offered in place of the personalized histories and perspectives of the 311,600,000 Americans.

For these reasons it is necessary to place the facts about America into some form of context and perspective which can be deemed, to some measure, to be fair, accurate, and consistently applied.

This book uses two different contexts in the presentation of facts and data about the state of Current America, the Years 2010-2012. These are referred to as the "horizontal" context and the "vertical" context.

The first context of presentation is referred to as "horizontal" because it is sideways in nature. This comparative context compares facts about Current America to parallel information about other nations. This context is meant to assist us in evaluating a given fact or piece of data about Current America relative to and as compared with parallel information about other selected countries. For example, it is interesting and accurate that the average life expectancy of an American at this time is approximately 79.9 years. However, this fact has more meaning—and gains more context and perspective—when compared with other countries. The U.S. life expectancy takes on more meaning when we recognize that it is only 32nd in the world and that it is substantially less than, for example, Japan (83.7 years) and Switzerland (82.5 years).[2]

Comparing Current America to other countries also helps us understand our relative strengths and achievements. For example, especially over the last decade, there has been a growing concern and passionate debate about the diminishment of America's manufacturing capacities. However, the fact that U.S. Manufacturing Output is $1.8 BB[3] has more meaning, gains more context, and even offers more comfort, when it is compared with other countries and thereby understood that the U.S. manufacturing output remains the highest in the world and that, except for China and Japan, no other nation has even one-third the current size of the U.S. manufacturing output.

For purpose of both brevity and meaningfulness, not all other countries are used in the presentation of comparable data. There are currently 196 countries in the world,[4] but most of them are so different from America

---

2. *The Economist Pocket World in Figures—2012 Edition.*

3. *The Economist Pocket World in Figures—2012 Edition.*

4. This number is used although there is some debate about the correct manner of counting countries depending upon the counting of places, i.e., "countries," such as Taiwan, Vatican City and Kosovo.

in terms of size, resources, economic development, and social organization that they have de minimus contributive utility in understanding our country's current condition. Without over-stating the obvious, comparing the manufacturing output of the U.S. to that of Liechtenstein or Papua New Guinea is not a fair fight. Comparing the levels of heterogeneity or the population growth of the U.S. to those of Djibouti or Nepal is not useful. Therefore, since the purpose of this book is to achieve both a more accurate and more comprehensive understanding of this country, the use of comparative countries is narrowed and focused.

Such narrowing of the comparative countries which are used is achieved in several ways. In some instances, there is an inclusion (with respect to any given topic, for example, GDP, urbanization levels, or literacy rates) of a listing of the "Top 5 Nations" or the "Top 10 Nations." If with respect to such topical listing contexts, the U.S. is not in such Top 5 or Top 10 Nations, then the U.S. and its ranking are inserted together with, in most instances, the identification of some of those countries immediately above or below the U.S. ranking.

In addition, certain nations are used more frequently as reference nations because of their closer social, developmental, or economic similarity to the U.S. These nations and agglomerations include the usual suspects of nations. For example, there are relatively frequent references to many of the thirty-four nations which are members of the Organization for Economic Cooperation (OECD)[5] and/or members of the

---

5. The Organization for Economic Cooperation and Development (the "OECD") is the successor international agency to the Organization for European Economic Co-operation (the "OEEC") which was formed in 1948 to assist in the administration of the post-World War II Marshall Plan. The OECD was formed in 1960 in order to "provide a forum in which (member) governments can work together to share experiences and seek solutions to common problems." *oecd.org.* The initial OECD members were the eighteen founder countries of the OEEC plus the U.S. and Canada. Since that time an additional fourteen countries have become members of the OECD. Most of the OECD countries are highly-developed, high-income economies with high HDI (Human Development Index) ratings, however some emerging countries such as Mexico are also members. The OECD is designed to provide a forum

(Continued on next page.)

G7, G8, and G20.[6] Comparative references are also made to many of the twenty-seven member nations of the European Union, those nations increasingly referred to as the BRIC nations—Brazil, Russia, India, and China,[7] to Canada and Mexico, our North American neighbors, and to certain other nations which, for varying reasons, have been in the news or have had particular importance or unique relevance to the U.S. over the last several years such as Iraq, Iran, and in a few instances Afghanistan.

This "horizontal" context for comparing data about America to parallel time-frame period data of other nations is simple and straightforward. The "vertical" context for comparing recent data about America to our own national historical data is arguably far more relevant, important, and interesting. However, it is also far more complicated and difficult.

---

committed to democracy and market economies. It publishes numerous books and reports, provides an on-going stream of statistics about many key economic, market and other social performance indices, including, for example, the OECD Economic Outlook (published twice a year) and PISA (the Program for International Student Assessment), which compares the decisional performance of the respective member countries. *oecd.org.*

6. The G7 is an international finance group composed of the now seven finance ministers representing some of the most heavily industrialized nations (U.S., Canada, France, Germany, Italy, Japan, and the United Kingdom). Initially the G7 was "an informal gathering of heads of state and governments of the then-world's most advanced economies," but it became more formalized in 1975. The finance ministers of the respective nations now meet regularly about three times a year, and all of the Members of the G7 are also Members of the OECD as described immediately above. In 1998 Russia joined "what then became the G8." A similar organization is the G20 which is an "informal forum" which includes both the G8 industrialized members and a number of emerging nations. The G20 creates an opportunity for the emerging nations to participate in an ongoing matters with respect to global economic discussions. See European Commission on Economic and Financial Affairs, *ec.europa.eu.*

7. Acronyms for, respectively, the top emerging markets (BRIC) Brazil, Russia, India and China and the "up-and coming economies" (MIST) of Mexico, Indonesia, South Korea, and Turkey. The terms were believed to have been originally used by Jim O'Neill, an economist employed by Goldman Sachs. Padgett, T., "Day of the Dead. The Drug War Is Mexico's Tragedy," *Time,* July. 11, 2011, p. 24.

The "Vertical" Context
and
The Distinctions Between Current America and Modern America

The second context of presentation and perspective is chronological or "vertical" in nature. This context offers a backwards perspective and is used for two separate, but inter-related reasons: (1) To more easily identify trends and patterns in American history, and (2) To thereby better recognize our shortcomings and more fully appreciate our successes.

The use of a relevant historical context also allows us to contain the impact of aberrational facts and to recognize when a fact has been twisted, unduly dismissed, or dangerously buried as we hear so frequently during debates and discussions about America's social, political, and economic issues. This context and perspective helps us to know when to ignore the self-serving, misguided or alarmist rumblings within the media echo chamber.

This vertical context is used to present data about Current America, defined as the last three years (2010-2012), amidst and in comparison to parallel data about Modern America, defined as the last fifty-five years of American history (1957-2012).

Thus, two differentiated, but overlapping, time periods in America's political, economic, and social life are addressed in this book: Current America and Modern America. While these periods are more thoroughly discussed below, very summarily, the concepts of Current America and Modern America are used in order to distinguish between two recent Americas:

Current America is the world in which we are currently living. It is the convoluted worlds of Obama and Rubio, of fallen heroes and rising stars, and of fiscal cliffs, sequestration, and slippery slopes. It is the world of culture wars and inspirational stories; public distrust and personal perseverance. It is the world of Superstorm Sandy and the senseless tragedies of Newtown and the Boston Marathon bombing. It is the world of Apple iPad sales, Facebook's IPO, and of our troops (finally) coming home.

Modern America is more difficult to define. It is roughly the post-World War II period. For some Americans, it is the America of our parents and grandparents. For others, it is the world of their youth and the world when America held a position as one of, but not the only, world power.

Current America

Current America encompasses the most recent years and events of our American life. It is that period of time which we readily recall; about which the news is still fresh and the debates are still lively. It is that period of time when the victories are well-remembered and the disappointments are still painful. Current America is defined as our last three years. While any such definition of Current America is somewhat arbitrary, the concept of Current America is used, more specifically, for three separable and distinct reasons.

First, Current America is used to help narrow the focus the information and the data presented in this book to those aspects of American social and cultural life which have attracted our most recent interest and concern. These are the aspects of American life which have been at the center of our most recent conversations; have dominated our headlines; have consumed our attention; and have taken our energy.

Second, Current America is use to reflect the reality of American's short memory and even shorter attention span. This short three-year span is not intended to imply criticism of American life. Instead, it merely acknowledges that life in Current America is busy, fast-paced, highly distracted, and, for most, hectic. We all have competing claims upon our time—from our spouse, our children, and our employer. It is not even surprising that most Americans read too fast and remember too little. For better or worse, many Americans have become accustomed to live for the moment and in the present. Especially since 2008, most Americans have been in a place of *trying*. We try to plan for tomorrow. We try to save for rainy days. We try to look to the future. Closer to home, we do better. We still remember the date of our marriage (or, statistically for most, our marriages); we honor the births of our children; and we mourn the deaths of our loved ones. We hold closely (and usually privately) those few moments and occasions in our lives which are precious and special and, even as a society, we remember certain days sometimes with a special glee such as on the 4th of July and sometimes with great and shared sorrow, or even horror such as 9/11.

But mostly, time passes, and it does so quickly. History quickly becomes just that—history. It is far beyond the scope of this book to analyze whether or not the reality of short memories is good or bad, but certainly it is not surprising. The shortness of our memories and the limits of our recall are not here noted with any intended criticism. They are merely realities of modern life.

Thus and excepting only those matters of national tragedy or calamity, those matters of special personal interest, or those matters which have *directly* affected our lives or those of our loved ones, Americans are routinely lured into believing that the facts, data, and events of our American life will each be overtaken by the mere passage of time; by the intervention of new developments; or by the replacement of newer interests, concerns or distractions.

A darker version of this theory is that waiting-it-out reflects the growing culture of indifference in which matters need not be adequately addressed or fully resolved. By this theory, the problems facing our country are the problems of others. By this theory, we need only to survive Current America. If we do that, then the rest can be written off, willingly shelved, begrudgingly accepted, or conveniently forgotten. The time boundaries of our living and our attention are becoming ever-narrower. Thus, the focus of America's attention is that which is happening now, and that "now" is defined in this book as Current America.

There is an admitted level of arbitrariness to the use of the last three years, however, as noted above, this time frame is used because most Americans (in the context of reflecting upon the state of our country) can readily and accurately go back three years. Most Americans can easily recall the nature of the issues, the alternative theories, the posed arguments, and, albeit with varying degrees of accuracy, the competing bodies of evidence offered by the various proponents.

Obviously, this definition of Current America is meant to address America as it exists long after the initial shock of 9/11; long after the invasions of Afghanistan and Iraq, long after the Bush Presidency; and long after—but still amiss the consequences of—the financial collapse of 2008 and the Great Recession; and long after Obama's 2008 and 2012 elections.

However, it is important to recognize that none of these events occurred in isolation from one another. Just like events in our personal lives, our nation's events criss-crossed and overlapped with one another. Even Current America arrived amidst a tangle of headlines and as the subjects of our chatter. The fancy historian's word for this concept is that of "integrated" history. In other words, we do not live our lives in a compartmentalized fashion. Neither our lives nor the events which affect them can be easily slotted as between our economic life, our political life, our social life, our family, our health, and on and on. Instead, the world's events come at us—together and at once.

In addition, the recent events in American society occurred in the context of a bigger, more aged America. Current America is itself a part of a deeper perspective. The last three years, Current America, are merely the most recent insert pages of a more expansive American history. The events of Current America and ascertaining the state and condition of our country can best, if not only, be understood in the context of a more expansive period of American history which is referred to as "Modern America." The words of our Constitution, the writings of our Founding Fathers, the debates about slavery, the Western expansion and the rise of industrialism, and the agonies and the liberal re-directing of our country which arose from the Great Depression remain relevant. But it is the last part of our American history, our Modern America, which is most critical to identifying current data trends, to highlighting (and isolating) aberrational facts, and to measuring the existence, the nature, and the extent of our successes and our shortcoming.

Modern America and Its Importance As Contextual Reference

Just as the last three years is referred to as Current America and is used to define the time period of our country's most recent events, the fifty-five year period, 1957-2012, is referred to as Modern America. It is used as the point of context and reference for better understanding the facts and data about Current America which are presented in this book.

The selection of this fifty-five year time period as the year parameters of Modern America, just like the definition of Current America, is somewhat arbitrary, but the importance of such context, almost however defined, cannot be over-stated.

Examples abound, for example, in both politics and economics.

In politics, nearly one-half of this nation has grown up only in an America political system which is characterized by extreme partisanship. To this one-half of America, the utility of compromise and the spirit of bipartisanship are far less understood. It is difficult for them to imagine the social congeniality, the mutual goodwill, and even the friendships which existed just a few decades ago among many political adversaries. It is hard for them to imagine that despite all of their political differences Republican President Reagan and the Democratic Speaker of the House Tip O'Neill were friends. Such levels of social friendship and even open displays of mutual respect between Gingrich and Clinton, between Pelosi and Bush, or between Boehner and Obama are, for many, unfathomable. Only the context of Modern America, enveloping Current America, can display how much and how quickly we have changed.

In economics, more and more Americans are growing up in an America which is highly innovative and entrepreneurially driven. However, it is also characterized by a Darwinian, almost survivalist environment. Too many people believe (and sometimes with sad justification) that it is acceptable, if not necessary, to round the truth and cut in line in order to get ahead. While the barbarians may not be at the gate, too many people believe (again, sometimes with sad justification) that the at-any-cost protection of one's self or one's family is necessary in an economic environment in which loyalty is rarely rewarded and long-term employment, lifelong careers, and financial security are rarely assured. Some economists argue that these changes have been unavoidable and may be unalterable especially in our post-recession, global economy. However, in order to understand some of the economic tensions and socio-political realignments existent in Current America, it is important to understand that this environment is relatively new. It may or *may not be* unalterable. This is not the way it used to be. This may not be the way it has to be.

Thus, a time frame of context, reference, and comparison, almost however defined, is necessary for several reasons.

First, the concept of Modern America offers a thin-wall defense to our Age of Big Data in which there is, literally, too much information with too many facts, rumors, opinions, and theories all stirred together as one; google-presented and data-dumped without organization or sorting. We live in a world in which the mere volume of facts and data is capable of edging out both reflection and reason. As Burton Malkiel wrote in his review of Nate Silver's recent book, *The Signal and the Noise*, the trick is to extract the correct signal from the noisy data.[8] The fifty-five year definitional concept of Modern America may help with extracting the "correct signals" from the "noisy data." It allows us to narrow the focus of our historical perspective. It allows the necessary tailoring of the sheer volume of information and comparative data to that which is most useful to our understanding of our current state, our current condition, our Current America. This narrowing of contextual reference is also due both to the capacity of this writer and to the patience of you, the reader. However, even this is far more than a mere matter of brevity.

Second, the concept of Modern America reflects the fact that for many Americans history is of limited interest. The subject of history is oftentimes perceived as having limited relevance. This is not intended as an absolutist statement, and in fact many Americans evidence a continuing, great interest, for example, in the personal details and lives of certain historical figures[9] and in the political thoughts and theories of our Founding Fathers. However, for many Americans, history has been assigned to the province of academics and historians. For some Americans, history has been relegated to the stuff of

---

8. Malkiel, B., Review of Nate Silver's book, *The Signal and the Noise*," (Malkiel), *The Wall Street Journal*, September 25, 2012.

9. For example, there are now more than 16,000 books which have been written about Abraham Lincoln alone, and there are another "20 new books (about Lincoln) coming soon." Cohen, S., "Fourscore and 16,000 Books," *The Wall Street Journal*, October 12, 2012. It is highly likely that this interest will become even more resurgent with the November, 2012 release of Steven Spielberg's film, *Lincoln,* starring Daniel Day-Lewis as Lincoln and based upon Doris Kearns Goodwin's 2005 biography of Lincoln entitled *Team of Rivals.*

curiosities and trivia, and certainly—within limits—there is nothing wrong or even disrespectful with that. Sometimes, history is just that. History. It is merely interesting. It does merely put life and color and texture into our past. Some parts of history have little or no current relevance or use.

For example, the fact that James Madison had a wife named Dolly who, like Johnny Cash, only wore black might be curiously interesting, but it is not necessarily meaningful. The fact that nearly 200 years ago John Quincy Adams became President "by a fluke" or that he routinely walked down to the Potomac River each morning for some nude bathing tells us how much Washington, D.C. has changed, but these facts do not help us in understanding Current America. The fact that 68-year-old William Henry Harrison delivered a two-hour Inauguration Speech, caught pneumonia, and died a month later is now only a matter of historical curiosity or familial interest. The facts that James Polk was nominated by his party on the 9th ballot and Franklin Pierce on the 49th ballot are certainly of limited relevance in our current age of pre-packaged, fully-scripted political conventions. The fact that Daniel Webster referred to Zachary Taylor as nothing more than a "swearing, whiskey-drinking, fighting frontier colonel," that Rutherford B. Hayes was correctly and routinely referred to as "His Fraudulency," and that Grover Cleveland was derided for his "ugly honesty" might give us some perspective and even comfort in knowing that neither partisanship nor coarseness of political speech are new. However, such facts—even if technically relevant—are easily dismissible as being too old and too outdated.[10] These types of facts remain appropriately relegated to matters of curiosity, trivia, and detail. They tell us nothing about emerging China, trade imbalances, or the proverbial price of beans.[11]

Even facts and matters of great import and deep substance sometimes fade in importance. Like you and me, they age with time. They seem to

---

10. The provision of more information about President Taylor such as the fact that he died just days after laying the cornerstone to the Washington Monument as the result of partying too much on iced milk and cherries are merely examples of historical trivia. However, none of these facts—historically accurate and verified facts—still tell us much about Daniel Webster, Zachary Taylor, or "iced milk and cherries."

11. For a fine, light collection of interesting facts about our country's presidents, see Boller, Paul. F., *Presidential Anecdotes* (1981).

lessen in relevance over the years. Memories fade, arguments get settled, issues get resolved, and—except for the stubborn outliers living deep within the woods or who are time-trapped in their own clouded minds— history moves on. For example, the income tax debates surrounding the ratification of the Sixteenth Amendment[12] were both raucous and important, but these debates are now seen by nearly all Americans as distant and archaic.[13] The arguments challenging the right of women and minorities to vote and the importance of their open access to education, housing, and employment seem to be and for most Americans are from another era. Especially in light of the recent financial collapse, some economists and politicians have argued for a re-analysis of the wisdom of Keynesian economics and the advisability of many aspects of FDR's New Deal programs, but even this debate is best presented in the context of Current America and Modern America. To go too far back in time challenges history too much. The players have changed. Daniel Day-Lewis is Lincoln—Lincoln isn't Lincoln.

And the world and the issues have changed as well. The size and nature of our country and the twists and turns and details of the issues have changed dramatically. Even since the Presidency of FDR, empires have fallen, Hitler and Stalin and Mao are dead. The Colonial Era has expired.

---

12. It is commonly (and conveniently) forgotten that the first income tax was proposed by President Lincoln in order to pay for the Union's war effort in the Civil War. Nearly 30 years later, the Democrats passed the first peacetime income tax in 1894, but it was not until 1913 that the 16th Amendment clarifying that "Congress shall have the power to lay and collect taxes on income ...." was ratified by the requisite number of states.

13. While the power of the federal government to impose a progressive form of income taxation has been long resolved and accepted by nearly all Americans, albeit possibly begrudgingly, there are a few who still object. See, e.g., the meritless, but stubbornly repeated claims made by William J. Benson's December, 2007 "Defense Reliance Package" or his (with Martin J. "Red" Beckman) 1985 book *The Law That Never Was: The Fraud of the 16th Amendment and Personal Income Tax* in which they set forth arguments claiming that the 16th Amendment was never properly ratified. These 16th Amendment non-ratification arguments are a somewhat common theme among income tax protestors. However, they have been consistently rejected by the courts and were rejected in the criminal case against Benson personally just before he (and later some of his followers) were convicted and imprisoned for tax evasion and willful failure to file tax returns.

Communism has fallen. The EU has been formed. The Third World has emerged. Technology and science have advanced beyond anyone's imagination. With the greatest regard for Constitutional history and for the words and intents of our Founding Fathers, with respect to most matters of the day, it is Modern America which serves as the best and the most relevant context for assessing the true state of Current America.

Third, the concept of Modern America allows readers to draw directly upon their personal memories, recollections, and experiences of some or even all of this period. It reminds us how quickly things can change in America. Modern America extends backwards just a couple of generations; a mere five decades. Certainly not all that came before was good, but some of it was. Especially, for example, in the contexts of communities, the role and importance of civility, and the expectations of our political and economic leaders, some of it was better than that which we endure today.

Thus, the references to Modern America are not just academic or definitional for many Americans. For many Americans, it is the life and the America which they lived; which they experienced; which they knew. Approximately 45,000,000 Americans, nearly 1 in 6, were born prior to 1950. They have formative or cognitive memory of the entire reach of this 1957-2012 Modern America. The balance of Americans, depending upon their age, have direct knowledge and memory of some parts of this period as well—the '60s, the '70s, the '80s or the '90s. The comparative references of Current America to periods of Modern America are therefore included in order to build upon *their* American years, and to remind them of the data and details of *their* Modern America; and to affirm its continuing relevance to understanding the state and condition of our country as it exists today.[14]

---

14. It is impossible to list the many fine, even seminal, books which have been written about these years, but for general (and sometimes colorful and evocative) reading about the some of the earlier decades of the period 1957-1980 see, for example, David Halberstam's *The Fifties* (1993) and *The Best and The Brightest* (1972); William Manchester's *The Glory and the Dream—A Narrative History of America 1932-1972 (Parts III—V)*; and Arthur M. Schlesinger, Jr's *A Thousand Days* (1965) and *The Imperial Presidency* (1973).

(Continued on next page.)

For a more biographical perspective, see, for example, Doris Kearns Goodwin's *Lyndon Johnson and the American Dream* (1991) and Robert Caro's *The Years of Lyndon Johnson (The Path to Power* (1982); *Means of Ascent* (1990); *Master of the Senate* (2002); and *The Passage of Power* (2012)). See also, Tom Brokaw's *Boom* (2007), and Peter Carroll's largely unrecognized, but interesting, *It Seemed Like Nothing Happened—The Tragedy and Promise of America in the 1970s* (1982). Lastly, for more generalized and summarized reading, see, e.g., Peter Jennings and Todd Brewster's *The Century* (1998), and Chronicle Publications' *Chronicle of America* (Jacques Legand, Clifton Daniel, and John W. Kirshon).

CHAPTER 4

An Introduction to The Baseline— Modern America

The Concept of Ages and Eras

The phrase Modern America, as used in this book, is defined as the fifty-five year period from 1957 to 2012, but such year selections are not mandated. To the contrary, there is rarely any wide consensus as to the beginning or even the ending of ages and eras. Instead, their definings and namings remain, at best, an imprecise science for rather obvious reasons.

Ages don't arrive with a parade. Eras aren't announced with a press release. There is no easy or quick consensus about the proper years or the correct titling of any age or era even though some commentators are relentless in their scurry to define and name-tag them—the Age of Jackson, the Ante- and Post-Bellum Era, the Reconstruction Era, the Industrial Age, the Gilded Age, the Great Depression, the War Years, the Modern Age, the Cold War Era, the Age of Affluence, the Age of Technology, the Computer Age, the Information Age, the Age of Entitlement, the Age of Indifference, the Age of Terrorism, and on and on.

Especially in the academic world, the significance of events are the subject of endless academic papers and scholarly debates. Various alternatives are floated around one after another, and they are one-by-one considered. After intervening decades of reflection, thick academic research and lengthy analyses combined with the distilling blend of perspective, sometimes—but even then only sometimes—a consensus evolves.

In Current America, where most of us live and work, it is the same. Some degree of consensus may evolve but the real dating and naming of eras usually arrive more by the habit of repetition than by any exacting application of underlying science or studied history.

Thus, I willingly recognize that there is no tight academic or scientific implication associated with the use of the phrase "Modern America." It will be argued that 1957 was an extraordinary year, but it is the concept of a reference point more than the associated dates which is important. And to that extent, the year selection, the significance of varying events, and the naming of our eras and ages can remain, usually without problem or consequence, a fun, but notoriously subjective, parlor game.[1]

But there are a few exceptions. Even though history is both endless and patient, with a new page being written each day, there are special dates. Occasionally, an event of such singularity and consequence occurs that a new age is triggered. Excepting for the prickly academic or stubborn contrarian, these events and their associated dates are recognized by everyone as unique. For better or worse, with memories of joy or sadness, these dates hold special distinction. These dates oftentimes deserve and receive names of their own.

In the early 20th Century, before the beginning of Modern America, there were many such events and dates—Black Tuesday,[2] Pearl Harbor Day—the Day of Infamy,[3] D-Day and V-E and V-J Days.[4] More recently,

---

1. Lest it not be obvious, unlike the beginning dates of an era, the ending date both for Modern America and for Current America are *not* difficult. It is today, now. Even more precisely, the ending moment of our Current America for purposes of this book is the moment you are reading this passage.

2. On October 29, 1929, America incurred the most devastating stock market crash in its history signaling the beginning of the Great Depression.

3. On Sunday, December 7, 1941, "a day which will live in infamy," the Japanese attacked Pearl Harbor and the formal U.S. involvement in World War II began.

(Continued on next page.)

the moon landing would have been a candidate but for the raucous cacophony of the '60s in which it was buried. The obvious, most recent candidate is the tragedy of 9/11.

Thus, there are a few eras which arguably do begin or end with specificity—but not many. Even though it is hard to determine the beginning of a baseline Modern America and even though 1957 was chosen for the many detailed reasons discussed below, there are admittedly any number of worthy, alternative beginning dates which are worthy of consideration.

The Many Alternative Definitions Of Modern America

Working backwards, some could claim that Modern America began just a few years ago—in 2008 when the financial collapse exposed the

---

This phrase was used by President Franklin D. Roosevelt in his address to Congress the very next day, December 8, 1941. The speech was brilliant and short. It was a mere seven minutes in length. The speech was broadcast live by radio, and it is estimated that more than four out of five Americans—more than 80% of all Americans—listened to Roosevelt on that mid-day Monday. Within an hour, 33 minutes to be precise, a formal Declaration of War was passed by Congress, and America entered World War II. The Declaration was passed nearly unanimously with only one Representative, Jeannette Rankin, the first women ever to be elected to the House of Representatives and a lifelong pacifist from Montana, voting against the Declaration. Nearly sixty years later, another "Pearl Harbor Day" struck America on 9/11. While it is still too early to know, some believe that historians will someday reach consensus that Monday, September 11, 2001 marked the beginning of a new age, the Age of Terrorism.

4. The invasion of Normandy by the Allied Forces sealed the fate of Germany's Third Reich and the end of the war, but on that day nearly 12,000 men died (2,700 British, 949 Canadians, and 6,600 Americans) and tens of thousands more were wounded. It was not until 1945 that Germany, and three months later, Japan, surrendered and World War II ended. VE Day (Victory in Europe) was May 8, 1945, and VJ Day (Victory of Japan) was August 14, 1945 (most commonly remembered by as a result of Alfred Eisenstaedt's famous photograph of the American sailor kissing a woman in a white dress in Times Square, New York City). Over the next eighteen months men came home, families were re-united, and new lives began—in a sense, literally, with the arrival of the Baby Boomers.

weakness and literal fragility of the American economy. The financial collapse and the Great Recession which followed decimated the corporate balance sheets of thousands of companies and the personal finances of millions of American households. It simultaneously escalated the debate about both the proper role and the necessary limits of the federal government. It once again exposed the poor, indeed irresponsible, financial condition of both our federal and state governments. Debt ceilings and fiscal cliffs aside, it put the entire construct and logic of Keynesian economics back into play.

Seven years earlier, the attacks of 9/11 revealed a new and different kind of American vulnerability when nineteen terrorists commandeered commercial airlines and caused them to crash—all within 51 minutes of each other—into the World Trade Center in New York, into the Pentagon on the outskirts of the District of Columbia, and into a lonely field near Shanksville, Pennsylvania. With these attacks a new and deeper kind of fear was injected into the American psyche. The attacks led directly to the American invasion of Afghanistan and a few months later Iraq. The war in Afghanistan now holds the dubious distinction of being the longest war in American history. More than 6,500 American soldiers have lost their lives in Afghanistan and Iraq, and many tens of thousands more have been injured or impaired for life.[5] The 9/11 attacks further altered the way many Americans viewed the world. It changed our concepts of national security. It re-defined the boundaries of our personal privacies. It contributed to the massive increase in the American deficit. It further elevated (at least for a period of years) the influence of American neo-conservatism, and for a multitude of interwoven reasons it strained our nation's relations with many countries both within and without the Muslim world.

---

5. The Department of Defense reports that as of December 31, 2012, 6,587 military personnel have died in the Afghanistan War (Operation Enduring Freedom) and the Iraq War (Operation Iraqi Freedom). Another over 56,679 are currently being reported by the DOD as wounded in action. However, these numbers materially underestimate the true scope and extent of injuries suffered by U.S. troops, their families, and their loved ones as their result of injuries incurred during action or from the cumulative effect of multiple tours of duty.

A far weaker, but viable, candidate as the beginning of Modern America could be 1992. Its claim is more tepid and rests largely upon it being a year of disproportionate significance because it, better than other years, marked the beginning of the far more discordant and ideological era in American social and political life. This year signified the closing of the Reagan (and Bush Sr.) Era. Ross Perot had said his piece and left the stage just as cocksure of himself as when he arrived. A young former Governor from Arkansas, Bill Clinton, was elected. However, far more than that changed. Both coincidentally and partly resultantly, the major political parties became more ideological and more partisan. The media and especially "talk radio" became more harsh, more coarse, and less restrained. A new and hardened style of intransigence was injected into American politics which, as of this writing, remains unabated.

Nineteen eighty-nine can also lay claim as the beginning of Modern America. Nineteen eighty-nine marked the end of the Cold War. A moderated form of Chinese Communism survived the pro-democracy Spring protests, but the world watched in awe and silence as the solitary, young man stood and blocked the tank in Tiananmen Square. Just a few months later and on the other side of the world, the Berlin Wall came down, and the dismembering of the Soviet Union began. George H.W. Bush, Sr., who is increasingly and possibly correctly viewed by some as the Second Eisenhower, exercised his Presidency with a certain calmness, steadfastness, decency, and decorum. The peace dividend from the collapse of Communism never arrived and the bounce didn't long last, but for a brief period there was a nearly universal belief that the virtues of democracy and capitalism had finally prevailed as the political and economic models for the world's nations.

Nineteen eighty was also an extraordinary and transformational year. The rise and the power of the Moral Majority was becoming more apparent as the Rev. Jerry Falwell exhorted Americans to "get in step" with conservatism. Ronald Reagan won in a landslide, and many welcomed the "new day in America" even though this was also the year in which the prime interest rate climbed to 21.5% and a crazy man killed John Lennon outside of the Dakota apartments on the Upper West Side of New York.

In Christian Caryl's fine and thoughtful book *Strange Rebels*,[6] a case is made for 1979 as being "the transformational year." Relying heavily upon an internationalist analysis Caryl notes that this was the year "that brought Iran's Islamic revolution, the siege of the U.S. embassy in Tehran, the Soviet invasion of Afghanistan, and the emergence of four leaders who, (Caryl) argues, changed the course of history: Margaret Thatcher, the Ayatollah Khomeini, Deng Xiaoping and Pope John Paul II."[7] While these are remarkable and significant events and while these are dominant (and even transformational) figures in recent world history, they are not—even collectively, enough. It is not yet clear, for example, as to the outcome of the Islamic Revolution or the sustaining influence of Islamic fundamentalism as opposed to, for example, the significance of 2010's Arab Spring. Similarly, it is not obvious that the transformative force was the influence of Margaret Thatcher as opposed to the congealing powers of Ronald Reagan's brand of conservative politics and free market economics. More significantly, an over-emnphasis on 1979 underestimates the structural changes made to our political and economic systems that resulted from the rise of libertarianism, partisanship, the evolution (or devolution, depending upon one's perspective) of America's social structures, and even the more aggressive forms of modern capitalism which have come to dominate American economic life.

The deeper historians might lay a serious, albeit far quieter and less recognized, claim to 1971 as the year of the beginning of Modern America. In 1971, wedged in between the 1970 killings at Kent State[8] and

---

6. Caryl, C., *Strange Rebels – 1979 and the Birth of the 21ˢᵗ Century* (2013).

7. Karl, J., "Where Were You in 1979," (A Review of C. Caryl's Book), *The Wall Street Journal*, May 4-5, 2013.

8. From another "grassy knoll," the second grassy knoll in less than a decade, the Kent State Shootings occurred on May 4, 1970 at Kent State University in Ohio. On that day students had assembled to protest America's invasion of Cambodia which President Nixon had disclosed five days earlier on April 30, 1970. In the usual ebb and flow of these types of protests, students protested and a march began, and the police (and in this case the national guard) had been called out to preserve and protect. But this time

(Continued on next page.)

the 1972 break-in at the Watergate apartments, *All in the Family* debuted in Hollywood and Disney World opened in Orlando. Although it would be another couple of years until the helicopters would lift the last escapees off the roof of the American Embassy in Saigon,[9] by 1971 America and the world came to know, if not accept, that the Vietnam War was starting to

---

things went wrong. The guardsmen fired 67 rounds in 13 seconds. Four students were killed and nine others wounded. The political significance of the Kent State Shootings was in the nation's response. More than 4.0MM students went on strike. Hundreds of universities, colleges, and high schools were closed throughout the United States. Many believe that this was one of the turning points, one of those cathartic moments borne of both clarity and exhaustion, when public opinion coalesced even stronger against America's role in Vietnam (and now Cambodia). Others would go farther and suggest that on that day in May, at Kent State and with the wide distribution of John Filo's Pulitzer–Prize winning photograph of Mary Ann Vecchio kneeling over the body of Jeffrey Miller, the '60s ended—appropriately dazed, confused, aimless, adrift, and saddened with its dearth of achievements. See Laurant, D., "Kent State—A History Lesson That He Lives and Teaches…," *Accent on Living,* Health Publications, Spring, 2001 (about Dean Kahler who has his own memory of Kent State. He was shot and paralyzed from the chest down on that day so many years ago. He still lives and teaches in Ohio.) In October, 2012 and more than forty years after the shooting, Kent State University opened a "May 4 Visitors Center" to help visitors "better understand the events of that day set against the political and cultural changes of the times." Associated Press, October 18, 2012. See also, Porter, C., "Four Decades Later … Embracing the Tragedy as Part of University's History," *The Wall Street Journal*, November 24-25, 2012.

9. The fall of Saigon occurred on April 30, 1975, almost exactly five years to the day from the tragedy of Kent State discussed immediately above. The capture of Saigon, the capital of South Vietnam, by North Vietnamese armies led to the strangely named Operation Frequent Wind, the largest helicopter evacuation in history. In the chaos of the last days and the last Operations (Operation Babylift which evacuated about 2,000 orphans from the country, Operation New Life which evacuated over 10,000 Vietnamese refugees, and Operation Frequent Wind) many thousands of Vietnamese were evacuated out of Vietnam. But many of our allies remained. They were left behind. Even according to the new Communist government which took over, over the next years more than 200,000 South Vietnamese government officials, military officers and soldiers were sent to deadly "re-education camps." And thus America's longest war (at least until our current, now longer Afghanistan War) ended poorly, incompletely, and with a degree of confusion, sadness and indeed bitterness which remains with America to this day.

wind down. In addition, the longer term political and social consequences of that tortuous war—such as a heightened skepticism of both the media and governmental leaders—were also beginning to come into view.

In 1971 close observers of American political and social life recognized the early, nascent signs of the rise of both the size and potential power of the conservative and the evangelical movements. Possibly even more significant is the fact that 1971 was the beginning of the more thorough entwining of the private and the public sectors. It was subtle at first. For most Americans it was below or even off-radar. However, in 1971 Lewis Powell, while still a practicing attorney in Virginia and before his 1972 appointment to the Supreme Court by Richard Nixon, wrote his now-famous Memorandum challenging businesses to organize and take steps "to change both the policy and political mainstream in Washington."

The significance of Powell's recommendations were both massive and immediate. In 1970, for example, there were only about 200 lobbyists in Washington. Within ten years the number of business lobbyists in Washington would increase more than ten-fold to over 2,400 lobbyists. The membership base of the National Federation of Independent Businesses increased from 300 to over 600,000. A couple of years later, in 1974, the conservative Heritage Foundation (now one of the most influential, right-wing think tanks in Washington, D.C.) was started with $250,000 of seed money from the beer magnate Joseph Coors[10] for a very specific purpose and with a tightly-defined, specific audience— to influence "Congress and congressional staff."[11] Soon thereafter, the Heritage Foundation was generating ten to fifteen page position papers,

---

10. According to Ed Feulner, who eventually served for 35 years as the President of The Heritage Foundation, there are now more than 600,000 donors. In December, 2012 Senator Jim DeMint (R-S.C.) announced his retirement from the U.S. Senate in order to become the new President of The Heritage Foundation. Henninger, D., "A Lesson in Conservative Optimism—The Weekend Interview with Ed Feulner," *The Wall Street Journal*, December 8-9, 2012.

11. Henninger, D., "A Lesson in Conservative Optimism—The Weekend Interview with Ed Feulner," *The Wall Street Journal*, December 8-9, 2012.

which it called "Backgrounders," further evidencing that the modern age of focused, organized, targeted, business-influenced, if not business-driven, conservatism had begun. The consolidation of the public and the private sectors is the real merger and acquisition of the 20th Century, and it began in 1971. Businesses organized. First, they asserted their political influence. Then, in the opinion of many, they asserted their control of many aspects of our public life. Congress was no longer a public house. K Street was no longer just an address.

For other writers and historians 1968 was The Year—the year of Boom,[12] the year of tumult and tragedy; the year of the transformation, if not the unwinding, of America. The Vietnam War waged ferociously with the January, 1968 Tet Offensive in which the Viet Cong launched a massive offensive throughout South Vietnam. 1968 was the year of the assassination of Martin Luther King, Jr. on April 4 in Memphis, Tennessee. Both grief and riots besieged the nation for weeks, and just two months later Bobby Kennedy was assassinated on June 6 in Los Angeles. It was the second Kennedy assassinated in five years. In retrospect, it is almost weirdly appropriate that this was the year in which 911 lines were first tested and installed. But back then, nothing seemed to help the cause or calm the storm. President Johnson announced that he would not seek a second term, and Hubert Humphrey was nominated in August, 1968 at the "whole world is watching" Democratic Convention in Chicago. Just a few months later, Humphrey (and George Wallace from Alabama) were defeated by the again resurgent Richard Nixon who claimed the Presidency with a mere 49,257 votes out of 59,403,000 cast, by less than 1/10th of 1%. And there were other segments of the population committed to their own, sometimes overlapping causes—the student radicals and the war protestors, the civil rights activists rightly emboldened by the Voting Rights Act of 1965 and other legislation,[13]

---

12. See Brokaw, T., *Boom—Talking About the Sixties* (2008).

13. The eloquent historian James T. Patterson in his new book *The Eve of Destruction* also presents a compelling case for identifying 1965 as one of the "hinge years—when history turns and goes in another direction." Patterson argues that 1965, a year of

(Continued on next page.)

and the hippies who were still coming off of (or down from) the Summer of Love in the Haight-Ashbury District of San Francisco. But neither wild chaos nor horrendous tragedy necessarily signifies change. Modern America had begun earlier.

For example, it is hard to remember or to understand that in 1962 the spirit of Camelot was in the country. JFK, at the age of 43, was the youngest president ever elected, and the White House was alive with Jackie, John-John and Caroline. There was a certain magic to it all. Many thought of JFK as a "hero-president" whose deliverance was nothing less than "existential" as described by then young and star-struck Norman Mailer. America was, at once, both young and virile. America had no limits. The sky was the limit.

John Glenn may have been strapped and cramped in his Friendship 7 capsule, but in 1962 he became the first American to orbit the Earth and going to the moon *was* next. A little closer to home, Andy Williams was singing his first signature hit, *Moon River,* and he could now be seen be in more places due to America's launching of Telstar, one of our country's first telecommunications satellites which, while no longer functional, is still orbiting the Earth—lonely and only occasionally remembered.

In this relatively more orderly, if not more just and peaceful, time following the exhaustions of World War II and the Korean War, concepts of community were stronger. The neighborhood was not yet "the hood," and the word "gang" connoted young friends more than it did guns and drugs. Things were *not* perfect, as will be discussed below, but the times and the tones were different. Milk was still home delivered, and the milk cartons

---

hopeful optimism, low unemployment, phenomenal economic GDP growth, and great legislative achievement (Voting Rights, Medicare and Medicaid, the formation of the Departments of Housing and Urban Development and Transportation), was the last year before "the Sixties" began. Gordon, J., "When the Sixties Began," *The Wall Street Journal*, Dec. 24, 2012 review of Mr. Patterson's book. See also, Patterson, James, *Restless Giant—The United States From Watergate to Bush v. Gore*, (2005) which, in effect, picks up America's story where William Manchester's magnificent *The Glory and the Dream—A Narrative History of America—1932–1972* leaves off.

were not adorned with the haunting faces of abducted children. Kids still roamed neighborhoods and played "until the street lights came on," supervised "playdates" were largely unheard of, and for many American families there still unknowingly existed a full six degrees of separation from their lives and that of the fearful paranoias of the 21st Century world.

In 1962 James Bond, a character who arose from Ian Fleming's typewriter ten years earlier in England, finally came to life with the premiere of the first of twenty-three Bond films, *Dr. No,* starring Sean Connery and Ursula Andress.[14] In the same year two far more serious and real doctors received the Nobel Prize in Physiology or Medicine and launched the field of stem-cell science even though they could not anticipate that fifty-five years later this science would remain in America the subject of both hope and controversy.[15] However, in 1962, all was not perfect. No year ever is.

In 1962, like now, the signs of both threat and change were everywhere. Americans were starting to pull out their maps and find this place called Vietnam. Dominos was still just a board game in 1962, and some Americans were already wondering why we should be sending more "military advisors" to the place so far away. With the 1961 Bay of Pigs fiasco still in America's recent memory, in October, 1962 the U.S. and the Soviet Union gambled with future of the world as our navy took blockade positions around Cuban. The world survived, but we all knew that things had gone too far; that the end had actually been in sight.

Domestically, in 1962, there were early signs of other significant changes as well. James Meredith, accompanied by federal marshals, became the first black man to enroll in Ole Miss. The Supreme Court banned prayer in school. Rachel Carson released her book, *Silent Spring,* "and in the process (lent) inspiration ... to the then nascent global environmental

---

14. Sean Connery with his looks, charm and style became an instant star; a god-like hero beyond reproach. But both the times and the tolerances were different then, and co-star Ursula Andress caused a stir and Hollywood journalist wrote that "tawny 26-year-old Ursula Andress should have been billed not by her last name, but as "Undress.' " Kamp, D., The Birth of Bond, *Vanity Fair,* October, 2012, p. 249.

15. The recipients were Dr. Shinya Yamanaka of Japan and John Gurdon of Great Britain.

movement."[16] Almost concurrently, Michael Harrington released his book, *The Other America*, which helped reveal the plight of America's poor and helped set the stage for Lyndon Johnson's War on Poverty. With little notice at the time, the recently formed Students for a Democratic Society (the "SDS") ratified what it referred to as the Port Huron Statement calling for "a more egalitarian, horizontal society." The SDS would soon become recognized as one of the most vociferous and radical political organizations of the decade, and its formation was, in the opinion of some, the theoretical beginning of radicalization of U.S. college students.[17]

---

16. The book *Silent Spring* was derided by some at the time as an "emotional and inaccurate outburst," and others accused Ms. Carson of being a communist. While Ms. Carson's book was relatively narrow in its focus and merely "challenged the practices of agricultural scientists and the government and warned against overuse of synthetic pesticides (and DDT in particular)," its reverberations were extensive. Without question, this book was at least partially responsible for the 1972 banning of DDT by the then newly-formed Environmentally Protection Agency, but some critics still maintain that Ms. Carson's "extreme rhetoric generated a culture of fear, (resulting) in policies that have deprived many people access to life-saving chemicals…" In her defense, some argue that this attack may be, however, partly disingenuous since "Carson took pains to make it clear she was not calling for the banning of all pesticides, especially those that might be able to protect (humans) against insect-transmitted diseases," such as malaria. Walsh, B., Rites of Spring," *Time*, October 1, 2012, p. 56. See also, Souder, William, *On a Farther Shore: The Life and Legacy of Rachel Carson*, which describes "the moment when a gentle, optimistic proposition called 'conversation' began its transformation into the bitterly divisive idea that would come to be known as 'environmentalism'." In 1964, less than two years after the publication of *Silent Spring*, Ms. Carson died of cancer at the age of 57.

17. See Corbin, I. "From Port Huron to Zuccotti Park" *The Wall Street Journal*, August 3, 2012 (Reviewing *Take It Big: C. Wright Mills and the Meaning of Political Intellectuals* by Stanley Aronowitz). Interestingly, a very different had crowd made its own "statement" just a couple of years earlier when William F. Buckley Jr. invited about 100 conservative activists to the Buckley family estate in Sharon, Connecticut. The conference "would mark the founding of the Young Americans for Freedom (YAF)" and would issue what came to be known as the "Sharon Statement." Unlike the SDS's Port Huron Statement and almost parroting the views of Buckley's relatively new conservative publication *National Review*, the Sharon Statement "affirmed the importance of limited government, the efficacy of the free market, and the need to seek victory over rather than coexistence with Communism." Edwards, L., *William F. Buckley Jr.— The Maker of a Movement*, p. 75.

In 1962, Douglas MacArthur, as an aging soldier and leader from an earlier age, delivered his famous and eloquent Farewell Address at West Point.[18] However, other voices were starting to be heard as well. Only two hundred miles down the Hudson River from the hallowed, sacred halls of West Point, another very different type of society was beginning.

Forty-year-old Helen Gurley Brown published *Sex and the Single Girl* and to the shock and dismay—(this earlier generation's variation of our "shock and awe") of "decent society," the book quickly became a 1962 best seller.[19] And not far away and for reasons some of us still don't understand, Andy Warhol "vaulted Campbell's red-and-white tomato soup cans to icon status."[20] In Hollywood, Marilyn Monroe, aka Norma Jean Baker, the last of the Hollywood love goddesses, was found dead by suicide at the age of 36, and Joe DiMaggio, though divorced from her at the time of her death, began his many decades of grief. He would never remarry, and he would live another 37 years.

A hop, skip, and a Central Valley away from Marilyn Monroe's Hollywood, George Lucas was just graduating from high school in Modesto, California. It would still be fifteen years until Obi Wan and his crew were born in 1977 and another several years after that before the real beginning of the personal computers age, but by 1962 the first wave of video technology—television—had already started to change America dramatically.

By 1962 many American families had televisions. Most of the pictures were grainy, and the televisions had "rabbit ear" antennas sitting on top. Most of the shows were in black and white since color television (i.e., "living color" as opposed to, I guess, the other kind of color) was just starting to become commercially available. It was still an optional feature.

---

18. MacArthur, who would pass away just two years later, told the young cadets in the almost dated eloquence of his, an earlier, generation that "…in my dreams I hear again the crash of guns, the rattle of musketry, the strange, mournful mutter of the battlefield."

19. Ms. Brown would go on to be the Editor of *Cosmopolitan* for 32 years.

20. Now, 50 years later, the soup company is "returning the favor" by changing its can design and by now offering its soups in various colors just as Warhol had envisioned. *Time,* September 17, 2012, p. 52.

Color televisions were still a luxury. They were owned by the rich people down the street. But by 1962 televisions were already a part of American life. No one minded that programming still signed off each night and was replaced (usually at midnight) with a test pattern. But that, too, would soon change. In October, 1962 late night television was introduced with Tony Bennett, Joan Crawford, and Rudy Vallee being the first guests on Johnny Carson's new "Heeeeere's, Johnny" Tonight Show which aired that month. The show lasted for another 30 years and 4,531 shows.[21]

For all of these reasons, 1962 is, among all of the valid candidates, the second best candidate for defining the beginning of Modern America. But there are multiple reasons to go back a bit further to 1957 in order to find The Year which, in the opinion of this writer, is the unquestioned beginning of Modern America. Nineteen fifty-seven was The Year when the old yielded to the new; when Modern America was birthed; when the America began which we still see and feel (and at times endure); and when the pace of American life, for better or worse, began to accelerate.

1957—The Beginning of "Modern America"

As precisely as one can measure sea changes and detect epochal shifts, 1957 was the end of one era, and it was the beginning of another. It was in that year that the confusion, the wildness, and the most recent (and so far stubbornly irreversible) set of changes in American life had begun.

The Fifties was "an older, stiffer world, with Britain just (a few) years removed from food rationing and America still in an era of Kramdens, Eisenhowers, and finned Cadillacs."[22] While World War II was not a distant memory, at least some its horrors had been by then contained.

The dead had been buried. The survivors had come home. Squad by squad and company by company, the American soldiers—our fathers,

---

21. Johnny Carson aired his last show on May 22, 1992. At the end of that show he quietly thanked Ed McMahon and Doc Severinsen "and the people watching" and closed his last show by saying "I bid you a very heartfelt goodnight." In 2005, 13 years later, Carson died at the age of 79.

22. Kamp, D., "The Birth of Bond," *Vanity Fair*, October, 2012, p. 243

uncles, grandfathers, …. were released from the military.[23] For the loved ones at home, the waiting and even the rationing of gas and rubber and nylon were over. The last of the other transitions from the war were over as well. The Nazi concentration camps had long since been shut, the relocation camps in Europe had been emptied, and the long rebuilding had been started. Even the tragic existence (albeit not the pain) of America's own ten Japanese internment camps had come to an end.[24]

The world had been divided and re-aligned. The new ascendant powers were clear. The modern state of Israel had been founded on the southeastern shore of the Mediterranean. The Marshall Plan had been adopted. The Berlin airlift of 1948 was over. And in 1949 China had been "lost" to Communism.

The wartime alliance between the Soviet Union and the West had long since been dissolved, and "(a) new edgier, political era had begun."[25] America's monopoly of the atomic bomb was short-lived, and any hope of a post-war, unilateral domination by the West evaporated when the Soviet Union tested its own nuclear weapon in early September of 1949 and when, over the next decade, it continued to impose its forced dominion over Eastern Europe. Especially after the Soviet army and tanks crushed Hungary's brief 1956 uprising,[26] the Soviet Union came to be

---

23. By 1947, just two years after the end of the war, the size of our armed forces had been cut by nearly 90%—"from their wartime strength of 12 million to 1.5 million." Halberstam, D., *The Fifties,* p. 27.

24. The "relocation centers" were located in isolated areas in seven states and housed over 120,000 Japanese and Japanese-Americans (including about 2,200 Japanese who were transported from South America at the outbreak of the war). Adding insult to injury, most of them were located on Native American lands. The last center at Tule Lake, California, was closed on March 20, 1946, and the powers of the War Relocation Authority were officially terminated by President Truman shortly thereafter. Only two of these former camps remain and are open to visitors—the incongruously named Heart Mountain, located just east of Cody, Wyoming, and Manzanar, located at the base of the Sierra Nevada Mountains between Long Pine and Independence, California.

25. Halberstam, D., *The Fifties,* p.52.

26. The Hungarian uprising, though long-coming, was spontaneous in origin. However, it lasted only 18 days, although sporadic violence and periodic economic

(Continued on next page.)

seen—correctly, by all and just as the Soviets wished—as a real threat; as a dominant and imposing world power.

It is not surprising that America had welcomed Eisenhower to the White House in 1953. Americans were busy to get on with "their" own lives. There was an almost literal need for his calm style and his well-earned confidence.

Just a few months after Eisenhower had entered the White House, Josef Stalin, after having purged millions of his fellow citizens to their exile and eventual death, had finally died himself—further and more finally closing the War Years.[27] In 1956 Nikita Khrushchev had delivered his "Secret Speech" to the Soviet's 20th Congress in which he denounced Stalin's purges and the personality cult which had arisen around Stalin himself. By 1957 the Kremlin shuffle was over with the rigid, square Georgian face of Josef Stalin replaced with the seemingly less intimidating and almost disheveled Nikita Khrushchev. However, in November, 1956, just six weeks before the beginning of Modern America, Khrushchev used his now-infamous phrase "we shall bury you." Americans were crudely reminded that while the Cold War was closing out its first full decade, it was still real. It was still dangerous.

---

interruptions continued through the middle of 1957. Within less than two weeks Soviet forces entered Budapest and other parts of the country in the early morning hours, and within days thereafter relative peace was imposed, and the world came to understand that the uprising never had a realistic chance of succeeding. Over 2,500 Hungarians and 700 Soviet troops were killed. More than 350 Hungarians were later executed, another 13,000 were imprisoned, and many were deported to the Soviet Union. See generally, Applebaum, A., *Iron Curtain: The Crushing of Eastern Europe 1944-1956* (2012).

27. I admit caution in the use of this phrasing as it relates to even the death of Stalin. As some Americans considered in the context of the U.S.'s killing of Osama bin Laden in Abbottabad, Pakistan in 2011, it may cross the boundaries of propriety and possibly even morality to express joy or happiness in the passing of another person. However, the phrasing here seems both narratively and morally permissible when one considers the enormity of Stalin's crimes against his own people—for which he never paid and for which he was never called to atone for in any court of international jurisdiction.

Despite the implications of Khrushchev's statement,[28] both the Soviet Union and even the prospect of nuclear war remained largely outside the view (or at least beyond the focus) of most American families. The decision to start proceeding with the development of the far more powerful H-Bomb had been made at the beginning of the decade, but it was left to Edward Teller and his team to move from the atomic bomb to the hydrogen bomb. In 1957 most Americans happily chose to remain largely and almost consciously ignorant of the nuclear threat. The threat seemed distant, and parents were at peace with, or at least accepting of, their children duck-n-covering under their desks at school.

No one was digging bomb shelters in their backyards yet. No one was getting scanned at our airports or patted down at our borders. There were no nuclear missiles in Cuba, and for the most part the Russian Bear seemed a long ways away. It was unsettling (and for some even terrifying with that "Russian eye in the sky") when in October, 1957 Russia launched the world's first orbiting satellite, Sputnik, across the bow of our terrain and our psyche. But despite the unsettling stir of Sputnik in 1957, Americans remained confident and steady in their embrace of their willing ignorance and their sense of long-earned bliss. Most Americans only took casual and passing notice that the Treaty of Rome which was signed that year by six European countries and by which the history-defying European Economic Community came quietly into being.

Americans were happy that much of the prior decade's tensions had seemed to ease. They were happy that both the reality and the paranoia of the House Un-American Activities Committee investigations had long since expired. By 1957, it had even been seven years since Joe McCarthy, at the time a deservedly little-known Senator from Wisconsin, had given

---

28. Despite the warlike implications of this phrase and despite its widespread interpretation by most Westerners, Premier Khrushchev insisted that this was not a statement of intimidation or a nuclear threat. Instead, several months later (and again in the U.S. several years later) he stated that this phrase was merely a reference of the Marxist saying that "(t)he proletariat is the undertaker of capitalism." Disingenuously, he insisted that the phrase was merely an expression of competing values between the worker society of the Soviet Union and the bourgeois West.

his now-infamous "I-have-here-in-my-hand-a-list" speech in Wheeling, West Virginia. By 1957, the "circus" and the "carnival-like four-year spree of McCarthy's accusations, charges, and threats" had come to an end.[29] And America was happy that the carnival had closed. Americans were pleased that the fears had seemed to lessen; that the pains had started to fade; and that some of the scars had started to heal.

America was happy that World War II and, by 1957, the Korean War had ended. While World War II obviously remained etched in both the collective memory of the country and while the personal memories of all of its citizens grieved at the loss of another 54,200 American war deaths in Korea, the Forgotten War,[30] Americans were tired of war. By 1957, they wanted to move on. And they did. They had no idea that Vietnam was coming. They had no idea that they were, once again, merely in a brief period of respite.[31]

For most Americans—but, as will be discussed, not all—it was a time of perceived security and welcome stability. However, these types of historical summaries can be dangerous. They can easily be misread as odes to days gone by; as misplaced, almost nostalgic remembrances of previous (good) times. However, be assured that this description of 1957 is *not* so intended. There is no delusion that 1957 was a perfect year; the beginning of some kind of perfect era. It was not. No year ever is. No era ever is. To the contrary, in 1957 there were many problems. There was a stench of

---

29. Halberstam, D., *The Fifties*, p. 52.

30. Although the actual hostilities occurred from June, 1950 until July, 1953, the war period was extended until January, 1955 due to the uneasy and protracted peace negotiations. Of the 54,200 American deaths, 33,700 "were actual battle deaths." See Korean War Statistics, Veterans of the Korean War, *veteransinfo.net.*

31. Americans had no idea that they would come to care about Southeast Asia. Most Americans had never heard of Vietnam. They didn't know where it was. They had no idea that in less than a decade, would have to be fought by their young sons; and that the war would be shown to them in another kind of living (and dying) color. In 1957 Americans didn't yet have to struggle with trying to understand how a small country, so many miles away, could devastate the American psyche and community. After all they had been through, it was inconceivable that a distant war in a small county would, in many cases, break-up Americans families and turn generation against generation. In 1957, this was all unknown; unforeseeable.

wide discriminations and the sadness of poverty—especially rural poverty. But it is also true that by 1957 millions of veterans, with their young families in tow, had taken advantage of the GI Bill. It cannot be denied that they had survived much, and by 1957 many of them emerged—energetic, enthusiastic, and educated.[32]

Americans were holding jobs, building families, buying houses, and mowing yards. They were making up for lost years. They were enjoying an economy characterized by job security and relative economic equality.

1957 was also one of the last years in which the traditional systems and allocations of authority were still holding. It was an orderly era even for young people. *The Wild One* with Marlon Brando had been released in 1953, and *Rebel Without a Cause* with James Dean had been released in

---

32. It is estimated that by the time the original GI Bill ended in 1956, nearly one-half of the 16,000,000 World War II veterans had taken advantage of some of the benefits conferred by the GI Bill. The impact of the "blandly and bureaucratically named Servicemen's Readjustment Act of 1944 (the "GI Bill")" cannot be overstated. At the time of its enactment, the Congressional debate about this legislation "rarely penetrated the public awareness." At the time of its enactment "the nation's focus was upon the daily advances, setbacks and genuine horrors of the war...." In addition, Congress estimated that only about 7% would take advantage of the GI Bill's education benefits since college was still then viewed as a bastion of the elite. It was believed that only a small number of GIs would take advantage of the college-access benefits if for no other reason than less than one-half of the GI's who served in World War II had even finished high school. But Congress was wrong, and millions of vets came home anxious, ready and eager to go to college. They saw the GI Bill as an opportunity to change the lives. And they took it. For millions of veterans and for their young families and their newly-built communities, everything changed. It is not easy to measure the impacts of the GI Bill—"14 ... Nobel Prize winners, 3 Supreme Court Justices, 3 Presidents, a dozen Senators, 2 dozen Pulitzer price winners, 238,000 teachers, 891,000 scientists, 67,000 doctors, 450,000 engineers, 240,000 accountants, 17,000 journalists, 22,000 dentists ....." It altered the dreams of millions of vets. It moved their horizon. It created their success. It generated a new kind and a new level of affluence never before experienced by any country. It changed "both the aspirations and the expectations of all Americans, veterans and nonveterans alike. A nation of renters (became) a nation of homeowners." Suburbs were built. Highways were laid. Almost unwittingly, "(t)he Cold War (found) its warriors—not in the trenches or the barracks, but at the laboratory and the wind tunnel and the drafting table." Humes, E., *Over Here—How the G.I. Bill Transformed the American Dream* (2006), p. 5-6 and 33.

1955. But they were still just movies. The real world for most Americans was still more sedate; more controlled; more controllable. The concept of "teenagers" had not yet fully come of age, and hardly anyone noticed that Jack Kerouac finally got around to publishing his book *On the Road* even though he had written it several years earlier. Young people were still "largely accepting of the given social covenants,"[33] and even though many Americans (and especially many American women) knew that it wasn't always so, families sat together, without debate or discord, and watched *Father Knows Best* on TV every week.

Just as the traditional family structures and the authoritarian roles of parents still dominated, the American dream—especially in the context of economic terms—was coming true. Many families were beginning to possess a sense of the economic security which had been so cruelly eviscerated by the Great Depression and so long postponed by the War.

For many Americans, at least for many white Americans, there seemed to be a real chance of having a good life. The bounce of optimism was nearly everywhere, and Henry Luce and others started talking about "the American Century."[34] From today's perspective, from the perch of

---

33. Halberstam, D., *The Fifties*, p. x.

34. Halberstam, D., *The Fifties*, p. 117. Possibly more interesting and more accurate was the characterization by Maohirior Amaya, a Japanese intellectual and high-level civil servant "… that the American Century was the same thing as the Oil Century—an era in which the economy was driven by oil instead of coal and in which, for the first time, the worker became a consumer as well." Id., p. 117. The dominance of oil in the 20th Century cannot be easily over-stated. It contributed, if not assured, the affluence and relative ease and mobility of life of citizens in developed nations. It fueled—both figuratively and literally—the development of automobile industry and the construction of massive highway infrastructures. It created the possibility and cost-effectiveness of air travel. As a mere by-product it created the concept of tourism and the development of the worldwide hospitality industry. Oil enabled a plethora of derivative innovations and products—especially, for example, plastics. It led to the formation of OPEC and was an omnipresent influence upon international politics in general and to the enhanced geopolitical significance of the Middle East. It also was a major source of certain forms of environmental degradations such as global warming and major spills and resultantly, albeit indirectly, helped to trigger, especially in the last quarter of the 20th Century, the growth and importance of the environmental movement.

our hyper-accelerated, attention-deprived, multi-tasking, and techno-wired life, the country at the beginning of Modern America was moving at a much slower, so-yesterday, snail-mail pace. But part of the amazement of 1957 is that it wasn't that long ago. Modern America is new. It is recent. And in that sense as well, the concept of Modern America remains a valid basis by which to analyze and compare the facts and data about Current America.

It was an almost naive; uninformed; secure; and non-reflective period. But it made sense. It felt good. There were dead serious exceptions, but overall there was an "(era) of general good will" and by 1957 and for many Americans economic security was morphing into something even better—affluence. Few could see and even fewer would accept the seemingly counter-intuitive notion that affluence could have a downside even though John Kenneth Galbraith up in Massachusetts was writing his soon-to-be-famous book, *The Affluent Society,* arguing just that. Leave it to an ivory tower dude to ruin the day. Instead, in 1957 and for most Americans, affluence was good and still uncomplicated. The parents of the late 1950's had no idea that Galbraith's book would soon be read by their children—all ensconced years later in their college dorms. They had no idea that conformity was to be condemned or that the role of women would soon be a matter of serious and passionate debate.

To the contrary, the '60s hadn't arrived yet. In 1957 young boys were still wearing Davy Crockett coonskin hats. *Leave It to Beaver* premiered on TV, and on Sunday nights families gathered around their new TV to watch the *Ed Sullivan Show* or to listen to the real-deal Uncle Walt introduce the week's *Wonderful World of Disney.*[35] TV was watched as a family and usually it was watched without the interruptions of telephones and text messages. Instead, just like their one TV, most families had only

---

35. Disneyland, which had opened in Anaheim, California just a couple of years earlier in 1955, was stilling getting its kinks out. However, by 1957 Disneyland welcomed 4.0MM visitors with admission prices they could afford. The rest of the Disney entourage—Disney World in Florida (1971), the Disney TV Channel (1977), the Disney Cruises (1995), and the cross-marketing land of Disney—would be introduced to a changed America over the next five decades of Modern America.

one phone—and the phone was itself almost always in the other room, tethered to the wall.

In 1957 politics had a tarnished, but not buffoonish, history. Like now, politicians were not seen as the most honest bunch, but politics was still deemed an honorable profession. Politicians did their jobs and, within limits and with some conspicuous exceptions, they could be believed. The press was not disdained. Reporters wore hats, smoked relentlessly, and drank too much. However, by and large, they did their job. They collected the news, and they reported the news.

Thus, the late 1950s was an "era of general good will and expanding affluence, (and) few Americans doubted the essential goodness of their society."[36] Americans were not all grumpy and entitled or as "pushy and self-aggrandizing"[37] as many believe we are today. Americans weren't all frustrated and angry as many believe we are today. Americans weren't all in-your-face cocky or whatever-dismissive as many believe we are today. Certainly disagreements were real and tensions existed, but cynicism was not honored as an independent, badge-of-honor virtue. In 1957 motives were not doubted as a matter of practice.

Sports, like today, were big, but it was less "professional." There was a more personal relationship between the fans and their idols. The NBA on

---

36. Halberstam, D., *The Fifties,* p. x.

37. Noonan, P., "The I's Have It," *The Wall Street Journal*, November 17-18, 2012. Ms. Noonan laments in this column that "(w)e are becoming a conceited nitwit society" in which we are "pushy and self-aggrandizing" and "(n)o one is ashamed to brag now. And show off." She notes, possibly correctly, that we have lost our culture of modesty and that, in its place, there is "(a)n epidemic of egomania (which has stricken) America's civilian and military leadership." In the context of the tragic 2012 General David Petraeus debacle, she cleverly compares, for example, how neither General Ulysses S. Grant nor General Dwight Eisenhower ever decorated their uniforms. Noonan notes that Grant "wore his uniform with four stars on his shoulder and nothing else. And that was a fellow who'd earned a few medals," whereas now generals, such as General Petraeus and his fellow officers routinely display their "fruit salad" rows and rows of awards and ribbons. These small military examples arguably pale in comparison to the rough parallels of brash self-aggrandizement and self-promotion which are now both common and even expected in American politics and business.

television was still in its infancy. The NBA made its network television debut in the 1955-1956 season,[38] and it was starting to attract more interest due to the introduction of the game-accelerating 24-second rule and the ascendance of the amazing Boston Celtics when Bill Russell joined Bob Cousy and Coach Red Auerbach in 1957.[39] In terms of national dominance as a sport and especially as a television sport, the NFL was also still in its infancy. The first major NFL television contract wasn't signed until 1962, and, more importantly, college football games, just like college basketball games, held far greater fan loyalties and interest than professional league games.

Although off-camera and out of the spotlight, 1957 was a big year for boxing. In that year Angelo Dundee, while in Louisville, Kentucky with light heavyweight champion Willie Pastrono, got a call from a young man named Cassius Clay, who in 1964 changed his name to Muhammad Ali upon his joining the Nation of Islam. Ali and Dundee were "one of the most successful pairings of trainer and athlete in modern sport" ever launched.[40] But none of this—basketball, football, the rivalry of Russell and Chamberlain, the teaming of Dundee and Muhammad Ali—compared in 1957 with the dominance of baseball.

In 1957, baseball, and only baseball, remained the only real national pastime. Kids from Kansas to New York tracked batting averages. They knew every score. They counted every RBI. The players were idolized, and some of them—especially Mickey Mantle—were gods. It was said of Mickey Mantle that "even his aura had an aura." Buddy Holly had his fans,

---

38. Except for a brief period during the 1953-1954 long-defunct Dumont television network, the NBA was not presented on network television until the 1955-1956 season. Interest in the NBA grew steadily and eventually gained a stalwart television audience on NBC and other network stations, on ESPN, and NBA programming which was launched in 1999.

39. With Bill Russell as their dominating Center, the Boston Celtics won eleven NBA titles over the next thirteen seasons. When 7'1", 250-pound Wilt Chamberlain (after playing for a year (1958) with the Harlem Globetrotters) joined the then-Philadelphia Warriors (the team moved to San Francisco in 1962) the Russell-Chamberlain rivalries, one of the greatest sports rivalries in history, began.

40. Memorium for Angelo Dundee. *Time*, December 19, 2012.

and there were the usual Hollywood gaggle of stars, but for most American boys baseball players were the real American celebrities. Baseball players were the real American heroes. Their partying was not the stuff of scandal. It was the stuff of legend.

Baseball was serious business, but there was an easy fun to it all as well, such as the night in May, 1957 when Mickey Mantle, Yogi Berra, Hank Bauer, and Whitey Ford and their wives all went out to celebrate Billy Martin's 29th birthday. They ended up at the Copacabana to see Sammy Davis Jr. The Copa "billed itself as 'the hottest club north of Havana'" (which was still a place you could travel to back then). Before the night was out, a melee broke out. Noses got broken when a bunch of upper Manhattan guys started with the "little black sambo" catcalls at Sammy. But times were different. No arrests were made. No breaking-news reports were made. No lawyers got involved. Instead, the players' legends grew.[41] It was just a different era.

But other realities were also in play by 1957. The nature and capacities of transportation was changing. Travel was getting easier. By 1956 the interstate highway system, the "largest public works system since the Pyramids,"[42] had started to be built. By 1957, the network of roads could be well-imagined even though the entire project wouldn't be technically finished until 1992 with the completion of I-70 through Glenwood Springs, Colorado. By 1957, even mass transit was so common and so widely used that it wouldn't be until 2011 that the ridership number of 10.4BB trips would again be approached.[43] Curiously, the high mass transit ridership in 2011 was largely seen as attributable to the high price of gasoline.

41. Leavy, J., *The Last Boy—Mickey Mantle and the End of America's Childhood*, p. 164. This wonderfully titled and brilliantly written book encapsulates the era—the last days of "America's Childhood."

42. See, e.g., Weingroff, R., "The Genie in the Bottle: The Interstate System and Urban Problems, 1939—1957," quoting Fishman, R., "The American Metropolis at Century's End: The Past and Future Influences," Housing Facts and Findings, Winter, 1999.

43. *The Week,* March 23, 2012, citing S. Hargreaves, *CNNMoney.com.* See also, *Time,* March 26, 2012, p. 5.

And air travel had arrived as well. As of 1957 less than 1% of Americans had travelled internationally by air, but non-stop transcontinental air travel was becoming routine. While air travel had not yet kickstarted the destination travel and hospitality business, the conduct of American business had changed. The nation had gotten smaller. The East and the West had gotten closer.

By 1957, diesel power on U.S. railroads for the first time eclipsed steam power, but because of the burgeoning air travel, Americans no longer needed to rely upon the slow chug of the trains even if it was a "diesel chug" rather than a "steam-powered" chug. While in hindsight it was probably inevitable, it was still a shock when both the New York Giants and the Brooklyn Dodgers moved to California in 1957. The Brooklyn Dodgers played their last game at Ebbets Field on September 24, 1957, and some say that Brooklyn never fully recovered.

The Brooklyn Dodgers are but one obituary entry for 1957. Normally obituaries are tempting, but dubious, markers for identifying the ends of any era. But 1957 was a peculiar year. Many lives from the prior eras came to an end. Many chapters of American history seemed to close. In 1957 Joe McCarthy died of cirrhosis of the liver. Bugsy Moran died of lung cancer. Elliot Ness died broken and penniless since his book, *The Untouchables,* was not released until the summer after his death. And Oliver Hardy and Humphrey Bogart died. Even the Hudson Bay Company, after 275 years of operation, closed its doors.

And conversely there were births and new beginnings. In 1957 Hanna-Barbera began productions. Both the Marriott and Hyatt hotel chains opened their doors. After five years of trying different motel designs (room size, gift shop, swimming pool, "Kids Free," TVs "In *Every* Room"), Holiday Inns finally went public. Ski resorts were opened for the rich—but the rich were envied, not vilified. They were not derisively referred to as "the 1%."

A little company named Wham-O Manufacturing introduced the Frisbee to the delight of kids and the confusion of parents. Toys-R-Us started selling toys. Franchising started to accelerate, and McDonald's was still selling its 15-cent hamburgers. In 1957 McDonald's only had 40 franchises while today it doubles as a Disney cross-marketing store and has 25,163 worldwide and 12,804 in the U.S. alone—or 257 per state for anyone who is still counting. Outside of Minneapolis, Minnesota, America's first covered and heated mall was opened. For better or worse, it was all starting to come together.

And possibly the most important and best-remembered of all, the '57 Chevy, the "hot one," was born. With no intended offense to Mustangs or Corvettes, the '57 Chevy still owns American automobile history. It remains "the most popular used car in history."[44]

In 1957 Merv Adelson's Paradise Homes in Las Vegas was selling houses as fast as they could be built during the booming, early Mob days of Las Vegas,[45] while far away—quietly, without flair, and without any expectations of the Vegas-style bow-downs—Warren Buffett was also just getting started. In that year and at the age of 27, he bought the 5-bedroom stucco house in Omaha, Nebraska, where he still lives today. About 710 miles to the southeast another young man, but the near anti-thesis of Warren, was also buying his first home. He would name his new home *Graceland,* and Elvis Presley would call it home until his death 20 years later. On the West Coast, Bill Gates and Steve Jobs, born within eight months of one another, were still toddlers just hanging around and waiting to excel in pre-school. Sixteen-year-old Bob Zimmerman was up in Hibbing, Minnesota living with his parents. It would be another two years until he started using the name Bob Dylan. On the other side of the water in 1957 and in Liverpool, another sixteen-year-old, John Lennon, met Paul McCartney. Shortly thereafter they started playing together in their newly-formed band, the Quarrymen.[46] A few years later they would change their name to The Beatles.

---

44. Holmes, *Ultimate Classic Cars*, Kandour, Ltd., p. 33-35.

45. Burrough, B., "Remembrance of Wings Past," *Vanity Fair*, March, 2013, p. 254, relating the fascinating story of the downfall of Merv Adelson—one of the first large homebuilders in Las Vegas, one of the former owners of Rancho La Costa in San Diego, and one of the founders of Lorimar Productions, According to this article, Adelson, now 83, is "broke and living in a one bedroom apartment in Santa Monica, California."

46. George Harrison would join the group the next year, and in 1962 Ringo would join The Beatles and round out the Fab Four.

The American world was anticipatory, alive, exciting, rock-n-roll, innovative, and energetic. Americans didn't yet realize how much the world would shrink over the next decades, but in Greenwich, England in 1957 Daniel Day-Lewis, who 55 years later would become America's visual personification of our own Abraham Lincoln, was born. More historically important was the birth of another child. In that same year and many continents away, Osama bin Laden was born in Riyadh, Saudi Arabia, the nth son of a billionaire construction magnate. Decades later, near the other end of Modern America, this child would bring fear, cause destruction, and introduce the word "jihad" to America. However, in 1957, the birth of Osama bin Laden held little significance. The rise of terrorism couldn't be imagined, and most Americans—or at least most white Americans— hadn't even noticed or couldn't come to believe that all was not well. The failure to notice was not, for most Americans, a matter of convenience or an instance of stubborn and willful blindness. The answers were simpler and literally more obvious.

At the beginning of Modern America, in 1957, most Americans—or at least their parents and grandparents—had gone through the Depression. They had gone through the War. They had buried uncles and brothers. Most Americans had seen too much. They held too many and too recent memories. They had already lived through too much. It is not even surprising that many Americans, consciously or otherwise, decided to start anew, and by 1957 the 122.7 births per 1,000 women birth rate among U.S. women was higher than at any time before—or since.[47]

The younger, newer members of the Baby Boomer generation were ensconced in their childhoods, but they only heard stories from their parents and from their grandparents. They did live them. They were unaware that they were in familial proximity with and blood descendants of what would be later referred to as the Greatest Generation.[48]

---

47. This 122.7 birth rate at the peak of the baby boom compares with the more recent birth rate of 64 births per 1,000 — an all-time U.S. low, as of 2007-2010. Jordan, M., *The Wall Street Journal,* November 30, 2012, citing the Pew Research Center.

48. Brokaw, T., *The Greatest Generation,* 1998.

Intellectually, most Americans—and certainly the Americans in the Negro communities as they were then referred to then—knew that all was not perfect. Americans knew that there were poor people. Americans knew that minorities, especially in the South, were too often ignored or mistreated. They knew that their children were beginning to show signs of insolence, indulgence—and worse yet, independence. They knew about McCarthyism, about the Cold War and the Russkies and the Hungarian Revolution. They knew about the stunning failure of Edsel, and they'd eventually find out that the Africanized bee had been released in that year. But, largely, in 1957, at that time and for that brief moment in American history, most were anxiously willing to believe that much was good. From the perspective of those who had lived through the War Years and especially for those who had also lived through the Depression of the 1930s, it wasn't hard to see, to feel, and to believe that the '50s were "better."

This perception was due to many other factors as well. It was due partly to the fact that communities were tighter and the country was smaller. In 1957 there were (only) 172,000,000 Americans—about 55% of Current America's population. But the benevolent and widely shared perception that things were "better" was also partly due to the fact that at least a measure of public civility was commonplace. Civility was expected, and manners still mattered.

But apart from the then smaller population, America seemed—to itself—to be in other ways big. In 1957, at the beginning of Modern America, the world was a vastly different place, but America's financial and economic position in the world was un-rivaled.

Even though America's GDP in 1957 was a mere $461 MM (only 3% of today's GDP), America possessed one-half of the world's wealth; more than one-half of its productivity; and two-thirds of the world's machines. "The rest of the world (lay) in the shadow American industry."[49] Americans welcomed and embraced this long-awaited era of national economic dominance and personal job security. Possibly because it so strongly sensed, correctly, that it was both powerful and on the move, Americans neither

---

49. Halberstam, D., *The Fifties*, p.116 quoting British historian Robert Payne.

noticed nor cared about the relative lack of innovation. They weren't bothered by the relative absence of booming entrepreneurship. They weren't bothered by what would seem today to be poor rates of return. Both their dreams and their expectations were more modest.

They didn't notice the relative absence of consumer choice. Instead, they were enthralled with the multitude of new things which *were* available for the first time and for *them*—houses, cars, dishwashers, washers and dryers, air-conditioning, televisions, and above all—*hope.* In sum, there was a certain, albeit overstated and partly misplaced, contentment and even enthusiasm in America and for all things American.

In 1957 Eugene Burdick and William Lederer were busy writing *The Ugly American.* By 1958 it was a bestseller. However, most American's weren't bothered by the title. Most Americans weren't offended by the thinly-veiled condemnation of America's arrogance overseas. Even fewer Americans at the time noticed the prescient setting of the book—Southeast Asia.[50] But the cracks in the wall were there. As in any society as diverse as America—racially, ethnically, educationally, economically, culturally—there were problems. Looking back, the problems were there then; just as they are today. Everywhere.

Some of the cracks in the wall were not inherently matters of serious social concern. Instead, they were mere matters of evolution; almost matters of preference and taste. For example, in 1957 the sixteen-piece Count Basie Band was still playing at the Waldorf-Astoria Hotel in New York, but most of the country was moving (far) beyond and away from Big Bands. On January 6, 1957 more than 60,000,000, 82.6% of the American television audience, watched Elvis Presley's 3rd and final performance on *The Ed Sullivan Show*, or, more precisely, 2/3 of his performance since he was only shown above his waist in order to conceal his "gyrations." The new American bands were smaller. The band members were younger. They didn't wear tuxedos, and they practiced in their parents' garages. The clarinets had been traded in for electric guitars. Presley's top hits in the year were *Jail*

---

50. In 1963 the movie, *The Ugly American,* was also released starring Marlon Brando as Ambassador Harrison MacWhite.

House Rock and, appropriately named for the emerging teenager generation, *All Shook Up*. The battle between the Big Bands and Rock n Roll was on. And Rock n Roll won. There was no easy bridge between Count Basie and Bo Diddley. Folk singers and balladeers put up a fight, and Count Basie, God bless him, performed with his orchestra until his death in 1984. But rock n roll won.

The music was hot, lively, and not just new. It was a different, questionable kind of music. A young, respectable, "clean-cut as was said back then, 15-year-old Canadian named Paul Anka had spent most of the 1950's touring with Chuck Berry, Little Richard, (and) Eddie Cochran," and in 1957 Anka released his first signature hit, "Diana."[51] But for all of the traditional respectability, even if such a concept could be defined, it was obvious that Chuck Berry and Ozzie Nelson were never going to be good friends. They came from different places. They had different interests. More importantly, they were headed in different directions, and by 1957 most parents had started to notice. Some parents had started to (futilely) disapprove. But it came. It came all at once. And it came from everywhere.

The British invasion of The Beatles wouldn't arrive until the early 1960s, but in 1957 *American Bandstand*[52] was born, and a whole new sub-generation was born. They were called "teenagers." They hadn't yet been radicalized, but they had become identifiable as both a market and almost as a generation. *Possibly* more important for our consideration of Current America, many of them had tasted relative luxury. They had had an easy life. They had been indulged. They were the first derivative beneficiaries of America's new wealth. Their expectations weren't tempered by memories or burdened by patience.

Other issues, other "cracks in the wall" were more serious; far more so. Other issues within American society were of greater importance. They were of longer consequence, and they were not mere matters of familial structure, generational association. They were not mere matters of musical

---

51. Weintraub, J., "Paul Anka – A V.F. Portrait," *Vanity Fair*, May, 2013, p. 184.

52. *American Bandstand* remained on television for 32 years until 1989. For many, Dick Clark, until almost the end of his life in April, 2012, remained the ageless teenager.

preference or taste. They were matters of right and wrong; good and evil. These issues lay just below the surface of busy, bustling America.

In 1957, even amidst the consumerism, confidence, and enthusiasm for all things American, the ferment of change was present. The winds of change were everywhere. Collectively, the continuing relevance of many of these issues today is another reason for identifying 1957 as being the beginning of Modern America.

In that year, about 55 years ago, Senator Kefauver held Senate hearings about the activities of American pharmaceutical companies. With far less fanfare but arguably with greater long-term significance, two scientists in La Jolla, California reported that fuels increased atmospheric carbon dioxide. In that year the U.S. Surgeon General for the first time reported a link between smoking and lung cancer.

And then, as now, the issues and moralities of race and civil rights were dominant. On a Spring day in April of 1947, 28-year-old Jackie Robinson broke the color line and started at first base for the Brooklyn Dodgers. A year later President Truman by Executive Order had mandated the integration of the U.S. military. In 1954 the Supreme Court in the case of *Brown vs. Board of Education* went far further and tossed out the convenient, but disingenuous "separate but equal" 1896 reasoning of *Plessy v. Ferguson.* By a powerful vote of 9-0 the Supreme Court ordered that American public schools were to be integrated. The momentum changed, and the inevitability of the civil rights movement began.

On December 21, 1956, just four days before Christmas and eleven days before the beginning of 1957, the City of Montgomery, Alabama finally agreed to permit the integration of the City's buses and Montgomery's Negro community agreed to end its year-long boycott which had begun when a 42-year-old seamstress, named Rosa Parks, had refused to yield her seat on a Montgomery, Alabama city bus to a white man. She had been arrested about a year earlier and the long and momentous bus strike that was led by young Rev. Martin Luther King, Jr. began. Shortly thereafter, but with little notice outside of the black community, the Rev. Martin Luther King, Jr. was selected to be the first President of the newly formed Southern Christian Leadership Conference. Within a mere six years, the Rev. King would be delivering this "I Have a Dream" speech in Washington, D.C. to the gathered hundreds of thousands.

Also in 1957 Lyndon Johnson, largely for his own political, aspirational reasons, ramrodded through a civil rights bill.[53] While this legislation is almost more famous for the 24 hours, 18-minute filibuster of Senator Strom Thurmond, the longest-filibuster in the history of the U.S. Senate, and while the legislation made little meaningful change in and of itself, it was significant in several respects. First, it was the first civil rights bill since 1875. More importantly, it presaged the powerful civil rights legislation that would be enacted within the next decade.[54]

Things were amiss in 1957 when President Eisenhower nationalized 1,000 paratroopers and 10,000 Arkansas National Guard troops in order to help Gov. Orval Faubus step aside and allow nine brave young black children to enter the Little Rock Central High School.

And there were still many more issues on their way which would need to be addressed—such as the still unarticulated, feelings of emptiness and abandonment felt by many women, the draft and anti-war movements of the '60s, the scourge of drugs, the rise of crime, and the waves of alternative lifestyles and Hippies and countercultures which would soon be introduced into American life.

---

53. Caro, Robert *The Passage of Power* (2012), p. xiv.

54. Senator Thurmond of South Carolina opened his filibuster on August 28, 1957 by denouncing the proposed Civil Rights Bill as "cruel and unusual punishment." Over the next 24 hours and 18 minutes "(t)he senator, armed with throat lozenges and malted milk tablets, recited the voting rights laws of every state to (supposedly) show (that) adequate protection existed. He also recited the Declaration of Independence and launched into a history of Anglo-Saxon juries to counter the bill's proposal to allow judges to punish cases of civil contempt without a jury trial." The Southerners didn't rise up and convince the other Senators to block the legislation, and thus Thurmond finally stopped his filibuster after a strong denunciation of "those nine men" on the Supreme Court who had, three years earlier in the case of *Brown v. Board of Education* outlawed school segregation." With that closing denunciation, he finally quit and left the chamber. The bill passed less than two hours later by an overwhelming vote of 62-15. *Associated Press,* June 27, 2003, quoting Nadine Cohodas' biography entitled *Strom Thurmond and the Politics of Southern Change* (1995).

And so it is that 1957 is the good place to begin our understanding of Current America in the context of Modern America. While culture wars and their "language of catastrophe"[55] remained still a thing of the distant future, it was back then that things started to become astir. It was then—in 1957—that maybe not knowing fully why, Congress ordered with little objection, notice or fanfare, that the words "In God We Trust" be emblazoned, for the first time, on U.S. Currency.

---

55. Frank, T., "Easy Chair—Social Studies," *Harper's Magazine*, October, 2011, p. 11.

CHAPTER 5

Assumptions, Sources,
and Methodology

Fundamental Assumptions

Chapters regarding the methodology of a book—the use, number, and nature of underlying assumptions, the selection of topics, facts, and sources, and the organization and structuring of one's presentation of information, are too frequently dismissed as unnecessary. Sometimes they are kept hidden by the author almost as inside information about his writing of a book.

However, this is at best imprudent. At worst, it is dangerous because the methodology will, in all cases influence, and in extreme cases control, the quality of the book itself. The methodology and rigor of the writer can drive the conclusion and ultimately dictate the usefulness of the book itself. Especially in our age where the application of motivated reasoning on the part of any commentator is far too often both practiced and even expected, the honest presentation of my methodology should be offered. This is humbly done here.

Attempts at the pure objectivity, even the sincere, well-meaning kind, are not enough since no writer can fully escape his own predispositions, interests, knowledge, and experiences. Even though I acknowledge that absolute objectivity is beyond my reach, this chapter is intended to honor the necessary burden of disclosure. Many of the facts and much of the data presented in this book may be surprising to the reader—even to the reader who thought that he or she knew "their" America well. But the methodology relating to the writing of this book and assemblage of these facts this should not be either surprising or hidden from the reader. They are willingly and candidly shared.

For all of these reasons, in this short chapter, the methodology of this book is set forth. It is likely that you will find the methodology to be both admittedly and intentionally unique.

As discussed in the prior chapters, the basic purpose of this book is to assist Americans—that broad swath of people commonly known as "citizens" and periodically identified as "voters"—in better understanding the state and condition of Current America by the organized presentation of hard facts and measured data.

The fundamental assumption is that, for a multitude of reasons, most Americans do not have a clear and accurate understanding of the actual state and condition of our country. This applies to those many Americans who have out of resignation, frustration or exhaustion withdrawn from the public square. Especially over the last couple of decades, this growing number of Americans have reached a place of near disinterest with our own society. They are no longer inclined to stay abreast, let alone become involved. Their perceptions vary. They may believe that the forces of changes in this country are beyond their reach and influence. They may have concluded that the economic and political systems are unalterably rigged. They may believe that they are "on their own" and that any meaningful concepts of social contract and relative income equality, such as it ever was, have long since been dissolved or (especially over the last several decades) have been torn asunder by the Darwinistic forces of our advanced capitalism.

However, the feeling that we do not have a clear understanding of the actual state and condition of our country also applies, albeit to a lesser degree, to even those Americans who dutifully try to follow the news and try to keep abreast of the major issues of the day. They, too, are having difficulty seeing our nation's greatness, remembering our achievements, identifying our failures, and measuring our shortcomings.

Some of the reasons for this difficulty in knowing the true state of our country are obvious. They are the subject of frequent comment and justified criticism about both the quality and objectivity of American journalism and media. This line of criticism is based upon the argument that it is increasingly difficult to find the news; to learn the facts; to get the data. In this sense, Americans correctly perceive that honest news and objective facts are hard to find.

Ignorance or willful disinterest can also be rooted, almost strangely, in our American sense of individualism—that stubborn individualism whereby people are free to draw their own almost personalized conclusions or free to remain steeped in their own ignorance and disinterest.

Some of the difficulties in knowing our own country have more to do with simpler, albeit powerful, things. They have nothing to do with the conservative bias of Fox or the "lean forward" nature of MSNBC. They have nothing to do with talking heads or the Honey Boo Boo, Duck Dynasty quality of American television. They have to do with misperceptions about our country which have been allowed to harden into firm beliefs and convictions. These misperceptions are understandable, but they are not necessarily rooted in any cold bias or stubborn ignorance. Instead, the misperceptions and misunderstandings about our country result more from age or generational associations, from the impact and subtle influences of parochialism or regionalism, from their varying levels of education or capacities of reason or recall, from the nature of their employment, from race, ethnicity, religion, interests and inclination, or—in some instances— from just idiosyncratic stubbornness.

Other difficulties stem from the sheer size and complexity of our country and its populace—313,900,000 people, five generations of citizens drawing upon radically different memories and experiences, 50 states, over 3,000 counties, over 20,000 towns,[1] nearly 3,800,000 square miles, every type of climate, every nature of topography, urban, suburban, ex-urban, rural and remote, rich and poor, educated and uneducated, and on and on.

---

1. This number refers to towns with populations in excess of 30,000. National League of Cities.

America is just hard to know. And just to complicate matters, it changes—constantly—sometimes slowly and sometimes daily. America, like every nation, is vulnerable to the whims of nature, the results of discovery, the wonders of innovation, and from time to time even the ruination of wars and the aberrational events of the fanatics and terrorists. It exists simultaneously as a part of the world and also alone and separate from the world. It exists ensconced in problems of its own history and making, but it is entangled with an ever-shrinking world in which the economics of Greece and Spain and Cyprus and our relations with distant countries are matters of serious interest and consequential effect.

But none of this means that we cannot know America better and especially in the last several decades of our grumpy, entitled America, our knowledge of our country—both the good and the bad—has become increasingly limited and closed. It has fallen prey to obstinate and closed beliefs. Complicating matters, some Americans have become unduly sensitive to criticism or critique while others fail to recognize or remember our greatness—even now.

This book is one modest attempt to "see" America as objectively as possible. The target audience for this book is wide and expansive. It is not written for the narrow reading of experts, professionals, and academics. Their roles in resolving America's problems are critical. However, while their commentary and guidance should not be ignored, neither should it be blindly followed. Instead, democracy is unique. A wide and informed population is necessary. It is not a coincidence that the farmer in Kansas, the cab driver in Chicago, and the bartender at the Cosey Inn in Dutch Harbor all have the same vote as the President of MIT and the CEO of Goldman Sachs. The democratic sharing of the power and the sharing of voting is certainly not efficient, but it is the *only* way in which America can work.

As explained above, the references to data about Modern America are included in order to assist in our understanding of the state and condition of Current America, the nature and extent of our country's successes, and, if and where applicable, the nature and extent of our failures. This book is intended to be only narrative and observational. Neither the data selection nor the textual commentary is intended to argue a position, to make a case, or to further a cause. Americans are more in need of facts than commentary.

Each of us—especially, for example, in the context of our recent presidential elections—have suffered through enough hours of motivated reasoning; biased reporting; conspicuous omissions, twisted logic, and calculated phrasings. Americans have suffered enough from the theories and words used have been slimmed, trimmed, packaged, and spun by the best trained professionals. It is not that I, like you, do not have deeply held beliefs about what our country must do. However, that is neither the subject nor the manner of presentation of this book.

To the contrary, once more, the purpose of this is narrower. For that reason, the facts and data about America are presented "coldly"—without interpretation or commentary. The occasional inclusion of comparative data between Current America and the preceding years of Modern America are presented solely for the reader to analyze and reach his or her own conclusions.

Sources of Incorporated Facts and Data

The facts and data presented in this book are not derived from what are commonly known as "primary" sources—original letters and writings, authentic transcripts and ancient texts, raw data painfully assembled and scrupulously reviewed by devoted researchers and specialists boring deeply into their target subjects.[2] Instead, this book takes an entirely new approach. It comes from a different direction. While this book has taken a painful two years to write, no tedious, dusty-book, hunch-back reading was done in its preparation. Instead, this book largely rests primarily upon a careful selection, analysis and use of "secondary" sources. It comes from the articles, papers, and writings of carefully reporters and columnists, from certain carefully selected and intentionally "balanced" periodicals, and

---

2. To take just one example, in the course of research for his latest book about Thomas Jefferson, (Meacham, J., *Thomas Jefferson: The Art of Power* (2012)) writer Jon Meacham comments in his book-tour speeches how he, God bless him, read every one of the 128 + letters written between Thomas Jefferson and John Adams.

from the data assembled and presented by certain governmental agencies, private institutions and organizations.

At first blush, this approach may seem shallow, short-cutty, and even unprincipled. However, there is a method to the madness. There is a logic to the approach. Researchers and specialists are commendable. We need them. Their research is conducted with precision, and their works are written with detail. They bore deeply into each subject. But the problem is that we Americans live in an accelerated, brevity-obsessed, bottom-line society. This is not necessarily an issue of commitment; it is a matter of time. Even if an individual wants to become informed and well-read—a possibly somewhat wide and dangerous assumption, time does not seem to permit. We Americans may give a light read to Carl Honore's *In Praise of Slowness* or even his newer, *The Slow Fix,*[3] but we are neither convinced nor seemingly capable of changing "our pill-popping, speed-yoga, retail-therapy, drive-thru-funeral, rent-a-pal, high-frequency-trading world."[4] It is downright counter-intuitive to promote—in another book of all places—a gentler pace when there are already too many books; too many subjects, too many developments; too many opinions, and too many perspectives. Complicating the whole issue is that America is in trouble; that there is much to do, and that the only place to begin is *everywhere.*

With some reluctance, but with assured correctness, this book accepts that Americans live in that highly-accelerated, brevity-obsessed, bottom-line society. For that reason this book seeks to describe Current America from numerous perspectives and in many contexts with the nearly-impossible mix of breadth, accuracy, and brevity. There is an admitted fear that the objective may be nobler than the result. However, this approach is the only way to grasp a more accurate and fuller understanding of America. We just cannot see America from our front porches, from talking with friends,

---

3. Honore, Carl, *In Prasie of Slowness: How a Worldwide Movement Is Challenging the Cult of Speed* (2004) and *The Slow Fix: Solve Problems, Work Smarter and Live Better in a Fast World* (2013).

4. Poole, S., "Not So Fast There," *The Wall Street Journal*, March 14, 2013, somewhat critically reviewing Carl Honore's latest book, *The Slow Fix.*

or through the portals of our televisions and laptops. This book further seeks to integrate and organize the facts and data about Current America. It relies, albeit cautiously and with comparative cross-checking, upon the writings and articles as presented by certain selected media sources.

No matter how narrowly or widely one wishes to define the media—newspapers, periodicals, opinion journals, wire services, television news, talk radio, or Internet bloggers—it can be relied upon only with caution. Its reporting needs to be closely evaluated. Over especially the last several decades, some aspects of reporting have become unquestionably diminished and some parts of the media have been unquestionably compromised. This diminishment and compromise are the result of the constant press for profitability, the competitive desire for attention and audience, and the raw demands of commercialism. Nevertheless, unalterably and excepting only for those few individuals who see the events or are at the center in the story, it is still the media that speaks first and regularly to the American people. Enhanced by its omnipresence and its power of digital repetition (and in the case of political elections it seems, repetition *ad nauseum*), the media retains a critical and commanding role in informing the public, in defining the issues, and in framing the perceptions, beliefs, and opinions of the American people.

In another sense, a more honorable sense, newspapers and magazines are the first drafts of history. Rarely are reporters or columnists able to present the thoughtful styles or the researched thoroughness of historians. Rarely do their articles even purport to incorporate the multiple perspectives of history. But the better articles and columns, these better first drafts of history, *are* written with thought, consideration, and informed knowledge. The better articles and columns do try to honor the truth as it is then understood, and they are printed only after a certain degree of proofing, fact checking and dutiful confirmations. In some instances, their articles are even more. In some instances, they are the result of the more thorough forms of investigative reporting. However, they are always, by definition, contemporary in nature and influenced by the commercialism of the media.

The articles are oftentimes written with relentless speed and under the pressures of mandated tight deadlines. Even the better investigative writings are rarely written with the advantages (and thus sometimes the accuracy) which come from the discovery, assemblage, or analysis of all of the relevant facts. They rarely incorporate all of the distanced and informed perspectives. Thus, the articles contained in newspapers and magazines rarely resemble—either in substance or in style—anything approaching the detailed thoroughness of academic writings. But they do address, they do have knowledge about, they do write about Current America. And Current America is where we live. Current America is what we need to change.

One further preliminary observation should be made. It is beyond the purpose of this book and the intent of this author to defend the state of the American media, and journalism in particular, but broad-brush criticisms of the press and of journalism in general are both naïve and wrong. Some publications *are* better than others. By almost any measure, certain publications *are* better than others. Some *are* even good. Some publications and writers are deserving of our respect—begrudging or otherwise. When the base standards of accuracy, thoroughness, and objectivity are combined with clarity of reasoning and quality of articulation, it also becomes obvious that certain writers and columnists are better than others; some are good; and some are even excellent.

To some lock-minded souls, any statement of commendation about the media is anathema regardless of how deserved or qualified the statement. However, the constantly repeated and derisive statements about the "mainstream, drive-by media," the "talking heads," and the "tabloid press" are dangerously simplistic. In some instances, they are fundamentally wrong.

The role and the influences of perspective, predisposition, and even bias in the media are far more difficult to isolate and evaluate. Certainly newspapers and magazines exhibit differing perspectives and biases. Sometimes they do so unabashedly. Sometimes those perspectives and biases bleed far beyond the editorial pages. Sometimes matters of perspective, predisposition, and bias influence, if not wholly decide, which writers are hired and whose writings are most prominently presented. These matters govern the selection of subjects and dictate the tone of the writing and the emphasis and presentation of the articles. But once again, the application of broad-brush thinking in the evaluation of the media is just too simplistic. Dennis Miller is not Don Imus. NPR is not Howard Stern. The Associated Press is not the Drudge Report. NBC is not the Christian Broadcasting Network. Peter Jennings is neither Glenn Beck nor Ed Shultz. *Field & Stream* is not *Hustler*. *The Wall Street Journal* is not the *National Inquirer*. *The New York Times* is not the *American Spectator*. The *National Review* is not *The Nation*. And on and on.

Before proceeding, it should be noted that apart from presenting the news, facts, and data about Current America, this book relies upon certain carefully selected newspaper and magazine for another reason—their de facto sorting role in identifying and addressing those subjects which are, for whatever reason, of greatest contemporary interest to the American people. This is essentially the reflective, responsive role of the media in American society. In part, exactly because the media is in the business of *selling* the news, the media addresses (albeit, once again, with varying levels of emphasis and prioritization) those subjects which are of interest to its readers. In that sense and to that degree, the media merely mirrors the conversations, thoughts, interests, opinions, and sometimes the concerns of the American people at a given point in time. For this reason, in trying to accurately describe the state and condition of Current America, many of the facts presented in this book are selected not upon the basis of what I or what any group or association believes American *should* be focused upon or *should* be considering, but upon what Current America has of late and in fact been focusing.

Recognizing that various publications have certain real or perceived biases, this book draws heavily from four intentionally disparate publications: *The Wall Street Journal, The Economist, Time Magazine,* and the newcomer, *The Week.* Obviously many other publications could have been selected, and there is an admitted so-shoot-me, my-bad dimension to this perilous science of selection. Most of the magazines have a small, tight subscription base, but there are plenty from which to choose from— about 2,815 to 20,207 magazine and publications in North America alone depending on whether member-only circulations and business-to-business and trade journals are included.[5] But selections, nevertheless, had to be made. I didn't pick *The New Yorker* or *The Atlantic.* I steered away from opinion magazines such as *National Review, The Nation, The Weekly Standard,* or the *New Republic.* I didn't select the *Washington Post* or *The New York Times.* I viewed the *Confederate Veteran, Real Simple, Game Informer,* and *Wired* as too narrow in their focus and subject matter. And I didn't pick *The Watchtower* or *Field and Stream.* Instead, I elected to closely, but certainly not exclusively, review these four publications for much of the last two years.[6]

The facts and data from a review of these publications are heavily supplemented with contextual and supporting data from many sources such as the U.S. Bureau of Labor Statistics, U.S. Census Data, the OECD, the World Economic Forum, the CDC, Pew Research Center, the National Center on Addiction and Substance Abuse, the U.N. Department of Economic & Social Affairs, and other publications and sources including, in some instances, *The New York Times, Vanity Fair, Harper's, CSMonitor.com, BloombergNews.com,* and *The New York Review of Books.* International comparisons are, in some instances, drawn from *The Economist's Pocket World in Figures—2012.* The list of the literally hundreds of articles and sources is included at the end of this book at Appendix C.

---

5. There can be material variances in the number of magazines published since different sources include (or exclude) varying types of materials. For example, magazines which are limited to member-only circulation and business-to-business and trade magazines are oftentimes not included in the tally of "general circulation" magazines. As of 2010, the total number of magazines available in North America, depending upon such qualifications, varies from 2,815 (Standard Rate and Data service) to 20,207 (according to the count of the obviously far more inclusive National Directory of Magazines). The Association of Magazine Media; *magazine.org.*

6. In 2009 *The Wall Street Journal* with a 2012 total average circulation of 2,294,000 passed *USA Today* (Circulation: 1,714,000) which had been the largest daily newspaper for the prior decade. Numbers 3 and 4 in circulation are, respectively, *The New York Times* (Circulation: 1,614,000) and the *Los Angeles Times* (Circulation: 641,400). Audit Bureau of Circulation.

Nevertheless, the primary source data and research are drawn from these above-referenced four publications. They are used in order to aggregately center this presentation of Current America for two reasons. First, they were selected because they deemed themselves to be and they are news publications which collectively address those subjects which have drawn, for whatever reason, the interest and attention of the American people. Second, especially when read together, they assist in presenting an accurate, albeit abbreviated, description (and reflection) about the condition of Current America.

The Wall Street Journal was founded in 1874—nearly 140 years ago— by reporters Charles Dow, Edward Jones, and Charles Bergstresser. It was selected here partly because it is the largest U.S. daily newspaper with a total average total circulation (both print and digital) of about 2,294,000. It was also selected because of its reach and influence. It is perceived by some (especially after its 2007 purchase by Rupert Murdoch's News Corp) as presenting a free-market, business and conservative political bias in both its topical selection and its tone and presentation. However, *The Wall Street Journal* also holds a long and largely deserved reputation for both accuracy and relative thoroughness.

The Economist was founded in 1843 by the Scottish businessman and banker James Wilson and is printed in the United Kingdom. It is highly regarded for its "serious trend coverage," accuracy, and precision of language.[7] It focuses heavily upon weekly news and international affairs with regular special reports on other subjects and has long had the tradition of printing nearly all of its articles "without bylines in a unified voice of the magazine."[8] Thus, the names of any writer or columnists are rarely identified. Over the last decade *The Economist,* unlikely nearly all other publications, increased its North American circulation "by more than 130% to 830,000."[9] The average reader of *The Economist* (43.7 years)

---

7. Pew Research Center's Project for Excellence in Journalism, The State of the News Media—2011, p. 6.

8. *Id.,* p.6.

9. *Id.,* p. 9.

is slightly younger than U.S. average age (45.4 years) and has an annual household income (appr. $119,400) which is approximately double the U.S. average household income (appr. $59,500).

Time was founded in 1923 by Henry Luce and Briton Hadden, and it has long been a mainstay, mainstream U.S. news magazine. *Time* magazine was selected because (especially with the 2010 cessation of the print news magazine edition by *U.S. News and World Report* and the more recent December, 2012 cessation of *Newsweek)* it is now the largest news magazine in the U.S. with a circulation of appr. 3,300,000. By subject category, *Time* presents articles on national affairs (29.1%), global and foreign affairs (19.5%), culture (11.3%), entertainment and celebrity news (10.4%), and business and industry (5.3%). The average reader of *Time* (age 47.3 years) is slightly older than U.S. average age (45.4 years) and has an annual household income (appr. $75,600) which is slightly larger than the U.S. average household income (appr. $59,500).

The Week is the wild-card selection. Unlike all three of the other publications, *The Week* is new. It has little history and no pretension. It also has a much smaller circulation (517,200). The U.S. edition of *The Week* was launched in 2001, and despite industry trends, it has been steadily gaining in popularity and circulation. It is somewhat like *Time* magazine in that it is a weekly news magazine which purports to present a balanced view of the news. However, by its unique, heavy use of an aggregation and attribution style of reporting, it presents a wide-range of disparate perspectives, thoughts, and data. As reported in 2011, "(w)hile magazines like *Time* ... published heavy essays, distinguished guest columnists and artful photo spreads, *The Week* (has) embraced magazine journalism at its most functional and stripped down."[10] The average reader of *The Week* has an annual household income (appr. $145,000) which is even higher than *The Economist* and is nearly 2.5 times the U.S. average household income (appr. $59,500).[11]

10. Peters, J., "The News, In Bright Bits," *The New York Times,* March 13, 2011.

11. Peters, J., "The News, In Bright Bits," *The New York Times*, March 13, 2011, citing Mendelsohn Affluent Survey.

I am aware that America, for better or worse, has become a scorecard nation, and thus I believe the reader will be pleased to find, as noted above, that the relative percentage distribution of sourcing citations as between these publications (excepting in this book, *The Economist*) and, collectively, the many other sources is nearly equal.

Methodology, Neutrality of Presentation, and Identification of (Multiple) Sources

Organization of Facts and Data

The facts and data presented in this book are topically organized into the following categories and chapters:

- Demographics, Geography, Climate, and Weather

- Crime and Punishment, Law and Litigation, Ethics and Accountability

  – Crime and Punishment

  – Law and Litigation, Ethics and Accountability

- Housing, Education, and Health

  – Housing, Cities and Communities

  – Education and Literacy

  – Health, Health Care, and Health Insurance

- American Life, Entertainment, Religion and Culture

For ease of location about any subject, a summary Table of Contents is included at the beginning of each chapter, and the facts and data are cross-referenced in detail in the Index.

In addition, in order to intrigue the reader and to better introduce each subject matter chapter, I have taken the liberty of including some exemplar facts about the state of Current America at the beginning of each topical chapter.

Attributions and Citations

Every effort has been made to include attributions and detailed reference citations. For the convenience of the reader and to assist in the reader's de facto evaluation of the entry itself, the citations are included immediately after each entry as opposed to the back of the book. Because article titles and headings are rarely written by the article's author and because they oftentimes do not necessarily assist the reader in understanding the subject or scope of the article, article titles and headings are normally as a part of the reference citation.

Neutrality of Presentation
Without Commentary, Criticism, or Critique

Many of the facts and data are presented with some explanation and expansion, but they are presented without criticism or critique. In order to try to achieve the intended objectivity and neutrality of presentation, adjectives and adverbs are rarely used. For example, while to some it may be surprising that the percentage of foreign nationals on the Boards of Directors of U.S. corporations is 7%, this fact is *not* presented with the prefatory word "*only* seven percent (7%)."

The New Words, Phrases, and Colloquialisms
of Current America

In the fast-paced, accelerated world of Current America, new words, phrases and colloquialisms are constantly being added to the lexicon of our American life. Some of these evidence staying power and durability. They eventually become widely known, commonly understood, and frequently used. Others quickly evaporate. At the end of this book at Appendix B is a partial listing and definition of some of these new words, phrases, and colloquialisms. Also included at Appendix B is a list of those abbreviations used in the text of this book (e.g., DOD (Department of Defense), SEC (U.S. Securities and Exchange Commission), TARP (Troubled Asset Relief Program), and OECD (The Organization for Economic Cooperation and Development).

Rounding

Sometimes exact, decimal point precision matters. The late Astronaut Neil Armstrong used to point out to audiences the "reliability specifications" which were necessary in the Apollo 11 Mission—namely, 0.99996%—"which means that you have (or are 'permitted') four failures in 100,000 operations."[12] This kind of reliability and precision is terribly impressive, but neither this book nor the facts contained herein are going to get you to the Moon (or back). Decimal-point accuracy and precision specificity are at times both useful and even important, however in the context of presenting the state of Current America, assisting the reader in understanding, and, when necessary, recalling data and identifying trending patterns are far more important.[13]

Furthermore, it is rarely useful to bury anyone in the literal minutiae of single dollar or small percentages, and orders of magnitude are far more critical than anything Dewey decimal has to offer. For example, the current average college annual expenses of $20,902 are rounded to $21,000 in order to improve ease of one's retention of the data and to simplify this data's comparison. For those reasons and simply because too many numbers (and especially those with lengthy decimal points)

12. The late Neil Armstrong, astronaut and ever the modest and "reluctant hero," speaking about the 1969 Apollo 11 mission to the moon from NASA's Johnson Space Center Oral History Project, quoted in *The Wall Street Journal*, August 27, 2012, a day after his passing.

13. The utility of rounding and the use of numerical ranges are widely recognized as a means of presenting certain types of information in a more meaningful manner in many varying contexts. However, rounding and ranges are useful not just in the context of demographics or economics, for example, but also they are useful in the context of even off-target information about weather forecasting. See, Malkiel, B., "Telling Lies From Statistics," Review of Nate Silver's book, *The Signal and the Noise*," *The Wall Street Journal*, September 25, 2012 ("The best forecasts don't contain specific numerical expectations but define the future in terms of ranges (the hurricane should pass somewhere between Tampa and 350 miles west) and probabilities (there is a 70% chance of rain this evening"). Thus, in this context ranges of predictions, like orders of magnitude, are oftentimes better and more useful.

can be mind-numbing, rounding is commonly utilized. Rounding is the norm—not the exception.

The Sustained Relevance of Presented Data

This data will retain a sustained relevance for a long time. Unquestionably, cataclysmic world-changing events occur. But they occur only rarely. We all remember the shock of 9/11 and the altering devastation impact of Hurricane Katrina. We have heard about or, in some cases even remember Black Monday and Black Thursday. However, things rarely occur "overnight." Financial collapses do not occur overnight. Wars are not won by a single invasion or by a sky-lit display of shock and awe. The truth is that despite the perceived pace of American life, its political, economic, and social life changes slowly. Politicians change, new legislation is passed, new products are introduced, and events occur, but most societal matters of American life are matters of ebb and flow; trends and evolutions.

Thus, the relevance and import of this data about American society will not fade quickly. Much of it will remain both useful and relevant for years. Just as with the rounding which is discussed above, tight precision certainly can at times matter. However, orders of magnitude and trending lines are of more significance. Numbers should be checked—and re-checked. And, yes, it is wonderful that there is always some spring-butt in the back row who is anxious to cite yesterday's exact, up-to-the-moment, just-released, press-hot data. I recognize that as I wrote this paragraph the population of this country changed and many of the data percentages slightly adjusted here and there, but in nearly all cases, it is the assembled data, the evaluated patterns, and the identified trends usually matter more.

For that reason, fascinating facts and even the thick plods of good data can rarely be dismissed with an oh-so-yesterday sigh. The facts and data of this book will retain great meaning far past their release date. I believe that you will find that they almost have a life span and a shelf life all of their own. However, for various reasons and in certain contexts, some data has been intentionally omitted from this book. They are discussed in the next section.

Excluded Data

This book focuses almost exclusively upon "facts and data"—of which there is plenty. However, not all "facts and data" are the same, and some categories thereof have been intentionally omitted.

Estimates, Forecasts, and Projections

Most estimates, forecasts and projections have been excluded. For example, it may correctly and appropriately be viewed as both interesting and important that it is *estimated* that Americans spent 7.64BB hours "negotiating tax-related paperwork" and in complying with mandates of federal and state tax reporting and compliance requirements. However, this estimate would not be included in this book since it is based upon dangerous self-reporting and because it is far beyond any measurable margin of error.[14]

Similarly, an inclusion/exclusion distinction is made between observational studies vs. randomized, controlled studies. Data based upon *observational studies* may be interesting, but it inevitably depends upon the treacherous fallibility of having to rely upon the accuracy and completeness of the participants' recall and reporting. Contrariwise, data relying upon the more complex, albeit more costly, *randomized, controlled studies* may be included due to the fact that they are far more accurate.

Surveys and Polls

Surveys and polls are rarely cited for several reasons. First, they can fluctuate far too impulsively and too frequently. Unlike sustained relevance of hard data discussed above, polls have horrendously short shelf-lives. They are highly vulnerable to whims, moods and even extraneous, intervening, but well-publicized events. Surveys and polls can be invaluable in designing political and marketing campaigns, but they are poor sources of reality- and factual-based data. They oftentimes address matters of public perception and mood, but they are oftentimes a function of polling mechanics and quality—the polling procedures, the question designs, and the size and

---

14. *The Week*, April 27, 2012 citing *Reason.com*.

definitional correctness of the sampling group itself. For these reasons, survey and poll data can be easily manipulated, and such data is routinely and intentionally result-driven in both its purpose and result. Therefore, while a few polls such as right way-wrong way polls and issue polls are included, most consumer confidence polls, exit polls, name recognition and candidate popularity polls, and accountability polls (purporting to assign relative political or economic accountability for the state of American affairs) are excluded.

Legislative and Political Proposals, Editorials, Opinion Magazines, and Marketing, Promotional and Advertising Statements

For many of the same reasons which relate to surveys and polls, the facts and data contained in this book rarely incorporate legislative or political proposals or the projected costs and effects thereof. In most instances, these types of analyses are definitionally too hypothetical because the legislative has not yet been finalized and because the number and volatility of the necessary underlying assumptions.

In addition, since the purpose of this book is to present an objective and accurate presentation of Current America and to rely as heavily as possible upon neutral, balanced and authoritative writings, facts are rarely drawn from either editorials or from opinion magazines such as *The Nation, The New Republic, The Weekly Standard*, and the *National Review*. These may be fine and useful publications however they are too often written from a fixed point of view. In their rawest form. they are written almost as push-pieces about their given subject. The expressed opinions tend to be presented as conclusionary in nature, and the facts which are used are too often presented without a full, or at least balanced, presentation of countervailing theories, opinions, and information.

Lastly, facts are rarely cited from marketing, promotional, or advertising statements or from political party or campaign materials since in these contexts facts are prepared with even less restraint. These facts are presented, unabashedly, in order advance a defined (and, in some cases, paid) objective of the writer, campaign, company, group or association. These facts are too often self-serving to the advertisement's or the campaign's objectives and are offered only in blind support of the subject product or in order to advance the objectives of the subject campaign or candidate.

Trivia and Minutiae Facts

Minutiae facts are those facts and records such as sports statistics (wins/ losses, pitcher ERAs, golf handicaps, racing records etc), meteorological records (record weather high and lows, humidity levels), and the millions of the other factoids which are literally known for their curiosity or accuracy. Nevertheless, they are here excluded simply because they are of interest to relatively small and usually contained groups of Americans and because they rarely, if ever, influence the direction, the nature, or the speed of the necessary changes in our society. These facts are both honored and honorable, but for the purposes addressed in this book, they are irrelevant.

Regionally Idiosyncratic Data

Slightly more problematic is the inclusion or exclusion of regionally idiosyncratic data such as the data relating to average or median incomes, the educational levels, or the housing valuations in various regions of the country. In some instances this data is included in order to underscore, literally, the reasonableness of our differing perceptions of America. It does matter "from whence you come," and the marked variances from region to region within this country are sometimes best evidenced by the inclusion of comparative regional data. In other instances, such data is excluded, however, because it is so narrowly regional or because it does not have any meaningful national implications.

Highly Time-Sensitive Data

Certain types of highly time-sensitive (and usually highly volatile) data such as daily stock values, balance of trade and international monetary accounts information, event attendance, travel, and weather data are normally not included except in the context of identifying trending patterns. This type of data may not be matters of trivia or minutiae, but they are facts which are uniquely characterized by their volatility.

Closing

Every reasonable attempt has been made to avoid the inclusion of any erroneous or misquoted facts, data, information or attributions. Nevertheless, it is highly likely that despite all best efforts some errors are contained herein. Be assured that I shall welcome both your comments and your corrections, and I thank you in advance as we, together, try to understand the state of Current America.

There is much to do to make our country even greater. Fortunately, there is much that can be done. Over the last several political cycles, the words *change* and *hope* have been repeatedly invoked. I suggest that upon any serious evaluation of either Modern America, this nation's existence since 1957, the word *achievement*, even more than change and hope, may seem most appropriate.

Based upon this country achievements, there is every informed and reasonable basis to be optimistic about our country's ability to address its problems and to meet its challenges. This small book like it's companion book, *The Relevance of Reason—Business and Politics,* is humbly offered as one place to begin.

PART II

Demographics, Geography, Climate, and Weather

CHAPTER 6

Demographics, Geography, Climate, and Weather

Exemplar Facts About Current America From This Chapter

(Details and Source Citations Below)

The U.S. median age is 37.2 years—State with oldest median age population is Maine (42.7 years); State with youngest median age population is Utah (29.2 years).

Since 1960, the average height of American men has increased by 1 ½"—from 5' 8" to 5' 9 ½".

More than 50% of all U.S. childbirths to mothers under 30 years of age are outside of marriage.

8% of U.S. childbirths are children of illegal immigrants.

U.S. parental and maternal leave policies are dramatically fewer than those of other countries.

Canada is the only other advanced country that, like the U.S., offers birthright citizenship, whereby a child born in the country is automatically a citizen thereof.

The U.S. population density is 87.4 persons per square mile (Europe: 134 ppsm; Asia: 203 ppsm).

The distance/driving time from Dutch Harbor, Alaska, to Key West, Florida, is 6,115 miles/122 hours.

Nearly 50% of all Americans are now unmarried—more than double the 22% in 1950.

The average cost of a wedding in the U.S. is $27,000.

1 in 7 U.S. marriages is inter-racial or inter-ethnic.

There are more Puerto Ricans living in the U.S. (55%) than living in Puerto Rico (45%).

The teenage pregnancy rate has almost consistently declined over the past 20 years.

In 2012 there were 3,215 daily-high temperature records set in the U.S.

Table of Contents
Of The Data Contained in This Chapter

Age, Height, and Weight—U.S. Population Averages.
- Age.
    - Adult U.S. Population—Over 15 and as Percentage of U.S. Population.
    - Age Groups—U.S. Population By—Number and as Percentage of U.S. Population.
    - Age Dependency Ratios—Under 18 and Over 65.
    - Median Age—5 States With Highest and 5 States With Lowest Median Ages.
    - Median Age—U.S. and Comparisons With Global and Other Selected Countries and World Regions.
    - Percentage of People in U.S. Under 15 and Over 65.
- Height and Weight—U.S. Averages and Changes of Since 1960.

Childbirths, Fertility, and Birth Rates.
- Assisted-Reproduction Technologies—Frequency of Use Of.
- Childbirths—Illegal Immigrants—Percentage of Children Born in U.S. Whose Parents Were Illegal Immigrants.
- Childbirths—Outside of Marriage.
  - Age of Mother—Percentage as Function of Age of Mother.
  - Education of Mother—Percentage as Function of Level of Education of Mother.
  - Race of Mother—Percentage as Function of Race.
- Fertility and Birth Rates.
  - Fertility Rates of Top 10 Countries by GDP.
  - Impact of Recession.
  - U.S. Compared With Other Countries.
  - U.S. Replacement Rate Compared With Fertility Rate.
- Race and Ethnicity.
  - Latino—Percentage of All Children Born in U.S.
  - Non-White Births Percentage Higher Than White Births.

Children, Childcare, Child Rearing, and Related Public Policies (Including Parental/Maternal Leave Policies).
- Allowances—Weekly—Percentage of Parents Who Pay and Average Amount.
- Breast-Feeding—Commonness of in U.S.
- Childcare and Childcare Public Policies (Including Parental/Maternal Leave Policies).
  - Fathers' Growing Involvement In—Percentage of Fathers Who Routinely Care for Children Under the Age of 15.
  - Parental and Maternal Leave in U.S.—Amount Of—Compared With Other Countries.
- Children's Savings Accounts—Importance of and Correlation to Likelihood of College Attendance and Graduation.
- Corporal Punishment of Children.
  - Number of Regions in U.S. Where Remains Legal in Schools.
  - Spanking—Percentage of Adults Who Believe in Giving Children an Occasional "Good, Hard Spanking."
- Sleep—Recommended Amount of Sleep for Children.

Citizenship and Naturalization, Immigrants and Immigration, Emigration and Migration, Non-Deportation Rights and Employment Visas.
- Citizenship and Naturalization.
  - Citizenship.

- – Birthright Citizenship—Number of Other Advanced Countries Which Offer Birthright Citizenship.
- – Citizenship Applicant's Knowledge of American History and Government.
    - ◦ Naturalization—Immigrants Becoming Citizens Through Naturalization—2010—Number Of.
- Emigration and Migration.
    - ◦ Emigrant Populations—Biggest Emigration Populations and Percentage of Populations.
    - ◦ Emigration and Renunciation of Citizenship.
        - – Number of Days Per Year Person Allowed to Return to the U.S. Even After Renunciation of Citizenship.
        - – U.S. Citizens Who Gave Up U.S. Citizenship in 2011— Number Of.
    - ◦ Migration—Mexico—Net Migration From U.S. to Mexico—2005–2010.
- Immigrants and Immigration.
    - ◦ Economic and Educational Generational Progress of Adult Children of Immigrants.
    - ◦ Immigrant Populations—Biggest Immigrant Populations and Percentage of Populations.
    - ◦ Legal Immigrants—Number and as Percentage of All Immigrants in U.S.
    - ◦ Ratio of Family Reunification and Work-Based Immigration.
    - ◦ U.S. Immigrant Population Percentage—Compared With Other Countries.
    - ◦ U.S. Permanent-Resident Visas—Percentages Based Upon Skills vs. Family Unification.
- Non-Deportation Rights and Employment Visas.
    - ◦ DACA—Number of Young Immigrants Eligible for Application for DACA Non-Deportation Rights.
    - ◦ Employment Visas.
        - – H1-B Visa Skilled Workers Programs—Annual Caps On.
        - – H1-B Recipients—Breakdown of Which Industries in Which They Work.
- Undocumented Workers.
    - ◦ Countries and Regions of Origin.
    - ◦ Deportation of Illegal Immigrants—Level of Public Support For.
    - ◦ States with Highest Percentage Of.

       ° Total Number of Undocumented Workers Currently In U.S.

       ° Work-Force—As Percentage of U.S. Workforce.

Density.

- U.S. Population Density and Five States With Highest and Five States With Lowest Population Density.
- World Population Density and Density by Countries (10 Countries with Highest and Lowest Population Density) and by Continents.
    - ° World Population Density.
    - ° Population Density—By Continents.
    - ° Population Density—By Countries.
    - ° Population Density—By Highest Density Megacities.

Displaced Persons and Refugees.

- Displaced Persons—Number and Percentage of Persons Classified as Refugees or "Displaced" as of 2010.
- Refugees—Number of Refugees in U.S. and as Percentage of U.S. Population.

Fastest and Slowest Growing Continents or Regions of World.

Generations.

- Contemporary American Generations—Names Of.
- Generations—U.S.— As Percentage of Total U.S. Adult Population.
- Multi-Generational—Adult Children—Ages 25–34—Living in Multigenerational Households.
- Youth Generation of World—Percentage of World Population Under Age 25.

Geography of U.S.

- Deserts—Number of U.S. Deserts in Top 10 Largest in World.
- Drives—Most Scenic and Most Scenic Coastal.
- Lakes—U.S. Lakes in Top 10 Largest Lakes In World.
- Mountains.
- Rivers.
- Size of U.S.
    - ° Distance and Driving Time from Compton, California, to Caribou, Maine.
    - ° Distance and Driving Time from Dutch Harbor, Alaska, to Key West, Florida.
    - ° U.S. and U.S. Compared to Largest 5 Nations.
    - ° U.S. Land Size—In Square Miles and Acres.
- States—Names—Origins Of—Native American, British, French, and Spanish—Number Of.

Homeless Persons.
- Age and Race.
- Disability—Instances of Among Persons and Families in Emergency or Transitional Shelters.
- Household Size—Individuals and Families.
- Homelessness Rate Compared With Poverty Rate.
- Newly Homeless—Percentage Coming from Institutional Setting.
- Personal Characteristics and Subpopulations – Chronic Substance Abusers, Severely Mentally Ill, Etc.
- Single-Night Sheltered vs. Unsheltered Homeless Persons Nationwide.
- Veterans In Emergency or Transitional Shelters.

Households.
- Economics Of.
    - Economic Well-Being—Correlations with Education, Employment, Age of Marriage, and Marriage Before Paternity.
    - Economic Well-Being—Disposable Income—Use of for Debt.
    - Household Budgets—Automobile—Annual Costs; Percentage of Annual Household Budget; Highest Weekly Outlay.
    - Household Debt Burdens.
        - As Percentage of Household Income —1980–2012.
        - Current Amounts vs. 2008.
        - Median Debt Burden for Households as a Function of Age of Head of Household.
        - Mortgage Debt—Older Families (Ages 55–64)—Percentage of Families Still Carrying Mortgage Debt and Their Median Mortgage Debt Amount.
        - Percentage of Households Without Debt.
        - States with Highest and Lowest Average Per-Household Debt.
    - Young Adults' Total Debt—"Total Debt" and Credit Card Debt Dropping Substantially.
- Married-Couple Families—Supported Financially by Husband Alone.
- Housework Chores—Performed By Working Mothers vs. Working Fathers.
- Number of Households in U.S. and Average Size Of.
- Single-Person Households.
    - Chance That U.S. Child Lives in Family Headed by Single Mother.
    - Singledom and Unmarried—Number of Households in U.S.
- Young Adults Returning Home to Live—Number of and Financial/ Retirement Effects on Parents.

Language—Other Than English Spoken At Home.

Marriage and Divorce.
- Divorce Rate.
- Inter-Racial/Inter-Ethnic—New Marriages—Percentage Of.
- Marriage—Cost Of.
- Online Dating and Effect of Social Networking—Percentage of U.S. Couples Who Met Online.
- Percentage Drop Over Last Appr. 40 Years in Women Who Are Married.
- Plural Marriage—Est. Number of U.S. Families Which Practice.
- Same-Sex Marriages.
    - College Freshmen Percentage Approval Of.
    - States and Growing International and Business Recognition Of—Number of States and Examples of Major Corporations Recognizing Same-Sex Marriages.
    - Voter Referendum Approvals Of.

Population.
- U.S. Population—Adult and Minors, By Age Category, By Gender.
- U.S. Population; World Population; U.S. Population as Percentage of World Population; and Population of Selected Countries.
- World's Largest 10 Countries—Current (2009).
- World's Largest 10 Countries—2050 (Projected).

Race and Ethnicity.
- Diversity and Dispersion Within Society.
- Diversity—Lack Of—Places Where Whites Make Up At Least 90% of Population.
- Diversity—Most Diverse Metropolitan Area in U.S.
- Percentage of U.S. Population—By Race.
- Puerto Ricans—Number of Puerto Ricans Living in Puerto Rico Compared with Living in U.S.

Sex Ratio—Males per 100 Females—Number of Countries Where M:F Ratio Exceeds 120 Men Per 100 Women.

Teenage Girls—Sexual Activity.
- Average Children per American Woman Age 15–19.
- Abstinence—Age 15–19.
- Pregnancy Rate—Age 15–19.

Weather.
- Drought.
    - Economic Effect Upon U.S. Farmers—Percentage of Farmers With Crop Disaster Insurance.

- Percentage of Country in 2012 Drought and Year of Last Drought of Similar Size and Extent.
- Hurricanes and Superstorms—Superstorm Sandy—Size and Impact Of.
- Temperatures.
  - First Six Months of 2012.
  - Number of High Temperature Records—June 2012.

Data

Age, Height, and Weight—U.S. Population Averages.
- **Age.**
  - **Adult U.S. Population—Over 15 and as Percentage of U.S. Population.** Appr. 249MM or 20% of the U.S. total population. PRB World Population Data Sheet, *prb.org.*
  - **Age Groups—U.S. Population By—Number and as Percentage of U.S. Population.** The number and percentages by alternative age grouping are as follows:

Age Group	Number	Percentage of U.S. Population
Under 5 years	20.0 MM	6.5%
5–17 years	54.0 MM	17.5%
18–24 years	30.7 MM	9.9 %
25–44 years	82.1 MM	26.6 %
45–64 years	81.5 MM	26.4 %
65 years and Over	40.3 MM	13.0 %

A slightly different age grouping is as follows:

Age Group	Number	Percentage of U.S. Population
Under 18 years	74.2 MM	24.0%
18–44 years	112.8 MM	36.5%
45–64 years	81.5 MM	26.4%
65 years and Over	40.3 MM	13.0%
18 and Older (Adults)	234.6 MM	76.0%

U.S. Census Bureau (2010 Census Summary).

  - **Age Dependency Ratios—Under 18 and Over 65.** The age dependency ratio roughly calculates the percentage of the population that is, as a result of age, dependent. The overall age dependency ratio, for example, is calculated by dividing the combined under-18 and 65-and-over population by the 18–64 population and multiplying by 100. The respective Age Dependency Ratios are as follows:

Overall Age Dependency Ratio: 58.8   (in other words, out of 100 people, 58.8 of them are "age dependent" upon the balance of the population)

Old-Age Dependency Ratio   20.8

Child Dependency Ratio   38.0

U.S. Census Bureau, 2009–2011 ACS 3-Year Estimates.

○ **Median Age—5 States With Highest and 5 States With Lowest Median Ages.** The five states with populations which have, respectively, the highest and the lowest median ages are as follows:

Five States With Highest Median Age		Five States With Lowest Median Age	
Maine	42.7 years	Utah	29.2 years
Vermont	41.5 years	Texas	33.6 years
West Virginia	41.3 years	Alaska	33.8 years
New Hampshire	41.1 years	Idaho	34.6 years
Florida	40.7 years	California	35.2 years

United States Median Age: 37.2 years

U.S. Census Bureau.

○ **Median Age—U.S. and Comparisons With Global Other Selected Countries and World Regions.** The U.S. median age is 37.2 years old (compared with the global median age of appr. 28 years and the U.S. median age of 35.3 years just 12 years ago in 2000). The median age is defined as the age at which there are an equal number of people above and below such age. The nation with the highest median age is Japan (44.7) and 21 countries (nearly all European countries) have median ages above 40 years. Conversely, 40 countries (nearly all in Africa or the Middle East) have a median age of less than 20 years. U.S. Census Bureau and *The Economist, Pocket World in Figures—2012.* See also, *The Economist,* December 22, 2012—January 4, 2013, p. 102, citing Pew Research Center. See also, Perry, A., "Africa Rising," *Time,* December 3, 2012, p. 48 (Average age in Sub-Saharan Africa is 18.6 years, and there is a projected increase of 108MM African schoolchildren expected within the next decade).

○ **Percentage of People In U.S. Under 15 and Over 65.**

	United States	World
Under 15:	20.0%	26.0%
Over 65:	13.0%	8.0%

PRB World Population Data Sheet, prb.org.

- **Height and Weight—U.S. Averages and Changes of Since 1960.** While there are substantial differences in height and weight among different ethnic groups of Americans, the overall average height and weight of Americans are set forth below. They evidence that Americans have gotten taller by about 1.5" in the last 50 years (e.g., for men: from 5'8" to 5'9 ½") and heavier (e.g., for men: from 166 lbs to 191 lbs). The 1960 numbers are indicated below in parentheses.

	Men (Aged 20-74 Years)		Women (Aged 20-74 Years)	
	Height	Weight	Height	Weight
All Americans	5'9 ½"	191 lbs	5'4"	164 lbs
	(1960: 5'8")	(1960: 166 lbs)	(1960: 5'3")	(1960: 140 lbs)

U.S. men's weights have increased since 1960 disproportionately with age (e.g., Men 60–74 showing a 33 lbs increase). The increases in the U.S. women's rates are just the reverse. Since 1960, most of the weight increases have been disproportionate among women aged 20–29 years (nearly 29 pounds heavier than in 1960). *usgovinfo.about.com* and citing report from CDC.

Childbirths, Fertility, and Birth Rates.

- **Assisted-Reproduction Technologies—Frequency of Use Of.** Appr. 5MM children have been born in the U.S. through some form of assisted-reproduction technologies since the first test-tube baby was born in 1978, 34 years ago. *Time,* July 23, 2012, p. 5.
- **Childbirths—Illegal Immigrants—Percentage of Children Born in U.S. Whose Parents Were Illegal Immigrants.** 8%. (2008). *Time,* August 30, 2010.
- **Childbirths—Outside of Marriage.**
    - ○ **Age of Mother—Percentage as Function of Age of Mother**. More than 50% of all births to mothers under the age of 30. Lowry, R., "Just Not the Marrying Kind," *Time,* March 5, 2012, p. 13 citing *The New York Times.*
    - ○ **Education of Mother—Percentage as Function of Level of Education of Mother.** The strong correlation between education of mother and the likelihood that the child will be born outside of marriage is as follows:

Education Level	Percentage of Children Born Outside of Marriage
Non-College-Educated Women	60%
(Some College Education)	(30%)
College-Educated Women	10%

The Week, July 27, 2012, p. 16 citing David Brooks and Jason DeParle in *The New York Times*. See also, Lowry, R., "Just Not the Marrying Kind," *Time*, March 5, 2012. (70% of births to high school dropouts, 51% to high school graduates, 34% to mothers with some college education, and 8% to mothers with college degree).

○ **Race of Mother—Percentage as Function of Race.**

Race of Mother	Percentage of Children Born Outside of Marriage
Blacks	73%
Latinos	53%
Whites	29%

Compare this to data contained in "the controversial 1965 report on the perilous state of the black family authored by liberal intellectual Daniel Patrick Moynihan," in which at that time "24% of births among blacks (vs. the current 73%) and 3% of births among whites (vs. the current 29%) were out of wedlock." Lowry, R., "Just Not the Marrying Kind," *Time*, March 5, 2012 citing *The New York Times*. This substantial increase in the percentage of children born out of wedlock parallels the increases of such births in the U.K. as well. The percentage of English children born out of wedlock increased from 1/5 in 1981 to 1/2 in 2011—just 30 years later. Harper's Index, *Harper's Magazine*, June, 2013, p. 156, citing Office of National Statistics, Newport, England.

• **Fertility and Birth Rates.**
  ○ **Fertility Rates of Top 10 Countries by GDP.** The total fertility rates of the top ten GDP countries (average from 2005-2010) are as follows:

Ranking	Country	Total Fertility Rate	Ranking	Country	Total Fertility Rate
1.	India	2.07	6.	China	1.64
2.	*United States*	*2.07*	7.	Russian Fed.	1.44
3.	France	1.97	8.	Italy	1.38
4.	Brazil	1.90	9.	Germany	1.36
5.	United Kingdom	1.83	10.	Japan	1.32

Last, J., "America's Baby Bust—The Nation's Falling Fertility Rate …," The *Wall Street Journal*, February 2-3, 2013 citing data from the United Nations.

  ○ **Impact of Recession.** The steep decline in birth rate, especially among immigrant women, is the driving force behind the record low U.S. birthrate. The annual number of births per 1,000 women (ages 15–44) peaked in 1957 during the Baby Boom at 122.7 and it dropped down to 64 births per 1,000 in 2007–2010. The 8% drop from 2007 to 2010 (and 19% for immigrants of Hispanic origin during this period) strongly suggests an impact-of-recession correlation and parallels similar drops during the Great Depression and during the oil shock years of the 1970s. Jordan, M., *The Wall Street Journal,* November 30, 2012, citing data from Pew Research Center.

○ **U.S. Compared With Other Countries.** The U.S. fertility rate (i.e., the estimate of the number of children a woman will have in her lifetime) is appr. 2 children per woman.

> Highest in Last 40 Years: 2007—2.12 children per woman
> Most Recent: 2011—1.9 children per woman
> Lowest: 1976—1.74 children per woman

Arguably, more significant, the birth rate, number of children per 1,000 women ages 15–44, fell in 2011 to appr. 63 per 1,000, which is "the lowest level since at least 1920, the earliest year for which reliable data is available." Bialik, C., *The Wall Street Journal,* December 8–9, 2012, citing data from Pew Research Center and CDC. This data can also be compared with other nations in which the birth rates are below 1.5 children per woman such as in Italy, Spain, Greece, the nations of Eastern Europe, Russia, South Korea, and Japan. Wattenberg, B., "What's Really Behind the Entitlement Crisis," *The Wall Street Journal,* July 13, 2012. The average worldwide fertility rate estimated by Population Reference Bureau is 2.4. PRB 2012 World Population Data Sheet, *prb.org.* See also Wattenberg, B., *The Wall Street Journal,* May 24, 2012 (Noting that while birth rates are dropping significantly in other modern or developing nations (e.g., Japan and Poland birth rates dropped to 1.3; Brazil and China birth rates dropped to 1.9), American fertility rates remain quite high.). But see, McGurn, W., *The Wall Street Journal* (Review of J. Last's book *What To Expect When No One's Expecting*), February 21, 2013 (Comparing the low fertility rates in Germany (1.36) and Japan (1.4) to that of the 1.6 fertility rate of white, college-educated women whom Mr. Last identifies as a "proxy" for the U.S. middle class).

○ **U.S. Replacement Rate Compared With Fertility Rate.** The U.S. replacement rate, the childbirth rate necessary to sustain the current U.S. population, is 2.1. Because the current U.S. fertility rate is 1.93 (down slightly from the 2.07 Years 2005-2010 average), the U.S. population may begin to shrink absent immigration etc. Furthermore, the fertility rate has not exceeded the replacement rate "since the early 1970s." Despite "the conventional wisdom" about the forthcoming dangers of global population, this author states that the global population will begin to shrink in about 60 years. Last, J., "America's Baby Bust—The Nation's Falling Fertility Rate …," The *Wall Street Journal*, February 2-3, 2013.

- **Race and Ethnicity.**
    - ○ **Latino—Percentage of All Children Born in U.S.** 25% (i.e., one in four births). Scherer, M., "Why Latino Voters Will Swing the 2012 Election," *Time*, March 5, 2012, p. 22, citing Pew Hispanic Center, U.S. Bureau of Labor Statistics; U.S. Census Bureau.
    - ○ **Non-White Births Percentage Higher Than White Births.** For the first time in U.S. history, the percentage of non-white children born (50.4%) exceeded those of white children born in the U.S. (49.6%). *Time,* June 4, 2012, p. 11, citing data from U.S. Census Bureau for the time period July 2010 through July 2011.

Children, Childcare, Child Rearing, and Childcare Public Policies (Including Parental/Maternal Leave Policies).

- **Allowances—Weekly—Percentage of Parents Who Pay and Average Amount.** An estimated 61% of parents pay allowances to their children—with "more than half (of U.S. parents paying allowances) … when their children are just 8 years old." The average allowance is $15 per week. *The Week*, September 14, 2012, p. 18 citing *CNN.com.*
- **Breast-Feeding—Commonness of in U.S.** U.S. mothers who breast-feed—73.9% (compared with France and Ireland, "where it seems to be viewed as mildly disgusting."), Johnson, D., "Mothers Beware!," *The New York Review of Books,* June 21, 2012.
- **Childcare and Childcare Public Policies (Including Parental/Maternal Leave Policies).**
    - ○ **Fathers' Growing Involvement In—Percentage of Fathers Who Routinely Care for Children Under the Age of 15**. 32% of fathers with working wives. Thomas, S., "Are Dads the New Moms?" *The Wall Street Journal*, May 12–13, 2012 citing recent U.S. Census Bureau report.
    - ○ **Parental and Maternal Leave in U.S.—Amount Of—Compared With Other Countries.** Under federal law, public employees and workers at private companies with 50 or more workers have the right to receive 12 unpaid weeks. Some states have mandated paid leave laws. Comparisons with paternity and maternity leave in other nations are as follows:

Parental and Maternal Leave Policies

Selected Countries	Parental and Maternal Leave
Australia	18 weeks at federal minimum wage (appr. $606 a week)
Belgium	15 weeks at appr. 75%–82% of pay
South Africa	4 months at 60% of pay
Sweden	13 months (at least 2 months of which must be paternity leave) at 80% of parent's salary up to $65K

United States   12 weeks (unpaid)

Hansegard, J., "For Paternity Lease, Sweden Asks If Two Months Is Enough," *The Wall Street Journal*, August 1, 2012. See also, *The Week*, October 12, 2012, p. 8 (German government proposed grandparental leave for up to three years without risk of job loss or credit towards retirement benefits—but without pay).

- **Children's Savings Accounts—Importance of and Correlation to Likelihood of College Attendance and Graduation**. "Children with savings accounts are 7 times more likely to attend college" and "are also twice as likely to graduate or be on track" to do so than children who do not have savings accounts. *The Week,* July 27, 2012, p. 33 citing *The Washington Monthly.*

- **Corporal Punishment of Children.**
    - **Number of Regions in U.S. Where Remains Legal in Schools**. Only one—"The South." "Corporal Punishment: The Ugly Reality," *The Week,* November 18, 2011, p. 17, citing P. Jonsson in *CSMonitor. com.*
    - **Spanking—Percentage of Adults Who Believe in Giving Children an Occasional "Good, Hard Spanking."** 70% as of 2008 (down from 83% in 1986). "Corporal Punishment: The Ugly Reality," *The Week,* November 18, 2011, p. 17, citing P. Jonsson in *CSMonitor.com.*

- **Sleep—Recommended Amount of Sleep for Children.** The recommended sleep for children by age range is as follows:

Age	Recommended Hours of Sleep
Babies (3 months to 11 months)	14–15 hours
Toddlers (1 to 3 years)	12–14 hours
Preschoolers	11–13 hours
Elementary Schoolers	10–11 hours

Rochman, B., "Please, Please Go To Sleep," *Time,* March 26, 2012, p. 47, citing National Sleep Foundation.

Citizenship and Naturalization, Immigrants and Immigration, Emigration and Migration, Non-Deportation Rights and Employment Visas.
- **Citizenship and Naturalization.**
  - ○ **Citizenship.**
    - – **Birthright Citizenship—Number of Other Advanced Countries Which Offer Birthright Citizenship.** One other advanced nation, Canada, still offers birthright citizenship. Neither European nations nor China or Japan do so. Stengel, R., "One Document, Under Siege," *Time,* July 4, 2011, p. 42.
    - – **Citizenship Applicant's Knowledge of American History and Government.** 93% of immigrants applying for U.S. citizenship correctly answer six out of ten questions on these subjects correctly. (Survey indicates that only about 65% of native-born Americans can match the rate). *The Week*, May 18, 2012, p. 18, citing *USA Today.*
  - ○ **Naturalization—Immigrants Becoming Citizens Through Naturalization—2010—Number Of.** 610,000 now-citizens passed examinations in English and about civics. Stengel, R., "One Document, Under Siege," *Time,* July 4, 2011, p. 42.
- **Emigration and Migration.**
  - ○ **Emigrant Populations—Biggest Emigration Populations and Percentage of Populations.** The ten nations with the largest emigrant populations (defined as the number of a country's nationals who have emigrated as of 2010) are as follows:

Ranking	Country	Total Emigrant Population (2010)	Emigrant Population as Appr. Percentage of Total Population
1.	Mexico	11.9 MM	10.6%
2.	India	11.4 MM	0.9%
3.	Russia	11.1 MM	7.8%
4.	China	8.3 MM	0.6%
5.	Ukraine	6.6 MM	14.4%

  The range of those nations with the highest immigrant populations as a percentage of population are 68.3% (No. 1—West Bank & Gaza) to Portugal (No. 10—20.8%). *The Economist, Pocket World in Figures: 2012 Edition*; Population Data from World Bank.
  - ○ **Emigration and Renunciation of Citizenship.**
    - – **Number of Days Per Year Person Allowed to Return to U.S. Even After Renunciation of Citizenship.** 120 days per year.

– **U.S. Citizens Who Gave Up U.S. Citizenship in 2011— Number Of.** 1788 persons (compared with appr. 400 persons in 2009). Expressed as a percentage of U.S. population: 0.0000057%. Wolverson, R., Walt, V., "Take the Money and Run," *Time*, July 30, 2012, p. 13.

o **Migration—Mexico—Net Migration From U.S. to Mexico— 2005–2010.** For the first time since the 1930s, there was a net migration of Mexicans (legal and illegal) *from the U.S. to Mexico* between 2005–2010. *The Week*, May 4, 2012, p. 8, citing the Pew Hispanic Center.

• **Immigrants and Immigration.**

o **Economic and Educational Generational Progress of Adult Children of Immigrants.** Adult Americans who are children of immigrants progress significantly by several economic and educational measures and in one generation are able to achieve relative parity with native-born Americans. Examples of such single-generational progress are as follows:

	Median Household Income	College Degree	Home Ownership Rate	In Poverty
Immigrants	$45,800	29%	51%	18%
Adult Children Of	$58,100	36%	64%	11%
All of U.S.	$58,200	31%	65%	13%

Differences Among Children of Varying Immigrant Groups
Asian Children	55%
Hispanic Children	21%

Self-Reporting By Adult Children of Immigrants That Their Standard of Living Is Better Than That of Their Parents at Parallel Stage of Life

Children Of:
Asian-American Immigrants	75%
Hispanic Immigrants	67%
Compare: All U.S. Population	60%

Jordan, M., *The Wall Street Journal*, February 8, 2013, citing Pew Research Center.

o **Immigrant Populations—Biggest Immigrant Populations and Percentage of Populations.** The five nations with the largest immigrant populations are as follows:

Ranking	Country	Total Immigrant Population (2010)	Immigrant Population As Appr. Percentage of Total Population
1.	*U.S.*	*42.8MM*	*13.7%*
2.	Russia	12.3MM	8.7%
3.	Germany	10.8MM	13.2%
4.	Saudi Arabia	7.3MM	26.0%
5.	Canada	7.2MM	20.9%

The range of those top 20 nations with the highest immigrant populations as a percentage of population are 86.5% (No. 1, Qatar) to Oman (No. 20, 28.4% with West Bank and Gaza (at No. 11 with 43.6% and Luxembourg (No. 17 with 35.2%). *The Economist, Pocket World in Figures, 2012 Edition*; Population Data from World Bank, U.S. Census Bureau.

○ **Legal Immigrants—Number and as Percentage of All Immigrants in U.S.** There are currently appr. 29.4MM legal immigrants in the United States. In other words, appr. 73% of all immigrants (i.e. appr. three out of four immigrants) currently in the United States are residing here legally. See also Jordan, M., "The Costs and Benefits of an Immigration Overhaul," *The Wall Street Journal*, February 4, 2013.

○ **Ratio of Family Reunification and Work-Based Immigration.** Since the 1960s, family preferences (including the very broad definition of "family reunification" including not only spouses and minor children but also parents and siblings) account for nearly two-thirds of all legal immigrants—far exceeding the work-based immigration. This creates what is sometimes referred to as "chain migration." Bush, J., Bolick, C., *The Wall Street Journal,*, January 25, 2013. See also, Cannato, V., *The Wall Street Journal*, March 12, 2013, review of the book, *Immigration Wars* by Jeb Bush and Clint Bolick (Noting that only 20% of yearly visas are reserved for skilled workers and nearly two-thirds of all immigrations are now based upon the family reunification policies. Thus, family reunification is itself "(t)he eight-hundred-pound gorilla in immigration reform.").

○ **U.S. Immigrant Population Percentage—Compared With Other Western Countries.** The U.S. immigration percentages increasingly parallel and resemble those of many other Western European countries. For example, "France, Germany and the U.K. have only slightly fewer foreign-born residents than [the U.S.]" and Canada and Australia (and also the U.K. and Singapore), who aggressively seek certain highly skilled immigrant workers and their families, "(now) have a higher percentage of foreign-born citizens than the U.S." Zakaria, F., "Broken and Obsolete—An Immigration Deadlock Makes the U.S. a Second-Rate Nation," *Time,* June 18, 2012, p. 24.

o **U.S. Permanent-Resident Visas—Percentages Based Upon Skills vs. Family Unification.** The bases for issuance of permanent resident visas in the U.S. are as follows:

	U.S.	Canada
Skills-Based	13%	62%
Family Unification	66%	38%
Other	21%	

Zakaria, F., "Broken and Obsolete—An Immigration Deadlock Makes the U.S. a Second-Rate Nation," *Time,* June 18, 2012, p. 24.

• **Non-Deportation Rights and Employment Visas.**

  o **DACA—Number of Young Immigrants Eligible for Application for DACA Non-Deportation Rights.** Appr. 800,000 and possibly as many as 1,700,000 immigrants under the age of 30. *The Economist,* August 25–31, 2012, p. 24.

  o **Employment Visas.**

    – **H1-B Visa Skilled Workers Programs—Annual Caps On.** Under "the H1-B program, which accounts for nearly all [U.S.] legal skilled immigration," there is a cap of 85,000 such visas per year—65,000 with at least a BA degree and 20,000 with at least a master's degree. Seen by some as aggravating matters, even this program has been "further tightened." For example, "(b)uried" in 2009 legislation in response to the financial collapse is the Employee American Workers Act, "which restricted H1-B hiring at any U.S. company that received government support from either TARP or new Federal Reserve credit facilities." See Seib, G., "Visa Plan Poses Bipartisan Test," *The Wall Street Journal,* May 1, 2012 ("In 2008 the legal (H-1B visas) quota was filled in one day, according to the GAO"), and Slaughter, M.J., "How Skilled Immigrants Create Jobs," *The Wall Street Journal,* June 21, 2012. Even assuming the continuation of the 85,000 annual cap, this would mean that only 1,020,000 H1-B visas could be issued *per decade,* representing appr. 0.3% of the U.S. population. See also, *The Economist,* October 13-19, 2012, p. 17 (Start-Up Chile instituted in Chile, in which immigrants are sought, including entrepreneurs "with a good idea can get a visa in a couple of weeks," and where "since 2010, when Start-Up Chile began, it has attracted some 500 companies run by whizz-kids from 37 countries"). Almost humorously, see *The Week*, May 31, 2013, p. 34, citing *Bloomberg.com* (As recently as 2010, fashion models were nearly twice as likely to get their H1-B visas approved as computer programmers. More than 50% of fashion-model visa applications were approved as compared with 28% of visa requests for computer-related occupations).

  – **H1-B Recipients—Breakdown of Industries in Which They Work.** In 2010 the H1-B skilled worker visas were granted to individuals working in the following fields:

Computer-Related Occupations	47.5%
Engineering, Architecture, Surveying	10.3%
Education	10.3%
Administrative Specialties	8.6%
Medicine and Health	7.8%
Other	15.3%

Seib, G., "Visa Plan Poses Bipartisan Test," *The Wall Street Journal*, May 1, 2012, citing U.S. Citizens and Immigration Services.

• **Undocumented Workers.**
  ○ **Countries and Regions of Origin.** The top three countries of origin of undocumented workers are Mexico (59%), El Salvador (6%), and Guatemala (5%) for a combined total of 70% of all undocumented workers. In addition, appr. 1.0MM (8.7%) are from Asia and the Pacific Islands, 800,000 (or about 7%) are from South America, and 300,000 are from Europe (2.6%). Vargas, J., "Not Legal—Not Leaving," *Time*, June 25, 2012, p.34.

  ○ **Deportation of Illegal Immigrants—Level of Public Support For.** As of February 2007 the following percentages indicate the stated beliefs of polled U.S. citizens with respect to the advisability or correctness of deportation of the estimated 11.0 MM illegal immigrants currently in the U.S.

"All" should be deported	23%
"Most" should be deported	30%
(i.e., 53% believe "all" or "most" should be deported)	
"Most" should be allowed to remain in the U.S. legally	31%
"All" should be allowed to remain in the U.S. legally	5%
(i.e., 36% believe that "all" or "most" should be allowed to remain legally).	

usnews.nbcnews.com citing Reuters/Ipsos Poll, February 20, 2013.

○ **States with Highest Percentage Of.** The top three states which have the highest percentage shares of undocumented workers are Nevada (7.2%), California (6.89%), and Texas (6.7%), for a combined total of 20.7%. Vargas, J., "Not Legal—Not Leaving," *Time,* June 25, 2012, p.34.

○ **Total Number of Undocumented Workers Currently In U.S.** 11.5MM or appr. 4% of the U.S. population. Vargas, J., "Not Legal—Not Leaving," *Time,* June 25, 2012, p. 34.

○ **Work-Force—As Percentage of U.S. Workforce.** As of 2010 undocumented workers represent appr. 5.2% of the U.S. workforce (or about 1 in 20 workers) as compared with 3.8% (or about 1 in 26 workers) in 2000. Vargas, J., "Not Legal—Not Leaving," *Time,* June 25, 2012, p.34.

Density.

- **U.S. Population Density and 5 States With Highest and 5 States With Lowest Population Density.** U.S. Population Density: 87.4 person per square mile.

5 States With Highest Density		5 States With Lowest Density	
(p/sq/mile = persons per square mile)			
New Jersey	1,196 p/sq. mile	Alaska	1.2 p/sq. mile
Rhode Island	1,018 p/sq. mile	Wyoming	5.8 p/sq. mile
Massachusetts	839 p/sq. mile	Montana	6.8 p/sq. mile
Connecticut	738 p/sq. mile	North Dakota	9.7 p/sq. mile
Maryland	595 p/sq. mile	South Dakota	10.7 p/sq. mile

The above listing includes only states. It does not include, for example, the District of Columbia (9,857 p/sq. mile). U.S. Census Bureau; *Bloomberg.com*; *About.com/geography.*

- **World Population Density and Density by Countries (10 Countries with Highest and Lowest Population Density) and by Continents.**

○ **World Population Density:** 105 persons per square mile (115 persons per square mile if Antarctica (which has zero population) is excluded.

Population Density—By Continents:

Listed in order of highest to lowest population density:

Asia	203 persons/sq. mile
Europe	134 persons/sq. mile
U.S. Population Density:	**87.4 persons per square mile**
South America	73 persons/sq. mile
Africa	65 persons/sq. mile
North America	32 persons/sq. mile

Australia   6 persons/sq. mile

Antarctica   0 persons/sq. mile

o **Population Density—By Countries** (Excluding microstates such as Macau (20,910 persons/sq.mi), Singapore (7.447 persons/sq. mile), and Hong Kong (6,418 persons/sq. mile):

Countries With Highest Population Density		Countries With Lowest Population Density	
Bahrain	1,818 p/sq. mile*	Mongolia	1.8 p/sq. mile
Malta	1,318 p/sq. mile	French Guiana	2.6 p/sq. mile
Bermuda	1,225 p/sq. mile	Namibia	2.8 p/sq. mile
Maldives	1,060 p/sq. mile	Australia	2.9 p/sq. mile
Bangladesh	1,033 p//sq. mile	Iceland	3.1 p/sq. mile

U.S. Population Density: 87.4 person per square mile

* *"p/sq.mile" means "persons per square mile.* Because of the small land size of many of these countries with high densities, Bangladesh is often considered the country with the highest population density. *The Economist, Pocket World in Figures: 2012; About.com/geography.*

o **Population Density—By Highest Density Megacities.** A "megacity" is usually defined as a city with a population of more than 10MM. The 10 densest megacities in the world are as follows:

Ranking	City/Country	Population (MMs)	Persons Per Sq Mi	GDP Per Capita
1.	Dhaka, Bangladesh	14.4MM	115,200	$3,100
2.	Mumbai, India	17.3MM	82,000	$5,900
3.	Karachi, Pakistan	20.9MM	67,300	$3,500
4.	Manila, Philippines	21.2MM	38,300	$9,200
5.	Lagos, Nigeria	12.1MM	34,500	$3,300
6.	Kolkata, India	14.6MM	31,500	$3,800
7.	Delhi, India	22.8MM	30,400	$9,500
8.	Seoul-Inchon, S Korea	22.9MM	27,400	$32,200
9.	Mexico City, Mexico	20.0MM	25,400	$19,900
10.	Tehran, Iran	19.3MM	25,400	$17,800

Reference U.S. City

New York, New York   8.3MM   26,400

realestate.msn.com (June 11, 2013)

Displaced People and Refugees.

• **Displaced Persons—Number and Percentage of Persons Classified as Refugees or "Displaced" as of 2010.** 44MM or 0.63%. *Time*, July 4, 2011,

p. 15, citing UNHCR report with Germany as the only industrialized, developed nation of the top five nations that "host the most refugees."

- **Refugees—Number of Refugees in U.S. and As Percentage of U.S. Population.** The U.S. has the 9th most refugees of all nations, with 275,000 persons, which constitute appr. 09% of the U.S. population. This compares with Pakistan (the nation with most refugees) with 1.7 MM refugees, or about 1% of its population. *The Economist, Pocket World in Figures: 2012 Edition*; Population Data from World Bank.

Fastest and Slowest Growing Continents or Regions of World. Based upon analysis of the top 20 fastest and showing regions of the world (Population Change—Years 2005–2010), the following are the fastest and slowest growing regions:

Fastest Growing Regions or Continents	Slowest Growing Regions or Continents
Africa (12 of 20)	Eastern Europe and Baltics (14 of Top 20)
Arab Peninsula/Middle East (7 of top 20)	Caribbean (3 of Top 20)
	(Puerto Rico, U.S. Virgin Islands, and Cuba)
	SE Asia (1 of Top 20) (Singapore)
	Western Europe (1 of Top 20)(Germany)
	Eastern Asia (1 of Top 20)(Japan)
	Africa (1 of Top 20)(Zimbabwe)

The Economist, Pocket World in Figures, 2012 Edition.

Generations.

- **Contemporary American Generations—Names Of.** While there is widespread agreement upon the age boundaries of the Baby Boomers (1946–1964), the names and year delineations of other generations are, at best, a rough science. Generation names and inclusionary years vary and sometimes overlap. Many demographers refer to the following:

Years	Generation Name(s)
2000–2012	Generation Z (New Baby Boomers)
1980–2000	Millennial or Gen Y
1965–1979	Generation X
1946–1964	Baby Boomers

Also common are the following generation names:

Years	Generation Name(s)
1995–2007	New Silent Generation
1978–1990	Generation Y (or, jokingly, sometimes referred to as "Generation Why?")

1965–1985	Generation X	
1965–1980	Gen X—Baby Busters	
1975–1985	Gen X—MTV/Boomerang Generation	

The generation names and definitions sometimes used by the Pew Research Center are as follows:

Generation Name	Date of Birth Range	Current Age Range (As of 2012)
GI Generation	Born Prior to 1936	76+
Silent Generation	1937–1945	67–75
Older Boomers	1946–1954	58–66
Younger Boomers	1955–1964	48–57
Gen X	1965–1976	36–47
Millennials	1977–1992	20–35

See also, Carlson, Elwood, "20th Century U.S. Generations," Population Bulletin 64, No. 1 (2009) which identified and references the Baby Boomers (1944–1964) ("median member born in 1955"), Generation X (1965–1982) ("median member born in 1974"), and the New Boomers (1983–2001) ("median member born in 1982"). Lastly, there is also widespread agreement about the duly earned use of the phrase "The Greatest Generation" for those Americans born between 1901 and 1945. *prb.org* (Population Reference Bureau), *About.com;* Pew Research Center's Internet and American Life Project.

- **Multi-Generational—Adult Children—Ages 25–34—Living in Multi-generational Households.** 20%—"1 in 5." This is "roughly double the rate in 1980." Ford, A., *Time,* April 9, 2012, p. 16, citing Bureau of Economic Analysis, Bureau of Labor Statistics, Pew Research Center, and the American Assembly of Columbia University. See also, Wolverson, R, "Now What?" *Time,* June 13, 2011, p. 34, citing Twentysomething Inc. (85% of U.S. graduates are "taking shelter under their (parent's) roof.").

- **Youth Generation of World—Percentage of World Population Under Age 25.** Appr. 3BB or about 43% of the world's 7BB population (World Bank), which makes this youth generation "the largest generation in human history." *The Week,* August 24–31, 2012, p. 18, citing the *Los Angeles Times.*

Geography of U.S.

- **Deserts—Number of U.S. Deserts in Top 10 Largest in World**. There is some substantial disagreement about the propriety of inclusion or exclusion of the Arctic and Antarctic deserts and about the separate identity and size of certain desert areas, however, based upon the more consensus lists of the 10 largest deserts. The appr. 190,000 sq. mi. Great Basin Desert in Nevada is the only U.S. desert that would be included. The 130,000 sq. mi. Colorado Desert and the 15,000–54,000 sq. mi. Mojave Deserts would be ranked Nos. 13 and 20, respectively.

- **Drives—Most Scenic and Most Scenic Coastal.** Each of us has our own bucket list of things to do and places to visit before we die, and there is certainly no absolute criteria for the preparation of any list of "most scenic drives." Nevertheless, as offerings of two places to begin, the following lists were assembled and presented by *msn.travel.com.* March 20, 2013. The following top 10 lists are **not** listed in any order of priority:

Most Scenic Spring Drives in the U.S.—Top 10

1. Colorado. The Million Dollar Highway, Red Mountain Pass, Colorado.
2. Washington. Loop from Seattle on WA-580 near Arlington, through the North Cascades Highway to Skagit Tulip Festival, Washington.
3. Virginia. Shenandoah National Park and Skyline Drive (105 miles and 75 overlooks).
4. Texas. Texas Hill Bluebonnet Tour (Austin, Highway 183 N to FM 1431 West and end at Burnet, Texas).
5. Yosemite National Park Drive (180 miles starting at CA Hwy 49 and continue on CA 120 to top of Tioga Pass).
6. California. Anza Borrego Desert State Park (Two-hour drive through the desert).
7. Virginia. George Washington Memorial Parkway, Washington, DC (Initial stretch on the Mt Vernon Memorial Parkway).
8. California. Antelope Valley (Located right outside of Los Angeles; take I-5 N and exit on CA 138 (Lancaster Road)).
9. New York. Route 9A out of New York City up the Hudson Valley to Sleepy Hollow and on to Hyde Park and see the two-century-old Vanderbilt Mansion.
10. Connecticut. Merritt Parkway (Called the "Queen of the Parkways" with 69 art deco bridges and forested surroundings).

Most Scenic Coastal Drives in North America—Top 10

1. California. Highway 1, Big Sur (137 miles from San Luis Obispo to Monterey).
2. North Carolina. Cape Hatteras National Seashore (Pea Island National Wildlife Refuge and from Points Harbor to Ocracoke).
3. Canada. Central Coastal Drive. Prince Edward Island (Green Gables Shore Region and Red Sands Shore).
4. Hawaii. The Hana Highway (68 miles from Kahului over 59 bridges to Haleakala National Park).

5. Florida. Daytona Beach. (On the beach with a $5 vehicle pass and a 10 mph speed limit).

6. California. 17-Mile Drive, Pebble Beach (with Fanshell Overlook, Point Joe and Lone Cypress).

7. Virginia. Chesapeake Bay Bridge-Tunnel (Connecting Chesapeake Bay with the Virginia portion of the Delmarva Peninsula).

8. Oregon. U.S. Highway 101 (363 miles from Cannon Beach through Tillamook and south to Haystack Rock).

9. Mexico. The Michoacán Coast (201 miles from Manzanillo to Playa Azul).

10. Massachusetts. Route 6A, Cape Cod (63 miles along Old King's Highway from Bourne to Provincetown).

Romano, T., *local.msn.com*, March 20, 2013.

- **Lakes—U.S. Lakes in Top 10 Largest Lakes In World**. Three of the top ten largest lakes are located in the U.S.

Ranking	Name (and Location)	Size in Square Miles
1.	The Caspian Sea ("lake")(Asia)	143,000 sq. mi.
2.	*Lake Superior (U.S./Canada)*	*31,800 sq. mi*
3.	Lake Victoria (Africa)	26,800 sq. mi.
4.	*Lake Huron (U.S./Canada)*	*23,000 sq. mi.*
5.	*Lake Michigan (U.S.)*	*22,000 sq. mi.*

- **Mountains—Number of U.S. Mountains Amongst Highest 100 Mountains in the World; Highest Mountain in U.S.; Highest Mountain in Lower 48 States; Number of Highest 20 U.S. Mountains Located Outside of Alaska.**

Number of U.S. Mountains Amongst Highest 100 Mountains in the World:	None
Highest Mountain in United States:	Mt. McKinley, Alaska—20,320 ft
Highest Mountain in Lower 48 States:	Mount Whitney, California—14,494 ft.
Number of Highest 20 U.S. Mountains Located Outside Alaska:	One—Mt. Whitney, CA.

geography.about.com and *americasroof.com.*

- **Rivers—Number of U.S. Rivers Amongst Longest 10 Rivers in the World; Longest Five Rivers in U.S.** One—if one includes the Mississippi-Missouri systems. The longest five rivers in the U.S. are as follows:

Ranking	Name	Length
1.	Missouri River	2,540 mi.
2.	Mississippi River	2,340 mi.
3.	Yukon River	1,980 mi.
4.	Rio Grande River	1,900 mi.
5.	St. Lawrence River	1,900 mi.

ga.water.usgs.gov/edu (citing Kammerer, J.C., U.S. Geological Survey Fact Sheet OFR 87-242 rev.) and *The Economist: Pocket World in Figures, 2012 Edition.*

- **Size of U.S.**
  - **Distance and Driving Time from Compton, California to Caribou, Maine.** 3,241 miles and about 53 hours driving time according to Google Maps. *Googlemaps.com.*
  - **Distance and Driving Time from Dutch Harbor, Alaska to Key West, Florida.** 6,115 miles and about 122 hours driving time according to Google Maps. *Googlemaps.com.*
  - **U.S. and U.S. Compared to Largest 5 Nations.**
    United States: 3.7 MM square miles
    The largest nations in world, listed in order of size, are as follows:

Ranking	Name	Size
1.	Russia	6.6 MM sq. mi.
2.	Canada	3.9 MM sq. mi.
3.	***United States***	***3.7 MM sq. mi.***
4.	China	3.7 MM sq. mi.
5.	Brazil	3.3 MM sq. mi.

  - **U.S. Land Size—In Square Miles and Acres.** Appr. 3.5 MM sq. miles or 2.2 BB square acres.
- **States—Names—Origins Of—Native American, British, French, and Spanish—Number Of.** While the name origin of a couple of states (Oregon and Rhode Island) are unknown or in dispute, there is consensus that the origin of the names of more than one-half of the states (26) are Native American, 13 states are of or derived from British or French origin, and 6 states are from or derived from Spanish words.

Homeless Persons.

(Preliminary Note: All data regarding homeless populations must be accepted and reviewed with some caution (a) because, almost definitionally, it is extremely difficult to obtain and maintain accurate demographic reporting, and (b) because data oftentimes must rely upon self-reporting of person's histories, condition and state. Nevertheless, and especially with respect to orders of magnitude and point-in-time data, there are numerous collectively accurate and responsible reports and data generated by agencies and bodies such as the *Annual HUD Report (the Annual Homeless Assessment Report)*, the Hunger and Homelessness Survey released by the U.S. Conference of Mayors, and various reports of the National Alliance to End Homelessness such as "The State of Homelessness in America 2013."

- **Age and Race.** The age and race of those persons and families in emergency or transitional shelters is as follows:

Age: Under 18:	21.8%	**Race:** White, non-Hispanic/Latino	41.6%
Age 18-30	23.0%	Black	37.0%
Age 21—50	37.0%	White, Hispanic/Latino	9.7%
Age 51-61	14.9%	Other Single Race/Mltpl Races	11.7%
Age 62 or older	2.8%		

HUD, Annual Homeless Assessment Report to Congress.

- **Disability—Instances of Among Persons and Families in Emergency or Transitional Shelters**. Appr. 36.8%, or nearly four out of ten are intellectually or physically disabled. HUD, Annual Homeless Assessment Report to Congress.

- **Household Size—Individuals and Families.** Of those persons and families in emergency or transitional shelter is the respective household sizes were as follows:

Single persons/1-person "households":	63.0%
2-person households:	10.1%
3- or more person households:	26.9%

HUD, Annual Homeless Assessment Report to Congress.

- **Homelessness Rate Compared With Poverty Rate.** While to some persons the 0.2% homelessness rate may not seem like a lot (unless you or a friend are the homeless persons in question), this rate equates to appr. one homeless person for every 500 Americans. This 0.2% homelessness rate equates to roughly 625,000 homeless and compares with the 15.9% poverty rate (which increased from 15.3% between 2010 and 2011). National Alliance to End Homelessness, "The State of Homelessness in America—2013." See also, National Coalition for the Homeless Reports.

- **Newly Homeless—Percentage Coming from Institutional Setting.** Prior to entering the shelter facility, 11.0% reported that they were coming from a psychiatric facility or substance abuse center (6.4%), from an incarceration facility (4.4%), or from a foster home (0.2%).

HUD, Annual Homeless Assessments Report to Congress.

- **Personal Characteristics and Subpopulations—Chronic Substance Abusers, Severely Mentally Ill, Etc.** The percentages of the sheltered homeless, by certain subpopulations, and from data collected by a point-in-time methodology are as follows:

Chronic Substance Abusers	34.7%
Severely Mentally Ill	26.2%
Veterans	15.1%
Victims of Domestic Violence	12.3%
Persons with HIV/AIDS (Adults)	3.9%
Unaccompanied Youth	1.1%

HUD, Annual Homeless Assessments Report to Congress.

- **Single-Night Sheltered Homeless Persons Nationwide.** Appr. 1.6 MM of the 46.2 MM Americans living in poverty. See also, *Time,* March 18, 2013, p. 13, citing Coalition for the Homeless (50,000 reported in New York City's shelters "each night in January (2013)" which was "a record high that included 21,000 children. …").
- **Veterans In Emergency or Transitional Shelters.** Nearly 12%, or about one in nine, were veterans. See also the data from the point-in-time methodology set forth immediately above and reporting the veterans percentage as 15.1%.

Households.
- **Economics Of.**
  - **Economic Well-Being—Correlations with Education, Employment, Age of Marriage, and Marriage Before Paternity.** An individual has only a 2% chance of "being in poverty" and has a 72% "chance of joining the middle-class *if* they finish high school, are fully employed, wait until age 21 to become married, and get married prior to having a child. The numbers are "almost precisely reversed for people who (violate) these…rules." Notable and Quotable, *The Wall Street Journal,* June 11, 2012, based upon analysis of U.S. Census data and citing testimony of Brookings Institute Senior Fellow Ron Haskins' testimony before the Senate Finance Committee on June 5, 2012.
  - **Economic Well-Being—Disposable Income—Use of for Debt.** Appr. 11% "to pay down all forms of debt." This is down from a 14% peak in 2007 and the lowest debt service ratio in nearly 20 years (since 1994). Schoen, J.; *economywatch .nbcnews.com,* August 9, 2012, citing Federal Reserve data.
  - **Household Budgets—Automobile—Annual Costs; Percentage of Annual Household Budget; Highest Weekly Outlay.** It costs appr. $8,600 per year, according to the AAA, for an owner of a

"midsize sedan who drivers 15,000 mile a year" (including finance costs, depreciation, repairs, insurance taxes, and gas). This amount would represent appr. 16% of an average family budget. Gross, D., "Renting Prosperity," *The Wall Street Journal*, May 5-6, 2012. See also, *The Economist*, September 22-28, 2012, p. 29.

o **Household Debt Burdens.**

  – **As Percentage of Household Income: 1980–2012.** In the 3rd Quarter, 2012 U.S. households spent only 10.6% of their after-tax income on debt payments—the lowest percentage since 1983. If other monthly payments, such as rental payments and auto leases, are included the percentage increases to only 15.7%, which is also "near a 30-year low." The financial obligations, by year, are as follows:

Year	Appr. Financial Obligations (Note 1) as Percentage of After-Tax Income
1980	16.0%
1985	17.8%
1990	17.0%
1995	17.0%
2000	18.1%
2005	18.3%
2007	19.0%
2012	15.7%

  Note 1: Ratio of estimated required payments on mortgage and consumer debt plus automobile lease payments, rental payments, and household insurance to disposable after-tax personal income. Casselman, B., *The Wall Street Journal*, December 24, 2012, citing Federal Reserve and Commerce Department.

  – **Current Amounts vs. 2008.** 118% of disposable household income. This is "11% down from its (2008) peak" of 129%, and this lessening of household debt is considerably more than the households in other countries (Spain drop, 4%; U.K. drop, 6%). Foroohar, R., "Digging Out of the Debt Hole." *Time,* July 16, 2012, p. 26, citing McKinsey & Company's global deleveraging report. See also, Mitchell, J., "U.S. Chips Away at the Debt on Their Homes," *The Wall Street Journal*, August 30, 2012 (noting that "household debt peaked in the fall of 2008 and has fallen nearly every quarter since, by a total ... of almost $1.3 trillion."). See also, Shah, N., *The Wall Street Journal,*

March 1, 2013 (Although for the first time in more than two years, overall consumers took on slightly more debt in the 4th Quarter of 2012 and despite the rather substantial increases in student loan debt, the aggregate U.S. debt level still remains $1.3 trillion *lower* than the U.S. peak of $12.7 trillion in late 2008), and *The Economist*, June 1-7, 2013 (Evidencing that the average 2012 U.S. household debt (gross debt as a percentage of disposable income) is materially less than that of Netherlands, Canada, Britain, Spain, and Japan and only slightly higher than Greece, France, and Germany).

– **Median Debt Burden for Households as a Function of Age of Head of Household.** The median debt burden of U.S. households is partly a function of the age of the head of the household.

Age—Head of Household	Median 2010 Household Debt Burden
Under 35	$39,600
35-44	$108,000
45- 54	$91,800
55-64	$76,900
65-74	$45,000
75 and Older	$30,000

Ensign, R., Wealth Management—Journal Report, *The Wall Street Journal*, February 25, 2013 citing Experian, Federal Reserve, and Zillow.

– **Mortgage Debt—Older Families (Ages 55–64)—Percentage of Families Still Carrying Mortgage Debt and Their Median Mortgage Debt Amount**. Appr. 54% of older families (up from 37% in 1989) are still carrying mortgage debt, and the median size of that debt is $97,000 (substantially higher than the $34,000 median debt in 1989). Tergesen, A, *The Wall Street Journal*, December 10, 2012.

– **Percentage of Households Without Debt.** 25.1% as of 2010 (slightly more than the 23% in 2007). Ensign, R., Wealth Management—Journal Report, *The Wall Street Journal*, February. 25, 2013.

– **States with Highest and Lowest Average Per Household Debt.**

Highest Average Debt Load State	Alaska	$29,700
Lowest Average Debt Load State	Maine	$23,800

Ensign, R., Wealth Management—Journal Report, *The Wall Street Journal*, February 25, 2013.

- o **Young Adults' Total Debt—"Total Debt" and Credit Card Debt Dropping Substantially.** The average young adult (someone under the age of 35) now has the lowest "total debt" since 1995—down to $15,000. "Total debt" includes mortgage loans, credit cards, auto lending, student loans and other consumer borrowing." In addition, 22% of young adults had zero debt and fewer carried credit cards. This data was deemed surprising to some since student borrowing has ballooned and the percentage of student loan delinquencies has increased. Shah, N., *The Wall Street Journal*, March 5, 2013, citing the Pew Research Center.
- **Married-Couple Families—Supported Financially by Husband Alone.** Less than one in five. Mundy, L., "Women, Money and Power," *Time*, March 26, 2012, p. 28, citing U.S. Bureau of Labor Statistics, Families & Work Institute, the Hamilton Project at the Brookings Institute, Current Population Survey, National Vital Statistics Reports; analysis by Reach Advisors of the American Community Survey, public-use microdata sample from 2008–2010; National Center for Education Statistics, and Pew Research Center.
- **Housework Chores—Performed by Working Mothers vs. Working Fathers.** 55% of working mothers do housework chores on an "average day" as opposed to 18% of working fathers. *The Week*, April 5, 2013, p. 17, citing U.S. Bureau of Labor Statistics.
- **Number of Households in U.S. and Average Size Of.** As of August 2012, there were appr. 14.3MM households in the U.S. Based upon the current U.S. population the average household size is approximately 2.7 people per household. U.S. Census Bureau.
- **Single-Person Households.**
  - o **Chance That U.S. Child Lives in Family Headed by Single Mother.** One in four. Harper's Index, *Harper's Magazine*, October 2012, p. 15, citing U.S. Census Bureau. This ratio represents a 133% increase in the last appr. 40 years since 1970. Harper's Index, *Harper's Magazine*, June, 2013, p. 15.
  - o **Singledom and Unmarried—Number of Households in U.S.** 28% (i.e., appr. 32MM Americans and "about 15MM of them between the ages of 24 and 65), "the highest level in U.S. history." *The Week*, February 10, 2012, p. 32, citing *Fortune*. See also, *The Week*, February 17, 2012, p. 14, citing Klinenberg, E., *The New York Times*. This pattern of increase is consistent with the worldwide trends—especially amongst the rich nations. Nearly 50% of all American adults are

now unmarried. This percentage is more than double the percentage (22%) who were unmarried in 1950. *The Economist*, August 25-31, 2012, p. 47.

- **Young Adults Returning Home to Live—Number of and Financial/Retirement Effects on Parents**. 22.6MM young adults (ages 18-34) representing appr. 32% of all such young adults were living at home in 2012. As a consequence, 26% of parents with home-living adult children have added new debt, and 7% of such parents have delayed retirement. Grind, K., *The Wall Street Journal*, May 4-5, 2013, citing data from the U.S. Census Bureau and the National Endowment for Financial Education (recommending consideration of the following courses of action: (1) "make them pay" (surprisingly, only 25% of such parents have asked the children to contribute to household expenses), (2) "set a time limit," (c) "make them work," and (d) "think before you cosign.").

Language—Other Than English Spoken at Home. Appr. 20.1% or 62.6MM persons. U.S. Census Bureau.

Marriage and Divorce.

- **Divorce Rate.** Appr. 40%, although this is only an estimate since many states do not collect data on divorce. Furthermore, this percentage figure can be heavily skewed depending upon the education levels and the ages of the parties at the time of their marriage. For example, the divorce rate for college-educated persons who marry after the age of 26 "has been dropping for the longest period in U.S. history." Luscombe, B., "The End of Alimony," *Time*, May 27, 2013, p. 44., citing Arizona State University Law Professor Mark Ellman.

- **Inter-Racial/Inter-Ethnic—New Marriages—Percentage Of.** 15% (or about one in seven) of all new U.S. marriages which is "nearly twice the rate of 30 years ago." Such marriages are much more common in Florida and the West (excepting Montana, Idaho, and Utah). The most common interracial marriages are between white and Hispanic (43.0%), white and Asian (14.4%), and white and black (11.9%). *Time*, March 3, 2012, p. 10, citing Pew Research Center Report. See also, *The Week*, May 11, 2012, p. 18 citing *The Washington Post* and stating that "about 10% of married couples are now interracial."

- **Marriage—Cost Of.** Appr. $27,000, excluding the aggregate flight, lodging, presents, and other costs incurred by attendees. Gill, A., *Vanity Fair*, September 2012, p. 202.

- **Online Dating and Effect of Social Networking—Percentage of U.S. Couples Who Met Online.** 30% (From 2007–2009). *Time*, August 30, 2010.

- **Percentage Drop Over Last Appr. 40 Years in Women Who Are Married**. Down 20% (However, the percentage of high-income women who are married has increased 12% over the same time period). Mundy, L., "Women, Money and Power," *Time*, March 26, 2012, p. 28, citing U.S. Bureau of Labor Statistics.
- **Plural Marriage—Est. Number of U.S. Families Which Practice.** From 30,000 to 100,000, taking "into account fundamentalist Mormons and the growing number of Muslim immigrants." Luscombe, B., "I Do, I Do, I Do, I Do," *Time,* August 6, 2012, p. 42 and citing *Columbia Law Review.* But see, Anapol, A. author of *Polyamory in the 21st Century*, cited in the same article, who estimates the percentage of polyamorists ("which can roughly be defined as having multiple lovers by mutual agreement") at 0.5% to 3.5% of the (U.S.) population. Converted into population numbers, this estimate range is far, far higher—from about 1.6MM to 10.9MM. However, this range appears to be greatly inflated acknowledging the difficulty of obtaining accurate data due, in part, to the fact that under-reporting occurs as a result of the illegality of polygamy in the U.S.
- **Same-Sex Marriages.**
    - ○ **College Freshmen Percentage Approval Of**. 71.3% (up from appr. 65% in 2009). *The Week*, February 17, 2012, p. 20, citing *TheDailyBeast.com.*
    - ○ **States and Growing International and Business Recognition Of—Number of States and Examples of Major Corporations Recognizing Same-Sex Marriages.** As of Spring 2013, twelve states ("up from zero less than a generation ago") recognize same-sex marriages, *The Week*, April 5, 2013, p. 2, citing *The Wall Street Journal;* Peters, M., *The Wall Street Journal,* May 14, 2013. In addition, the result of the USSC's June 2013 decision with respect to California's 2008 Prop 8 is that same-sex marriages will now be permitted in California. There also *may* be some nascent signs of increasing international recognition of same-sex marriage. Thirteen countries have now legalized gay marriage (e.g. Canada, Spain, Sweden, France, Uruguay, and New Zealand). However, at the same time Australia in 2012 rejected a similar proposal, and there are also rising signs of homophobia—stirred in part by American conservative Christians working abroad—in certain parts of, for example, Africa (Kenya and Uganda) and the Ukraine (laws proposed seeking to criminalize gay "propaganda"). See generally, *The Economist*, May 4-10, 2013, p. 61. With respect to major corporation, over 60 major

U.S. corporations ("including Apple, Xerox, Levi Strauss, Morgan Stanley, and Nike") filed amicus curie (friend-of-the court) briefs with the Supreme Court encouraging the reversal of California's same-sex ban, Proposition 8. *The Week*, March 15, 2013, p. 36, citing Davidson, A., *NewYorker.com*.

o **Voter Referendum Approvals Of.** After having lost 32 times previously, in November 2012 and for the first time in U.S. history, voter initiatives approving of equal-marriage rights for same-sex couples were passed in three states in November 2012—Maryland, Maine, and Washington. In addition, Minnesota voters refused to amend the state constitution to define marriage as the union between a man and a woman. *The Week*, November 16, 2012, p. 8.

Population.

• **U.S. Population—Adult and Minors, By Age Category, By Gender.**

General Category	Sub-Category	Percentage of U.S. Population	Number (Appr.)
Adults and Minors			
	Total Population	100.0%	311.6 MM
	Persons Under 5	6.5%	20.3 MM
	Minors (Under 18)	23.7%	73.8 MM
	All Adults	76.3%	237.8 MM
Working Age, Minors, and Seniors			
	Minors (Under 18)	23.7%	73.8 MM
	Working Age (18–64)	63.0%	196.3 MM
	Seniors (65 and Over)	13.3%	41.4 MM
Gender			
	Male	49.2%	153.3 MM
	Female	50.8%	158.3 MM

• **U.S. Population; World Population; U.S. Population as Percentage of World Population; and Population of Selected Countries.**

U.S. Population: 311,591,917 (July 2011) (U.S. Census Bureau)

World Population 6,974,000,000 (Appr.) (World Bank)

U.S. as Percentage of World Population: 4.5% (U.S. Census Bureau and World Bank)

- **World's Largest 10 Countries—Current (2009).**

Ranking	Country	Population	Percentage of World Population	Density Per/Sq.Mi.	U.S. as X Times As Large
1.	China	1,346 MM	19.3%	365 p/sm	.23 X
2.	India	1,198 MM	17.2%	943 p/sm	.26 X
3.	**United States**	**315 MM**	**4.5%**	**84 p/sm**	
4.	Indonesia	230 MM	3.3%	351 p/sm	1.4 X
5.	Brazil	194 MM	2.8%	58 p/sm	1.6 X
6.	Pakistan	181 MM	2.6%	551 p/sm	1.7 X
7.	Bangladesh	162 MM	2.3%	2,850 p/sm	1.9 X
8.	Nigeria	155 MM	2.2%	375 p/sm	2.0 X
9.	Russia	141 MM	2.0%	22 p/sm	2.2 X
10.	Japan	127 MM	1.8%	836 p/sm	2.5 X
11.	Mexico	110 MM	1.2%	45 p/sm	2.9 X
14.	Egypt	83 MM	1.2%	295 p/sm	3.8 X
16.	Germany	82 MM	1.2%	609 p/sm	3.8 X
21.	France	62 MM	0.9%	289 p/sm	5.1 X
36.	Canada	34 MM	0.5%	9 p/sm	9.3 X
39.	Iraq	31 MM	0.4%	160 p/sm	10.2 X

Population rounded to nearest MM. *The Economist, Pocket World in Figures: 2012 Edition; state.gov.*

- **World's Largest 10 Countries—2050 (Projected).**

Projected Ranking	Country Ranking	Current
1.	India	2.
2.	China	1.
3.	**United States**	**3.**
4.	Pakistan	6.
5.	Nigeria	8.
6.	Indonesia	4.
7.	Bangladesh	7.
8.	Brazil	5.
9.	Ethiopia	15.
10.	Congo-Kinshasa	20.

The Economist, Pocket World in Figures, 2012 Edition.

Race and Ethnicity.
- **Diversity and Dispersion Within Society.** U.S. is becoming far more evenly and more widely diverse as nation's minorities—"driven largely by

a surge in the Hispanic and Asian populations—move beyond traditional, 'gateway' cities (or large cities) into smaller cities and towns." In many cities and towns there has been a "surge" in the "diversity index"—an index which "weighs how a place's population is spread across five groups"—white, blacks, Hispanics, Asians, and others. Dougherty, C., Jordan, M., "Stirring Up the Melting Pot," *The Wall Street Journal,* September 7, 2012, citing U.S. 2010 Project at Brown University.

- **Diversity—Lack Of—Places Where Whites Make Up at Least 90% of Population**. Only 36% in 2010 as opposed to nearly 66% just 30 years ago in 1980. Dougherty, C., Jordan, M., "Stirring Up the Melting Pot," *The Wall Street Journal,* September 7, 2012, citing U.S. 2010 Project at Brown University.

- **Diversity—Most Diverse Metropolitan Area in U.S.** Vallejo, CA, with a diversity index score (100% equals a "perfectly diverse place") of 89.3, "with a population that was 41% white, 24% Hispanic, 15% Asian, 14% black, and 6% other." Other sample diversity index scores are Miami, FL—74.9, Gainesville, GA—59.5, and Fayetteville, AK—49.6. Dougherty, C., Jordan, M., "Stirring Up the Melting Pot," *The Wall Street Journal,* September 7, 2012, citing U.S. 2010 Project at Brown University.

- **Percentage of U.S. Population—By Race.**

Race		Percentage of U.S. Population
White Person (Not Hispanic	64%	(about 6.5 out of 10 people)
Latinos	16%	(about 1 out of 6 people)
Black	12%	(about 1 out of 8 people)
Asian	5%	(about 1 out of 20 people)

Scherer, M., "Why Latino Voters Will Swing the 2012 Election," *Time,* March 5, 2012, p. 22, citing Pew Hispanic Center, Bureau of Labor Statistics; Census Bureau. See also, Meckler, L., *The Wall Street Journal,* December 12, 2012 (Based upon Census Bureau estimates, by 2043 (i.e., appr. 30 years) "whites will no longer be in the majority among racial groups" and by 2060 (appr. 50 years) Hispanics "will account for nearly one in three people in the U.S.).

- **Puerto Ricans—Number of Puerto Ricans Living in Puerto Rico Compared with Living in U.S.** Living in Puerto Rico: Appr. 3.7MM; Living in U.S.: 4.6MM. Stated as a percentage, more than 55% of all Puerto Ricans live in the U.S. *Time,* June 27, 2011, p. 16. In November 2012 and for the first time, a majority of the Puerto Rican electorate voted to seek full statehood. Previously, in 1993 and 1998, only 47% so voted. *The Economist,* November 17–23, 2012, p. 28.

Sex Ratio—Males per 100 Females—Number of Countries Where M:F Ratio Exceeds 120 Men per 100 Women. Six countries—All in the Arab Peninsula. They are as follows, in order from highest:

Country	Male:Female Ratio
Qatar	311 males to 100 females
United Arab Emirates	228 males to 100 females
Bahrain	166 males to 100 females
Kuwait	148 males to 100 females
Oman	142 males to 100 females
Saudi Arabia	124 males to 100 females

The Economist, Pocket World in Figures, 2012 Edition.

Teenage Girls—Sexual Activity.
- **Average Children Per American Woman Age 15–19.** 3.4 children per 100 women, which is "the lowest rate since the CDC started tracking (these) birthrates in the 1940s." *Time*, April 23, 2012, p. 7.
- **Abstinence—Age 15–19.** 57% of girls in this age group have *not* had sexual intercourse. *The Week*, May 18, 2012, p. 18 citing report by the CDC and as initially reported by the Associated Press (increase from 49% in 1995).
- **Pregnancy Rate—Age 15–19.** Appr. 7% in 2006. The teenage pregnancy rate has "consistently declined over the past 20 years except for a small spike from 2005–2007." Sun, F., "Baby Mamas—Teen Moms Are Reality TV's New Stars. Is This A Good Thing," *Time*, July 18, 2011, p.59.

Weather.
- **Drought.**
    - **Economic Effect Upon U.S. Farmers—Percentage of Farmers With Crop Disaster Insurance.** Appr. 85% of U.S. farmers now carry some form of private crop disaster insurance, which is materially subsidized by the federal government. Walsh, B., "When the Rains Stop," *Time*, August 6, 2012, p. 34.
    - **Percentage of Country in 2012 Drought and Year of Last Drought of Similar Size and Extent.** 56% of U.S. (*The Week*, July 20, 2012, p. 6) and the worst drought since 1956. Walsh, B., "When the Rains Stop," *Time*, August 6, 2012, p. 34. But see, Harper's Index, *Harper's Magazine*, October 2012, p. 15, citing National Oceanic and Atmospheric Administration (60% of country and 1954 as last year with comparable drought).
- **Hurricanes and Superstorms—Superstorm Sandy—Size and Impact Of.** The October 2012 storm was 900 miles across—the largest ever recorded in the Atlantic Ocean. More than 106 Americans were killed, cars floated

on lawns, shorelines were re-aligned, the subways were flooded, and homes demolished. More than 15,000 flights were cancelled at JFK and LaGuardia, and 90% of the homes on New York's Long Island were without power. The NY Stock Exchange remained closed for two days, which was the longest weather-caused closure in 124 years. The preliminary damage estimates are from $30-$50 BB.

- **Temperatures.**
    - ○ **First Six Months of 2012.** "First 6 months of 2012 were the hottest ever recorded—4.5 degrees above the 20th Century average." *The Week,* July 20, 2012, p. 6, citing the National Climate Data Center. See also, *Time,* July 23, 2012, p. 10 (Drought was "the highest level in the U.S. Drought Monitor's 12-year history").
    - ○ **Number of High Temperature Records—June 2012.** 3,215 daily high temperature records were set in America in June 2012. *Time,* July 23, 2012.

PART III

Crime And Punishment,
Law And Litigation,
Ethics And Accountability

CHAPTER 7

Crime and Punishment

Exemplar Facts About Current
America From This Chapter
(Details and Source Citations Below)

Although U.S. homicide rates have decreased substantially in recent years (by 16.7% in U.S. cities), the homicide rates in U.S. suburbs have increased by almost exactly the same percentage.

The U.S. is 1 of only 20 nations, including China, Iran, Japan, Iraq, and Saudi Arabia, which imposes capital punishment, and the U.S. is the only G-8 country that does so.

Since 2002 appr. 300,000 fingerprints per day are collected at U.S. airports and borders.

There are currently as many as 9,000,000 identity thefts each year in the U.S.—about 1 for every 35 people.

The number of presidential pardons has declined substantially over the course of Modern America, from about 190 per year during the Eisenhower/Kennedy era to less than 50 per year during and since the Reagan presidency.

The $2.1 trillion cost of crime worldwide makes it one of the world top 20 economies.

Even excluding unique federal incarceration prisons such as Guantanamo Bay, the per-prisoner costs of incarceration at federal prisons vary considerably from appr. $30,000 at "average" federal prisons to as much as $60,000-$70,000 at super-maximum security prisons.

There are current no U.S. laws limiting the data collection by biometric technology or the sharing of biometric data between federal agencies.

There are appr. 6,000,000 (about 1 for every 50 people) in U.S. prisons or jails, which is a higher number than the Soviet Union imprisoned in the gulags during Stalin's regime.

Table of Contents
Of The Data Contained in This Chapter

911 Calls—Number of per Year.

Arrests for Violent Crimes—By Race—Perceptions vs. Reality.

Capital Punishment.
- Cost of Successful Death-Penalty Prosecutions Compared to Capital-Eligible Cases Where Death Penalty *Not* Sought.
- Cost Per Year of Housing a Death-Row Inmate.
- Countries, Including the U.S., That Impose Capital Punishment.
- Defendant IQ—Generally Accepted Minimum IQ Required by States as Condition for Imposing Death Penalty.
- Executions and Death Sentences Declining in U.S.
- Executions—Number of per 100,000 Population—States With Highest and Lowest Number.
- G-8 Countries—Number of Countries, Other Than the U.S., That Impose Capital Punishment.
- Public Opinion About Use of Death Penalty.
- States—Number and Identity of States Which Have Abolished Death Penalty Since 1957.
- States—Number of States That Have Abolished or Retained Capital Punishment in Last Five Years.
- States—Number of States Which Retain Right to Impose.

Cigarette Smuggling—Smurfing—Rising Extent of and Cost to Federal, State, and Local Governments.

Cost of Crime—Worldwide.

Crime Prevention—Biometrics.
- Biometric Data Collection Laws—Number of U.S. Laws Limiting Data Collection by Biometric Technology or Sharing Thereof Between Federal Agencies.
- FBI Biometrics Database—Number of Americans to Be Included In.
- Fingerprinting—Number of Fingerprints Collected Daily at U.S. Airports and Borders.
- Iris Scans—Number of Persons Who Can Be Simultaneously, Remotely Scanned.

Crime Rates.
- Bank Robberies—Declining Number Of—Average Amount per Heist.
- Crime Rate—Most Dangerous U.S. Cities.
- Increase of Crime Rates in U.S. Suburbs.
- Murder/Mortality Rate Decline vs. Gunshot Attack Rates Increase—U.S.
- Murder Rate of Washington, D.C. Compared With Mexico City, Mexico, and El Salvador.
- Murder Rates for Three Largest U.S. Cities.
- Murder Rate—U.S. Compared to Other Countries.
- Violent Crime Rate—Percentage Drop in Last Two Decades.

Drugs—Marijuana—Public Support of Legalization Of.

Fears of Being a Victim of Violent Crime or Terrorism.
- Fear of Being a Victim of Violent Crime.
- Fear of Being Victim of Terrorism.

Federal Criminal Statutes—Number Of.

Guilty Pleas—Entry Percentage and Resolution of All Federal Cases Prosecuted to Conclusion.

Homosexuality—Criminal Prosecution Of.
- Countries That Criminally Prosecute Homosexual Acts—Number Of.
- Countries That Impose Death Penalty In Criminal Prosecution of Homosexual Acts—Number Of.

Identity Thefts—Annual Number of in U.S.—Concentrations of Theft Rings in Certain States.

Immigration and Border Control Enforcement.
- Deportations.

       ○ Minors Sent Back to Mexico by U.S. Immigration Authorities in 2010; Percentage Sent Unaccompanied by an Adult.

       ○ Number of from the U.S. in 2.5 Years—2009–June 2011.

- States With On-Demand Identification Laws.

Insider Trading.
- Civil SEC Fines and Penalties.
- Number of Prosecutions Since August 2009.

Mass Shootings.
- Average Age of Mass Killer.
- Definition of, Distinction from "Random" Mass Shootings, and Average Number per Year.
- Eight Deadliest Incidents of Mass Shootings Since 1976.

Presidential Pardons—By President—In Modern America (1957–2012).

Prisons and Incarcerations.
- Aging Populations of Inmates.
- Costs of Incarcerations.
- Number of Inmates—U.S. Prisons and Jails.
- Number of New State Prisons Built Annually by Texas in Last Two Decades.
- Number of Prisons in U.S. Closed Within Last Two Years.
- Prison Sentencing—Extent of Disparities Based Upon Race.

Rape—Number Reported Each Day in U.S.

Sexual Abuse of Children—Roman Catholic Officials—Number of Convicted in U.S.

"Social Host" Laws—Number of States Which Have Adopted.

Tax Evasion—Relative Leniency for Offshore Tax Cheats.

Victims—Correlation to Race—New York City Shooting Victims and New York City Murder Victims—Percentage Racial Minorities.

Data

911 Calls—Number of per Year. Since the introduction of 911 in 1968, the use of 911 emergency lines has now grown to cover 96% of the U.S. and receives 240MM calls per year—appr. 658,000 per day. Kenneally, C., "How to Fix 911," *Time*, April 11, 2011, p. 36.

Arrests for Violent Crimes—By Race—Perceptions vs. Reality. In one survey, appr. 38% of those surveyed believe that 60% of those arrested for violent crimes were black. In fact, only appr. 38% of those so arrested were black. Toure, "Inside the Racist Mind," *Time*, May 7, 2012, p. 20. Nevertheless, the 38% percentage is still disproportionately high compared with the appr. 12% percentage of Americans who are black.

Capital Punishment.

- **Cost of Successful Death-Penalty Prosecutions Compared to Capital-Eligible Cases Where Death Penalty *Not* Sought.** According to one study, it costs $3MM for a successful death-penalty prosecution in state of Maryland vs. $1.1MM "to prosecute a capital-eligible case in which the state didn't seek the death penalty." Jones, A., "New Death Sentences Fall to Lowest Level in 35 Years," *The Wall Street Journal*, December 15, 2011, citing 2008 Washington, D.C. Urban Institute study.

- **Cost Per Year of Housing a Death-Row Inmate.** Appr. $100,000 per year. Since death-row inmates are housed alone, they require a higher level of security. Jones, A., Eder, S.," Death Penalty Costs Get Close Look," *The Wall Street Journal*, October 6–7, 2012, citing a study by Arthur Alarcon, a federal appellate judge for the Ninth Circuit in Los Angeles, California.

- **Countries, Including the U.S., That Impose Capital Punishment**. 20 nations as of 2011, including China, Iran, Saudi Arabia, and Iraq. *Time*, April 9, 2012, p. 13, citing data from Amnesty International. Contrariwise, while capital punishment, by law or practice, has been declining substantially throughout the world, capital punishment in Japan has risen "dramatically in the past two decades" in response to, according to one writer, the 1995 doomsday cult, which killed 13 people "by releasing poisonous sarin gas in the Tokyo subway." *The Week*, November 16, 2012, p. 18, citing H. Nagano, *Mainichi (Japan) Daily News*.

- **Defendant IQ—Generally Accepted Minimum IQ Required by States as Condition forImposing Death Penalty.** An IQ threshold of 70 after USSC banned executions of mentally deficient prisoners in 2002. The only exception is Texas, which executed a prisoner in 2012 with a claimed IQ of only 61. *The Week*, August 17, 2012, p. 5.

- **Executions and Death Sentences Declining in U.S.** 43 prisoners were executed in 2011 and 2012. This is substantially fewer than the year 2000 (85 executions and 224 death sentences). Although 33 states still have the death penalty, more than 75% of the 2012 death sentences were carried out (all by lethal injection) by just four states: Texas (15), Arizona (6), Oklahoma (6), and Mississippi (6). *msn.com*, December 18, 2012, citing the Death Penalty Information Center (the "DPIC"); Jones, A., Eder, S., "Death Penalty Costs Get Close Look," *The Wall Street Journal*, October 6–7, 2012, citing

DPIC, and *Time,* April 9, 2012, p. 13, citing data from Amnesty International. See also, Jones, A., "New Death Sentences Fall to Lowest Level in 35 Years," *The Wall Street Journal,* December 15, 2011, quoting Richard Dieter, Executive Director of the Death Penalty Information Center, that this is "the first time [the U.S. has] had fewer than 100 new death sentences in a year in the modern era of capital punishment."

- **Executions—Number of per 100,000 Population—States With Highest and Lowest Number.** The number of executions per 100,000 population varies radically amongst the states. The states with the highest and lowest ratable numbers over the last appr. 35 years (since 1976) are as follows:

Highest Ranking	State	No. Per 100,000 Population	Lowest Ranking	State	No. Per 100,000 Population
1.	Texas	493	1.	North Dakota	0
2.	Virginia	110		Kansas, Minnesota, Iowa,	
3.	Oklahoma	102		Wisconsin, Michigan, West Virginia	
4.	Florida	74		New York, Vermont, Maine, New	
5.	Alabama	55		Hampshire, Massachusetts, Rhode	
				Island, New Jersey, Alaska, Hawaii	

Jones, A., *The Wall Street Journal,* March 7, 2013 citing the Death Penalty Information Center.

- **G-8 Countries—Number of Countries, Other Than the U.S., That Impose Capital Punishment.** Zero. *Time,* April 9, 2012, p. 13, citing data from Amnesty International.

- **Public Opinion About Use of Death Penalty.** A majority of Americans still support the use of the death penalty. However, this support has consistently diminished over the last few decades. The percentages of Americans favoring the retention of the death penalty for the following respective year are as follows:

Year	Percentage of Americans in Favor of Death Penalty
2011	61%
2007	69%
1994	80%

Jones, A., "New Death Sentences Fall to Lowest Level in 35 Years," *The Wall Street Journal,* December 15, 2011, citing Gallup Poll.

- **States—Number and Identity of States Which Have Abolished Death Penalty Since 1957.** In addition to Michigan, Wisconsin, Maine, and Minnesota, which states abolished the death over a hundred years ago, the following additional states, by decade, have now abolished the death penalty:

Decade	No. of States	Name of States
1950s	2 states	Alaska, Hawaii
1960s	3 states	Vermont, Iowa, and West Virginia
1970s	1 state	North Dakota
1980s	2 states (+ DC)	Massachusetts, Rhode Island, and Washington, DC
1990s	0 states	
2000s	5 states	New York, New Jersey, New Mexico, Illinois, and Connecticut

TOTAL: 13 states

Jones, A., *The Wall Street Journal*, March 7, 2013 citing the Death Penalty Information Center.

- **States—Number of States That Have Abolished or Retained Capital Punishment in Last Five Years.** Five states (Connecticut, Illinois, New Jersey, New Mexico, and New York) have voted to abolish the death penalty. Jones, A., Eder, S., "Death Penalty Costs Get Close Look," *The Wall Street Journal*, October 6–7, 2012. In November 2012, California voters rejected a ballot measure (Prop. 34) by a vote percentage of 53% to 47% to repeal the death penalty. The California death penalty had been reinstated by a 1978 ballot measure, which had then passed by 71% to 29%. With the reinstatement 34 years ago, only "13 of the more than 800 convicts sentenced to death have been executed" since then. *The Week*, November 16, 2012, p. 5.

- **States—Number of States Which Retain Right to Impose.** 33 states, or 66% (two out of three). Jones, A., Eder, S., "Death Penalty Costs Get Close Look," *The Wall Street Journal*, October 6–7, 2012.

Cigarette Smuggling—Smurfing—Rising Extent of and Cost to Federal, State and Local Governments. Due largely to the significant variances in state-imposed taxes and because the criminal penalties are far lighter than those associated with smuggling drugs (e.g., a maximum of five years under federal law), the rise of cigarette smuggling and re-selling (referred to by the police as "smurfing") has been substantial and is now costing governments "nearly $10BB per year." For example, an estimated 40% of all cigarettes sold in New Jersey, which imposes a tax of $2.70 per pack, have been smuggled in from low-tax states. *The Economist*, November 24–30, 2012, p. 32.

Cost of Crime—Worldwide. $2.1 trillion, according to estimate of United Nations, making crime one of the world's top 20 economies." *Time,* May 7, 2012, p. 7.

Crime Prevention—Biometrics.

- **Biometric Data Collection Laws—Number of U.S. Laws Limiting Data Collection by Biometric Technology or Sharing Thereof Between Federal Agencies.** None. Currently, even "private companies could collect a person's biometric data without his consent and use it to track (the person's) movements." *The Week*, June 7, 2013, p. 11.

- **FBI Biometrics Database—Number of Americans To Be Included In.** 100MM, or appr. 31.3% of the U.S. population. The consolidation database is scheduled for completion in 2014. *The Week*, June 7, 2013, p. 11.

- **Fingerprinting—Number of Fingerprints Collected Daily at U.S. Airports and Borders.** Appr. 300,000 per day. The U.S. government started collecting fingerprints of all foreign visitors in 2002. *The Week*, June 7, 2013, p. 11.

- **Iris Scans—Number of Persons Who Can Be Simultaneously, Remotely Scanned.** "Widely used" at U.S. military bases and federal agencies, an advanced form of this technology can now remotely scan up to 50 persons simultaneously. *The Week*, June 7, 2013, p. 11.

Crime Rates.

- **Bank Robberies— Declining Number Of—Average Amount Per Heist.** The number of bank robberies has declined by almost 50% in the last decade to a current annual rate of about 5.1 bank robberies per 100 banks. This decline is substantially greater than the decline in the overall crime rate during this period. The number of U.S. bank robberies peaked in 1991 with 9,400 robberies as compared with only about 3,900 in 2011 (with 88 injured and 13 dead). These 3,900 bank robberies in 2011 compare with over 314,000 incidents of Internet crime in the same year. Similarly, the average amount stolen per heist has dropped in 2012 to a mere $7,600 (from $12,400 about 13 years ago) for an aggregate $29.5 MM stolen (as compared with the estimate of $1.8 BB stolen via check and debit-card fraud in 2010). Nicas, J., *The Wall Street Journal*, February. 5, 2013, citing data from the FBI and the American Bankers Association.

- **Crime Rate—Most Dangerous U.S. Cities.** The crime rates in U.S. cities can be compared by measuring the cities' respective "crime rate index." The index is a "weighted average of six crime categories (murder, rape, robbery, aggravated assault, burglary, and motor vehicle theft). The national rate is 1 and any number higher than 1 indicates a higher than average incidence of crime." Based upon the review of FBI data by the Congressional Quarterly, the following is a list, in order, of the most dangerous U.S. cities.

Ranking	City	Population	Crime Rate Index	Murder Rate (Per 100,000)
1.	Detroit, MI	713,200	4.71	48.2
2.	St. Louis, MO	320,500	3.63	35.3
3.	Oakland, CA	395,300	3.49	26.3
4.	Cleveland, OH	397,100	3.09	18.6
5.	New Orleans, LA	347,000	2.84	57.6
6.	Newark, NJ	278,100	2.82	33.8
7.	Atlanta, GA	425,500	2.66	20.7
8.	Baltimore	626,800	2.61	31.1
9.	Memphis, TN	652,700	2.28	17.9
10.	Kansas City, MO	461,500	2.13	23.4

Christie, L., CNN Money, *money.cnn.com* (January 23, 2013).

- **Increase of Crime Rate in U.S. Suburbs.** Although U.S. homicide rates have decreased substantially (e.g., 16.7% in cities), the homicide rates in suburbs have increased by almost exactly the same percentage and are up, for example, 23% in Atlanta's suburbs despite a 49% drop in the city of Atlanta. Suburban homicides now make up appr. 21% of all U.S. homicides. McWhirter, C., Fields, G., "Crime Migrates to Suburbs," *The Wall Street Journal,* December 31, 2012.

- **Murder/Mortality Rate Decline vs. Gunshot Attack Rates Increase—U.S.** While the murder rate in the U.S. has been "falling for two decades," the number of gunshot victims has increased substantially. Thus, the murder/mortality rate as of 2010 was appr. 14,800, which reflected a substantial decline from prior years (e.g., in 2007 the number was 16,900). However, this decline may merely reflect improvements in the availability of and treatment at emergency rooms since the number of gunshot victims and serious knife stabbings has risen substantially during the same period. Fields, G., McWhirter, C., *The Wall Street Journal,* December 8–9, 2012.

- **Murder Rate of Washington, D.C. Compared With Mexico City, Mexico, and El Salvador.** The Washington, D.C. murder rate is more than double that of Mexico City, Mexico (*The Week,* April 20, 2012, p. 16), but the murder rate in El Salvador (due in large part to the country's *maras,* or street gangs) has "a rate per head 15 times higher than in the United States." *The Economist,* May 12–18, 2012, p. 43.

- **Murder Rates for Three Largest U.S. Cities.** The murder rates of the three largest U.S. cities are as follows:

Chicago, IL	18.6 per 100,000
Los Angeles, CA	7.8 per 100,000
New York City, NY	5.0 per 100,000

Von Drehle, D., "His Kind of Town," *Time*, June 10, 2013, p. 36.

- **Murder Rate—U.S. Compared to Other Countries.** Four times higher than Britain and six times higher than Germany. *The Economist,* December 22, 2012–January 4, 2013, p. 12.

- **Violent Crime Rate—Percentage Drop in Last Two Decades.** 41%. *The Week,* August 3, 2012, p. 4, quoting B. Doherty in *Reason.com.* See also, *The Economist,* August 25–31, 2012, p. 21 (violent crime has dropped by 38% from its 1992 peak). The reasons for such dramatic fall in the crimes rates have been attributed, among other factors, (i) to improved policing techniques and technologies, (ii) to the legalization of abortion in the 1970s, (iii) to the demographics of the population, and, more specifically, the aging of the population, (iv) to increases in immigration (immigrant communities in nearly all large U.S. cities have experienced demonstrably lower crime rates), (v) to the high incarceration rates in certain states, and (vi) to the introduction and wide availability of video games and social-media technology.

Drugs—Marijuana—Public Support of Legalization Of. In 2013, and for the first time, a majority of Americans (52%) purported to support the legalization of marijuana. This 52% compares with 41% just three years earlier in 2010. *The Week,* April 19, 2013, p. 19, citing Pew Research Center.

Fears of Being a Victim of Violent Crime or Terrorism.

- **Fear of Being a Victim of Violent Crime** According to a recent poll, the following percentages of respondents identified these places as those which they most worried about being a victim of a violent crime:

Place	Percentage of Respondents
Bad Neighborhoods	44%
Theaters, Stadiums, and Theme Parks	14%
Airplanes, Subways, Buses	8%
At Home	5%
At School	4%

The 60 Minutes/Vanity Fair Poll, *Vanity Fair*, April, 2013, p. 68.

- **Fear of Being Victim of Terrorism**. In appr. the last 18 years (starting with the 1995 Oklahoma City Bombings and ending with the 2013 Boston Marathon bombings), the percentage of Americans who fear that they (or a family member) would be a victim of terrorism has fluctuated between appr. 25% (Year 2000) to 59% (October 2001) with a relatively stable average of about 35% to 40% since 2002. See, Calabresi, M., Crowley, M.,

"Homeland and Insecurity," *Time*, May 13, 2013. Rather consistently, appr. 60% of Americans believe that "terrorists will always find ways to launch major attacks no matter what the U.S. does." *Time*, May 13, 2013, p. 22, and citing a Time/CNN/ORC poll.

Federal Criminal Statutes—Number Of. Arguably substantiating the need for a re-organization and simplification of the federal criminal statutes, there are currently over 4,500 federal criminal statutes and "tens of thousands of regulations that carry criminals penalties, including prison." Fields, G., King, N., *The Wall Street Journal*, May 6, 2013.

Guilty Pleas—Entry Percentage and Resolution of All Federal Cases Prosecuted to Conclusion. 97% (up from 84% in past 22 years since 1990) with some consensus that this high and increasing entry of guilty pleas is the result of the "growth in the number of federal criminal laws(,) the stiffening of sentences by U.S. Congress and the U.S. Sentencing Commission," and the fact that the Federal guidelines have "formalized a system to reward defendants who plead guilty if they accept responsibility or cooperate with prosecutors, among other things." Fields, G., Emshwiller, J., "Federal Guilty Pleas Soar as Bargains Trump Trials," *The Wall Street Journal*, September 24, 2012.

Homosexuality—Criminal Prosecution Of.
- **Countries That Criminally Prosecute Homosexual Acts—Number Of.** 76 countries. *Time,* August 10, 2010. See also, *The Economist,* November 17–23, 2012 (referencing 78 countries, "mostly in the Muslim world, Africa and other developing states" despite the powerful trend toward giving homosexuals full marriage or civil union rights).
- **Countries That Impose Death Penalty in Criminal Prosecution of Homosexual Acts—Number Of.** Seven countries. *Time,* August 10, 2010.

Identity Thefts—Annual Number of in U.S.—Concentrations of Theft Rings in Certain States. "As many as 9MM " identify thefts, and there are appr. 10,000 identity theft rings currently operating in the U.S. The highest concentration is mostly in Delaware and the southern states of Alabama, North and South Carolina, Georgia, Mississippi, and Texas. *The Week*, December 7, 2012, p. 36, citing *Time.com*.

Immigration and Border Control Enforcement.
- **Deportations.**
  - **Minors Sent Back to Mexico by U.S. Immigration Authorities in 2010; Percentage Sent Unaccompanied by an Adult.** In 2010, appr. 20,400 minors were returned to Mexico by the U.S. immigration

authorities, and 57% of these minors were sent back unaccompanied by an adult., Harper's Index, *Harper's Magazine*, October 2011, p. 15.
  ○ **Number of Deportations from the U.S. in 2.5 Years—2009–June, 2011.** Appr. 1MM. *Time*, June 27, 2011, p. 16.
- **States With On-Demand Identification Laws.** Arizona (until portions of state law were struck down by federal order), Georgia, Alabama, and South Carolina. *The Week*, May 4, 2012, p. 5. Relatedly, State Senate President Russell Pearce, "the author of Arizona's controversial immigration law, is the only state legislator to be recalled in Arizona history." *The Week*, November 18, 2011, p. 5.

Insider Trading.
- **Civil SEC Fines and Penalties.** The number and size of civil SEC fines and penalties have been increasing in recent years. Examples of some of the largest civil penalties are as follows:

American International Group, Inc.	2006	$800MM
WorldCom, Inc.	2003	$750MM
SAC Capital Advisors LP	2013	$616MM
Goldman Sachs Group, Inc.	2010	$550MM

Rothfeld, M., Eaglesham, J., Bray, C., *The Wall Street Journal*, March 16-17, 2013. See also, Rivkin, D., Carnbey, J., *The Wall Street Journal*, March 15, 2013 (discussing the *Gabelli v. SEC* case and arguing that while civil litigation claims may seek to compensate victims of corporate fraud and other unlawful behavior, the SEC fines are merely punitive in nature and may "do more harm than good.").
- **Number of Criminal Prosecutions Since August 2009**. Eighty-one cases have been brought in the last four years by federal prosecutors in Manhattan and by FBI agents. Of these 81 cases, guilty pleas or convictions have been obtained in 73 cases (i.e., 90.1%). The longest sentences in this "four-year crackdown" are as follows:

Matthew Kluger	12.0 years
Raj Rajaratnam	11.0 years
Zvi Goffer	10.0 years
Garrett Bauer	9.0 years
Anthony Chiasson	6.5 years
Joseph Contorinis	6.0 years

Bray, C., "Long Jail Term for Manager (Anthony Chiasson)," *The Wall Street Journal*, May 14, 2013, citing data from U. S. Department of Justice and staff reports.

Mass Shootings.

- **Average Age of Mass Killer.** 27 years old. Cloud, J., "Preventing Mass Murder—Can We Identify Dangerous Men Before They Kill?" *Time,* August 6, 2012, p. 33, citing a 2004 paper by a team of psychologists headed by Professor Reid Maloy of the University of San Diego, as published in the *Journal of Behavioral Sciences & the Law.*

- **Definition Of, Distinction from Random Mass Shootings, and Average Number per Year.** One definition of "mass shooting" is a shooting in which there are four or more fatalities, and while the number of such mass shootings has not changed materially over the last 30 years (appr. 20 mass shootings per year since the late 1970s), the number of random mass shootings has gone up substantially from 18 in the 1980s, 54 in the 1990s, and 87 in the 2000s. See two varying and thoughtful perspectives: Klein, J., "How the Gun Won," *Time,* August 6, 2012, p. 26, citing James Alan Fox, professor of criminology, law, and public policy at Northwestern University; and Kopel, D., "Guns, Mental Illness, and Newtown," *The Wall Street Journal,* December 18, 2012.

- **Eight Deadliest Incidents of Mass Shootings Since 1976.** The eight deadliest incidents of mass shootings since 1976 are as follows:

Ranking	Year	Place	Number Killed
1.	2007	Virginia Tech, Blacksburg, Virginia (Student kills students in campus dorm and classroom)	32 dead
2. (Added)	2012	Sandy Hook Elementary School, Newton, CT (Students, Principal, others killed by rampaging youth)	28 dead
3.	1991	Killeen, Texas (Shooting at Luby's Cafeteria, a restaurant)	23 dead
4.	1984	San Ysidro, California (Shooting at McDonald's Restaurant)	21 dead
5.	1986	Edmond, Oklahoma (Mail carrier shoots co-workers)	14 dead
6.	1999	Columbine, Colorado (Colorado high school)	13 dead
6.	2009	Fort Hood, Texas (Military processing center)	13 dead
6.	2009	Binghamton, New York (Shootings in immigration community center).	13 dead

Klein, J., "How the Gun Won," *Time,* August 6, 2012, p. 26, citing data from James Alan Fox, a professor of criminology, law, and public policy at Northwestern University.

Presidential Pardons—By President—In Modern America (1957–2012). The number of presidential pardons has declined dramatically during Modern America beginning with President Reagan.

President	No. Of Pardons	Ave. No. Per Year	President	No. Of Pardons	Ave. No. Per Year
Eisenhower[1]	1,157	145	Reagan	406	51
Kennedy	575	192	Bush, GHW.	77	19
Johnson	1,187	198	Clinton	456	57
Nixon	926	185	Bush, GW	176	22
Ford	409	136	Obama[2]	23	8
Carter	566	142			

Note 1: 1953–1961;   Note 2: 2008–2011. *Infoplease.com.*

Prisons and Incarcerations.

- **Aging Populations of Inmates.** Between 2007 and 2010, there was a 63% increase in the number of prisoners (men and women) who are age 64 and over. *The Week,* February 10, 2012, p. 16, citing *The New York Times.*

- **Costs of Incarcerations.** The per-prisoner costs of incarceration vary radically depending upon the size of the prisoner populations and the nature of the incarceration facility. The following list compares some of such incarceration costs:

Type of Institution/Facility	Average Annual Per-Prisoner Cost
All Federal Prisons	$30,000
Super-Maximum-Security Prisons	$60,000–$70,000
Guantanamo Bay	$900,000

  The Week, May 17, 2013, p. 18 citing *Reuters.com*

- **Number of Inmates—U.S. Prisons and Jails.** Appr. 6MM or about 1.9% of our population (1 in 50 people)—"a higher number than the Soviet Union imprisoned in the gulag archipelago during Stalin's regime." *The Week,* April 6, 2012, p. 18, citing *Time.*

- **Number of New State Prisons Built Annually by Texas in Last Two Decades.** Three per year. During the years 1990 to 2011. Strumpf, D., "With Fewer to Lock Up, Prisons Shut Doors," *The Wall Street Journal,* February 11, 2013, citing Texas Department of Criminal Justice.

- **Number of Prisons in U.S. Closed Within Last Two Years.** Partly as a result of the fact that the inmate population fell in 2010 (for the first time in 40 years) and again in 2011, "35 adult correctional facilities in 15 states" have been closed in the last two years. Strumpf, D., "With Fewer to Lock Up, Prisons Shut Doors," *The Wall Street Journal,* February 11, 2013, citing data from the National Conference of State Legislatures.

- **Prison Sentencing—Extent of Disparities Based Upon Race.** According to an analysis by the U.S. Sentencing Commission "(p)rison sentences of black men were nearly 20% longer than those of white men for similar crimes in recent years...." The analysis concluded that the "racial gap has widened since the (USSC) restored judicial discretion in sentencing" in the consolidated cases of *United States v. Booker* and *United States v. Fanfan*. Palazzolo, J., *The Wall Street Journal*, February 15, 2013. See also, Albonetti, C., "Judicial Discretion in Federal Sentencing," *Criminology & Public Policy*, Vol. 10, Issue 4 (2011).

Rape—Number Reported Each Day in U.S. 232 per day, or about 84,700 per year. While "the federal code refers to 'aggravated sexual abuse,' rape definitions vary by state, for example, on whether force must have been used." International and inter-societal comparisons are very difficult to make. For example, because of the levels of violence against women (e.g., in Botswana) or possibly the relatively broad definition of rape (e.g., in Sweden) some countries have massively greater reports of rape per 100,000. The level of reported rapes in the U.S. is slightly less than that of the U.K. and slightly more than that of France. *The Economist*, September 1–7, 2012, p. 59.

Sexual Abuse of Children—Roman Catholic Officials—Number of Convicted in U.S. Only one as of August 2012. Monsignor William Lynn, age 62, sentenced for 3–6 years.

"Social Host" Laws—Number of States Which Have Adopted. "Social host" laws impose criminal or civil penalties upon those persons, "hosts," who permit underage drinking on their property. As of 2012, 28 states have adopted some variant of these laws—up from just 18 in 2005. In addition, some states now impose liability in the event anyone is harmed as a result of such drinking, and "many" cities and counties are considering such ordinances. Levitz, J., "Party Laws Put Hosts on Hook," *The Wall Street Journal*, September 12, 2012.

Tax Evasion—Relative Leniency for Offshore Tax Cheats. Despite the increase in the number of offshore tax evasion cases which have been initiated since 2009, the average incarceration sentences for these 71 taxpayers has been less than 15 months—approximately one-half of the average 30-month sentences which have been imposed in other tax evasion cases. While the reason for the relative leniency is hard to determine, some suggest that it is merely because of the large monetary penalty amounts which such defendants have had to pay. Saunders, L., *The Wall Street Journal*, May 6, 2013.

Victims—Correlation to Race—New York City Shooting Victims and New York City Murder Victims—Percentage Racial Minorities. "In [NYC in 2011], 96% of all shooting victims and 90% of all murder victims were racial minorities. *The Week*, April 6, 2012, p. 16, citing *The New York Times.*

CHAPTER 8

———•••———

Law and Litigation, Ethics and Accountability

Exemplar Facts About Current America From This Chapter
(Details and Source Citations Below)

There have been more than 400 terrorism or terrorism-related trials held in U.S. federal courts as of May 2012.

62% of U.S. college undergraduates admit to cheating in the course of their academic studies.

More than 80% of the 500 allegations of child sexual abuse involving Boy Scout leaders were *not* reported to police over several decades.

Except for election consequences, no elected official or government regulator has been the subject of a civil fine, penalty, sanction, or criminal prosecution resulting from the 2007–2008 financial collapse.

U.S. major banks legal costs as a percentage of pre-provision profits during the first six months of 2012 varied considerably from, for example, Wells Fargo's low 1.0% to JPMorgan Chase's 14.5%. The average legal costs of sixteen major banks was 4.0%.

Following a relatively steady trend over the last several years, the number of annual applications to law school dropped from appr. 100,000 annually in 2004 to appr. 54,000 in 2012.

Although certain fines and sanctions have been imposed, no major banking executive has yet been imprisoned as a result of the financial crisis.

Table of Contents
Of The Data Contained in This Chapter

- ○ Guilty Pleas—BP to Plead Guilty to Numerous Felony Counts and to Remit Appr. $4.5BB to Federal Government and $525MM to SEC.
- Business Suspensions from Federal Government Contracts—Number Of.
- Great Recession.
  - ○ Business People—Civil Fines, Penalties and Sanctions Upon— Imposition and Number Of.
  - ○ Credit-Rating Firm Sued—S&P as "Enablers" of Financial Meltdown.
  - ○ Elected Officials or Government Regulators—Civil Fines, Penalties, Sanctions, and Consequences or Criminal Prosecutions Of.
  - ○ Failed Institutions—Number of FDIC-Filed Lawsuits and Prosecutions Against Bank Officers and Directors Since 2010 and as Compared With Late 1980s Savings and Loan Crisis.
  - ○ Major Banking Executives Imprisoned as Result of Financial Crisis—Number Of.
  - ○ SEC—Settlements With and Collected Fines from Financial Institutions and Class-Action Lawsuits—2011.
- Health-Care-Fraud—Largest Penalty in American History.

Law and Litigation.

- Civil Charges—5-Year and 10-Year Federal Statute of Limitations Applicable to Most Alleged Violations of Laws Enforceable by SEC and Other Federal Agencies.
- Law School—Application For Admission—Extent of Drop In—Average Annual Tuition.
- Law School Graduates—Current Annual Number Of.
- Litigation—NFL—Football Concussion Injuries.
- Overlapping and Potentially Duplicitous Litigation—Number of Legal Orders Received Each Week by Wells Fargo Bank.
- Terrorism and Terrorism-Related Trials—Federal Courts—Number of Tried In.
- U.S. Major Banks Legal Costs as Percentage of Pre-Provision Profits.

Data

Constitutional Law—The Four Dominant and Competing Theories of Constitutional Theory. Per Wilkinson's book, Cosmic Constitutional Theory, there are the following four dominant theories of constitutional interpretation:

No. 1. Living Constitutionalism, in which an "aggressive expansion" of constitutional protection is pursued in order to achieve a wide-ranging series of liberal political reforms, "ranging from racial integration to expanded rights for criminal defendants."

No. 2. Originalism Interpretation of the Constitution based upon the Framers' intents.

No. 3. Political Process Theory whereby the Constitution is to be interpretted to promote "well-functioning and equitable democratic processes [and] preventing majorities from oppressing minorities."

No. 4. Pragmatism which suggests the discarding (or at least containment and de-emphasis of) ideological theories and interpreting the Constitution in such way as will maximize the overall public good."

White, A., Review of J. Harvie Wilkinson III's book *Cosmic Constitutional Theory," The Wall Street Journal,* April 16, 2012.

Ethics and Accountability.

- **Attorney Disbarments and Misbehavior—Housing Crisis—Mortgage-Fraud Cases.** More than 25% of "a national database of 25,000 homeowner complaints regarding suspected, mortgage-related fraud" involved allegations of potential wrongdoing by attorneys. Since early 2009 the State Bar of California has itself received more than 11,000 such complaints, which have led to the disbarments or the imposition of other sanctions of more than 100 California attorneys. Emshwiller, J., "Lawyers Land in Hot Water—Criminal and Civil Mortgage-Fraud Cases Have Exploded Since Housing Crisis," *The Wall Street Journal,* September 19, 2012, citing data assembled by the Washington-based Lawyers' Committee for Civil Rights Under Law and Mr. Joseph Dunn, executive director of the State Bar of California.

- **"Behaving Badly"—Ranking of Things Which Keep Americans From "Behaving Badly."** The following differing principles, beliefs, or fears are deemed to be forces that can keep Americans "from behaving badly."

Principle, Belief, or Fear	Percentage of Americans Who Identified This Category as Keeping Them "From Behaving Badly"
Morals and principles	70%
Religion	8%
Fear of Getting Caught	7%
Undeterred—Do Bad Things Anyway	*2%*

"The 60 Minutes/Vanity Fair Poll," *Vanity Fair,* September 2012, p. 114.

- **Cheating—Student Cheating—Percentage of Undergraduates Admitting.** 62%. Webley, K., "Cheating Harvard," *Time,* September 17, 2012, p. 22, citing Donald McCabe, Rutgers University.
- **Child Sex Abuse.**
  - **Boy Scouts Failure to Report Allegations of Child Sex Abuse—Percentage of Non-Reported Cases.** More than 80% of the 500 allegations of child sexual abuse were not reported to police over several decades, according to a review of the Boy Scouts "perversion" files. "Most [accused] volunteers or employees … were allowed to quietly leave for false reasons, to protect the organization's reputation." *The Week,* September 28, 2012, p. 14, citing the *Los Angeles Times.* See also, *The Week,* November 2, 2012, p. 5, 2012. After "twenty years' of secret records detailing allegations of sexual abuse" involving more than 1,200 Scout leaders were revealed, it became apparent "one of the country's oldest young organizations systematically failed to report abuse and often covered up allegations." (Author's Personal Note: As a former Eagle Scout and as an attendee many years ago of the World Boy Scout Jamboree in Marathon, Greece, this entry about another institution's betrayal is particularly painful.)
  - **Penn State—Penalties Imposed by NCAA Upon Penn State After Conviction of Former Ass't Coach Jerry Sandusky on 45 Charges of Child Sex Abuse.** $60MM fine, a four-year ban for post-season play, and a reduction in the number of football scholarships that are allowed to be granted. *The Week,* August 3, 2012, p. 5. Former Penn State football coach Jerry Sandusky was sentenced to between 30 and 60 years in prison. See also, Johnson, KC, Taylor, Stuart Jr., "Penn State, Duke and Integrity," *The Wall Street Journal,* September 17, 2012 (Contrasting the different reactions of "two prominent American universities (Penn State and Duke)" in the context of their respective scandals (Penn State's Sandusky/child molestation charges and the disproven charges of a savage gang rape hurled at three Duke lacrosse players, with dozens more accused of complicity.). While the ultimate results of these two tragedies are radically different, they "grew out of a lack of courage to resist the demands of powerful special interests."). *The Wall Street Journal,* July 18, 2012.
- **Reputation—Preservation of One's Reputation Relative to Divorce or Bankruptcy.** Bankruptcy was deemed worse for one's reputation in the opinion of 63%–72% of those polled (with variations depending upon whether one is married, divorced, or has never been married). Divorce was

deemed worse for one's reputation by only 22%–30% of people. "The 60 Minutes/Vanity Fair Poll," *Vanity Fair,*" September 2012, p.114.

- **Sports and Sportsmanship.**
  - ○ **Basketball—Mike Rice—NCAA Coach Terminated for Abusing Players—Rutgers University.** The Coach was at first fined and then terminated after the wide release of practice videos in which Coach Rice was seen shoving and kicking players in a manner reminiscent, in the opinion of some, of former Indiana basketball coach Bobby Knight and the University of Alabama's football coach Bear Bryant. Shortly after the public release of the Rutgers videos, the Rutgers' athletic director was also terminated since it was determined that he had known about Coach Rice's behavior but had not sought harsher discipline. *The Week,* April 19, 2013, p. 19.
  - ○ **Cycling—Lance Armstrong—Stripped of Titles and Lifetime Bans.** The U.S. Anti-Doping Agency issued a "blistering [202-page] report," which concluded that Armstrong had been at the center of a "massive team doping scheme, more extensive than any previously revealed in professional sports history." As a consequence of its finding, the agency stripped Armstrong of all of his seven Tour de France titles and banned him for life from all professional cycling, despite the fact that he has continued to deny all doping charges and has never failed any of the over 500 drug tests that he has taken in his 25-year cycling career. Albergotti, R., O'Connell, V., "Drug Case Against Armstrong Detailed," *The Wall Street Journal,* October 11, 2012; *Time,* September 10, 2012, p. 7. Shortly thereafter, Armstrong was also banned from running in the Chicago Marathon for his charity Livestrong because the event is sanctioned by USA Track and Field, which itself must comply with and enforce bans imposed by the U.S. Anti-Doping Agency.
  - ○ **Football—NFL Professional Football Hitting Bounties— Amount New Orleans Saints Offered Players in Hitting Bounties.** $1,000 for any "hit that took a player off the field" and $10,000 'for delivering Brett Favre's head on a platter.'" *The Week,* March 23, 2012, citing Steve Chapman, *Chicago Tribune.*

Fines, Suspensions, and Accountability.
- **BP 2010 Oil Spill.**
  - ○ **Clean-up Costs and Monetary Pledges To Date; Civil and Criminal Penalties.** BP paid about $14BB in upfront cleanup and restoration costs and has pledged another $1BB for further restoration projects and

an additional $500MM for research. The civil and criminal sanctions, "which could reach the tens of billions of dollars," are still proceeding and the costs are to a degree awaiting further discovery analysis and the completion of the NOAA's Natural Resource Damage Assessment. Fowler, T., "Experts Weigh Spill's Lasting Effects," The *Wall Street Journal*, April 13, 2012.

○ **First Criminal Indictment—Number of Years After Spill.** Nearly two years after the Spring 2010 oil spill the U.S. Justice Department issued its first criminal indictment against Kurt Mix, a former BP engineer, for allegedly destroying evidence—namely "some 300 emails and text messages" relating to what BP knew about the true flow rate of the MaCondo well. *The Week*, May 4, 2012, p. 7.

○ **Guilty Pleas—BP to Plead Guilty to Numerous Felony Counts and to Remit Appr. $4.5BB to Federal Government and $525MM to SEC.** In resolution of all BP's federal criminal charges relating to the death of 11 workers, to its discharge of 206BB gallons of crude oil, and to its obstruction of Congress, BP has agreed (subject to final court approval) to plead guilty to a series of federal criminal charges and to pay a fine of $4.5BB over five years (and to the SEC over three years). This is the largest fine ever levied by the U.S. Justice Department. Expressing deep regret for the incident, Carl-Henric Svanberg, BP's chairman, said that the resolution was deemed to be in the "best interest of BP and its shareholders, [in that it] removes two significant legal risks, and allows us to vigorously defend (BP) against the remaining civil claims." Johnston, I., Eng, J., NBC News, *nbcnews. com*, November 15, 2012. *The Week*, November 30, 2012, p. 36.

• **Business Suspensions from Federal Government Contracts—Number Of.** More than 100 suspensions were imposed by federal governmental agencies during the 12 months ending in September 2012, such as the suspension of BP PLC from obtaining new contracts due to the finding that it lacked "business integrity" in the wake of its then-recent settlement of criminal and some civil charges. Fowler, T., "BP Blocked from Deals," *The Wall Street Journal*, November 28, 2012.

• **Great Recession.**

○ **Business People—Civil Fines, Penalties, and Sanctions Upon—Imposition and Number Of.** Although Countrywide Financial Corp. was one of the principal subprime lenders responsible for the 2008 financial crisis, its former CEO, Angelo Mozilo—himself "a tabloid-ready poster boy for general subprime quasi-criminality ... never spent a day in jail." He had imposed a $67.5MM fine, however, at the time this amount reportedly equaled only about 10% of his net worth. Editor's Letter (G. Carter), *Vanity Fair*, September 2012, p. 108.

○ **Credit-Rating Firm Sued—S&P as "Enablers" of Financial Meltdown.** The Justice Department (and soon to be joined by some State Attorneys General) is preparing to sue Standard & Poor's, one of the three largest bond-rating firms, based upon its allegations that S&P managers "pushed to weaken standards for rating mortgage-linked deals or ignored the standards entirely." This claim follows a three-year investigation and a conclusion by Congress's Financial Crisis Inquiry Commission that the "top credit-rating firms were 'key enablers' of the financial meltdown." Although S&P may assert a First Amendment defense, the Justice Department may file its action under the post-S&L crisis 1989 legislation which imposes a low burden of proof. Eaglesham, J., Neumann, J., Perez, E., *The Wall Street Journal*, February 5, 2013.

○ **Elected Officials or Government Regulators—Civil Fines, Penalties, Sanctions, and Consequences or Criminal Prosecutions Of.** None, unless one wishes to attempt to trace the results of subsequent elections or the post-Recession decisions of certain elected officials to retire or to not seek election.

○ **Failed Institutions—Number of FDIC-Filed Lawsuits and Prosecutions Against Bank Officers and Directors Since 2010 and as Compared With Late 1980s Savings and Loan Crisis.** In recent years and as a result of the Great Recession, "over 40 lawsuits against officers and directors of failed institutions (have been initiated)… (and) more actions are expected. However, there have been very few criminal prosecutions against high-profile bankers." This contrasts sharply with (a) the more aggressive prosecutions in other countries such as Iceland, Germany, and even Spain, and (b) even with the actions of U.S. prosecutors in the late 1980s during which over 800 bankers who were jailed for charges stemming from the savings and loan crisis. While German prosecutors are prosecuting some officers for offences such as Untreue (or breach of trust or derogation of duty which causes real damage), the laws are even stricter in Brazil. In Brazil, bank executives and directors are personally liable for repaying the debts of failed banks. *The Economist,* May 4-10, 2013, p. 71.

○ **Major Banking Executives Imprisoned As Result of Financial Crisis—Number Of.** Zero. In addition "Wall Street bankers seem not to have paid any social cost either." *The Week,* August 17, 2012, p.

35, citing J. Eisinger in *ProPublica.org*. See also, (i) *The Week*, June 8, 2012, p. 38 citing T. Keenan, *New York Post* and (ii) Orwall, B., Bray, C., "Ex-Banker Tried to Settle Charges," *The Wall Street Journal*, September 28, 2012 (Former Credit-Suisse Group AG investment-banking executive Kareem Serageldin, the highest-ranking Wall Street executive criminally charged to date, was arrested by police in the United Kingdom based upon a warrant from U.S. authorities.). To the criticism of some, U.S. Attorney General Eric Holder stated in March 2013 that big banks had not been indicted for their role in the financial crisis (unlike the huge accounting firm Arthur Andersen which was indicted and thereafter went out of business in the context of the October 2001 Enron scandal) "because such action could 'have a negative impact' on the economy." *The Week*, March 22, 2013, p. 34, citing Sorkin, A., *The New York Times.* See also, *The Economist,* May 4-10, p. 71, reporting upon U.K. consideration of the adoption of a "rebuttable presumption" that directors of a failed bank "should be automatically barred from running another unless they could prove they weren't at fault."

○ **SEC—Settlements With and Collected Fines from Financial Institutions and Class-Action Lawsuits—2011.** In Fiscal Year ("FY") 2011 and early 2012 the SEC, reached 13 settlement agreements of $5MM or more and in FY 2011 it collected $414MM in fines from financial institutions. In addition, there were class action settlements in the aggregate amount of $1.5BB in Calendar Year 2011. *The Economist*, October 13–19, 2012, p. 18, citing NERA, an economic consulting firm.

• **Health-Care-Fraud—Largest Penalty in American History.** $3BB imposed on British drugmaker GlaxoSmithKline and relating to Wellbutrin, Paxil, and Avandia. This sum represents appr. 11% of the total sales receipts from the sales of these drugs in prior years. *The Week*, July 20, 2012, p.36, citing *CNNMoney.com*.

Law and Litigation.

• **Civil Charges—5-Year and 10-Year Federal Statute of Limitations Applicable to Most Alleged Violations of Laws Enforceable by SEC And Other Federal Agencies.** The "time is running out for U.S. securities regulators to file civil charges" resulting from alleged financial wrongdoing in the context of the 2007–2008 financial collapse. Without obtaining a "tolling agreement," whereby the target defendant(s) agree to waive or to "toll" the applicable statute of limitations, the SEC and other agencies have only a limited number of months to file civil actions. Such target defendants often agree to such tolling agreements "in hopes of persuading the [SEC] not to proceed with formal enforcement action." In a few instances, agencies can rely upon a much longer 10-year statute of limitations, which exists under, for example, the federal Financial Institutions Reform, Recovery, and Enforcement Act (more commonly referred to as "FIRREA") which was passed after the savings and loan crisis in the late 1980s. Eaglesham, J., Neumann, J., Albergotti, R., "Clock Is Ticking on Crisis Charges," *The Wall Street Journal*, July 12, 2012.

• **Law School—Application For Admission—Extent of Drop In.—Average Annual Tuition.** The number of annual applications to law school has dropped precipitously from appr. 100,000 annually in 2004 to appr. 54,000 in 2012. At the same time the average annual tuition has increased to appr. $40,000. Epstein, R., Review of *The Lawyer Bubble* by S. Harper, *The Wall Street Journal*, May 6, 2013.

• **Law School Graduates—Current Annual Number Of.** 44,495 in 2012, or roughly one new lawyer for every 7,000 people in the country. Palazzolo, J. and Phipps, C., "Law Schools Apply the Brakes," *The Wall Street Journal*, June 11, 2012, citing the American Bar Association.

• **Litigation—NFL—Football Concussion Injuries.** The number of former players suing the NFL "in dozens of lawsuits for allegedly concealing the impact of repeated concussions on their brain." This number is now appr. 1,500. *The Week*, May 18, 2012, p. 4. See also, (i) *The Wall Street Journal*, June 8, 2012 (Consolidation of 86 lawsuits by 2,300 retired players); and (ii) Gregory, S., "Can Roger Goodell Save Football," *Time*, December 17, 2012, p. 36 (Describing certain football rule changes, such as eliminating kickoffs, which are being considered to increase the safety of NFL football).

• **Overlapping and Potentially Duplicitous Litigation—Number of Legal Orders Received Each Week by Wells Fargo Bank.** Possibly due in part to "the overlapping of regulators and litigators in state, federal, and contingency-fee-financed civil action(s)," the sheer volume of U.S. banking litigation (and especially in light of the 2008 financial collapse) has exploded. Wells Fargo Bank alone "receives around 300 state, federal and grand jury subpoenas a week on average" and "about 5,000 legal orders a week." In response, the bank has "two centers, one on each coast, devoted to processing them." *The Economist*, October 13–19, 2012, pp. 18 and 83.

• **Terrorism and Terrorism-Related Trials—Federal Courts—Number of Tried In.** More than 400 as of May 2012. *The Economist*, May 12–18, 2012, p. 36.

- **U.S. Major Banks Legal Costs as Percentage of Pre-Provision Profits.** Based upon data from the first six months of 2012, the following respective banks' legal costs (exclusion of fines, penalties, and awards) as a percentage of profits are as follows:

Bank	Legal Costs as Appr. Percentage of Pre-Provision Profits
Wells Fargo	1.0%
Average (of 16 Banks)	*4.0%*
Citigroup	6.0%
Bank of America	13.0%
JPMorgan Chase	14.5%

The Economist, October 13–19, 2012, p. 83.

PART IV

Housing, Education, and Health

CHAPTER 9

Housing, Cities, and Communities

Exemplar Facts About Current America From This Chapter
(Details and Source Citations Below)

Despite the devaluating impact of the 2008 Great Recession, the average U.S. home still appreciated 56% from 1997 to 2011.

Only three U.S. cities (New York (No. 2), Los Angeles (No. 14), and Chicago (No. 24)) are among the 26 cities in the world with populations above 8MM.

82% of the U.S. total population now lives in an urban area (compared with 50% of the inhabitants worldwide and 78% of the inhabitants of the more developed regions).

86% of the U.S. population commutes to work by car (with more than 75% driving alone) and only 5% use public transportation.

10% of all U.S. occupied homes are now in gated communities.

It is now cheaper (and more "socially acceptable") to rent in 72% of U.S. metropolitan areas.

Only 40% of Americans know the names of their neighbors (and only 24% know the names of their neighbor's children).

New Orleans now has a population equal to 79%
of its pre-Katrina population.

The average square footage of newly built U.S. homes
is 2,480 square feet.

Table of Contents
Of The Data Contained in This Chapter

House and Lot Sizes.
* House and Lot Sizes—Plymouth, Massachusetts (Year 1620) and Levittown, New York (Year 1952).
* Median—Newly Built Single-Family Dwellings ("SFDs")—Appr. 40 Years (1973–2010).
* Minimum Square Footage Required for Apartments in San Francisco.
* Percentage Increase of Newly Built Homes Over Last 35 and 55 Years.
* U.S. House Sizes Compared With Other Countries.

Housing Costs as Percentage of Family Budget.

Housing Units—Percentage of Which Are in Multi-Unit Structures (e.g., Apartments).

Neighbors' Names—Percentage of Americans Who Know Neighbors' Names.

New Orleans—Population Recovery Since Hurricane Katrina.

Sales of Newly Built Homes.

Data

Cities and Urbanization.
* **"Best Cities" to Live—U.S.** Using weighted criteria based upon the availability of leisure activities, education attributes, economic factors, crime, and air quality, the following cities were ranked the Top 20 by *Bloombergnews.com*

Top 20 "Best Cities" in America To Live

Ranking	City and State	Ranking	City and State
1.	San Francisco, CA	8.	Austin, TX
2.	Seattle, WA	9.	San Diego, CA
3.	Washington, DC	10.	St. Paul, MN
4.	Boston, MA	11.	Pittsburgh, PA
5.	Portland, OR	12.	Minneapolis, MN
6.	Denver, CO	13.	Nashville, TN
7.	New York, New York	14.	New Orleans, LA
15.	Kansas City, MO	18.	Raleigh, NC
16.	Atlanta, GA	19.	Honolulu, HI
17.	Madison, WI	20.	Columbus, OH

BloombergNews.com (October 12, 2012).

* **Cheapest and Most Expensive—U.S. Cities—Top 10 Respective Cities.** The cities listed below are based upon the Council for Community and

Economic Research's calculation of living expenses in U.S. with populations greater than 50,000. "The Cost of Living Index (COLI), which (is a city-to-city comparison index which) measures relative price levels for housing, utilities, transportation, grocery items, health care, and miscellaneous goods and services. A Cost of Living score of 100 reflects the national average. The further the score falls below 100, the lower the cost of living. Property and median household income data is from the Census Bureau. Average home prices were provided by the Council for Economic Research." Huddleston, C., *Kiplinger* posted on *realestate.msc.com*. (October 4, 2012). See also, *coli.org*.

Cheapest Cities in America			Most Expensive Cities in America		
Ranking	Cheapest Cities	Cost of Living Index Score	Ranking	Most Expensive Cities	Cost of Living Index Score
1.	Harlington, TX	82.8	1.	New York, NY	228.3
2.	Memphis, TN	83.7	2.	San Francisco, CA	166.5
3.	McAllen, TX	84.1	3.	Honolulu, HI	165.8
4.	Fayetteville, AR	84.6	4.	San Jose, CA	154.3
5.	Temple, TX	85.7	5.	Stamford, CT	147.4
6.	Conway, AR	86.2	6.	Santa Ana (Orange County) CA	144.7
7.	Pueblo, CO	86.2	7.	Washington, D.C.	144.6
8.	Wichita Falls, TX	86.9	8.	Boston, MA	139.4
9.	Springfield, IL	87.1	9.	Oakland, CA	137.4
10.	Winston-Salem, NC	87.5	10.	Anchorage, AK	134.9

Huddleston, C., *Kiplinger* posted on *realestate.msc.com*. (October 4, 2012)

- **Most Livable U.S. Cities in Top 50 Most Livable Cities Worldwide—Number of and Identity.** According to the Economist Intelligence Unit's Global Livability Survey, there are 13 U.S. cities in the Top 50 Most Livable Cities in the World. However, there are no U.S. cities listed in the Top 25 Most Livable Cities in the World. The Most Livable Cities are based upon an analysis of 140 cities worldwide and 30 indicators in "five broad categories: stability, health care, culture and environment, education, and infrastructure." The top three "most livable" cities were Melbourne, Australia; Vienna, Austria; and Vancouver, Canada. The U.S. "Most Livable Cities" and their respective rankings among the 140 most livable cities worldwide are as follows:

Most Livable U.S. Cities in Top 50 Most Livable Cities Worldwide

Ranking	City and State
26.	Honolulu, Hawaii
30.	Pittsburgh, Pennsylvania
34.	Washington, D.C.
36.	Chicago, Illinois; Atlanta, Georgia; and Miami, Florida.
40.	Detroit, Michigan. (Author's Note: Highly curious inclusion. See, Most Miserable Cities listed below).
41.	Boston, Massachusetts.
42.	Seattle, Washington.
43.	Minneapolis, Minnesota; Los Angeles, California (tie).
45.	Cleveland, Ohio.
46.	Houston, Texas.

eiu.com; cnngo.com. This survey evidences the level inconsistency that exists between polls based upon the inclusion or exclusion or weighting of various factors. See, e.g., Cities—Most Miserable, below, in which Miami, Florida, and Detroit, Michigan, were ranked the first and second "Most Miserable Cities" in the U.S. by *Forbes.com.*

- **Most Miserable Cities—Top 10 U.S. "Most Miserable" Cities.** *Forbes* Magazine's list of the Most Miserable U.S. cities, which is based upon *Forbes'* analysis of the 200 largest metropolitan areas and divisions, is set forth below. The stated criteria used by Forbes are 10 factors: violent crime, unemployment rates, foreclosures, taxes (income and property), home prices, political corruption, commute times, weather, and the performance of the area's pro sports teams. According to Forbes, "while sports, commuting, and weather can be considered trivial by many, they can be a determining factor in the level of misery for a significant number of people." *Forbes.com.* Based upon the selection and weighting of the above-described criteria, such rankings are, at best, a partially subjective listing. In the listing below, the primary basis for the rankings is provided:

Top 10 "Most Miserable" Cities in the U.S.

Ranking	City and State	Primary Basis for Such Ranking
1.	Miami, FL	Housing—364,000 houses in foreclosure since 2008; 47% of all houses "underwater."
2.	Detroit, MI	Closed schools, laid off police, housing prices collapse.

3. Flint, MI   High crime, 775 abandoned homes leveled in 2011.
4. West Palm Beach, FL Corruption and housing prices collapse.
5. Sacramento, CA   High foreclosure rates, sports team may be moving.
6. Chicago, IL   "Gridlock traffic," high property taxes, tough winters.
7. Fort Lauderdale, FL   Housing prices collapse—down 50%.
8. Toledo, OH   Political scandals, high income and property taxes.
9. Rockford, IL   High property—15th highest in U.S. at 2.4% per annum.
10. Warren, MI   Housing prices collapse—down 50% in median value.

Stockton, California, was the first city ever to be ranked by *Forbes* as the Most Miserable City for two years in a row. Stockton dropped (or improved) from No. 1 Most Miserable City in 2011 to No 11 in 2012. In fairness, however, the City of Stockton arguably moved only from "miserable" to "bankrupt," since the city filed for bankruptcy in early 2012. *Forbes.com.,* February 2, 2012, citing *RealtyTrac* with regard to housing price changes and percentages.

- **Number of U.S. Cities in Top 25 Largest Cities in World**. Only three cities—New York (No. 2 with 17.8MM), Los Angeles (No. 14, with 11.9MM), and Chicago (No. 24, with 8.3MM). There are a total of 26 cities in the world with populations estimated at above 8MM. The five largest cities in the world (sometimes more accurately referred to as "urban agglomerations") are as follows:

Ranking	City and Country	Est. Population
1.	Tokyo-Yokohama, Japan	33.2MM
2.	New York, New York, U.S.	17.8MM
3.	Sao Paulo, Brazil	17.7MM
4.	Seoul-Inchon, South Korea	17.5MM
5.	Mexico City, Mexico	17.4MM

The Economist: Pocket World in Figures, 2012; About.com/geography. See also, The World Factbook at *cia.gov,* which identifies a slightly different list in the following order: Tokyo (No. 1 with 36.7MM), Delhi, India (No. 2. with 22.2MM), Sao Paulo, Brazil (No. 3 with 20.3MM), Mumbai, India (No. 4 with 20MM), and Mexico City, Mexico (No. 5 with 19.5MM). New York is characterized as New York-Newark at No. 6 with 19.4MM.

- **States With Most Number of Fastest Growing Cities.** Texas has eight of the fifteen fastest growing cities. Dockterman, E., *Time,* July 16, 2012, p. 16, citing U.S. Census data.
- **Urbanization.**
    ○ **Level Of—United States.** 82% of U.S. total population now lives in an urban area (2010) as compared with approximately one-half

worldwide and 78% of the inhabitants of the more developed regions. The World Factbook at *cia.gov.*; U.N. Department of Economic and Social Affairs, Population Division (World Urbanization Prospects— The 2011 Revision). Distinguishing between "urban areas" and "suburbs," however, more than 50% of the population lives in suburbs, although there is a growing moving trend back to the city center with "51% (of the nation's) largest cities … seeing more growth in the core than outside of it." *The Economist*, September 22–28, 2012, p. 32, citing William Frey at the Brookings Institute.

○ **Level Of—U.S. Compared With Those Nations with Highest and Lowest Levels of Urbanization.**

Ranking	Highest Urbanization Rate		Lowest Urbanization Rate	
1.	Bermuda	100%	Burundi	11.0%
	Cayman Islands	100%	Papua New Guinea	12.5%
	Hong Kong	100%	Uganda	13.3%
	Macau	100%	Trinidad & Tobago	13.9%
	Singapore	100%	Sri Lanka	14.3%
6.	Puerto Rico	98.8%	Ethiopia	16.7%
	United States Urbanization Rate = 82%			
7.	Guadeloupe	98.4%	Niger	17.1%
	Kuwait	98.4%	Nepal	18.6%
9.	Belgium	97.4%	Rwanda	18.9%
10.	Qatar	95.8%	Malawi	19.8%
. . . . .				
19.	Argentina	92.4%		
20.	Israel	91.9%		
27.	Brazil	86.5%		
30.	France	85.3%		

The World Factbook at *cia.gov*; U.N. Department of Economic and Social Affairs, Population Division (World Urbanization Prospects—The 2011 Revision); *The Economist: Pocket World in Figures, 2012 Edition.*

World Megacities—Number of Located in U.S. in 1970 vs. 2011. In 1970, there were only two "megacities" in the world—Tokyo and New York. Now there are 23. Of these 23 megacities, 13 are located in Asia, 4 in Latin America, and 2 each in Africa, Europe (Moscow and Paris), and North America (New York-Newark, and Los Angeles-Long Beach-Santa Ana). U.N. Department of Economic and Social Affairs, Population Division (World Urbanization Prospects—The 2011 Revision).

Commuting, Means of Transportation, and Place of Work—Characteristics.

Category	Percentage of Total Population
Transportation to Work	
Car, Truck, or Van	86.1% (Drive alone–75.4%/Carpooled–9.7%)
Public Transportation	5.0%
Walked or Bicycled	3.4%
Worked at Home	4.3%
Place of Work	
In State of Residence	96.2%
Outside State of Residence	3.8%
Time Leaving for Work	
5:00 AM – 7:00 AM	27.1%
7:00 AM – 9:00 AM	44.3%
Other	28.6%
Travel Time to Work	
Under 20 Minutes	43.2%
Mean Travel Time to Work	*25.5 minutes*
20–45 Minutes	54.7%
More Than 45 Minutes	15.6%

U.S. Census Bureau—Commuting Characteristics, 2011 ACS Survey.

Detroit—Vacant Homes—Number of Razed in Last Two Years. 2,000 vacant homes. This is partly due to the shrinkage of the city by nearly 25% in the last decade from a population of 950,000 in 2000 to 715,000 in 2010. *Time,* May 7, 2012, p. 12, quoting fire commission Donald Austin's statement to local paper. In July, 2013 Detroit became the first major U.S. city to file bankruptcy.

Foreclosure Process—States Requiring Judicial Approval—Number and Effect Of. 24 States. The foreclosure backlog is 2.6 times larger in states requiring judicial approval of such foreclosures as compared with states where no judicial review is required. Compare the average no-judicial review foreclosure in Texas (90 days) with judicial review foreclosure in New York (1,019 days). *The Week,* April 13, 2012, p. 38, citing K. Mracek, *Kiplinger.com.*

Gated Communities—Percentage of Occupied Homes Now In. Appr. 10%. Increased number of houses in gated communities in last decade between 2001 and 2009: 53%. *The Week,* April 13, 2012, p. 20, citing *The New York Times.*

Home Ownership.

- **Compared with Renting—Relative Costs Of—Comparative Cost of in U.S. Metropolitan Areas.** Cheaper (and more "socially acceptable") to rent in 72% of U.S. metropolitan area ("up from 54% 10 years earlier"). Gross, D., "Renting Prosperity," *The Wall Street Journal*, May 5–6, 2012, citing Moody's and from his new book *Better, Stronger, Faster: The Myth of American Decline and the Rise of a New Economy* (2012). But see, Wolverson, R., "Welcome to the 'Sharing Economy," *Time*, September 24, 2012, p. 44, citing the real estate website *Trulia*, which found that "buying was less expensive than renting in 98 out of 100 major U.S. metropolitan real estate markets."

- **Rate—Peak Percentage and Year and Current Home Ownership Rate.** The record year for home ownership percentage was in 2006 when 69% of people owned homes. As of 2012, this percentage had fallen to 65.4%. Gross, D., "Renting Prosperity," *The Wall Street Journal*, May 5–6, 2012, citing the U.S. Census Bureau and adapted from his new book *Better, Stronger, Faster: The Myth of American Decline and the Rise of a New Economy* (2012). See also, *The Week*, September 14, 2012, p. 34, citing *Bloomberg Businessweek*, which states that home ownership percentage is currently at 62.1%, which is still "the lowest level since 1965."

Home Prices.

- **Changes—U.S.—Average—14 Years from 1997 to 2011.** Despite the material losses and devaluations of the last several years, the average U.S. home appreciated 56% over the 14-year period from 1997 to 2011. *The Economist: Pocket World in Figures, 2012 Edition.*

- **U.S. Cities With Highest Average Home Values**. Those cities, in descending order as follows:

Ranking City/State	Average Home Value	Ranking City/State	Average Home Value
1. Atherton, CA	$3,770,000	6. San Anselmo, CA	$2,170,000
2. Beverly Hills, CA	$2,900,000	7. Water Mill, NY	$2,165,000
3. New York, NY (10013)	$2,370,000	8. Los Altos, CA	$2,160,000
4. Santa Monica, CA	$2,360,000	9. Fisher Island, FL	$2,120,000
5. Rancho Santa Fe, CA	$2,240,000		

  The Wall Street Journal—Special Report, December 28, 2012, citing Zillow and presenting data that the 2012 was the beginning of the recovery for the $1MM+ sales price luxury homes in most parts of the U.S.

House Flipping—Volume Of, Recent Increase In, and Average Profit. Appr. 100,000 U.S. homes were "flipped" (i.e., bought and resold within six months) during the first six months of 2012, which represents a 25%

increase over the same period in 2011. While profitability can vary radically from region to region, one estimate of the average per flip profit is $29,000. Tuttle, B., "Home, Cheap Home," *Time*, November 5, 2012, p. 16, citing data from RealtyTrac and Arizona-based Colony American Homes.

House and Lot Sizes.

- **House and Lot Sizes—Plymouth, Massachusetts (Year 1620) and Levittown, New York (Year 1952).** For a basis of interesting historical comparison, the original lots mapped out by the Pilgrims in New Plymouth, Massachusetts, were 8 feet by 49 feet (i.e., 392 square feet). In 1952 (about 330 years later), the lots in Levittown, New York, averaged about 6,000 square feet and the average Levittown house was appr. 720 square feet (with two bedrooms and two bathrooms). *Chronicle of America,* p. 53; Halberstam, D., *The Fifties*, p. 135.

- **Median—Newly Built Single-Family Dwellings ("SFDs")—Appr. 40 Years (1973–2010).** Except for 2007–2010, the average and median sizes of newly built SFDs has increased with some regional distinctions (the Northeast consistently being the largest and the Midwest being the smallest). In addition, urban homes (i.e., those constructed inside MSAs (Metropolitan Statistical Areas) are generally appr. 10–15% larger (i.e., about 250–350 square feet larger).

House Sizes—Median Sizes—Newly Built Single-Family Dwellings—1973–2010

Year	Median Newly Built U.S. House Size	Year	Median Newly Built House Size
1950s	983 sf	1995	1,920 sf
1973	1,525 sf	2000	2,057 sf
1975	1,535 sf	2005	2,228 sf
1980	1,595 sf	2007	2,277 sf
1985	1,605 sf	2010	2,169 sf
1990	1,905 sf		

U.S. Census Bureau. Based upon data from the American Institute of Architects, in 2011 (and for the first time since 2009) house sizes started to again increase, and the *average* size in 2011 increased to 2,480 square feet—an 88-square-foot increase (appr. 3.6%). See, American Institute of Architects' Home Design Trends Survey, which reported slightly more than one-half (i.e., 52%) of the member architects reported in 2011 that home sizes were still declining.

- **Minimum Square Footage Required for Apartments in San Francisco.** Under San Francisco housing regulations, all new apartments must be at least 200 square feet. Harper's Index, *Harper's Magazine,* December 2012, p. 15.

- **Percentage Increase of Newly Built Homes Over Last 35 and 55 years.** The median size of U.S. newly constructed homes has increased 41% over the 35 years and appr. 121% over the last 55 years. U.S. Census Bureau and *Trulia.com*.
- **U.S. House Sizes Compared With Other Countries.** By any measure, the size of U.S. homes greatly exceeds that of other nations. The average floor space of newly built homes in the U.S. and selected other counties is as follows:

Country	Ave. Floor Space	Country	Ave. Floor Space
United States	*2,304 sf (Note 1)*	Spain	1,216 sf
Australia	2,217 sf	Ireland	1,044 sf
Denmark	1,475 sf	Ireland	947 sf
France	1,216 sf	United Kingdom	818 sf

Note 1: This is a slight variation from information in the 2,169 (Year 2010) data in above entry due to different reporting source. *policyexchange,* CABE, U.S. Census Bureau. See also, Wotapka, D., "Big Homes Are Back in Business," *The Wall Street Journal*, June 8, 2012 (2,480 sq. ft. (newly constructed homes)).

Housing Costs as Percentage of Family Budget. Appr. 32%—"the biggest single component of consumption in the U.S. economy. Gross, D., "Renting Prosperity," *The Wall Street Journal*, May 5–6, 2012, citing the Bureau of Labor Statistics and adapted from his new book *Better, Stronger, Faster: The Myth of American Decline and the Rise of a New Economy* (2012).

Housing Units—Percentage of Which Are In Multi-Unit Structures (e.g., Apartments). 25.9%. U.S. Census Bureau.

Neighbors' Names—Percentage of American Who Know Neighbors' Names. 40% (and only 24% knew their neighbors' children's names), according to a survey conducted by Harris Interactive on behalf of WhitePages.

New Orleans—Population Recovery Since Hurricane Katrina. 79%. New Orleans now has a population equal to 79% of its pre-Katrina population. Dockterman, E., *Time,* July 16, 2012, p. 16, citing U.S. Census data.

Sales of Newly Built Homes. 306,000 in 2011, "which is the lowest number since record-keeping began in 1963. Wotapka, D., "Big Homes Are Back in Business," *The Wall Street Journal*, June 8, 2012.

CHAPTER 10

Education and Literacy

Exemplar Facts About Current America From This Chapter
(Details and Source Citations Below)

9 states permit advertising on the sides of their yellow school buses.

19 of the top 25 universities in the world are located in the U.S.

The average amount spent by families for college expenses
is appr. $21,000 per year.

By at least one educational rating, the U.S. educational system remains
the most educationally competitive in the world.

Women now comprise 55%–60% of college attendees and are the
recipients of a majority of all master's degrees and doctorate degrees.

43% of all U.S. college grades are now "A's."

The graduation rates for U.S. colleges are very similar and very low:
30% for four-year colleges and 25% for two-year colleges.

The four highest–paid university presidents (Ohio State,
Texas A&M, Penn State, and the University of Kentucky) received
annual salaries from $970,000 to $1,990,000.

The aggregate amount of student loan debt in the U.S. now exceeds $1.1 trillion (about $942 billion in federal student loans and another $140 billion in private loans).

The U.S. spends an amount equal to 5.7% of its GDP on education, which places it 37th in the world in education spending as a percentage of GDP (slightly below Switzerland and Portugal and slightly above France, Poland, and Mexico).

The Department of Education Projects $51BB 2013 Profits From Student Loans. Appr. $51BB—"more than the profits of companies like Exxon Mobil and Apple, and roughly equal to the combined net income of the four largest U.S. banks."

85% of the U.S. adult population are high school graduates.

The K–12 U.S. average class size is 16.8, with the averages ranging from Virginia's 7.2 to Delaware's 24.2.

37 states (nearly 3 out of 4) cut public school expenditures in 2012.

Table of Contents
Of The Data Contained in This Chapter

- Perceived Value of College Education as Financial Investment—Change Between 2008 and 2011.
- Post-Graduation Employment and Salary Information—Growing State Assemblage and Publication of Data.
- Private vs. Public Schools—Respective Percentage of College Students In.
- Public Colleges and Universities—Number of and Attendance At.
- Quality Of—U.S. Engineering Graduates Immediately "Employable"—China and India Compared.
- Regrets of College Graduates About Their College Years.
- Salaries—University Presidents.
    - Highest Paid Public-University President.
    - Top 10 Highest Paid Presidents—Public and Private Universities—Median Compensations of All Public and Private Universities.
- SAT Scores.
    - Correlation Between Student's Scores and Family Income.
    - High School 2012 Graduating Class—SAT Average Scores.
- Student Loan Debt—Colleges and Universities.
    - Aggregate Amount Of.
    - Average Amount Of—Recent College Graduates.
    - College Students Who Drop Out With Student Loans.
    - Default Rate With Respect to Federal Student Loans.
    - Delinquency Percentage Rate.
    - Department of Education Projected Massive 2013 Profits From Student Loans.
    - Percentage of College Students Who Incur Student Debt.
    - Percentage of Student Loans Now Made Directly By Government.
    - Senior Citizens—Amount of Student Loan Debt Held by Americans Over Age 60.

Early Childhood Education.
- Impact Upon Child's Preparedness for Kindergarten.
- Poverty—Correlation to Early Childhood Preparedness for School.
- Pre-School.
    - Attendance—Percentage of U.S. Children Who Attend.
    - State-Funded Programs—Number of States With and Percentage of U.S. Children Who Attend.
    - States With Highest Percentage of 4-Year-Olds in State Pre-School Programs.
    - States Without State Pre-School Programs—Number and List Of.

- Class Size.
    - U.S. Average Class Size Compared With Other Countries.
    - U.S.—States' Class Size Disparities—States With Largest and Small Average Class Sizes.
- For-Profit K-12 Education—Continued Skepticism Of.
- Homeschooling.
    - Growth Of—Number of Children Homeschooled.
    - Reasons For—By Parental Motivational Category.
- K-12 Students—Number Of.
- Private K-12 Schools.
    - Annual Tuition—Average.
    - Students Attending the New "Avenues: The World School" in New York City.
    - Publicly Funded Scholarships For—States Which Allow Students to Attend Private K-12 Schools With.
- Public K-12 Schools.
    - Budget Cuts—States Which Cut Public School Expenditures in 2012—Number Of.
    - Charter Schools.
        - Families With Children In—Number Of.
        - States Which Limit the Expansion of Charter Schools—Number Of.
        - States Which Allow Parents to Send Their Children To.
        - Students—Number of Students in U.S. Charter Schools.
    - Common Core Standards—Adoption Of—Number of States.
    - Corporal Punishment—Spanking and Paddling In Schools—Number of States Where Permissible; Level of Public Support Of.
    - Employment in Public Education—Decline in Last 3 Years (2009—2012).
    - Gender Segregation—Permissibility in U.S. Schools.
    - "Parent-Triggers" Laws—States Which Have Adopted or Are Considering—Number Of.
    - Percentage of U.S. Children In Public K-12 Schools.
    - School Attendance—Chronically Absent Students—Percentage of U.S. Schoolchildren.
    - School Week—U.S. School Districts With 4-Day School Week—Number Of.
    - School Year—Increased by 300 Hours Under Pilot Program—Number of States.

- o Teacher Evaluations—Test Scores—States Which Have Adopted Teacher Evaluations and Student Test Scores Linkage Policies—Number Of.
- o Teachers—Number of and Teacher-to-Student Ratios.
- o Vouchers—Milwaukee, Wisconsin—Number of Years of Use In.
- Quality—Perceived Quality of Education—Private vs. Parochial vs. Home Schooling vs. Public Schools.

Public Libraries.
- All-Digital Library—First Ever.
- Digital Books and E-Readers—Prevalence of at U.S. Public Libraries.
- Number of in U.S.

Quick Summary and Comparison of U.S. Education Data With Other Nations.

Years of School—Average Number of Years—U.S. Compared With Other Countries.

Data

Advertising on Sides of Yellow School Buses—Number of States Which Permit. Nine states, as of appr. May 2012. In some instances, certain types of advertising, such as tobacco, alcohol, political, and junk food advertising, are specifically banned. *Time,* May 14, 2012, p.12.

Civics—Knowledge Of—By Americans. In response to polling of how many justices are on the U.S. Supreme Court, 65% of those without a college degree and 48% of those with a college degree either stated the wrong number or acknowledged that they did not know. "The 60 Minutes/Vanity Fair Poll," *Vanity Fair,* September 2012, p. 114.

College and Universities.
- **Best Universities.**
  - o **Attendance by Children from Low-Income Households**. "Only 3% of the students at the top 146 colleges come from families in the bottom (25%) of household income." Stengel, R., "Reinventing College," *Time,* October 29, 2012, p. 31.
  - o **U.S. Universities in Top 25 Universities in World.** While the identification and listing of the best universities is, at best, an imprecise standard and can be a function of with different or differently weighted criteria, *The Economist* makes its determination of

the top universities "based on academic peer review, employer review, faculty/student ratio, research strength and international factors." Of the 25 top-ranked universities, 19 are located in the U.S. Harvard University, University of California at Berkeley, Stanford University, and MIT are respectively ranked 1 through 4. (2010 Data). *The Economist: Pocket World in Figures, 2012 Edition.*

- **Business Schools—Summary Data About, Top 10 and Compared With European Business Schools.** Until recently, European business schools held distinct advantages over U.S. schools—cheaper, substantially shorter programs (11–16 months for some non-U.S. schools vs. 21–22 Months for U.S. schools), greater diversity of student bodies, easier post-graduation visa policies, and often higher post-graduation starting salaries. This has changed considerably over the past several years, and U.S. business schools have reasserted their relative preeminence.

The Economist's Business Schools 2012 Rankings (Full-Time MBA Programs)

Ranking	Name	Country	Ave. Salary of New Graduates	Ave. Age of Students
1.	Chicago (Booth)	U.S.	$113,200	27
2.	Virginia (Darden)	U.S.	$104,500	27
3.	Dartmouth (Tuck)	U.S.	$115,100	28
4.	Harvard	U.S.	$121,800	27
5.	Columbia	U.S.	$113,300	28
6.	UC Berkeley (Haas)	U.S.	$114,200	28
7.	MIT (Sloan)	U.S.	$115,400	28
8.	Stanford	U.S.	$127,200	—
9.	IESE	Spain	$126,800	27
10.	IMD	Switzerland	$145,300	31

U.S. vs. European business schools in Top 20—U.S., thirteen; European, seven. *The Economist*, October 6–12, 2012, p. 81.

- **College Graduates as Percentage of U.S. Population 25 or Older.** Appr. 27.9% of the U.S. population (or about 1 in every 3.5 Americans 25 or older) has a college Bachelor's Degree or higher. U.S. Census Bureau.
- **Community Colleges—Aggregate Enrollment in 2012.** Appr. 8MM U.S. students according to the Carnegie Corporation of New York and the Bill & Melinda Gates Foundation, co-sponsors of the TIME Summit on Higher Education.
- **Comparative Rankings—Criteria Used.** The college rankings and the relative weighting of each that was used by *Forbes* were based upon the following five general categories:

(1) Post-Graduate success (32.5%) (Alumni pay and prominence);

(2) Student satisfaction (27.5%) (Professor evaluations and freshman and sophomore retention rates);

(3) Student debt (17.5%) (Penalization upon occurrence of high student debt loads and default rates);

(4) Four-year graduation rate (11.25%); and

(5) Competitive awards (11.25%) (receipts of post-graduate awards such as Rhodes, Marshall, and Fulbright).

See *Forbes.com,* August 2, 2012, citing data assembled for Forbes by Center for College Affordability and Productivity.

- **Competency-Based College Degrees—Initiated Use Of.** While some universities offer competency-based credits or associate degrees, Wisconsin's public university system is the first to offer multiple, competency-based bachelor's degrees whereby "students are encouraged to complete their education independently through online courses," and no classroom time is required. Northern Arizona University is planning to offer a similar flat-fee competency-based degree program as well. Porter, C., "College Degree, No Class Time Required," *The Wall Street Journal*, January 25, 2013.

- **Conservative Studies—Number of U.S. Professors in Conservative Studies** Just one—at the University of Colorado at Boulder. The position, a "(privately-funded) visiting scholar in Conservative Thought and Policy," is "among the first of its kind on a U.S. campus" and was created in order to "broaden the intellectual diversity among the faculty" according to a Denver banker who sat on the selection committee. The creation of this post may have been in response to a 2008 survey of the Boulder campus faculty which found that "of the 825 faculty members, just 23 (i.e., 2.8%) were registered Republicans." Belkin, D., *The Wall Street Journal*, March 14, 2013.

- **Cost—Tuition and Fees.**
    - **Average Annual Amount Spent by Families for College Expenses.** Appr. $21,000, representing a 5% decline from 2011, due at least in part to the material increase in the number of students living at home. *The Week*, August 3, 2012, p. 16, citing *The New York Times*.
    - **Average at Four-Year Public Schools and Private, Nonprofit Institutions.** As of 2012, the respective college tuition costs (excluding room and board) are as follows:

Four-Year Private	$28,500	
Four-Year Public	$ 8,244	$5,189*
Two-Year Public	$ 2,963	

        *After institutional grants and scholarships.

Mitchell, J., "New Course in College Costs," *The Wall Street Journal*, June 11, 2012, citing the College Board, an advocacy group made up of universities, and Ripley, A., *Time*—Special Report, October 29, 2012, p. 33. See also, (i) Koppel, N., "Dispute Over College Tuition Roils Flagship Texas Campus," *The Wall Street Journal*, May 18, 2012 (this article includes sample undergraduate tuition and required fees such as University of California at Berkeley ($14,461), University of Michigan, Ann Arbor ($13,437), University of Texas at Austin ($9,792), and University of North Carolina, Chapel Hill ($7,009), citing data from University of Texas at Austin); (ii) *The Week*, November 2, 2012, p. 6 (which notes that the prices have risen again and, citing the College Board, the average annual cost is now $12,110 for in-state students and public four-year colleges and $23,840 at private nonprofit institutions); (iii) Thurm, S., "Who Can Still Afford State U?," *The Wall Street Journal*, December 15-16, 2012; and (iv) Ripley, A., *Time*—Special Report, October 29, 2012, p. 32.

o **Impact of Federal Aid for Students Upon Tuition and Fees— For-Profit Schools.** Tuition and fees are 75% higher at schools where students received federal aid compared with for-profit schools where students did not receive federal aid. Mitchell, J., "New Course in College Costs," *The Wall Street Journal*, June 11, 2012, citing study by National Bureau of Economic Research working paper by C. Goldin and S. Cellini.

o **Increases in Four-Year Public Schools.** The percentage increase in tuition and fees between 1990 and 2012 was 150%. Mitchell, J., "New Course in College Costs," *The Wall Street Journal*, June 11, 2012, citing a study by the National Bureau of Economic Research working paper by C. Goldin and S. Cellini.

o **Low-Cost College Degrees—Cost and Number of Texas Colleges Now Offering.** In response to calls for less-expensive undergraduate degrees and although there are numerous skeptics as to the feasibility and quality of the education that can be offered, ten Texas colleges are now offering college degree programs for $10,000, which is "a fraction of the roughly $30,000 that students at Texas public universities pay on average over four years." Koppel, N., Belkin, D., "Texas Pushes $10,000 Degree," *The Wall Street Journal*, October 8, 2012.

o **Pell Grants for Low-Income Students—Number of Recipients Since Their Introduction in 1972.** More than $270BB in grants has been awarded to an estimated 138MM students, according to the

Carnegie Corporation of New York and the Bill & Melinda Gates Foundation, co-sponsors of the Time Summit on Higher Education.

○ **Public Funding Of—Average State Funding per Student.** The average state funding per college student decreased more than 9% (with California's cuts the largest percentage at 14.3% in 2011) while the public tuition rose an almost parallel 8%. Simon, R., *The Wall Street Journal*, March 6, 2013.

○ **"Tuition Discount Rate"—Extent of Average Increase At Private Colleges.** The "tuition discount rate," the reduction off of the quoted tuition as the result of grants and scholarships given by colleges, has increased to "an all-time high of 45%" as of Fall 2012. These increases partly reflect the "buyers market" at private schools, and the fact that enrollment fell at nearly one-half (46%) of the 383 private universities in the survey conducted by the National Association of College and University Business Officers ("Nacubo"). Conversely, the average tuition discount rate declined slightly at public universities. Simon, R., *The Wall Street Journal*, May 6, 2013, citing Nacubo data.

• **Doctorates in Science and Engineering—Foreign-Born-Students—Percentage of Degrees Issued.** 42%. Huntsman, J., "A GOP Opportunity on Immigration," *The Wall Street Journal*, August 27, 2012, citing 2011 Kauffman Foundation Study. See also, *The Week*, April 20, 2012, p. 18, as corrected in May 4, 2012 issue (41% of MIT's graduate students in science and engineering are foreign-born).

• **Educational Competitiveness—Top 5 Nations**. Using Boston Consulting Group's new BCG E4 Index, which measures "expenditure (the level of investment in education by government and private households), enrollment (the number of students in the educational system), engineers (the number of qualified engineers entering the workforce), and elite institutions (the number of top global higher-education institutions), the ranking of the Top 5 educationally competitive countries are as follows:

Top 5 Educationally Competitive Countries

Ranking	Country	Main "Drivers" For Ranking
1.	*United States*	*(High spending, Dominance in globally ranked institutions, and qualified engineering rates)*
2.	United Kingdom	(High spending, Dominance in globally ranked institutions, and qualified engineering rates)
3.	China	(Enrollment; Relatively Low Spending)
4.	Germany	
5.	India	(Enrollment; Very Low Spending)

Silverstein, M., Singhi, A., "Can Universities Stay on Top?," *The Wall Street Journal*, September 29–30, 2012, citing Boston Consulting Group BSG E4 Index and analysis.

- **Enrollment and U.S. College Graduates—By Gender.** The enrollment percentages are as follows:

Men	Appr. 45%
Women	Appr. 55%

  The U.S. college graduates percentages are men, appr. 48.9%, women, appr. 51.1%. U.S. Census Bureau. See also, Mundy, L., "Women, Money and Power," *Time*, March 26, 2012, p. 28 (60% of U.S. college students and a majority of doctorates and master's degrees are women).

- **Enrollment Inducements—Newly Offered by Liberal Arts Colleges.** In order to attempt to counter the declining enrollment at private, four-year liberal arts colleges, the following enrollment inducements are now being offered (or at least market-tested).

  Post-graduation loan-repayment assistance for students earning $20,000–$37,000 (Spring Arbor University, Michigan);

  Four-year graduation or classes are free (Alma College, Michigan and Nebraska Wesleyan (Nebraska);

  Eighth semester tuition-free if 3.5 grade point average is maintained (Union College, Kentucky); and

  Statistical disclosure of use of all tuition dollars (Augustana College (Illinois).

  Belkin, D., Korn, M., *The Wall Street Journal*, March 12, 2013.

- **Enrollment—Total College—U.S. Compared With China and India.** The respective number of college students in order of the number of students are as follows:

  Total College and University Student Enrollment

Country	Number of Enrollees	Percentage of Total Population
India	244MM	20.2%
China	235MM	17.4%
United States	***67 MM***	***21.5%***

  Silverstein, M., Singhi, A., "Can Universities Stay on Top?," *The Wall Street Journal*, September 29–30, 2012, citing Boston Consulting Group analysis.

- **Foreign Students.**
  - **Enrollment in U.S. Universities—Number Of.** In the 2010–11 school year "about 723,000 foreign students were enrolled in U.S. universities." *The Week*, August 10, 2012, p. 16, citing *The Wall Street Journal*.

○ **Percentage of Graduate Science and Engineering Students Attending Massachusetts Institute of Technology Who Are Foreigners.** 41% are foreigners who are attending the university on visas. *The Week,* April 20, 2012, p.18, citing *Bloomberg.com.* and as corrected in *The Week,* May 4, 2012, p. 4.

○ **Percentage of Students Who Attend University Outside Their Home Country.** Appr. 2%. Foroohar, R., "Why the World Isn't Getting Smaller," *Time,* June 27, 2011, p. 20, citing Ghemawat, P., *World 3.0.*

• **For-Profit Schools—Percentage of U.S. College Students Who Attend.** Appr. 10%. However, (a) for-profit colleges also receive appr. "a quarter of all Title IV funding—$4BB in Pell Grants and $20 billion in guarantee loans in 2009," and (b) appr. 87MM Americans (about 28% of the U.S. population) lives, for example, "within 10 miles of one of University of Phoenix's nearly 200 campuses." Harper's Index, *Harper's Magazine,* October 2011, p. 15 and Beha, C., "Leveling the Playing Field," *Harper's Magazine,* October 2011, pp. 52–53.

• **Grade Inflation—Percentage of U.S. College Grades That Are "A's."** 43% of all U.S. college grades are now "A's." Harper's Index, *Harper's Magazine,* p. 15.

• **Graduation Commencement Addresses—Number of Republicans or Conservatives Invited to Address Top 50 U.S. Liberal Arts Colleges—2013.** None, at least with respect to the "top" 50 U.S. liberal arts college as identified by *U.S. News and World Report. The Week,* May 31, 2013, p. 6, citing the *Los Angeles Times.*

• **Graduation On-Time—Percentage of Students Who Complete Four-Year College in Six Years.** Only 58% of students graduate "on-time," which is (curiously) defined as six years for a four-year college, Ripley, A., *Time*— Special Report, October 29, 2012, p. 32.

• **Graduation Rates—U.S. Colleges and Universities.** The graduation rates for four-year and two-year colleges are very similar and very low. They are, respectively, as follows

U.S. College and University Graduation Rates

Type of College	Graduation Rate
4-Year Colleges	30%
2-Year Colleges	25%

Foroohar, R, "These Schools Mean Business," *Time,* April 9, 2012, p. 26 and Klein, J., "Learning That Works," *Time,* May 14, 2012, p. 36 (Stating that community college graduate rates are 23%). See also, *The Week,* June 8, 2012,

p. 38, citing R. Samuelson, *The Washington Post* (Stating that less than "60% of freshmen at four-year schools graduate within 6 years").

- **Online (MOOC) Courses.**
  - ○ **Major Universities Now Offering Free Through Coursera or edX—Number of.** Sixteen universities, including Stanford, Duke, and Princeton, are now offering "more than 100 free online courses this academic year in partnership" with Coursera. Harvard, MIT, and the University of California are offering online courses through edX. Despite the definitional absence of direct "face-to-face learning," professor-student interaction, and a high student attrition and course non-completion rate, such online courses can provide near-universal access to education. *The Week*, September 7, 2012, p. 11. See also, (i) Falk, A., *The Wall Street Journal*, August 29, 2012 (In some criticism of online programs, he states that "what really matters is [not the mere transmission of facts] but the set of deeper abilities—to write effectively, argue persuasively, solve problems creatively, and adapt and learn independently... and by far, the factor that correlates most highly with gains in these skills is the amount of personal contact a students has with professors. Not virtual contact, but interaction with live, human beings...Education is not a commodity. It's a social process..."); and (ii) Reif, L. "What Campuses Can Learn From Online Teaching," *The Wall Street Journal*, October 3, 2012 (discussing the "flipped classroom" in which a course can be readily "adapted and tailored" to a student's own learning style. In response to MIT's new online program, MITx, which began in December 2011, "150,000 people from 160 countries signed up for the prototype course, Circuits and Electronics.").
  - ○ **Origin and Growth Of.** The UK's Open University "started teaching via radio and (TV) in 1971, the for-profit University of Phoenix has been teaching online since 1989, (and) MIT has been posting lectures on the internet for a decade." However, in 2012, online teaching and courses exploded with the introduction and use of "massive open online courses" or "MOOCS," which were initially offered by two startups "spawned" by Stanford University, Udacity (475,000 users), and Coursera (over 2,000,000 users). Shortly thereafter, Harvard and MIT launched edX, a non-profit offering online courses from Ivy League schools. *The Economist*, December 2, 2012–January 4, 2013, p. 101.
  - ○ **Summary of Currently Available Free MOOCs Programs.** A summary of certain, currently available online MOOCs (massive open online courses), all of which were launched in 2012, is as follows:

	MOOC Udacity	Coursera	edX
Type	For Profit	For Profit	Not-for-profit
Schools–Ass'ns With	None *(Note 1)*	33 Universities *(Note 2)*	MIT, Harvard, Univ. of Texas, UC Berkeley
Number of Courses—			
Currently Available	14	198	7
Number of Students	400,000	1,400,000	350,000

Note 1: Founded by former Stanford professor; *Note 2*: Including Princeton, Stanford, Penn, Duke, Ohio State, and University of VA. Ripley, A., Special Report, *Time*, October 29, 2012, p. 33. But see newer data reported in Korn, M., *The Wall Street Journal*, February 7, 2013 (e.g., Coursera—217 classses with 2.5MM registered users).

- **Perceived Value of College Education as Financial Investment—Change Between 2008 and 2011**. The perceived value of college as a "good financial investment" has fallen from 81% to 57% in three years—from 2008 to 2011. Harper's Index, *Harper's Magazine,* October 2012, p. 15.

- **Post-Graduation Employment and Salary Information—Growing State Assemblage and Publication of Data**. Appr. ten states (including California (community colleges), Florida, Tennessee, Texas, and Virginia) have started or are expected to soon start publishing information about the post-graduation salaries of recent graduates by school and by programs. It is expected that this data disclosure trend will continue, and based upon Virginia's first release of data, the post-graduation salaries vary significantly between schools (e.g., $41,200 for graduates of George Mason University vs. $28,800 for graduates of Virginia State University). Even though the data is still incomplete since it, for example, does not include data relating to salaries of graduates who are self-employed, work for the U.S. government, or who have moved to another state, the data may be highly useful to students in their selection of schools and programs. Simon, R., Corkery, M., *The Wall Street Journal*, February 12, 2013.

- **Private vs. Public Schools—Respective Percentage of College Students In.** Only about 20% (down from 22% in 2006) of all college students in four-year colleges are now in private schools. Nearly 80% of all such college students are now enrolled in public college. Belkin, D., Korn, M., *The Wall Street Journal*, March 12, 2013.

- **Public Colleges and Universities—Number and Attendance At**. 678 public colleges and universities enrolling "more than 15MM students." As recently as 1951, a little before the beginning of Modern America, more Americans were enrolled at private than public universities. The GI Bill totally changed this. Now, more than three times the number of students attend public universities than private universities. Thurm, S., "Who Can Still Afford State U?," *The Wall Street Journal,* December 15–16, 2012.

- **Quality Of—U.S. Engineering Graduates Immediately "Employable"— China and India Compared.** 81% of U.S. engineering graduates are "immediately employable," compared with Indian engineering graduates (only 25%) and Chinese engineering graduates (only 10%). Silverstein, M., Singhi, A., "Can Universities Stay on Top?," *The Wall Street Journal,* September 29–30, 2012, citing World Economic Forum.

- **Regrets of College Graduates About Their College Years.** Based upon one recent poll, college graduates wish they had done more of the following during college:

More Studying	48%
More Networking	40%
More Sex	4%
More Drugs	1%

The 60 Minutes/Vanity Fair Poll, *Vanity Fair,* May, 2013, p. 52.

- **Salaries—University Presidents.**
    - **Highest Paid Public-University President**. In 2011 Ohio State University President E. Gordon Gee earned $1.9MM. In addition, it is reported that "he submitted $1.7MM in expenses for private jets, country club dues, and fundraising parties." *The Week,* December 28–January 4, 2012, p. 46.
    - **Top 10 Highest Paid Presidents—Public and Private Universities— Median Compensations of All Public and Private Universities.** The compensation of private university presidents is normally materially higher than that of public-university presidents.

Public Universities

Ranking	University	Name	Salary (Exclusive of Expense Reimbursements)
1.	Ohio State	E. Gordon Gee	$1,990,000
2.	Texas A&M	Michael McKinney	$1,970,000
3.	Pennsylvania State	Graham Spanier	$1,070,000
4.	Univ. of Kentucky	Lee Todd, Jr.	$970,000
5.	Univ. of Michigan System	Mary Sue Coleman	$845,100
6.	Texas Tech	Kent Hance	$757,700
7.	Univ. of Texas System	Francisco Cigarroa	$751,700
8.	Univ. of Minn-Twin Cities	Robert Bruininks	$748,000
9.	Univ. of Central Florida	John Hitt	$741,500
10.	Virginia Tech	Charles Steger	$738,600
	Median Pay—Public University Presidents:		**$409,500**

(Survey of 190 public universities)

Private Universities

Ranking	University	Name	Salary
			(Exclusive of Expense Reimbursements)
1.	Drexel Univ.	Constantine Papadakis	$4,912,100
2.	Johns Hopkins Univ.	William Brody	$3,821,900
3.	Univ. of the Pacific	Donald DeRose	$2,358,000
4.	Northwestern Univ.	Henry Bienen	$2,241,000
5.	Vanderbilt Univ.	Nicholas Zeppos	$1,890,000
6.	Mountain State Univ.	Charles Polk	$1,844,000
7.	Rensselaer Polytechnic	Shirley Ann Jackson	$1,772,000
8.	Swarthmore College	Alfred Bloom	$1,756,000
9.	Yale Univ.	Richard Levin	$1,628,000
10.	Chapman Univ.	James Doti	$1,542,000

Median Pay—Private University Presidents: $385,900
(Survey of 482 private universities)

Chronicle of Higher Education, December 5, 2011, *chronicle.com.*

• **SAT Scores.**
  ○ **Correlation Between Student's Scores and Household Income.**
  Out of a possible 2400 points, the household income correlations
  are as follows:

Household Income of Student	Average Score
Below $20,000	1322
Above $200,000	1722 (i.e., 30% higher)

  Harper's Index, *Harper's Magazine,* December 2012, citing the
  College Board (New York City, NY).

  ○ **High School 2012 Graduating Class—SAT Average Scores.** Out
  of a possible 800 on each section, the average scores for the following
  subject categories are as follows:

  Reading: 496 (34-point drop from 1972, the first year the College
  Board, the nonprofit group that administers the
  test, started tracking scores).

  Writing: 488 (Lowest score since this section was added in 2006).

  Math: 514 (Down four points from 2006).

  Banchero, S., "SAT Scores Fall as More Students Take Exam," *The
  Wall Street Journal,* September 25, 2012.

• **Student Loan Debt—Colleges and Universities.**
  ○ **Aggregate Amount Of.** $867BB. *The Week,* March 23, 2012, citing
  E. Pianin, *The Washington Post.* But see, (i) *The Week,* May 25, 2012,
  p. 18, citing *The New York Times* ($902BB in federal student loans

and $140BB in private loans for a combined total of 1.042 Trillion); and (ii) Mitchell, J., "Federal Student Lending Swells," *The Wall Street Journal,* November 28, 2012 (Noting a $42BB increase in the 3rd Q of 2012 to an aggregate student-loan debt of $956BB).

o **Average Amount Of—Recent College Graduates.** $16,932 (2010). Mitchell, J., "New Course in College Costs," *The Wall Street Journal,* June 11, 2012, citing Progressive Policy Institute, a "left-leaning think tank in Washington." But see, *The Week,* March 23, 2012, citing E. Pianin, *The Washington Post,* that the average, recent college graduate salary exceeds $25,000.

o **College Students Who Drop Out With Student Loans.** 30% (Estimated). *Time,* June 11, 2012, p. 5.

o **Default Rate With Respect to Federal Student Loans.** The current student loan default rate is 9.1% of all federal loans with respect to the most recent two-year reporting period (i.e., those which became due after October 2009). Mitchell, J., Ensign, R., "Student-Loan Defaults Mount Again," *The Wall Street Journal,* September 29–30, 2012, citing U.S. Department of Education. Possibly more significant is that (a) the three-year default rates has risen to 13.4% and (b) the default rates vary significantly as between public schools (11%), nonprofit private schools (7.5%, the lowest), and for-profit schools (22.7%, the highest). While the current 9.1% rate is the highest rate since 1996, it is still substantially below the 10%–22.5% default rates that existed from 1988–1996. See also, Nelson, L., "Two-Year Default Rates for Student Loans Increase Again," October 1, 2012, *insidehighered.com.*

o **Delinquency Percentage Rate.** 11% of student loan balances are 90 days or more delinquent. Ensign, R., "Wealth Management—Journal Report," *The Wall Street Journal,* February 25, 2013, citing Federal Reserve Bank of New York, "Quarterly Report on Household Debt and Credit," November 2012.

o **Department of Education Projected Massive 2013 Profits From Student Loans.** Appr. $51BB—"more than the profits of companies like Exxon, Mobil, and Apple, and roughly equal to the combined net income of the four largest U.S. banks." *The Week,* May 31, 2013, p. 34, citing *HuffingtonPost.com.*

o **Percentage of College Students Who Incur Student Debt.** 94% (appr. "double the percentage who needed to borrow two decades ago." *The Week,* May 25, 2012, p.18, citing *The New York Times.*

- ○ **Percentage of Student Loans Now Made Directly by Government; Caps on Loan Amounts.** 93%. Although in facilitation of this credit, no inquiry is made into the borrower's ability to repay and there is no inquiry of the type or course of study the applicant/ borrower wishes to pursue, most student loans are so-called Stafford Loans, which (a) are extremely hard to discharge in a later bankruptcy, and (b) are capped at $57,500 for undergraduate studies. Mitchell, J., "Federal Student Lending Swells," *The Wall Street Journal*, November 28, 2012.
- ○ **Seniors Citizens—Amount of Student Loan Debt Held by Americans Over Age 60.** $36BB. *The Week*, April 13, 2012, p. 20, citing *The Washington Post*.

Early Childhood Education.
- • **Impact Upon Child's Preparedness for Kindergarten.** Other factors being equal, early childhood education programs (i.e., pre-school programs) increase the child's preparedness by 15%. Other dominant factors include whether or not (i) the mother is married, (ii) the mother has been to college, and (iii) the child is a girl. *The Economist*, September 22–28, 2012, p. 40. See also, Dalmia, S., Snell, L., *The Wall Street Journal,* March 1, 2013 (presenting challenging evidence that the pre-schools programs of Oklahoma (which since 1998 spends about $8,000 per pre-school, about the same as it does on K-12 students) and Georgia (since 1995, all 4-year-olds) have not demonstrated major social benefits for their students).
- • **Poverty—Correlation to Early Childhood Preparedness for School**. Only 48% of "children born into poor families are ready for school by the time they start kindergarten," as opposed to 75% readiness with respect to middle-class and rich families. *The Economist,* September 22–28, 2012, p. 40, citing a Brookings Institute analysis.
- • **Preschool.**
  - ○ **Attendance—Percentage of U.S. Children Who Attend**. Appr. 59% of U.S. 3-and 4-year-olds attend some sort of pre-school. *The Economist*, September 22–28, 2012, p. 40. See also, Banchero, S., *The Wall Street Journal*, March 7, 2013, citing data from National Institute for Early Education Research and referencing "75% of the nation's (4MM) 4-year-olds are enrolled in public or private preschools."
  - ○ **State-Funded Programs—Number of States With and Percentage of U.S. Children Who Attend.** In addition to the federal Headstart Program, 39 states (appr. 80%) have state-funded preschool programs,

which aggregately enroll 28% of U.S. 4-year-olds and 4% of U.S. 3-year-olds. *The Economist*, September 22–28, 2012, p. 40, citing National Institute for Early Education Research.

o **States With Highest Percentage of 4-Year-Olds in State Preschool Programs.** The three states with more than 60% of all 4-year-olds in state pre-school programs are as follows:

Florida	76.0%
Oklahoma	73.5% (Adopted one of country's first state-funded preschool programs in 1998)
Vermont	66.9%

Banchero, S., *The Wall Street Journal*, March 7, 2013. (Author's Note: Arguably, Georgia should also be added to this list.)

o **States Without State Pre-School Programs—Number and List Of.** As of March 2013 there remain ten states (seven in the West or Northern Plains regions) *without* any state preschool programs. Those states are as follows:

Idaho	North Dakota
Montana	South Dakota
Wyoming	Indiana
Utah	Mississippi
Arizona	New Hampshire

Banchero, S., *The Wall Street Journal*, March 7, 2013.

Economic Advantages of Schooling—Lifetime Earnings as Function of Educational Achievement. The lifetime earnings as a function of educational level achievements are as follows:

	Lifetime Earnings	Amount Greater Than High School Graduate
Less Than High School	$1.0MM	–$400,000
High School Graduate	$1.4MM	Not Applicable
Some College	$1.6MM	+ $200,000
Associate Degree (2-Year)	$1.8MM	+ $400,000
Bachelor's Degree (4 Years)	$2.4MM	+ $1,000,000
Master's Degree	$2.8MM	+ $1,400,000
Doctoral Degree	$3.5MM	+ $2,100,000
Professional Degree	$4.2MM	+ $2,800,000

The income earning gap between high school and a Bachelor's degree was 50% in 1975; now it is 77%. In other words, a person obtaining a Bachelor's degree can now, on average, expect to earn 77% (not 50%) more than a person who only completes high school. Ripley, A., *Time,* Special Report, October 29, 2012, p. 32.

Education Spending.

- **Combined Annual Government and Private-Household Spending on Education—U.S. Compared With China and India**. The combined government and private-household spending on education, in order, of the following three countries is as follows:

Combined Government and Private-Household Spending on Education
(Year 2010)

Ranking	Country	Total Education Spending	Per Capita Education Spending
1.	***United States***	***$980BB***	***$3,145***
2.	China	$480BB	$357
3.	India	$180BB	$145

Silverstein, M., Singhi, A., "Can Universities Stay on Top?," *The Wall Street Journal*, September 29–30, 2012, citing Boston Consulting Group BSG E4 Index and analysis.

- **State Per Student Funding of Colleges—Biggest Increases and Decreases by State.** The changes in student funding of the various states between 2006 and 2011 have varied significantly. However, the U.S. average state funding change is a 13% decrease. The states which have increased per-student funding, and the states which have most significantly decreased such funding are as follows:

State Funding Increases		State Funding Decreases	
North Dakota	+18%	South Carolina—32% (the biggest decrease)	
Wyoming	>10%	Washington	Indiana
Alaska	<10%	Idaho	Georgia
Louisiana	<10%	Nevada	Florida
Illinois	<10%	New Mexico	Massachusetts
North Carolina	<10%	Minnesota	New Jersey
West Virginia	<10%	Iowa	Delaware
		Michigan	

Ripley, A., *Time*—Special Report, October 29, 2012, p. 32.

- **Teacher Pension Liabilities—Extent of Unfunded State Liabilities—Five States With Largest Pension Liabilities**. Though appr. one-half of the states have made "recent pension changes" (e.g., longer vesting periods, increased teacher contributions), the aggregate current unfunded teacher pension funds liabilities of all states are still $325BB. The states with the largest teacher liabilities are as follows:

States With Largest Teacher Pension Liabilities

Ranking	State	Amount
1.	Illinois	$43.5BB
2.	Ohio	$40.7BB
3.	Texas	$24.1BB
4.	Pennsylvania	$19.7BB
5.	Michigan	$17.6BB

Banchero, S., *The Wall Street Journal*, December 13, 2012.

- **Teacher Salaries.**
  - ○ **Public Schools vs. Charter Schools—Average Annual Base Teachers' Salaries and Average Hours Per Week.** The respective disparities between teachers at public schools and charter schools are as follows:

Type of School	Ave. Annual Base Salary	Ave. Hours Per Week
Public	$49,800 (22% more)	38.1 hours (4% less)
Charter	$40,800	39.7 hours

Banchero, S., Porter, C., *The Wall Street Journal*, April 16, 2013.

  - ○ **U.S. National Average and By State (With Ranking by Salary Comfort Index).** The average U.S. teacher salaries range from a high of $72,700 (NY) to a low of $39,900 (South Dakota).

U.S. Teacher Salaries—By State—Salary-Adjusted Top 5 and Bottom 5

(Note: The following data is ranked and adjusted by use of a "salary comfort index," which incorporates actual salaries with other factors such as area cost-of-living indices.)

Ranking By Salary Comfort Index	State	Average Salary
	Top 5	Top 5
1.	Connecticut	$69,200
2.	Michigan	$63,900
3.	Illinois	$64,500
4.	Pennsylvania	$60,800
5.	Ohio	$56,700
—	—	—
	Bottom 5	Bottom 5
46.	Vermont	$50,100
47.	Maine	$47,200
48.	South Dakota	$39,900
49.	Arkansas	$46,500
50.	Hawaii	$55,100

National Education Association (nea.org); National Center for Education.

- **U.S. Education Spending as Percentage of GDP and as Compared With Other Countries**. The U.S. is 37th in the world in its education spending as a percentage of GDP. The U.S. spending percentage compared with other select countries is as follows:

Ranking	Country	Education Spending As % of GDP	Ranking	Country	Education Spending As % of GDP
1.	Cuba	18.7%	34.	Switzerland/Portugal	5.8%
8.	Denmark	8.5%	*37.*	*United States*	*5.7%*
12.	Sweden	7.7%	40.	France and Poland	5.6%
17.	Israel	7.5%	46.	U.K. and Mexico	5.3%
23.	Finland and Tunisia	6.4%	78.	South Korea	4.2%

United Nations Human Development Programme.

Education Technology.
- **Amount Spent on Education Technology in U.S. in 2011**. $65.7BB or about 6.7% of total U.S. education spending. Webley, K., "Reboot School," *Time,* July 9, 2012, p. 36.
- **Computers Per Student.** Ratio of one computer for every three students (up from one for every 92 students 25 years ago). Webley, K., "Reboot School," *Time*, July 9, 2012, p. 36.
- **Internet Access by U.S. Schools—Percentage of Schools With**. "Nearly 100%." Webley, K., "Reboot School," *Time*, July 9, 2012, p. 36.
- **Online Education—Digital Lectures—(Salman) Khan Academy.**
  - **Number of Lectures in Repository.** 3,250 digital lectures. Webley, K., "Reboot School," *Time*, July 9, 2012, p. 36.
  - **Number of Countries Where Used.** 234 countries and territories. Webley, K., "Reboot School," *Time,* July 9, 2012, p. 36.
  - **Videos Watched in Last Five Years.** 160MM. Webley, K., "Reboot School," *Time*, July 9, 2012, p. 36.

High School.
- **Academically Selective Public High Schools—Number in U.S.** Academically selective public high schools, which use "quantitative evidence" such as test scores as the basis for admission, were deemed elitist and fell out of favor in the 1960s. However "in the wake of the 1983 commission that declared America to be a 'nation at risk' because of the poor quality of our education system," they have slowly started to re-appear. There are now used by 165 such high schools in the U.S. (i.e., appr. 0.7% of the national 22,568 high schools). See, Riley, N., "Dazed and Gifted," *The Wall Street Journal,*

October 15, 2012, reviewing Chester E. Finn and Jessica A. Hockett's book *Exam Schools: Inside America's Most Selective Public Schools.*

• **Dropout Rates—High School—Total and by Race and Ethnicity.** The high school drop-out rates vary significantly by race and ethnicity. They are as follows: Overall High School Dropout Rate: 7.4% in 2010 (12.1% in 1990).

High School Drop-Out Rate—By Race

(In order of lowest drop-out rate to highest)

Race	Drop-Out Rate	
	2010	1990
Asian/Pacific Islander	4.2%	4.9%
Whites	5.1%	9.0%
Blacks	8.0%	13.2%
American Indian/Alaska Native	12.4%	16.4%
Hispanic	15.1%	32.4%

National Center for Education Statistics. (Status Dropout rates used). See also, Schultz, G., Hanushek, E., "Education Is the Key to a Healthy Economy," *The Wall Street Journal,* May 1, 2012 (only 57% of Hispanic students in California finished high school and only 10% obtained a college degree.)

• **High School Class 2012—Percentage With Scores Indicating "College Readiness."** 43%. (ACT college-entrance data evidenced that about 25% met the college readiness standards.) Banchero, S., "SAT Scores Fall as More Students Take Exam," *The Wall Street Journal,* September 25, 2012.

• **High School Graduates—As Percentage of U.S. Population.** 85.0%. U.S. Census Bureau.

• **High School Graduates—Percentage Who Attend Some College.** 70% as opposed to appr. 5% of high school graduates in 1960. Penn, M., "In Search of the Changing American Voter," *Time,* July 2, 2012, p. 40.

• **High School Graduation Rates.** Despite the alarmist tone of the 2012 Council of Foreign Affairs-sponsored report, the, "high school graduation rates are at the highest point in history for students of all races and income levels." Ravitch, D., "Do Our Public Schools Threaten National Security?," *The New York Review of Books,* June 7, 2012, p. 45.

Information and Facts—Remembering—Capacity For—Lessened if Accompanied by Ability to "Look It Up Later." If a person believes that they *can* "look it up later," there is a 20% chance of remembering something. If the person does *not* believe they can look something up later, the chance of remembering increases from 20% to 33%. Harper's Index, *Harper's Magazine,* October 2011, p. 15.

K-12 Schools and Education.

- **Academic Performance—Top 10 Nations and U.S. Students' Scholastic Performance Compared With Other OECD Nations—Math, Science and Reading.** The Programme for International Student Assessment (PISA) is a worldwide study that has been performed every three years by the OECD to assess the scholastic performance of 15-year-old students in math, science, and reading. The study is conducted in OECD member and certain non-member nations. The respective 2009 rankings, by subject matter, are as follows:

Academic Performance (Math, Science, and Reading)—By Country

	Mathematics			Science			Reading	
Ranking	Country	Score	Ranking	Country	Score	Ranking	Country	Score
1.	China	600	1.	China	575	1.	China	556
2.	Singapore	562	2.	Finland	554	2.	S. Korea	539
3.	Hong Kong	555	3.	Hong Kong	549	3.	Finland	536
4.	S. Korea	546	4.	Singapore	542	4.	Hong Kong	533
5.	Taiwan	543	5.	Japan	539	5.	Singapore	526
6.	Finland	541	6.	S. Korea	538	6.	Canada	524
7.	Liechtenstein	536	7.	N Zealand	521	7.	N. Zealand	521
8.	Switzerland	534	8.	Canada	529	8.	Japan	520
9.	Japan	529	9.	Estonia	528	9.	Australia	515
10.	Canada	527	10.	Australia	527	10.	Netherlands	508
28.	U.K.	492	19.	Poland	508	15.	Poland	500
29.	Hungary	490	20.	Ireland	508	16.	Iceland	500
31.	*United States*	*487*	*23.*	*United States*	*502*	*17.*	*United States*	*500*
32.	Portugal	487	24.	Norway	500	18.	Liechtenstein	499
33.	Ireland	487	25.	Czech Rep	500	19.	Sweden	499

pisa2009.acer.edu. See also, the results of the Third International Mathematics and science study (TIMSS), involving appr. one-half million students in 41 countries. In the mathematics component of this study, the weighted average score was 498 and the U.S. students (442) came in 14th place behind No. 1 France (557), Cyprus (518), Greece (513), Canada (509), and Italy (474). Similarly, in the science component, the average weighted score was again 498 and the U.S. students came in 15th (423) behind No. 1 Norway (581), Germany (522), Latvia (488), Canada (485). The results of the most recent 2011 scores are very similar, wherein the U.S. students "either placed in, or tied for, the top 13 spots on all (TIMSS) exams." Banchero, S., *The Wall Street Journal*, December 11, 2012. While the U.S. has been making "steady progress since the exams first were given in 1995, "certain other nations (like Singapore and Japan) are "outpacing that progress." *Id.*

- **Class Size.**
  - ○ **U.S. Average Class Size Compared With Other Countries**. While classes vary significantly from school district to school district in the U.S., overall the U.S. is 15th in the world in terms of average class sizes. The countries with the largest average class sizes are as follows:

Average Public Education Class Sizes

Ranking	Country	Class Size (No. of Students)	Ranking	Country	Class Size (No. of Students)
1.	Japan	35.5	9.	France	21.6
2.	Hong Kong	31.9	—		
3.	Colombia	30.5	**15.**	**United States**	**18.3**
4.	Greece	24.8	—		
5.	Thailand	23.8	26.	Switzerland	11.9

Hanushek, E. (Senior Fellow at Hoover Institution of Stanford University), Luque, J., "Efficiency and Equity in Schools Around the World," April, 2002 (Data summarized at *nationmaster.com*.)

  - ○ **U.S.—States' Class Size Disparities Between—States With Largest and Small Average Class Sizes.** Average class sizes vary radically between the different states. The states with the largest and smallest class sizes are as follows:

Average Combined Grades School

Smallest Class Sizes			Largest Class Sizes		
Ranking	State	Class Size (No. of Students)	Ranking	State	Class Size (No. of Students)
1.	Virginia	8.6	50.	Delaware	24.2
2.	Maryland	7.2	49.	Kentucky	23.3
3.	West Virginia	9.3	48.	Michigan	22.8

United States Average: 16.8 students per class

National Center for Educational Studies (2007–2009)(Average Class Size for Teachers in Departmentalized Instruction).

- **For-Profit K-12 Education—Continued Skepticism Of.** Although K-12 education remains a $600BB+ business and although surveys indicate that "more than 75% of Americans are comfortable with the for-profit provisions of transportation and facilities," only about 33% of Americans support the privatization of K-12 education to for-profit entities. In the

15 years from 1996 to 2011, the number of for-profit charter schools increased from 6 to 758 schools, providing schooling to about 400,000. However, this is still "less than 1% of the 50 million" K-12 students. Hess, F., "The Irrational Fear of For-Profit Education," *The Wall Street Journal*, December 18, 2012.

- **Homeschooling.**
  - **Growth Of—Number of Children Homeschooled.** As recently as three decades ago, homeschooling was illegal in 30 states. Now, it is permitted in every state and "is probably the fastest-growing form of education in America …. the most radical form of privatization." In 1975, there were from 10,000–15,000 children homeschooled. Now there are appr. 2MM, which is about 3.6% of all children—"or about the same number as attend charter schools." *The Economist*, December 22, 2012–January 4, 2013, p. 40, citing Murphey, J., *Home Schooling in America* (2012).
  - **Reasons For—By Parental Motivational Category.** Homeschools are "overwhelmingly Christian" and 78% of their parents attend church frequently. The main stated motivations of the parents are as follows:

Religious or Moral Instruction	36%
School Involvement	21%
Quality of Instruction Available	17%
Also: Concerns about special education, distance of travel, and "nut allergies."	

    The Economist, December 22, 2012–January 4, 2013, p. 40, citing National Household Education Survey (2007).
- **K-12 Students—Number Of.** 48MM textbook-reading schoolchildren in 2011.
- **Private K-12 Schools.**
  - **Annual Tuition—Average.** $22,000. *The Week*, April 13, 2012, p. 38, citing A. Andriotis in *SmartMoney.com*.
  - **Students Attending the New "Avenues: The World School" in New York City.** 700 students are attending Avenues at a cost of "just under $40,000 a year." This New York private school will be joined by the planned opening of the next schools in Beijing (2014), Sao Paulo (2015), London (2016), and eventually as many as 15 more venues with "identical curriculum" and with the expectation that "pupils [will] be able to move freely between them." *The Economist*, September 1–7, 2012, p. 33.

    ○ **Publicly Funded Scholarships For—States Which Allow Students to Attend Private K-12 Schools With**. 16 states, plus the District of Columbia (i.e., about 30% of states). Manno, B., "Education Reform Gets a Hollywood Boost," *The Wall Street Journal*, September 29–30, 2012.

• **Public K-12 Schools.**

    ○ **Budget Cuts—States Which Cut Public School Expenditures in 2012—Number Of.** 37 states, which is nearly three out of every four states. *The Nation*, May 14, 2012, p. 4.

    ○ **Charter Schools**

      – **Families With Children In—Number Of.** There are currently about 2MM U.S. families with children in charter schools which, as an implemented concept rooted in its "two defining characteristics (of) accountability and freedom," celebrated its 20th anniversary since the opening of the first charter school in 1992 in Minnesota. Kenny, D. "Why Charter Schools Work," *The Wall Street Journal*, June 25, 2012.

      – **States Which Limit the Expansion of Charter Schools—Number Of.** 20 states still restrict the number of charter schools, although there is currently a movement to remove such caps. Hawaii, Idaho, and Missouri eliminated the caps last year, and Massachusetts, a recognized national leader in public education, is considering doing so in 2013. Levitz, J., *The Wall Street Journal*, March 11, 2013, citing data from the Center for Education Reform.

      – **States Which Allow Parents to Send Their Children To.** 41 states, plus the District of Columbia (i.e., 82% of all states). Manno, B., "Education Reform Gets a Hollywood Boost," *The Wall Street Journal*, September 29–30, 2012.

      – **Students—Number of Students in U.S. Charter Schools.** Appr. 2.3MM in the 2012–2013 school year. Levitz, J., *The Wall Street Journal*, March 11, 2013, citing data from the National Alliance for Charter Schools.

    ○ **Common Core Standards—Adoption Of—Number of States.** 46 states and the District of Columbia.

    ○ **Corporal Punishment—Spanking and Paddling In Schools—Number of States Where Permissible—Public Support For.** Corporal punishment is allowed in 19 states, although some district have limitations, such as (a) permitting only teachers of the same gender as the student to apply corporal punishment, or (b) requiring written permission from parents prior to administration of punishments, etc. Appr. 23% of adults "support spanking by teachers," although the general support for spanking has dropped from 94% in the 1960s to 71% as of 2004. *Time,* October 15, 2012, p. 17, citing AP, R. Larzelere, Oklahoma State University.

○ **Employment in Public Education—Decline in Last Three Years (2009–2012).** 266,000. *The Economist,* May 12–18, 2012, p. 34, citing Bureau of Labor Statistics.

○ **Gender Segregation—Permissibility in U.S. Schools.** Since 2006, gender segregation has been deemed permissible as long as it is "completely voluntary." This gender segregation is being fought in numerous jurisdictions, despite the voluntary nature of the program, and the number of schools still with same-sex classrooms is estimated to be between 500–1,000. Porter, C., "Suits Challenge Classrooms That Segregate Boys, Girls," *The Wall Street Journal,* September 5, 2012.

○ **"Parent-Triggers" Laws—States Which Have Adopted or Are Considering—Number Of.** Currently exist in 6 states, and parent-trigger laws were proposed in more than 20 states last year. Manno, B., "Education Reform Gets a Hollywood Boost," *The Wall Street Journal,* September 29–30, 2012.

○ **Percentage of U.S. Children In Public K-12 Schools.** Appr. 90%.

○ **School Attendance—Chronically Absent Students—Percentage of U.S. Schoolchildren.** Estimated at 12%. "Chronically absent" is defined as regularly missing one out of every ten school days. *Time,* September 17, 2012, p. 9.

○ **School Week—U.S. School Districts With 4-Day School Week—Number Of.** 292 school districts out of appr. 13,500 public school districts in the U.S. (about 2%) *The Nation,* May 14, 2012, p. 4.

○ **School Year—Increased by 300 Hours Under Pilot Program—Number of States.** 5 States—Colorado, Connecticut, Massachusetts, New York, and Tennessee. *Time,* December 17, 2012, p. 9.

○ **Teacher Evaluations—Test Scores—States Which Have Adopted Teacher Evaluations and Student Test Scores Linkage Policies—Number Of.** 26 states as of 2012. Banchero, S., "School-Test Backlash," *The Wall Street Journal,* May 16, 2012.

○ **Teachers—Number Of and Teacher-to-Student Ratio.** Appr. 3.2MM. *The Nation,* May 14, 2012, p. 4. The number of teachers has increased substantially since 1970, but the teacher-to-student ration has, contrary to popular perception, gone down.

Year	Number of Teachers	Teacher- to-Student Ratio
1970	2.1MM	1 Teacher : 22.3 Students
2012	3.3MM	1 Teacher : 15.2 Students

See also, Greene, J., "The Imaginary Teacher Shortage," *The Wall Street Journal,* October 9, 2012 citing the U.S. Department of Education's Digest of Education Statistics.

- ○ **Vouchers—Milwaukee, Wisconsin—Number of Years of Use In.** 21 years with minimal academic variance results, since "on average the students in the voucher schools achieve the same test scores as those in regular public schools." Ravitch, D., "Do Our Public Schools Threaten National Security?" *The New York Review of Books,* June 7, 2012, p. 45.

- **Quality—Perceived Quality of Education—Private vs. Parochial vs. Home Schooling vs. Public Schools.** Americans have very different perceptions about the probable quality of education offered at varying types of schools. These perceptions are as follows:

Type of School	Percentage of American Who Believe Children Receive Excellent or Good Education At
Private School	78%
Parochial Schools	69%
Home Schooling	60%
Public Schools	37%

The Week, September 14, 2012, p. 19, citing Gallup Poll.

Public Libraries.

- **All-Digital Library—First Ever.** Bexar County (includes San Antonio) in Texas will open the "nation's first entirely digital library... where people will be able to check out books only by downloading them to their own devices or borrowing electronic readers." The initial branch will have about 10,000 titles and 150 e-readers for library users to check-out, "including 50 designed for children." Bustillo, M., *The Wall Street Journal,* February 7, 2013.

- **Digital Books and E-Readers—Prevalence of at U.S. Public Libraries.** While all-digital libraries have not yet commenced, the frequency of these items is as follows:

Category	Percentage of U.S. Public Libraries Which Offer
Some Digital Books	Over 75%
E-Readers for Patrons to Borrow	39%

Bustillo, M., *The Wall Street Journal,* February 7, 2013, citing data from American Library Association.

- **Number of in U.S.** There are "an estimated 121,169 libraries of all kinds in the U.S. today;" however this remains an estimation because there is no single annual survey which provides statistics on all kinds of libraries. The major categories are as follows:

Library Category	Number	Percent of Total
School Libraries	99,180	81.9%
Public Libraries	8,951	7.4%
(About 179 per state average)		
Special Libraries	8,014	6.6%
(Corporate, Medicine, Law, Religious)		
Academic Libraries	3,689	3.0%
Government Libraries	1,060	0.9%
Armed Forces Libraries	275	0.2%

The American Library Association at *ala.org.*

Quick Comparison of U.S. Education Data With Other Nations The following is a highly abbreviated, quick-summary comparison of the U.S. standards and achievements in education compared with other national rankings. The actual rating of the U.S. is indicated in parentheses.

U.S. In Top 10 Comparative Ratings in World

Average Years of Schools of Adults	12 years	(1st)
Literacy		
Adults at High Level	19.0%	(9th)
Adults at Low Level	49.6%	(7th)
Primary Teaching Salary	$25,700	(5th)

U.S. In 11-20 Place in World in Comparative Ratings in World

Duration of Compulsory Education	12 years	(12th)
Grade 12 Advanced Students Math	442	(15th)
Grade 12 Advanced Students Science	423	(16th)
Literacy—Mathematical	493	(18th)
Literacy—Reading	504	(15th)
Literacy—Scientific	499	(14th)
School Life Expectancy	15.2 years	(16th)

U.S. Not in Top 20th Place in World in Comparative Ratings

Education Spending as Percentage of GDP	5.7%	(39th)

Years of School—Average Number of Years—U.S. Compared With Other Countries. The average years of school varies radically from country to country. Students in the U.S. go to school the longest (12 years), as compared, for example, to students in certain African countries like Mali

and Guinea-Bissau who go to school for less than one year. The top ten
countries are as follows:

Years of School—Top 10 Countries

Ranking	Country	Ave. Years of Schooling	Ranking	Country	Ave. Years of Schooling
1.	*United States*	*12.0 years*	6.	Australia	10.9 years
2.	Norway	11.8 years	7.	Switzerland	10.5 years
3.	New Zealand	11.7 years	8.	Germany	10.2 years
4.	Canada	11.6 years	9.	Finland	10.0 years
5.	Sweden	11.4 years	10.	Poland	9.8 years

Definition: Average years of schooling is the years for formal schooling
received, on average, by adults over the age of 15. UNESCO.

CHAPTER 11

Health, Health Care,
and Health Insurance

Exemplar Facts About Current America From This Chapter
(Details and Source Citations Below)

There are an estimated 45,000 deaths per year in the U.S.
resulting from a lack of health care.

The average American adult consumes appr. 250 pounds of meat
per year (compared with 10 pounds for the average adult in India
and 100 pounds for the average adult in China).

41% of Americans described themselves as inactive, (compared with
63% of people in the United Kingdom and 34% in Canada).

Appr. 10,800,000 Americans (about 1 in 30) receive disability benefits,
and this percentage represents a 53% increase over the past decade.

California has tasked only one person at its
California Department of Justice to monitor the State's
100 Million-Entry Prescription Drug Database.

More Americans die each year from opioids (15,000) than from heroin,
cocaine, and all other illegal drugs combined.

Graduates of foreign medical schools now account for more than 25% of all practicing U.S. physicians.

As of 2009, 4.7 MM (or appr. 1 out of every 66 Americans) were receiving Social Security Income or Social Security Disability Income because of mental illness.

The United States is the only major industrialized nation without comprehensive health care that is either free or inexpensive to its entire population.

Because Medicaid pays physicians only appr. 60% of the amount which is paid by private insurers, nearly 30% of physicians nationwide no longer accept new Medicaid patients.

The United States ranks 48th worldwide in infant mortality among all nations compared with 1960 when the United States ranked 12th.

The United States ranks 50th worldwide in life expectancy with 78.5 years (11 years less than Monaco's 89.7 years and 30 years more than Chad's 48.7 years).

There are 37,000 suicide deaths in the United States each year (more than the number of Americans killed annually in vehicle accidents).

Table of Contents
Of The Data Contained in This Chapter

- Health Care Spending (Medicare and Medicaid) as Percent of Federal Spending.

Deaths per Year Associated with Lack of Health Care.

Diet, Exercise, and Fitness.
- **Diet.**
  - Calories Per Day—Required by Many Active Adults.
  - Fastest Growing Beverage Category and Fastest Growing Food Product in Popularity in America.
  - Junk Foods—Elimination or Discouragement Of—By Major Corporations.
  - Meat—Average American Consumption of Meat.
  - "Pink Slime"—Amount of Beef Filler Purchases Annually for School Lunches.
- **Exercise and Fitness.**
  - Daily Exercise.
    - Amount Done by Marilyn Monroe in the 1950s to "Stay Toned."
    - Recommended Minimum Level of Exercise Per Week.
  - Inactivity and Television Viewing—Correlation with Health and Life Expectancy.
  - Lack of Exercise, Sedentariness, and Inactivity.
    - As Cause of Death—Number of Worldwide Deaths Per Year.
    - Percentage of Americans Who Engage in "Little or No Physical Activity."
    - Percentage of Americans Who Described Themselves as "Inactive"—Compared With Other Countries.

Diseases—Direct Medical Costs Of.

Disability Benefits.
- Americans Who Receive—Number Of.
- Disability Benefit Payment Amounts as Percentage of U.S. GDP.
- Disability Denial-of-Benefit Appeals—Backlog Of.

Doctors.
- Graduates of Foreign Medical Schools as Percentage of U.S. Practicing Physicians.
- Number of New Medical Schools in U.S.
- Projected U.S. Shortage by 2015 and 2025.
- Shortage of and Number of Years Since Increase in Government Funding of Residency Training.

Drugs, Addictions, and Substance Abuse.
- **Annual Consumption of Illegal Drugs (in Dollars) by Americans.**
- **Drug Prevention and Drug-Fighting Efforts.**
    - ○ Amount Spent Annually by U.S.
    - ○ Partial Success—Percentage Drop in Columbian Cocaine Production—Last Decade.
- **Marijuana.** *(See also Medical Marijuana Below)*
    - ○ Legalization of "Personal Use" Marijuana—2 States.
    - ○ Legalization of Marijuana—Percentage of Polled Americans Who Favor.
    - ○ Usage Ever Tried and Daily Usage.
- **Prescription Drugs.**
    - ○ California's 100MM-Entry Prescription Drug Database— Number of California Department of Justice Officials Currently Monitoring.
    - ○ Deaths—Drug-Related Deaths From Prescription Painkillers—Opioids.
    - ○ Most Prescribed Drug in U.S.
    - ○ Newborns.
        - – Duration and Medical Costs Associated with Resultant Neonatal ICU Care.
        - – Number of Infants Born Addicted to Opiates (Normally Oxycontin and Vicodin).
    - ○ States With Highest Rates of Prescription-Drug Abuse and Extent of Epidemic.
- **Substance Abuse—Extent of Teenage Abuse of Alcohol, Cigarettes, Marijuana, and Prescription Drugs.**

Employer-Mandated Health Incentives and Health-Based, Employer Penalties Upon Employees.

Employer Right to Deny Employment Based Upon Prospective Employee Tobacco Use—Number of States.

Employers—Percentage of Companies Which Offer Wellness Incentives or Financial Rewards or Prizes.

End of Life.
- Hospice and Palliative Care—Normal Length of in U.S.
- Last Days—Where Spent—Nursing Homes and Hospitals—Percentage of People In.

FDA—New Drugs—Annual FDA Approval Rates and Comparison of Approval Rates With Other Countries and Regions.

Health Care Rankings—U.S. Compared With Other High-Income Nations.

Health Insurance and Health Care Delivery System.

- Affordable Care Act.
  - ○ Exempted Persons—Categories of Persons Exempted from Requirement to Obtain Insurance.
  - ○ Penalties—Annual Penalties for Failing to Obtain Health Insurance—Amount Of.
  - ○ State Health Care Exchanges—Number of States Which Have Refused to Set Them Up.
- Americans Without Health Insurance.
- Americans Who Cannot Afford Any Health Care Insurance—Number Of.
- Defensive Medicine—Impact on Health Care Spending—Correlation With Malpractice Reform.
- Innovations in Delivery of Health Care—The 10 Innovations of 2012.
- Major Industrialized Countries Without National Health Care.
- Medicaid.
  - ○ Fraud, Waste and Abuse—Extent and Amount Of.
  - ○ Number of Low-Income Uninsured Americans Who Use Medicaid.
  - ○ Physicians—Medicaid Payments to Physicians—Percentage of Physicians Who Are Not Accepting New Medicaid Patients.
- Medical Services Technology.
  - ○ iPads and Tablets—Usage of by Physicians—Percentage of Doctors.
  - ○ Limited Correlation to Controlling Overall Health-Care Costs.
- Medicare—Success Rate of Denial-of-Payment Appeals.
- Nurse Anesthetists—Expanded Role in Treatment in Chronic Pain— Number of States Currently Allowing Nurses to Write Prescriptions for Controlled Substances.
- Patient Satisfaction and Procedural Metrics As New Factors in Medicare Payments to Hospital.
- Use of Premiums—Current Average Percentage of Insurance Company Premiums That Are Applied and Paid for Medical Care.
- Waste in Health Care Delivery System—Estimated Annual Monetary Amount Thereof.

Infant Mortality—U.S. Ranking Compared with Other Countries.

Leprosy—Number of Cases Diagnosed Annually in U.S. in 2001.

Life Expectancy.

- All Population (Males and Females)—U.S. Compared With Other Countries—10 Countries With Longest Life Expectancy and 10 Countries With Shortest Life Expectancy.

- Correlation Between Individual's Life Expectancy, Income, Wealth, and Ready Access to Health Care.
- Females—White U.S. Females and All Other U.S. Females—1850–2000.
- Females in U.S.—Life Expectancies Declining or Failing to Rise in Many U.S. Counties.
- Males—White U.S. Males and All Other U.S. Males—1850–2000.
- U.S. County with Lowest Life Expectancy.
- Worldwide Average Life Expectancy—Change in Since 1900.

Medical Marijuana.
- Legalization Of—Number of States.
- Los Angeles, California—Number of Medical Marijuana Dispensaries Closed by Vote of Los Angeles City Council.
- Medicinal Usage—Reasons For—Use by Cancer Victims vs. Pain Relief.

Medical Mistakes—Extent of Problem.
- Number of Annual Deaths and Percentage of Hospitalized Patients Who Will Suffer From.
- Ranking of Preventable Medical Errors as Cause of Death in U.S.

Mental Health.
- Anxiety—Number of American Sufferers.
- Failure to Treat.
  - Decline in Available Public Psychiatric Beds.
  - Number of Persons With Severe Mental Disorders Who Are Not Being Treated.
  - Persons With Severe Mental Disorders as Percentage of Homeless and Incarcerated Populations and as Percentage of Perpetrators of Homicides.
  - Ratio of Persons with Severe Mental Disorders in Prisons vis-à-vis in Hospitals.
- Homosexuality—Year of Deletion as Form of Mental Disorder by American Psychiatric Association.
- Memory Loss—Percentage of Baby Boomers.
- Mental Health Diagnoses.
  - Approval by APA—5th Edition—Diagnostic and Statistical Manual of Mental Disorders (the "DSM").
  - Newly Recognized Disorders—Examples of Changes in 5th Edition of DSM from Prior 2000 DSM.
  - Number of Diagnoses Listed in 2000 Version of APA's DSM.

- Mental Health Services—Number of Americans Who Receive Mental-Health Services "On Any Given Day."
- Social Security—Number of Americans Receiving SSI or SSDI Due to Mental Illness.
- State Mental Hospitals—Declining Number of Patients In—Effect of Federalization of State Mental Health Programs.
- Treatment—Electroshock Therapy—Number of Patients Receiving per Year.

Nursing Homes, Assisted Care, and Other Long-Term Care Facilities—U.S. Median Cost for Private Room—Interstate Variance.

Obesity.
- Calories per Day Which Child "Would Have to Cut to Achieve Federal Goals of Reversing Obesity by 2020."
- Children—Percentage and Adolescents Who Are Obese or Have Diabetes or Prediabetes.
- Countries with World's Heaviest Population—U.S. Compared With.
- Obesity Now a Greater Worldwide Health Threat Than Poverty—For First Time.
- Percentage of All Americans Who Are Obese or Overweight—Estimated Cost of "Obesity Epidemic."
- States—Number of States with Obesity Rate of 30% or Higher—States with Fattest and Skinniest Populations.
- States With Highest and Lowest Obesity Percentages.

Right to Die and Death with Dignity Legislation.
- Number and Percentage of Assisted-Suicide Deaths in Jurisdictions With Such Laws.
- States and Other Countries—Number With Such Legislation.

School Nurses—Current Prevalence and Reduction Of.

Sleep Deprivation—Extent of Among U.S. Workers.

Smoking.
- Adult Population—Percentage of and Decline of From 1965.
- Ingredients in Cigarettes—80MM Pages of Litigation-Released Documents.
- Prohibition in Bars, Restaurants, and Workplaces—U.S. Cities With.
- States Which Restrict Cities' Ability to Impose Their Own Anti-Smoking Laws and Ordinances—Number Of.
- Teen Smoking—Percentage Of.

Suicide.
- Annual Deaths By in U.S.—Number Of.
- Percentage of Deaths by Suicide—Civilian Men—Ages 17-60.

Vaccinations—Whooping Cough Cases in U.S. in 2012—Despite Availability of Vaccination.

Data

ADHD—Percentage of School-Age Children Diagnosed With. More than 10% of all school-age children and more than 20% of all high-school-age boys. This data represents an increase of over 41% over the last decade, but the increase may be attributable, at least in part, to "doctors yielding to pressure from parents" and to the increasing popularity of ADHD drugs such as Ritalin and Adderall as "study drugs" among college and high school students "with negligible symptoms." *The Week,* April 19, 2013, p. 21, citing *The New York Times.*

Boredom Causing Increased Likelihood of Dying from Heart Disease. As the result of a burgeoning interest in the formal psychiatric study of "boredom," it has been concluded that boredom has serious health consequences and is "linked to depression, overeating, substance abuse, ... gambling—and even mortality" since at least one study shows that the "boredom-prone" are more than twice as likely to die of heart disease. Silverman, R., *The Wall Street Journal,* February 26, 2013.

Childbirths—Midwives—Use Of—Proportion of Births. Appr. one in twelve, or 8.3%, as of 2009. *Time,* July 9, 2012, p. 7.

Circumcision—Rates of Hospital Circumcision in U.S. The 2010 rate was 55%—a drop from a high of 79% in the 1970s. Some attribute this drop in the circumcision rate to the elimination of Medicaid coverage for this procedure in 18 states and to the elimination of coverage by many insurance companies. *The Week,* November 2, 2012, p. 11, citing the CDC.

Cost of and Spending for Health Care.
- **Amount of Health-Care Spending—Per Person.** Current U.S. health care spending is appr. $2.6 trillion, or $8,402 per person. *The Week,* April 16, 2012, p. 16. The average annual health care spending by persons with employer-sponsored insurance in 2011 was appr. $4,500, a 4.6% increase from 2010. *The Week,* October 5, 2012, p. 6, citing the Health Care Cost

Institute. But see, Radnofsky, L., *The Wall Street Journal*, April 9, 2013 ($6,815 per person but also noting material differences between the different states ($5,031 in Utah compared with $8,341 in New York)).

- **Cost as Percentage of GDP.** Health care spending in the U.S. represents appr. 17% of U.S. GDP. Madrick, J., "Obama & Health Care: The Straight Story," *The New York Review of Books*, June 21, 2012. See also, *The Week*, July 20, 2012, p.13 and *The Economist*, September 8–14, 2012, p. 30, both stating that U.S. health care spending is appr. 18% of U.S. GDP.
- **Health Care Spending (Medicare and Medicaid) as Percent of Federal Spending.** Appr. 25% of all federal spending in 2011 was health care spending (as compared with appr. 9.5% just 30 years ago (i.e., 1981)). Wessel, D., "Everything You Ever Wanted to Know About The Budget* * But Were Afraid to Ask," *The Wall Street Journal*, July 21–22, 2012, citing his book, *Red Ink: Inside the High-Stakes Politics of the Federal Budget* (2012).

Deaths Per Year Associated with Lack of Health Care. Estimated 45,000 deaths. Madrick, J., "Obama & Health Care: The Straight Story," *The New York Review of Books*, June 21, 2012, citing Harvard Medical School study.

Diet, Exercise and Fitness.
- **Diet.**
  - **Calories Per Day—Required by Many Active Adults.** 2,200 calories a day for a "typical diet." Naik, G., "Big Calorie Cuts Don't Equal Longer Life, Study Suggests," *The Wall Street Journal*, August 30, 2012.
  - **Fastest Growing Beverage Category and Fastest Growing Food Product in Popularity in America.** Coconut water, "[more] than energy drinks," is the world's fastest growing beverage category (Mahr, K., "The Coconut Crazy," *Time*, December 17, 2012, p. 45), and yogurt is the fastest growing food product ($7.6BB industry at end of 2011) in popularity due largely to the growing popularity of Greek yogurt. *The Week*, July 27, 2012, p. 33, citing *The Los Angeles Times*. See also, Steinmetz, K., "How Chobani Spread Greek Yogurt Across America," *Time*, June 25, 2012, p. 70.
  - **Junk Foods—Elimination or Discouragement Of—By Major Corporations.** Walmart announced that it cut the percentage of sugar in its products by 10% and has "launched a (healthy foods) labeling program." Disney is eliminating the advertising of junk foods from its children's programming and improving the food served at its amusement parks. Restaurants are increasingly offering healthier dining options and even low sodium meals. Obama, M., *The Wall Street Journal*, February 28, 2013.

○ **Meat—Average American Consumption of Meat.** 250 lbs as compared with the average adult in India (less than 10 lbs) and China (100 lbs). Gandel, S., "Want to Make More Than a Banker? Become a Farmer?," *Time*, July 11, 2011, p. 38.

○ **"Pink Slime"—Amount of Beef Filler Purchases Annually for School Lunches.** 7MM pounds of this "gelatinous, ammonia-treated mix of low-grade beef scraps and connective tissue" used as filler in 70% of all supermarket ground beef. The industry refers to this material as "lean, finely textured beef trimmings." *The Week*, March 23, 2012, quoting N. Carnbone in *Time.com* and *The Daily*. When five retailers (Kroger, Stop & Shop, SuperValu, Safeway, and Walmart) announced that they would no longer sell ground beef "with ammonia-treated scraps and connective tissue," the two-decade practice essentially stopped. However, until this announcement, such pink slime scraps and tissue had been in 70% of supermarket hamburger. In April 2012, AFA Foods, a producer of such product, filed for bankruptcy, stating that demand for its product—"the "meat filler, dubbed 'pink slime'—had been cut." *The Week*, April 13, 2012, p. 36, citing *Bloomberg.com*. In September 2012, Beef Products, Inc., a South Dakota beef producer and a former maker of this "lean, finely textured beef" sued ABC News, seeking "at least $1.2BB in damages" as the result of ABC News' allegedly wrongfully and "unfairly disparag[ing] its beef additive by labeling it 'pink slime.'" The likelihood of any recovery may be slight since there "is no precedent of successful lawsuits based on the agriculture-libel statute, and, for example, a federal jury decided in 1998 that no damages were recoverable from TV host Oprah Winfrey as a result of her 1996 show about "mad cow" disease. Tomson, B. "ABC Sued for 'Pink Slime' Defamation, *The Wall Street Journal*, September 14, 2012.

• **Exercise and Fitness.**
  ○ **Daily Exercise.**
    – **Amount Done by Marilyn Monroe in the 1950s To "Stay Toned."** Ten minutes a day, according to an article she wrote 50 years ago about her fitness regime. *The Week*, August 17, 2012, p. 10, citing *The Daily Mail* (U.K.).
    – **Recommended Minimum Level of Exercise Per Week.** "30 minutes of moderate activity, like a brisk walk, 5 times per week." *The Week*, August 3, 2012, p. 19, citing *WebMD.com*.
  ○ **Inactivity and Television Viewing—Correlation with Health and Life Expectancy.** "For every 2 hours per day spent watching television,

the risk for developing Type 2 diabetes (increases) over 20% over 8.5 years … (the risk of) heart disease (about) 15% over (10 years),…and the odds of dying prematurely (increases) …13% during a 7-year follow-up." Park, A., "CSI TV," *Time*, June 27, 2011, p. 18, citing an analysis of eight separate studies as reported in *The Journal of the American Medical Association*. This article states that Americans watch appr. five hours of television a day, but other studies and surveys suggest the lower amount of appr. 2.5 hours. *See also, Society and Culture—Entertainment—Television.*

o **Lack of Exercise, Sedentariness, and Inactivity.**
  – **As Cause of Death—Number of Worldwide Deaths per Year.** 5.3MM deaths per year worldwide. *The Week*, August 3, 2012, p. 19, citing Harvard University researchers.
  – **Percentage of Americans Who Engage in "Little or No Physical Activity."** 40%. In Greece, the "most active country in the Western world," only 15% of the population was found to similarly engage in little or no physical activity. *The Week*, August 17, 2012, p. 4. The percentage of people who are sedentary "outside of work increased by about 40% between 1965 and 2009" as is partly evidenced by the fact that on average Americans take about 5,100 steps per day—far less than the minimum 10,000 steps per day recommended by the American Heart Association. *The Week*, March 22, 2013, p. 32, citing *The Wall Street Journal*.
  – **Percentage of Americans Who Described Themselves as "Inactive"—Compared With Other Countries.** Based upon survey responses of people 15 and older. 41% of Americans described themselves as inactive (i.e., not "meeting certain exercise criteria, such as 30-minutes of modest-intensity activity 5 times a week"). A comparison of America with other selected countries is as follows:

Inactivity and Sedentariness

Country	Percentage of Population Who Described Describe Themselves as "Inactive"
United Kingdom	63%
United States	***41%***
Canada	34%
India	6%

Bialik, C., "Don't Blame Sitting—Yet—For Shorter Lives of the Sedentary," *The Wall Street Journal*, July 21–22, 2012.

Diseases—Direct Medical Costs Of. According to a new RAND study, the relative direct 2010 medical costs of the following diseases are as follows:

Dementia	$109BB
Heart Disease	$102BB
Cancer	$ 72BB

The Week, April 19, 2013, p. 18, citing *The Wall Street Journal.*

Disability Benefits.

- **Americans Who Receive—Number Of.** Appr. 10.8MM or about 3.5% (appr. 1 in 30) of all Americans. This represents about a 53% increase over the past decade. *The Week,* May 4, 2012, p. 36, citing *The Daily Mail* (U.K.) and referencing data from the Social Security Administration. See also, *The Economist,* "Briefing—America's Jobless Men," April 30–May 6, 2011, p. 75. According to this article, "(t)he fraction of prime-age men on disability benefits… has more than tripled from 1.7% in 1970 to 4.9%" in 2011.

- **Disability Benefit Payment Amounts as Percentage of U.S. GDP.** Appr. $120BB or "almost 1% of (U.S.) GDP. *The Economist,* "Briefing—America's Jobless Men," April 30–May 6, 2011, p. 75.

- **Disability Denial-of-Benefit Appeals—Backlog Of.** Appr. 771,300, as of September 2011, compared with 392,400 in 2001—an almost doubling. Paletta, D., "Disability-Benefits System Faces Review," *The Wall Street Journal*, December 15, 2011.

Doctors.

- **Graduates of Foreign Medical Schools as Percentage of U.S. Practicing Physicians.** Graduates of foreign medical schools now account for more than 25% of all practicing U.S. physicians. In addition and due to fact that U.S. medical graduates "tend to prefer more lucrative specialties," more than 50% of primary-care doctors in the U.S. are graduates of foreign medical schools. Beck, M., *The Wall Street Journal*, March 14, 2013.

- **Number of New Medical Schools in U.S.** It is reported that twelve new medical schools are opening in the U.S. which, when combined with the growth in enrollment of existing medical schools, could generate as many as 5,000 additional doctors per year by 2019—i.e., six years from now. Beck, M., *The Wall Street Journal*, March 14, 2013.

- **Projected U.S. Shortage by 2015 and 2025.** Due partly to the mandated expanded coverage of Americans under the Affordable Care Act, it is projected that there may be a shortage of as many as 62,900 by 2015 and 140,000 by 2025. Beck, M., *The Wall Street Journal*, March 14, 2013 citing data from the Association of American Medical Colleges. See also, Beck, M., *The Wall Street Journal,* February 4, 2013, discussing the growing role of PAs, physician assistants (of whom appr. 80% have master's degrees) and other health professionals in response to the growing need for more medical care professionals and the loosening of some licensing and scope of permitted work restrictions by some states).

- **Shortage of and Number of Years Since Increase in Government Funding of Residency Training.** There is currently an estimated U.S. shortage of 63,000 doctors, and it has been appr. 16 years since the government funding for residency training was last increased in 1994. *Time,* July 30, 2012, p. 26, citing Association of Medical Colleges. See also, Beck, M., *The Wall Street Journal,* March 14, 2013 (Appr. 16 years, i.e., since 1997 when under the Balanced Budget Act of 1997 caps for Medicare-funded residencies (which account for most of U.S. medical residencies) were imposed.)

Drugs, Addictions, and Substance Abuse.

- **Annual Consumption of Illegal Drugs (In Dollars) by Americans.** Appr. $65BB. Padgett, T., "Mexico's Tragedy," *Time,* July 11, 2011, p. 24, citing the White House Office of National Drug Control Policy.
- **Drug Prevention and Drug-Fighting Efforts.**
  - ○ **Amount Spent Annually By U.S.** $15BB, including money spent for these purposes overseas. Catan, T., Barrett, D., Martin, T., "Prescription for Addiction," *The Wall Street Journal,* October 6–7, 2012.
  - ○ **Partial Success—Percentage Drop in Colombian Cocaine Production—Last Decade.** 72%. "due to joint drug-fighting efforts by U.S. and Columbia." *Time,* August 13, 2012, p. 9.
- **Marijuana.**
  - ○ **Legalization of "Personal Use" Marijuana—Two States.** In November 2012, as the result of ballot initiatives, Washington and Colorado legalized the possession of up to one ounce of marijuana by persons who are at least 21 years of age. The rules and regulations relating to the production, distribution, and sales are still being developed, and they are expected to be modeled after the state's existing liquor-sales laws. In addition to sales tax, the State of Washington will impose 25% excise taxes upon the growers, processors, and retailers. Because the possession of such small amounts is already treated as a low-priority, misdemeanor citation in most of the state, it is likely that the passage of this ballot measure is largely symbolic. Millman, J., *The Wall Street Journal,* December 7, 2012. Simultaneously, Oregon voters rejected a similar such proposal.
  - ○ **Legalization of Marijuana—Percentage of Polled Americans Who Favor.** With regard to personal-use quantities, 50% favored limited legalization, according to a 2012 Gallup poll. This percentage is greatly higher than the 12% in favor when Gallup started including

this question in its polling. Bustillo, M., Millman, J., "Voters Weigh Eased Pot Laws," *The Wall Street Journal*, September 24, 2012.

o **Usage—Ever Tried and Daily Usage.** An estimated one in three Americans admit to "having tried marijuana, and 5MM (or about one in every 62 Americans) use it almost every day." *The Week*, November 30, p. 11.

• **Prescription Drugs.**

o **California's 100MM-Entry Prescription Drug Database— Number of California Department of Justice Officials Currently Monitoring.** Only one person as of April, 2012. *Time*, April 23, 2012, p. 12.

o **Deaths—Drug-Related Deaths From Prescription Painkillers— Opioids.** Appr. 15,000 Americans per year—"more than from heroin, cocaine, and all other illegal drugs combined." As of 2009, and in part due to this rising abuse of opiates, drug overdoses— surpassing traffic accidents—have become "the single largest cause of accidental deaths in America." Catan, T., Barrett, D., Martin, T., "Prescription for Addiction," *The Wall Street Journal*, October 6–7, 2012, citing the CDC. See, Catan, T., Perez, E., "A Pain-Drug Champion Has Second Thoughts," *The Wall Street Journal*, December 15–16, 2012. Citing the National Vital Statistics, opioid-related deaths are now at about one person for every 1,800 people per year, or extrapolating to city populations, more than 60 deaths in Bismarck, North Dakota, annually, and more than 2,848 deaths annually in the Atlanta metro area.

o **Most Prescribed Drug in U.S.** Vicodin—or more precisely, the generic version thereof. In 2011, "pharmacies dispensed more than $9BB in prescription opioid painkillers, more than twice the amount a decade earlier." Catan, T., Barrett, D., Martin, T., "Prescription for Addiction," *The Wall Street Journal*, October 6–7, 2012.

o **Newborns.**

– **Duration and Medical (and Medicaid) Costs Associated with Resultant Neonatal ICU Care.** The babies' stay in the hospital ICUs "can stretch for weeks … and their treatment is costly—a mean of $53,400" per child, of which 78% is paid for by Medicaid. Campo-Flores, A., *The Wall Street Journal*, December 28, 2012, citing data from *The Journal of Medical Association*.

– **Number of Infants Born Addicted to Opiates—Normally Oxycontin and Vicodin**. 13,500 infants per year (about one per hour) are born addicted to opiates, a condition formally known as neonatal abstinence syndrome. This number has tripled between 2000 and 2009 and the scourge is "reminiscent of the 'crack babies' of the 1980s and 1990s." Campo-Flores, A., *The Wall Street Journal*, December 28, 2012; *The Week*, May 18, 2012, p. 21, citing report by University of Michigan.

○ **States With Highest Rates of Prescription-Drug Abuse and Extent of Epidemic.** The ten states, by region, with the highest rates on nonmedical use of prescription drugs are as follows:

Region	No. of States In Top 10 Nationally	State
West	7	Arizona, Colorado, Idaho, New Mexico, Nevada, Oregon, Washington
Midwest	1	Indiana
Northeast	1	Delaware
South	1	Arkansas

In Colorado alone, hospital admissions due to opioids grew to 7% of all admissions, and 6.5% of Oregon residents age 12 and over (almost one in every 13 persons) abuse opioids. The article also discusses how the South, whose states previously dominated the abuse-percentage lists, has experienced considerable success in cutting its previously-rampant use of opioids by the use of various approaches such as state task and drug strike forces, legislation limiting pain clinic ownership to health-care professionals, and the use of community awareness forums. Martin, T., *The Wall Street Journal*, March 11, 2013, citing data from Substance Abuse and Mental Health Services Administration and the National Survey on Drug Use and Health.

• **Substance Abuse—Extent of Teenage Abuse of Alcohol, Cigarettes, Marijuana, and Prescription Drugs**. The extent of teenage substance abuse of the following substance categories is as follows:

Substance	Percentage of Teenage Substance Abuse
Alcohol	75%
Cigarettes	46%
Marijuana	37%
Prescription Drugs	15%
Have tried all four categories	65%

Time, July 11, 2011, p.19, citing National Center on Addiction and Substance Abuse at Columbia University.

Employer-Mandated Health Incentives and Health-Based, Employer Penalties Upon Employees. In response to continuing, growing health-care costs and the perceived inadequacy of voluntary wellness programs, employers are making health-related demands upon employees and in some instances "penalizing workers for a range of conditions" such as the following:

    Demanding that employees share health-related information with employers (body-mass index, weight, and blood-sugar levels);
    Penalties for high blood pressure;
    Imposition of higher premiums or deductibles; and
    Punishing employees "who evade health screening."

Specific examples of such employer-mandated penalties are as follows:

General Electric:	$652	Penalty for employees who self-identify themselves as smokers.
Honeywell:	$1,000	Penalty "for workers who get certain types of surgery without seeking more input."
CVS:	$600	Annual penalty for failure to report weight, body fat, and cholesterol levels to company's benefits department.
Mohawk Industries:	$100	Monthly penalty for employees who do not participate in health-risk assessment.
Michelin:	$1,000	Maximum additional amount overweight employees or employees with high blood pressure must pay.
4 in 10 Employers:		Reward or penalize employees based upon tobacco use.

Kwoh, L. *The Wall Street Journal*, April 6-7, 2013.

Employer Right to Deny Employment Based Upon Prospective Employee Tobacco Use—Number of States. 21 states now permit such hiring bans. Kwoh, L. *The Wall Street Journal*, April 6-7, 2013 citing study by National Business Group on Health.

Employers—Percentage of Companies Which Offer Wellness Incentives or Financial Rewards or Prizes. "Nearly 90%." (up from 57% in 2009). Wieczner, J., *The Wall Street Journal*, April 9, 2013.

End of Life.

- **Hospice and Palliative Care—Normal Length of in U.S.** Two days to two weeks and is viewed by some as poorly designed and as merely a form of "brink-of-death care." See, *The Economist*, March 17–23, 2012, p. 94, citing Ira Byock, Director of Palliative Medicine at Dartmouth-Hitchcock Medicine Centre and a Professor at Dartmouth Medical School.

- **Last Days—Where Spent—Nursing Homes and Hospitals—Percentage of People In**. Appr. 30% of Americans spend their last days in nursing homes, and 50% spend their last days in a hospital—often intensive care units therein. *The Economist*, March 17–23, 2012, p. 94.

FDA—New Drugs—Annual FDA Approval Rates and Comparison of Approval Rates With Other Countries and Regions. Appr. 21 new drugs (or NMEs (New Molecular Entities)) were approved per year between 2001–2010 as compared with an annual new-drug FDA application rate of appr. 30 new drug per year. In the 12-month period ending on November 3, 2011, the FDA approved 35 new drugs, which was substantially higher than the decade average. Twenty-four of the 35 new drugs (nearly 70%) were U.S.-approved prior to any other country or region, including the EU. Almost one-half (16 new drugs) were approved under "'priority review," in which the FDA has a six-month goal to complete its review for safety and effectiveness. FDA News Release, dated November 3, 2011, (*fda.gov*). See, *The Economist*, September 29–October 5, 2012. The FDA fell from "a peak of 50 [new drug approvals] in 1996 to just 15 [new drug approvals] in 2008."

Health Care Rankings—U.S. Compared With Other High-Income Nations. In an analysis of the U.S. compared with thirteen developed nations (Europe, Australia, Japan, and Canada) the finding included the following:

Disease or Measure	U.S.'s Ranking
Diabetes	U.S. higher than most compared nations
Heart Disease	U.S. higher than most compared nations
HIV/AIDS	U.S. higher than most compared nations
Infant Mortality	U.S. highest of all compared nations
Life Expectancy—Men	U.S. worst with average of 75.6 years (compared with Switzerland's highest of 79.3—i.e., an "extra" almost 4 years)
Life Expectancy—Women	U.S. second to last with average of 80.7 years (compared with Japan's highest of 86.0 years—an "extra" 5.3 years)

However, some of these measures should be qualified and may even be a poor measures of a nation's health-care system For example, the U.S. life expectancy is "artificially" low due to the U.S.'s relatively high rate of fatal car accidents and murders. Likewise, the high infant mortality rate may be a misleading measure of the quality of the U.S. health-care system because in the U.S.—much more than in some of the other compared nations— doctors "are much more aggressive ... about trying to save premature babies," and thus the international comparisons are difficult to make. Pipes, S., *The Wall Street Journal*, February 5, 2013.

Health Insurance and Health Care Delivery System.
- **Affordable Care Act.**
  - ○ **Exempted Persons—Categories of Persons Exempted from Requirement to Obtain Insurance.** There are six categories of people exempt under the Affordable Care Act from obtaining health insurance without incurring a fine. Those six categories are as follows:
    1. Member of religious group that opposes health insurance;
    2. Undocumented immigrants;
    3. Persons in prison;
    4. Member of an Indian tribe;
    5. Person earning so little that such person is not required to file an income tax return; and
    6. Person unable to find health insurance that costs less than 8% of your income.

    Pickert, K., "What the Affordable Care Act Means to You," *Time,* July 16, 2012, p. 38.
  - ○ **Penalties—Annual Penalties for Failing to Obtain Health Insurance—Amount Of.** From $95 per individual in 2014 to $695 per individual by 2016 and thereafter. Pickert, K., "What the Affordable Care Act Means to You," *Time*, July 16, 2012, p. 38.
  - ○ **State Health Care Exchanges—Number of States Which Have Refused to Set Them Up.** 27 states, which means that under the Affordable Care Act such exchanges will have to be operated by the federal government. *The Week*, June 7, 2013, p. 4.
- **Americans Without Health Insurance.** One out of six Americans—appr. 50MM Americans, or 16% of the U.S. population, currently have no health insurance. Madrick, J., "Obama & Health Care: The Straight Story," *The New York Review of Books*, June 21, 2012; *The Week*, July 20, 2012, p.13.
- **Americans Who Cannot Afford Any Health Care Insurance—Number Of.** Appr. 17MM or about 5.5% of the U.S. population. *The Week*, July 20, 2012, p. 13.
- **Defensive Medicine—Impact on Health Care Spending—Correlation With Malpractice Reform.** Based upon comparative studies of those states which have enacted malpractice reforms, there is "a mere 2%-5% reduction in health-care spending compared to states that have not" enacted such reforms. These small percentages may understate the financial consequences of defensive medicine, however, because there is also evidence that the state

enactments of malpractice reforms may have done little to change "the physicians' perceptions of the risk of being sued." Chandra, A., Jena, A., Seabury, S., *The Wall Street Journal*, February 8, 2013.

- **Innovations in Delivery of Health Care—The 10 Innovations of 2012.** Correctly noting that health care innovations are not "limited to drugs and devises," the following is a list of 10 innovations that "took root in 2012."

  1. **Improved Bedside Manner.** Doctors adapting a better bedside manner. Institutions are putting doctors, nurses, and staff through customer-service training, and hiring patient experience consultants.

  2. **Heart Attack Treatment.** Heart attacks being treated faster. EMT are performing (and transmitting results) an increasing number of electrocardiograms en route to the hospital, materially improving survival rates.

  3. **Monitoring ER Patients**. Improved monitoring of ER patients to identify at-risk patients.

  4. **Access to Doctor's Notes.** Improved access to doctors' notes of meetings and consultations through trial programs, such as Open Notes.

  5. **Improved Health Apps.** Improved health apps by changing their focus from counting calories to monitoring contagiousness and providing ready and useful information on childhood infections.

  6. **Better Colon Cancer Screening**. Improved access to alternative, less arduous colon cancer screening.

  7. **End-of-Life Planning Dialogues**. Improved and more open communication programs relating to types of end-of-life treatments the patient wants through the use of, for example, of a program known as POLST—Physician Orders for Life –Sustaining Treatment.

  8. **Minimization of At-Hospital Illnesses.** Minimizing the number of illnesses that patients contract while they are at the hospital.

  9. **Medical-Training Robots.** Increased use of "lifelike electronic robots" at medical training schools.

  10. **Hospital Quality and Safety Data**. Increased and ready online access to data about the hospitals' quality and safety.

  Landro, L., "Ten Ways Patients Get Treated Better," *The Wall Street Journal*, December 18, 2012.

- **Major Industrialized Countries Without National Health Care.** Only the U.S. All of the other major industrialized nations provide comprehensive health care that is either free or inexpensive to its entire population. To most of the world (and especially to the industrialized and advanced nations) the entire national health care coverage debate is a "'toxic debate' that is simultaneously baffling." *The Week*, April 6, 2012, p. 16 (quoting Lee-Anne Goodman, Canadian Press) and p. 18.

- **Medicaid.**
  - ○ **Fraud, Waste and Abuse—Extent and Amount Of.** Arguably because of Medicaid's "pay-as-you-go, fragmented financing system, which is split roughly 60/40 between the states and the federal government," Medicaid is a "magnet for fraud." The GAO estimates that "fraud, waste, and abuse take close to 10% of the annual program spending, [and] other experts suggest the rate is 20% or 30%. Howard, P., Sykes, R., "Medicaid Is Broken—Let the States Fix It," *The Wall Street Journal*, October 11, 2012.
  - ○ **Number of Low-Income, Uninsured Americans Who Use Medicaid.** Appr. 65.2MM people, or 20% of the U.S. population.
  - ○ **Physicians—Medicaid Payments to Physicians—Percentage of Physicians Who Are Not Accepting New Medicaid Patients.** Medicaid pays physicians only about 60% of the amount which is paid by private insurers. Partly as a consequence of this fee payment disparity, at least one study by Health Affairs found that nearly 30% of physicians nationwide are no longer accepting new Medicaid patients. Howard, P., Sykes, R., "Medicaid Is Broken—Let the States Fix It," *The Wall Street Journal*, October 11, 2012.
- **Medical Services Technology.**
  - ○ **iPads and Tablets—Usage of by Physicians—Percentage of Doctors.** Appr. 62% of physicians "are now using tablets at the point of patient care." Gottlieb, S., Kleinke, J. D., "There's a Medical App for That—Or Not," *The Wall Street Journal*, May 30, 2012.
  - ○ **Limited Correlation to Controlling Overall Health Care Costs.** "Since 2009, almost a third of health care providers [vastly different from the 62% of physicians referenced immediately hereinabove] have installed at least some form of 'health-IT' technology." However, this article purports to analyze the prudence and effectiveness of the legislative health IT mandate which was part of the 2009 stimulus legislation. This legislative mandate required the installation of such health-care IT under the threat of de facto penalties imposed by reduced Medicare and Medicaid payments However, the authors argue that while the cost of adding such health IT technology are substantial, "the savings turn out to be chimerical" based in part upon the [counterintuitive] findings of a study by McMaster University in Hamilton, Ontario, which claims that there appears to be no correlation "between health IT and overall

health costs." Soumerai, S., Koppel, R. "A Major Glitch For Digitalized Healthcare Records," *The Wall Street Journal,* September 18, 2012

- **Medicare—Success Rate of Denial-of-Payment Appeals.** In 2010, the respective appellate success rates for Part A hospitalization appeals and Part B outpatient appeals were, respectively, 40% and 53%, suggesting that the appellants have, in effect, an almost 50/50 chance of prevailing in a denial-of-payment appeals. *The Week,* November 30, 2012, p. 37, citing M. Miller, *Reuters.com* and Centers for Medicare & Medicaid Services.

- **Nurse Anesthetists—Expanded Role in Treatment in Chronic Pain— Number of States Currently Allowing Nurses to Write Prescriptions for Controlled Substances**. 24 states currently allow nurses to write such prescriptions, but many more could be allowed to do so if nurse anesthetists were permitted by the Centers for Medicare and Medicaid Services ("CMS") to be reimbursed directly "for evaluating, diagnosing, and treating patients with epidural injections or prescription painkillers." The current guidelines are unclear and as a result in "2010, only about 4,000—or 0.017%—of the nearly 2.4MM Medicare claims for commonly billed chronic pain procedures were from anesthetists, according to CMS." Martin, T., "Nurses Seek Expanded Role," *The Wall Street Journal,* October 3, 2012.

- **Patient Satisfaction and Procedural Metrics as New Factors in Medicare Payments to Hospital.** As a part of the Affordable Care Act, more than $1BB in pay-for-performance bonuses will be paid by Medicare to hospitals based upon patient satisfaction and certain procedural metrics. The new payment rate for hospitals "combines patient-satisfaction scores (30% of the pay-for-performance score) with a measure of whether hospitals follow a dozen procedural metrics for treating such things as heart ailments and pneumonia (70% of the pay-for-performance score)." In some instances, hospitals have also "tied managers" compensation to satisfaction-survey scores. Adamy, J., "U.S. Ties Hospital Payments To Making Patients Happy," *The Wall Street Journal,* October 15, 2012.

- **Use of Premiums—Current Average Percentage of Insurance Company Premiums That Are Applied And Paid for Medical Care.** Appr. 70%. Madrick, J., "Obama & Health Care: The Straight Story," *The New York Review of Books,* June 21, 2012. Effective as of 2012, the Affordable Care Act requires 80%–85% of all premiums be used for medical care.

- **Waste in Health Care Delivery System—Estimated Annual Monetary Amount Thereof.** $750BB as estimated by the Institute of Medicine attributed mainly to "unneeded care, complicated paperwork, and fraud." *Time,* September 24, 2012, p. 11.

Infant Mortality—U.S. Ranking Compared With Other Countries. The U.S. ranks 48th among all nations compared with 1960 when the U.S. ranked 12th. Madrick, J., "Obama & Health Care: The Straight Story," *The New York Review of Books,* June 21, 2012. See also, Population Reference Bureau (6.1 deaths per 1,000 live births in U.S. vs. worldwide average of 44 deaths per live birth). *prb.org.*

Leprosy—Number of Cases Diagnosed in U.S. in 2011. 173 cases, as compared with appr. 250,000 worldwide. Appr. 95% of humans are naturally immune to leprosy and even with respect to the other 5%, leprosy has been "universally curable" as a result of medical breakthroughs in the early 1980s. Nevertheless, leprosy is still greatly feared and remains, as it was once called, "the separating illness" because of society's insistence upon isolation and quarantine for those afflicted. The former leper colony on the Hawaiian island of Molokai was closed in 1969, and now the nation's largest leprosy clinic remains open in Carville, Louisiana. As of 2013 there are only six patients still residing amidst the "silence at Carville." Solnit, R., "The Separating Sickness," *Harper's Magazine,* June 2013, p. 50.

Life Expectancy.

- **All Population (Males and Females)—U.S. Compared With Other Countries—10 Countries With Longest Life Expectancy and 10 Countries With Shortest Life Expectancy.** Of the 221 ranked countries, the following countries—listed in order—are the countries with the highest and the lowest life expectancy at birth in the world. The U.S. ranks No. 50.

Life Expectancy (All Population)

Ranking	10 Countries With *Highest* Life Expectancy		Ranking	10 Countries With *Lowest* Life Expectancy	
1(Best).	Monaco	89.7 years	212.	Mozambique	52.0 years
2.	Macau	84.4 years	213.	Lesotho	51.9 years
3.	Japan	83.9 years	214.	Zimbabwe	51.8 years
4.	Singapore	83.8 years	215.	Somalia	50.8 years
5.	San Marino	83.1 years	216.	Central A. Rep.	50.5 years
6.	Andorra	82.5 years	217.	Afghanistan	49.7 years
7.	Guernsey	82.2 years	218.	Swaziland	49.4 years
8.	Hong Kong	82.1 years	219.	South Africa	49.4 years
9.	Australia	81.9 years	220.	Guinea-Bissau	49.1 years
9.	Italy	81.9 years	221.	(Worst) Chad	48.7 years

Other Selected Countries and Countries With Life Expectancies Similar to The U.S.

Ranking	Country	Life Expectancy
12.	Canada	81.5 years
14.	France	81.5 years
18.	Israel	81.1 years
28.	Germany	80.2 years
—		
45.	Bosnia and Herzegovina	79.0 years
—		
48.	Denmark	78.8 years
49.	Portugal	78.7 years
50.	*United States*	*(78.5 years)*
51.	Taiwan	78.5 years
52.	Bahrain	78.3 years
53.	Chile	78.1 years
54.	Qatar	78.1 years
55.	Cyprus	78.0 years
—		
72.	Mexico	76.7 years
96.	China	74.8 years
121.	Egypt	72.9 years
123.	Brazil	72.8 years

CIA World Factbook at *cia.gov.* using 2012 estimates. See also (i) *data.world-bank.org.;* and (ii) Ohlemacher, S., "41 Nations Top U.S. Life Expectancy," Associated Press, August 12, 2007. These sources address (a) the volatility of such life expectancy ratings, and (b) the declining life expectancy ranking of the U.S. The U.S. was rated in 2007 at 41st in life expectancy at 77.9 years, as opposed to 50th (with a life expectancy of 78.5 years) just several years later. See also, Pallarito, K., "Life Expectancy in U.S. Trails Top Nations," June 16, 2011, *Health.com*, as reported at *cnn.com (*U.S. Ranked #38 in Life Expectancy—Worse Than the Virgin Islands, Martinique, and Costa Rica.). But see, *The Economist: Pocket World in Figures, 2012* stating that the U.S. life expectancy is 79.9 years and ranked 32nd in the world.

- **Correlation Between Individual's Life Expectancy, Income, Wealth, and Ready Access to Health Care.** While lifestyle (e.g., smoking, exercise, and diet) "is probably more important" than one's income, wealth, and access to health care, studies evidence that in the U.S. in the last 40 years there has been as much as a five-year divergence in the life expectancy between the rich and the poor. *The Economist,* December 22, 2012–January 4, 2013, p. 116.

- **Females—White U.S. Females and All Other U.S. Females—1850–2000** (Approximately and Rounded to Nearest Year).

Life Expectancy—U.S. Females

Year	White Females	All Other Females	Variation in Years Between "White Females" and "All Other Females"
1850	41 years	Unknown	Unknown
1900	51 years	35 years	16 years
1950	72 years	63 Years	9 years
2000	80 years	75 Years	5 years
2011	80 years (Compared to Worldwide Life Expectancy of 72 years for Females)		

Population Reference Bureau; PRB World population Data Sheet, *prb.org*.); Department of Health and Human Services, National Center for Health Statistics, National Vital Statistics Reports, Vol. 54, No. 19, June 28, 2006.

- **Females in U.S.—Life Expectancies Declining or Failing to Rise in Many U.S. Counties.** In roughly the last 15 years, U.S. female life expectancy has "slipped or failed to rise in more than 850 counties" (i.e., appr. 27% of the 3,143 counties or county equivalents in the U.S.), compared to just 84 counties for men. The female life expectancies have declined in 82% of the counties in Oklahoma, 66% in Tennessee, and 59% in Kentucky. In Mississippi, there are five counties where the life expectancy for women is on par with nations such as Honduras, El Salvador, and Peru." Pallarito, K., "Life Expectancy in U.S. Trails Top Nations," June 16, 2011, *Health.com*.

- **Males—White U.S. Males and All Other U.S. Males—1850–2000** (Approximately and Rounded to Nearest Year).

Life Expectancy—U.S. Males

Year	White Males	All Other Males	Variation in Years Between "White Males" and "All Other Males"
1850	38 years	Unknown	Unknown
1900	48 years	33 years	15 years
1950	66 years	59 Years	7 years
2000	75 years	68 Years	7 years
2011	75 years (Compared to Worldwide Life Expectancy of 68 years for Males).		

Population Reference Bureau; PRB World Population Data Sheet, *prb.org*.); Department of Health and Human Services, National Center for Health Statistics, National Vital Statistics Reports, Vol. 54, No. 19, June 28, 2006.

- **U.S. County with Lowest Life Expectancy.** Holmes County, Mississippi. Women—73.5 years (National Average = 80 years), Men 66 years (National

Average = 75 years). Pallarito, K., "Life Expectancy in U.S. Trails Top Nations," June 16, 2011, *Health.com*. The disparities cannot be well explained by demographic factors such as income or ethnicity. In fact, "(90%) of the variation … is not related to either (income or ethnicity), and so you need to look elsewhere (e.g., smoking, obesity, etc) to understand why some counties are keeping up and why others are falling behind." Pallarito, K., "Life Expectancy in U.S. Trails Top Nations," June 16, 2011, *Health.com.*, quoting Christopher Murray, M.D., Director of the Institute for Health Metrics and Evaluation at the University of Washington.

- **Worldwide Average Life Expectancy—Change in Since 1900.** The worldwide life expectancies at birth has more than doubled since 1900.

Medical Marijuana.

- **Legalization Of—Number of States.** Since California became the first state to legalize marijuana for medicinal purposes, there are now at least 14 other states that have done so despite the fact that the distribution of medical marijuana is still the subject of federal objection, crackdowns and there are numerous governmental regulations relating to the locations of dispensaries. Scherer, M., "Hot Pot," *Time*, May 14, 2012, p. 14. See also, Bustillo, M., Millman, J., "Voters Weigh Eased Pot Laws," *The Wall Street Journal*, September 24, 2012, referencing 17 states that permit the use of marijuana for medical purposes. This article also notes Connecticut which in June 2012 became the most recent state to allow for such medical use. But see, *The Week*, November 13, 2012, p. 11 which references 18 states and appropriately notes that there are radical differences in today's marijuana since today's marijuana contains as much as ten times the amount of active ingredient THC as that of several decades ago. See also, Campoy, A., "Medical-Marijuana Vote in Arkansas to Go Ahead," *The Wall Street Journal*, September 28, 2012. With the Arkansas Supreme Court clearing the way for the ballot measure, Arkansas "could become the first state in the South to legalize marijuana use for medicinal purposes."
- **Los Angeles, California—Number of Medical Marijuana Dispensaries Closed by Vote of Los Angeles City Council**. All of the city's 762 registered dispensaries. *The Week*, August 3, 2012, p. 7.
- **Medicinal Usage—Reasons For—Use by Cancer Victims vs. Pain Relief.** According to Colorado statistics, only about 3% of the "state's 140,000 medical marijuana users are cancer sufferers." The balance of the usage is used with respect to other forms of pain relief. *The Week*, November 30, 2012, p. 11.

Medical Mistakes—Extent of Problem.

- **Number of Annual Deaths and Percentage of Hospitalized Patients Who Will Suffer From.** 98,000 annual deaths from medical errors in U.S. (Institute of Medicine 1999 report) and 25% of all hospitalized patients "are harmed by medical errors." (*New England Journal of Medicine*). If medical errors were characterized as a disease, it would be the sixth leading cause of death in the U.S.—"just behind accidents and ahead of Alzheimer's." Makary, M., "How To Stop Hospitals From Killing Us," *The Wall Street Journal*, September 22–23, 2012. (Citing sources as indicated in parenthesis above.) See also,(i) Landro, L., "Hospital Horrors," *The Wall Street Journal*, October 4, 2012, review of Dr. Marty Makary's 2012 book *Unaccountable;* and (ii) Harper's Index, *Harper's Magazine*, December 2012, p. 15, citing Joint Commission Center for Transforming Healthcare (Oakbrook Terrace, IL). At an average rate of 40 instances per week, a U.S. surgeon operates on the wrong patient or body part and an estimated 6,000 patients a year "leave U.S. operating rooms with surgical sponges, forceps, and other surgical tools mistakenly left inside of them." *The Week*, March 22, 2013, p. 18, citing *USA Today*.

- **Ranking of Preventable Medical Errors as Cause of Death in U.S.** Preventable medical errors has been ranked as the Number Three cause of death in the U.S. Harper's Index, *Harper's Magazine*, December 2012, p. 15, citing Armstrong Institute for Patient Safety and Quality, Baltimore, MD.

Mental Health.

- **Anxiety—Number of American Sufferers.** More than 40MM Americans (or appr. 13% of the U.S. population) suffer from anxiety each year. Solomita, A., "The Wound-Up Nerd Chronicle," *The Wall Street Journal*, July 14–15, 2012, citing National Institute of Mental Health. See also, *The Week*, July 20, 2012, p.20. 31% of Americans suffer from some form of anxiety disorder. Americans are "more prone to anxiety than citizens of any other nation," according to a World Health Organization study.

- **Failure to Treat.**
  - **Decline in Available Public Psychiatric Beds.** Over the past 50 years, during the course of Modern America, the available number of public psychiatric beds have decreased by 92% from 559,000 to 43,000, though the population of persons with severe mental disorders has increased substantially. Torrey, E.F., Fuller, D., "The Potential Killers We Let Loose," *The Wall Street Journal*," December 19, 2012. See also, Kopel, D., "Guns, Mental Illness and Newtown, *The Wall Street Journal*, December 18, 2012. There has been a

"deinstitutionalization of the mentally ill" and the number of state hospital beds in America per capita has "plummeted to 1950 levels, or 14.1 beds per 100,000 people."

o **Number of Persons With Severe Mental Disorders Who Are Not Being Treated.** Data is excruciatingly difficult to obtain, but it is estimated that at least 3.5MM afflicted Americans are receiving no treatment and of these roughly 10% or 350,000 persons "become societal problems because of their untreated mental illness." Torrey, E.F., Fuller, D., "The Potential Killers We Let Loose," *The Wall Street Journal*," December 19, 2012, citing the National Institute of Mental Health.

o **Persons With Severe Mental Disorders as Percentage of Homeless and Incarcerated Populations and as Percentage of Perpetrators of Homicides.** It is estimated that it may be as high as 1/3rd of the homeless population and 1/5th of the prison population. Torrey, E.F., Fuller, D., "The Potential Killers We Let Loose," *The Wall Street Journal*," December 19, 2012. See also, Torrey, E.F., *The Wall Street Journal*, February 5, 2013 (Untreated mentally ill "are responsible for 10% of all homicides, constitute 20% of jail and prison inmates, and at least 30% of the homeless.").

o **Ratio of Persons with Severe Mental Disorders in Prisons Vis-à-Vis Hospitals.** There may be as many as three times as many persons with severe mental disorders in prisons than hospitals. Torrey, E.F., Fuller, D., "The Potential Killers We Let Loose," *The Wall Street Journal*," December 19, 2012, citing a 2010 survey by the Treatment Advocacy Center.

• **Homosexuality—Year of Deletion as Form of Mental Disorder by American Psychiatric Association.** 1974, by a vote of 5854 to 3810 (60.7% to 39.3%). Cloud, J., "What Counts As Crazy?," *Time.* March 19, 2012.

• **Memory Loss—Percentage of Baby Boomers**. Citing new data from the CDC, one in eight (i.e., 12.5%) of Americans over the age of 60 have self-reported increasing instances of confusion and memory loss. While the CDC is hesitant to yet draw conclusions from this self-reporting data because it is the first time this type of self-reporting data has been collected, the data at a minimum raises concerns about a possible looming Alzheimer's disease/dementia crisis. James, S., NBC News, *vitals.nbcnews.com,* May 9, 2013.

• **Mental Health Diagnoses.**

o **Approval by APA—5th Edition—Diagnostic and Statistical Manual of Mental Disorders (the "DSM").** Although it took "13 years and 1,500 mental-health experts to complete," the 5th Edition (replaced the Year 2000/4th Edition) was approved in 2012. Cloud, J., *Time*, December 17, 2012, p. 18.

○ **Newly Recognized Disorders—Examples of Changes in 5th Edition of DSM from Prior 2000 DSM.** The 2012 fifth edition recognizes hoarding, binge-eating, and skin pickers (known as excoriation) as disorders, and it also recognizes mourning as a treatable form of depression. Although it "reclassifies autistic disorder, it doesn't really improve doctor's understanding thereof." Conversely, the new edition rejects sex addiction and parent alienation syndrome (i.e., the difficulty that children go through after their parents divorce) as psychiatric disorders. Cloud, J., *Time*, December 17, 2012, p. 18.

○ **Number of Diagnoses Listed in 2000 Version of APA's DSM.** There are 350 psychiatric disorders listed in the 2000 version of the DSM, as opposed to 22 in the origina 1917 DSM. Cloud, J., "What Counts As Crazy?," *Time*, March 19, 2012, p. 42.

• **Mental Health Services—Number of Americans Who Receive Mental-Health Services "On Any Given Day."** 4.4MM or appr. 1.5 per 100 Americans. Cloud, J., "What Counts As Crazy?," *Time*, March 19, 2012, p. 42.

• **Social Security—Number of Americans Receiving SSI or SSDI Due to Mental Illness.** As of 2009, 4.7 MM (or appr. 1 out of every 66 Americans) was receiving Social Security Income or Social Security Disability Income because of mental illness. Torrey, E.F., *The Wall Street Journal*, February 5, 2013.

• **State Mental Hospitals—Declining Number of Patients In—Effect of Federalization of State Mental Health Programs.** Since 1963, when President Kennedy proposed that the federal government would fund community mental-health centers to take the place of state mental hospitals,, the number of state mental health patients has declined by about 75%—from appr. 504,600 to 132,200 patients. Some believe that little has changed since 1981, when President Reagan changed the nature of funding to block grants to the states. Torrey, E.F., *The Wall Street Journal*, February 5, 2013.

• **Treatment—Electroshock Therapy—Number of Patients Receiving Per Year.** There are appr. 100,000 patients a year currently receiving such therapy, albeit renamed from electroshock or "Edison's medicine" to the now more scientific name of "electroconvulsive therapy." *The Week*, "The Return of Electroshock Therapy," May 18, 2012, p. 11.

Nursing Homes, Assisted Care, and Other Long-Term Care Facilities—U.S. Median Cost for Private Room—Interstate Variance. The highly varying respective costs are as follows:

Nursing Homes Cost:

Highest	Alaska—$783 per day.
National Median	***$222 per day.***
Lowest	Missouri—$137 per day.

Assisted Care Facilities Cost:

Highest	Alaska—$224 per day ($6,813 per month).
National Median	***$108 per day ($3,300 per month).***
Lowest	Georgia—$49 per day ($1,500 per month).

Klein, Joe, "The Long Goodbye," *Time,* June 11, 2012, p. 18, citing Genworth 2012 Cost of Care Survey.

Obesity.

- **Calories Per Day a Child "Would Have to Cut to Achieve Federal Goals of Reversing Obesity by 2020."** 64 calories a day, "either by eating less or exercising more." *Time,* April 23, 2012, p. 18, citing *The American Journal of Preventive Medicine.*

- **Children—Percentage and Adolescents Who Are Obese or Have Diabetes or Prediabetes.** The percentage of children who are obese, who have diabetes or prediabetes are as follows:

Disease or Condition	Percentage of U.S. Children
Obese	Appr. 33% of all children
Diabetes or prediabetes	More than 20% ("up from 9% in 2000"—or about 1 in 11 children).

Kluger, J., Dias, E., "Does God Want You To Be Thin?," *Time,* June 11, 2012, p. 40.

- **Countries with World's Heaviest Population—U.S. Compared With.** The U.S. is the heaviest nation, outpacing the 137-pound "world average by 43 lbs." The U.S. and the next highest countries are as follows:

Ranking	Country	Average Weight of Population
1.	***United States***	***180 lbs***
2.	Kuwait	174 lbs
3.	Qatar	160 lbs
4.	Croatia	168 lbs
5.	United Arab Emirates	167 lbs
6.	Egypt	163 lbs

Time, July 9, 2012, p. 11, citing the Biomed Center of people 18 years of age and older.

- **Obesity Now A Greater Worldwide Health Threat Than Poverty—For First Time.** According to the medical journal *The Lancet,* in 2010 and for the first time in history, the number of deaths attributable to excess body weight exceeded those attributable to malnutrition. *The Week*, December 28, 2012–January 4, 2013, p. 16, citing *The Times (U.K.)*.

- **Percentage of All Americans Who Are Obese or Overweight—Estimated Cost of "Obesity Epidemic."** More than 25% (i.e., more than one in four) of Americans are obese. *Time*, August 10, 2010. It is estimated that the cost of the epidemic could rise to $66BB and that as many as 50% of all Americans will be obese by 2030. *Time*, October 1, 2012, p. 5. In addition, 70% of adults and 33% of children are currently either obese or overweight. *The Week*, May 25, 2012, p. 19, citing B. Stelter in *The New York Times*. See also, *The Week*, April 20, 2012, p. 6. According to the Brazilian government, and possibly a dubious byproduct of achieving BRIC development status, nearly 49% of all Brazilians are now overweight or obese.

- **States—Number of States with An Obesity Rate of 30% or Higher—States with Fattest and Skinniest Populations.** Nine states—up from three states in 2007—have an obesity rate in excess of 30%). *Time*, August 10, 2010. "For the sixth year in a row" Mississippi was determined to have the fattest population," followed closely by Louisiana and West Virginia. Colorado was "rated as the skinniest state." *The Week*, August 24–31, 2012, p. 4.

- **States With Highest and Lowest Obesity Percentages.** The states with the highest and lowest obesity percentages are as follows:

Highest Obesity Percentages		Lowest Obesity Percentages	
1. Mississippi	34.9%	1. Colorado	20.7%
2. Louisiana	33.4%	2. Hawaii	21.8%
3. West Virginia	32.4%	3. Massachusetts	22.7%
4. Alabama	32.0%	4. New Jersey/DC	23.7%
5. Michigan	31.3%	5. California	23.8%

Radnofsky, L., *The Wall Street Journal*, April 9, 2013.

Right to Die and Death with Dignity Legislation.

- **Number and Percentage of Assisted-Suicide Deaths in Jurisdictions With Such Laws.** In Switzerland, which has had assisted-suicide legislation since 1942, such deaths account for only appr. 300 deaths per year (i.e., 0.5% of all deaths). Similarly, in Oregon, which has had such legislation for the last 14 years, such deaths account for only 0.2% of all deaths. The percentages are very similar in Belgium (less than 1%) and the Netherlands (3%), which has a "notably relaxed approach to assisted suicide and voluntary euthanasia." *The Economist*, October 20–26, 2012, p. 55.

- **States and Other Countries—Number With Such Legislation.** Two states: Oregon (enacted in 1998) and Washington (enacted in 2009). In 2012, a "virtually identical" statute was the subject of a ballot initiative in Massachusetts. In addition, New Jersey introduced legislation to decriminalize the assistance which may be offered by physicians, and the Montana Supreme Court ruled that doctors cannot be prosecuted for prescribing lethal drugs to terminally ill patients. These statutes generally refer to and under certain circumstances permit "physician-assisted dying," as opposed to euthanasia. Since euthanasia involves the act of directly injecting medication to cause death rather than merely providing medication for the patient to take if he or she chooses, it is banned throughout the U.S. In addition to Oregon and Washington, Montana, as the result of a 2009 decision of the Montana Supreme Court, also permits physician-assisted dying. Angell, M., "May Doctors Help You to Die?" *The New York Review of Books*, October 11, 2012, p. 39. In related legislation, first California (pursuant to its Natural Death Act, which was enacted in the wake of Karen Ann Quinlan's death) and other states by separate legislation provide physicians "with general legal immunity if they complied with patient's living wills" or similar instructions. In 1990, Congress mandated that hospitals which "receive federal funds" (nearly all of them) must "inform patients of their rights to prepare advance directives, to refuse treatment for any reason, and to name a proxy to act for them if they lost the capacity to make such decisions." *Id.,* p. 40. There seems to be substantial public favor for these types of assisted-dying acts. There is 70% approval, according to a 2005 Harris poll, but the passage of legislation is not assured and as recently as 2000 the state of Maine voted against its. See also *The Economist*, October 20–26, 2012, p. 18. Assisted suicide already exists in seven countries and states, and "is now being debated in New Zealand, Quebec, Australia, and Britain."

School Nurses—Current Prevalence and Reduction Of. Although most "states don't require schools to have a nurse on site every day, about 75% of U.S. schools have a nurse on-site for at least a few hours a week. Audi, T., "School Districts Cut More Nurses," *The Wall Street Journal*, May 25, 2012, citing the National Association of School Nurses. Nevertheless, as noted in this article and in response to the need for further budget cuts, school nurses "are being cut from Philadelphia (appr. 35% of its school nurse positions) and San Diego (50% in 2012)."

Sleep Deprivation—Extent of Among U.S. Workers. Nearly 1/3 of U.S. workers are sleep-deprived. It is estimated that as many as 40MM U.S. workers get less than the recommended minimum of six hours of sleep per night. *The Week*, "America's Huge Sleep Deficit," May 18, 2012, p. 21, citing a report by CDC. See also, (i) *Time*, May 14, 2012, p. 7 (referencing

30%); and (ii) *The Week*, October 5, 2012, p. 18, citing *The New York Times* ("nearly a third of working adults" are sleep deprived).

Smoking.

- **Adult Population—Percentage of and Decline of From 1965.** Currently appr. 20.6% or about one in five U.S. adults. Melnick, M., "New Cigarette Warning Labels," *Time*, July 4, 2011, p. 25. See also, Hagerty, J., *The Wall Street Journal*, December 28, 2012, citing the CDC and referencing only 19% as of 2011 and the following data.

Decline In U.S. Smoking Percentages

	1965	2001	2011
Percentage of U.S. Adults Who Smoke Cigarettes	42%	23%	19%

See also, *The Economist*, June 1-7, 2013, p. 62, noting the general worldwide decline in cigarette smoking excepting in Central and Eastern Europe and in China where "(t)he average Chinese person smoked 30% *more* in 2012 than in 1990." (Emphasis added.)

- **Ingredients in Cigarettes—80MM Pages of Litigation-Released Documents.** Over 80MM pages of previously concealed and confidential documents have been obtained during the course of the Big Tobacco trials. The documents reveal that cigarettes contained a witches brew of ingredients. While the exact formulas of the respective companies' cigarettes remain trade secrets, the companies now disclose the added chemicals on their websites. For example, Phillip Morris "lists more than 100 different additives, Reynolds lists 158, etc." Some of the ingredients are merely flavorants, but others like menthol, "are added for physiological effects," and while nicotine "per se isn't typically added … ammonia is used in abundance … to push the nicotine molecule from a 'bound' to a 'free base' state.'" Chemicals like bleaches and glues are in the paper, and other chemicals are added to "adjust the color of the ash." Despite the known health risk, global consumption now exceeds 6 trillion cigarettes per year. Proctor, R., "What's Really in Your Cigarette?," *The Wall Street Journal*, September 1-2, 2012.

- **Prohibition in Bars, Restaurants, and Workplaces—U.S. Cities With.** Following the lead of San Jose, California, in 2000, smoking in these places are now prohibited in 30 of the 50 largest U.S. cities. *The Week*, November 30, 2012, p. 16, citing *The Hill*. See also, (i) *The Week*, December 7, 2012, p. 16, citing L. Gunter, *Toronto Star* (Gunther reports that in Alberta, Canada, smoking is now banned in any car in which a minor under the age of 18 is a passenger.); and (ii) Hagerty, J., *The Wall Street Journal*, December 28, 2012. As of December, 2012, North Dakota has banned smoking in public places and more corporations, such as 3M Corporation, have banned smoking on their corporate campuses in St. Paul, Minn., and Austin, Texas. *Time*, October 29, 2012, p. 10. A smoking ban has been adopted even in Russia, the world's second largest cigarette market, where currently one in three persons smoke, See Alpert, L., Martson, J., *The Wall Street Journal*, February 26, 2013 (Noting that Russian President Putin—despite "fierce resistance" from the world's largest four largest international tobacco companies -- signed the Russian Federan's "sweeping anti-tobacco bill" which bans smoking in most public places.)

- **States Which Restrict Cities' Ability to Impose Their Own Anti-Smoking Laws and Ordinances—Number Of.** "About 12 states, such as Florida and Oklahoma." Hagerty, J., *The Wall Street Journal*, December 28, 2012, citing C. Hallett, executive director of Americans for Nonsmokers' Rights.

- **Teen Smoking—Percentage Of.** Cited as a "pediatric epidemic," appr. 20% (600,000) middle school students, and 3MM high school students smoke "regularly." Of those who begin smoking, as many as 80% will continue smoking as adults. *The Week*, March 30, 2012, p. 25, citing report issued by U.S. Surgeon General's Office.

Suicide.

- **Annual Deaths By in U.S.—Number Of.** Appr. 37,000 Americans per year, which is greater than the number of Americans killed annually in vehicle accidents. *The Week*, October 5, 2012, p.18, citing *HuffingtonPost.com*. See also, Martin, T., *The Wall Street Journal*, May 3, 2013 (Noting (a) 31% increase in suicides in the 11 years between 1999 and 2010 (to appr. 38,400 in 2010 as compared with 33,700 vehicle deaths), and (b) that suicide is now the fourth most common cause of death for adults aged 35 to 64—"behind (only) cancer, heart disease, and unintentional injury such as drowning").

- **Percentage of Deaths by Suicide—Civilian Men—Ages 17–60.** 7%, compared with 20% of deaths among military personnel. Thompson, M., Gibbs, N., "Why Can't The Army Win the War on Suicide?," *Time,* July 23, 2012, p. 22, citing data from DOD and Centers for Disease Control and Prevention.

Vaccinations—Whooping Cough Cases in U.S. in 2012—Despite Availability of Vaccination. As of August 2012, there were appr. 18,000 cases of whooping cough reported in the U.S. despite the availability of a preventative vaccination. *Time*, August 6, 2012, p. 9.

PART V

American Life, Entertainment, Religion, and Culture

CHAPTER 12

American Life, Entertainment, Religion, and Culture

Exemplar Facts About Current America From This Chapter
(Details and Source Citations Below)

The average age of the Rolling Stones is older than the average age of the justices of the United States Supreme Court.

In 2011, states enacted a record-breaking 94 new laws restricting access to abortion services.

About 29% of Americans get their coffee at home and the rest get their coffee at Starbucks (25%), McDonald's (16%), Dunkin Donuts (11%), or some other place (19%).

Charitable giving as a percentage of disposable income has remained very consistent at appr. 2% of disposable income regardless of the marginal tax rates.

Similarly, charitable giving has remained at a steady 2% (1.7% to 2.3%) of GDP.

The United States ranks 16th in the world's best places to be born—below Canada and the Scandinavian countries and slightly above Israel, Italy, and Chile.

94% of the U.S. population now has access
to high-speed Internet service.

American consumerism may be on its way back—the 2012 Restoration
Hardware catalogue weighed 5.5 pounds and had 992 pages (but the
2012 cost for the 364 gifts referenced in the Twelve Days of Christmas
rose to $107,000 (plus an additional about $15,000 for shipping).

The U.S. is the only one of the 21 highly developed countries which
does *not* require employers to offer paid vacation time.

The average expected prom cost to U.S. families is now about $1,078.

Nearly one-half of the states now allow gambling casinos.

There are only 10 states where an athletic coach
(27 football coaches, 13 basketball coaches, and one hockey coach)
is *not* the highest paid public employee.

4,300,000 Americans are members of the National Rifle Association
(about 2.1% of the U.S. adult population).

The likelihood that people will move from their birth states
by the age of 30 is largely a function of education.

4% for college graduates, 27% for high school graduates, and 17%
for those without a high school diploma

English is required for obtaining a driver's license in 9 states.

Table of Contents
Of The Data Contained in This Chapter

Abortion.
- New State Laws Restricting Access to Abortion Services—Number and Type Enacted in 2011.
- Number of Abortions, Abortion Rate and Ratio, Percentage at Under 13 Weeks Gestation and Percentage Medical Abortions.

- "Pro-Choice"—Percentage of American's Identifying Themselves as "Pro-Choice."
- Prohibited—Only State.
- Time Limits On.
  - 12-Week Arkansas Ban—Adopted 2013.
  - Permissible Refusal to Perform—States With 20-Week Bans—Number Of.
- Waiting Periods.
  - Longest and "More Common" Mandatory Waiting Period in U.S.
  - States With—Number Of.

Absurdities.

- 24-Mile Space Jump by Daredevil Felix Baumgartner.
- Air Travel—TSA—Full-Body Pat-Down of 4-Year-Old.
- Air Travel—TSA—Age At Which Passengers Subject to "Less Stringent Searching."
- Amount of Money Bequeathed by the Late Leona Helmsley to Her Dog, Trouble.
- Anyone Going by the Name "The Situation" (aka Mike Sorentino) or "The Artist Formerly Known As …."
- Auction Prices—Art, Movies, Celebrity, and Sports Items.
  - Art—Highest Amount Ever Paid for an Artwork at Auction.
  - Chewbacca Headpiece Used in Original *Star Wars* Trilogy.
  - Diamonds—Recent Auction Prices of Large Diamonds.
  - Marilyn Monroe's Dress She Wore in Famous Scene in *The Seven Year Itch.*
  - Sports—Don Larsen's New York Yankee's Perfect Game Uniform.
- Congressional Appropriations—Homeland Security Department—Underwater Robot, Hog Catcher, Fish Tank.
- Garage Sale 690 Miles Long.
- Lady Gaga—Anything About.
- Lawsuit Regarding Claimed Free Speech Right to Yell Profanities At Football Game.
- Mayan Apocalypse—December 21, 2012.
- Pet Obesity Center Opened in Massachusetts.
- Security Cameras—Police in Prince George's County, Maryland, Setting Up Security Cameras to Monitor Their Speeding Cameras.
- Sports—Tennis—Decibels of Sharapova's "Screeches and Grunts."
- Whistleblower Award of $104MM to Convicted Felon.

Books.
- Nonfiction—Best-Selling Nonfiction Books in U.S. History.
- Nonfiction—First Megaselling Personal-Organization Book.

Caffeinated Society.
- Amount of Mgs of Caffeine Dispensed by Aeroshot, an Inhalable Caffeine Dispenser.
- Where Consumers Get Their Coffee—Home, Starbucks, McDonalds.

Celebrities, Heroes, and Powerful and Influential People.
- **Celebrities—American Obsession With.**
  - Jessica Simpson's Baby.
  - Kim Kardashian's Frustration With People "Questioning Her Right to Be Famous."
  - Lady Gaga—Number of Twitter Users Who Follow.
- **Heroes—Recipients of Carnegie Hero Fund Commission— Number Of.**
- **Rich, Powerful, and Influential People.**
  - 20 Most Powerful People in the World in 2012.
  - Listings and Trackings of the American Rich, Powerful, and Influential.
  - Person of the Year—*Time* Magazine—Modern America 1957– 2012—Names and Categories.
  - Person of the Year—2012—Top 5—Time Magazine.
- **Twitter Accounts—Comparative Trackings Of—Top 25 Accounts.**
- **Trusted Celebrities—America's 50 Most.**

Charity and Philanthropy.
- 2004 South Asian Tsunami Relief from Given by Americans and Comparison of Varying World Disaster-Relief Donations as Percentage of Total Incident Damages.
- Charitable Giving as Percentage of Disposable Income and Correlation of Charitable Giving to Marginal Tax Rates.
- Charitable Giving—Comparison of Giving by Low Income vs. High Income Individuals.
- Charitable Giving in U.S. In 2011.
- Giving Pledge—92 Billionaires Commit to Giving Away One-Half of Their Wealth.
- Government Fees and Grants as Percentage of Nonprofits' Revenues.
- Massive Personal Donation.
  - Central Park Conservancy—John Paulson—$100.0 MM— Arguable Distinction Between Absolute and Relative Donations.

       º Polio Eradication—Michael Bloomberg—$100MM and Bill and Melinda Gates $1.5BB Since 2008.
- Reported "Worst 10 Charities"—Lowest Percentage of Contributions Used for Intended Beneficiary Purpose.

Civility of Discourse.
- Cost of Civil Ticket for Swearing in Middleborough, Massachusetts.
- Harsh Words—The Growing List of Harsh Words and the Coarseness of American Political and Social Debate.
- Profanity—Impact Upon Likelihood of Employee Promotion.
- "Slut" Remark—Number of Advertisers Who Withdrew Sponsorship of Rush Limbaugh.

Compassion—Willingness of Surveyed Americans to Donate a Kidney.

Condition, Perception, and Popularity of Country.
- "Best Days" for America Ahead or Behind—Perception of Americans.
- Best Place to Be Born—Worldwide—Ranking of Top 80 Best Places to Be Born in 2013.
- Inter-Generational Expectation of Children's Jobs, Salaries, and Benefits—Negative Outlook.
- Popularity of U.S. Compared with Other Countries.
- Right Track/Wrong Track Surveys.
- Satisfaction/Dissatisfaction Surveys—Perception of Condition of Country.
- Year-End (2012) Surveys about U.S. Condition–Compilation Summary Of.

Consumerism.
- Black Friday—Average Amount Spent per Shopper.
- Black Friday/Thanksgiving Holiday—Number of People Who Visited Stores or Shopped Online—Total Sales.
- Children's Toys—Average Price of Items on Toys R Us 2012 Holiday Hot Toys List.
- Holiday Spending Amounts and Percentages—Winter Holidays Compared with Other Holiday and Back-to-School Spending Periods.
- Restoration Hardware 2012 Catalogue—Size in Weight and Pages.
- "Twelve Days of Christmas"—2012 Cost for the 364 Gifts Referenced in the Song.

Curiosities and Americana.
- Abraham Lincoln—One of America's First Historical Celebrities—16,000 Books And Counting.
- Aging—Average Age of Rolling Stones Exceeds Average Age of Justices of the U.S. Supreme Court.

- Cost of a Piece of History—Selling Price for George Washington's Annotated Copy of U.S. Constitution and Bill of Rights.
- Cost of "Triple Bypass (Pastrami) Sandwich" in New York City.
- Death and Dying—Number of Burials Compared with Cremations in U.S.
- Highest Paid Public Employees by State—Dominance of Athletic Coaches.
- Major Life Changes—Frequency of in Current America.
- Tooth Fairy—Average Amount Left by per Tooth in U.S.

Dating.
- High School Proms—Average Expected Prom Cost to Family of Teenager.
- On-Line Introductions and Dating—Number of Subscribers to *FarmersOnly.com*.

Divorce and Alimony.
- Alimony—Total Alimony Received Annually in U.S.—Legislation Limiting Availability or Duration Of.
- Marital Fault as Relevant Factor in Awarding Alimony—Number of States.
- Number of Americans Currently Receiving Alimony.

Entertainment, Music and Sports.
- Burning Man Festival—Current Size of Festival and Number of Years Held.
- Cruising—Number of Annual Cruise Passengers from North America.
- Gambling Casinos—Number of States Which Allow.
- Movies.
    ○ Demographics of Selectors of Academy Awards.
    ○ Least Favorite Types of Movies.
    ○ Quintessential Leading Male and Leading Female Actors.
    ○ Types—U.S. Preference for Great Films vs. Documentaries.
- Music.
    ○ Most Spending by Population on Music—By Nation and as Percentage of GDP.
    ○ *Rolling Stone*'s 500 Greatest Album Hits—Percentage of Recorded in the 1960s and 1970s.
- Sports.
    ○ Baseball.
        – Baseball History—Oldest Pitcher in Major League History to Win a Game.
        – Ticket Prices—Escalation of. MLB Tickets.
    ○ Basketball.
        – Colleges—U.S. Minimum Graduation Rate for NCAA. Basketball Team Qualification.

- – Education—Number of University of Kentucky National Championship Starters Who Quit College to Join the NBA Draft.
- ○ Collegiate Conferences—Number of Teams in The Big Ten Conference.
- ○ Golf and Golf Courses.
  - – Americans Who Play Golf—Percentage Of.
  - – Net Number of Golf Courses Closed Since 2005.
  - – Women—Augusta National Golf Club—Number of Women Admitted To.
- ○ Hunting—Active Hunters in U.S.—Number Of.
- ○ Olympics.
  - – Actual "Gold Contained in Olympics' "Gold Medal."
  - – Medals Count—All-Time Medalist Michael Phelps—Number of Medals.
  - – Medal Count—U.S. vs. Other Major Competitor Nations.
  - – Olympic 2012 U.S. Team—Size Of.
  - – Olympic Gold Medal—More Coveted Than Pulitzer Prize, Oscar, Grammy, and Tony Awards.
  - – Popularity—2012 Loss of U.S. Productivity Due to People Watching Olympics.
  - – Viewership—Olympics and Paralympics Opening Ceremonies—Number of Worldwide Viewers of 2012 Summer Olympics and Paralympic Opening Ceremonies.
  - – Viewership—Number of U.S. Viewers of Olympics' Opening Ceremony.
  - – Women—Olympic History—Number of Times More American Women Athletes Competing Than American Men.
  - – Women—Olympic History—Track and Field—Number of Years Women Competing in Track and Field.
  - – Women—Compared With Men—Speed in Running and Swimming Events.
- ○ Paralympic Games—2012—Size and History.
- ○ Professional Sports—Ticket Costs—Average Cost Of—Major League Baseball, NBA, and NFL.
- • Theme Parks—Ticket Costs—Top New U.S. Thrills and Theme-Park Attractions.
- • YouTube—Most Watched Clip in 2012—Psy's "Gangnam Style."

Food Resources—Wasted or Thrown Out—Est. Percentage Annually in U.S.

Groups and Associations.
- Boy Scouts.
    - Homosexuality.
        - Acceptance of Openly Gay Scouts—Policy Change.
        - Years of Internal Study Until Boy Scouts Announced Decision to Retain Exclusion Policy Regarding Openly Gay Scouts and Troop Leaders.
    - Membership Size.
    - Religious Sponsorship or Association—Extent Of.
- Militia and "Patriot Groups"—Number Of.
- National Rifle Association ("NRA")—Size and Growth Of.

Guns and Second Amendment Rights.
- College Campuses—States Varying Policies Regarding Permissibility Of.
- Concealed Weapons Laws.
    - Concealed Weapons Permits Issued and Permits Issued Monthly in Florida.
    - First State to Permit Citizens to Carry Concealed Weapons In Public and Year of Enactment.
    - States Which Have Considered Law Permitting Its Residents to Carry a Concealed Weapons Without Obtaining a Permit—Number Of.
- Deaths.
    - Americans (Excluding Military Personnel) Killed In U.S. With Guns in 2009—Number Of.
    - Children—Age 14 and Under—Killed and Injured in U.S. in 2010 as a Result of Gun Accidents.
- Enforcement of Proposed Federal Gun-Control Legislation—Percentage of U.S. Sheriffs Who Have Vowed Not to Enforce.
- "Guns in Trunk"—"Safe Commute" Laws.
- Guns Ownership Rate.
    - Number of and in Civilian Circulation in U.S.
    - U.S.—Compared With Other Countries.
    - U.S.—Drop in Household Ownership Rate since 1970.
- Guns and Annual Gun Purchases—Number of in U.S.
- "Open Carry" Laws—States With—Number Of.
- Purchase Access To—Refusal Rate under Federal Background Check Law and Percentage of Guns Purchased Without Requirement of Federal Background Check.

- "Stand Your Ground" Laws.
  - First State to Enact and Year of Enactment.
  - "Justifiable Homicides" Per Year—Increase in States With "Stand Your Ground" Laws.
  - States With "Stand Your Ground" Statutes as of 2012—Number Of.

Language.
- "English as Official Language" Statutes—Number of States.
- English Required for Obtaining Driver's License—Number of States.

Memoriam—2012—A Listing In Honor of Those Who Died in 2012.

Mistakes in U.S.'s Public and Social History—Examples Of.

Mobility in American Society—Geographic and Social.
- Geographic Mobility.
  - Frequency of Change of Address.
  - Impacts of Income and Education Upon Geographic Mobility.
  - Planned Relocations As Function of Age.
  - State to State Changes of Residence—Extent of California Exodus to Other States—Number Who Have Left in Last 20 Years.
- Social Mobility—Percentage Likelihood of One's "Social Status" (Pre-) Determined by One's Birth.
- "Success" and Optimism—Percentage of Americans Who Believe Success Achievable—Compared With Russians.

Nanny State.
- Disney Nutritional Standards.
- New York City's Attempted Ban on Sale of Sugary Drinks in Containers Larger Than 16 oz. and Examples of Other Legislative Bans.
- Political Correctness—New York City's Sensitivity Guidelines.
- Posting of Calorie Counts.
- Trans Fats.
- Outdoor Smoking Ban.

Pets—Monthly Cost of New TV Channel for Dogs.

Pornography vs. News Media Websites—Respective Page Views per Month.

Quality of Life.
- Basic Conveniences.
  - Air-Conditioning—U.S. Homes and Cars—Percentage of Homes and Cars With.
  - Air-Conditioning, Dishwashers, and Microwaves—Availabilities and Disbursement Of.

- o Internet—Percentage of Americans With Access to High-Speed Internet Service.
- Food and Dining Out—Percentage of Annual Income Spent On—As Function of Income Level.
- Friendships and Confidants.
  - o Close Confidants—Number of for Average Americans.
  - o Loneliness—Percentage of U.S. Adults Over Age 45 Who Are Chronically Lonely.
- Mail Delivery—Scheduled Elimination of Saturday Postal Delivery.
- States—10 Happiest and 10 Most Miserable States.
- U.S. Happiness Compared With Other 36 OECD Nations.
- U.S. Quality of Life Compared with Other Nations—U.N. Human Development Index.

Race, Ethnicity, and Diversity.
- College Education—Affirmative Action—Extent of Receipt of Admission Preferences.
- Judiciary—Diversity of Recent Appointments.
- Largest Minority Group in America.
- Misperceptions of Blacks—As Threat to Public Safety.
- Newborn Children—Percentage Who Are Whites of European Ancestry.
- Plight of Black Families and Males—School Drop-out Rates, Incarceration Rates, Fewer Two-Parent Families.
- Religion—Southern Baptist Convention (SBC)—Number of Times SBC Has Elected a Black Leader.
- Segregation—Continuation Of—First Integrated High School Prom— Mt. Vernon, Georgia, High School.

Regional, Political, Economic, Social Perspectives and Disparities.
- Alcohol Sales.
  - o Bars Per Capita—Variance by States—Top 5 and Lowest 5 Numbers of Bars per Capita.
  - o Government-Maintained Monopoly on Sale or Distribution Of— Number of States.
  - o Sales on Sunday—Counties in Georgia and Texas Where Still Illegal.
- Washington, DC Area—Unique Demographic Differences from Rest of Country.

Religion.
- Amish Population in America—Settlements—Number Of.
- Atheists, "Nones," and "Unaffiliated."

- ° "Nones" and "Unaffiliated" Percentage of Population in U.S. Who Self-Describe Themselves As.
- ° States Where Atheists Precluded from Holding Public Office—Number Of.
- ° U.S. Congressmen As of 2012 Who Identify Themselves as Atheistic—Number Of.
- Catholic Popes—Number from the New World—Number from Jesuit Order.
- Church Contributions—Amount Of—Aggregate and Average Per Capita per Church Member.
- Heaven—Percentage of Americans Who Profess Belief In.
- Largest Churches.
  - ° By Membership—U.S. and Canada—Top 10 in Size.
  - ° Fastest 5 *Declining* (Largest Churches) Memberships.
  - ° Fastest 5 *Growing* Memberships.
  - ° Top 25 Churches—Number Currently Growing in Membership Size.
- Reincarnation—Percentage of Americans Who Believe In.
- "Religious"—Percentage of Americans Who Profess To Be.
- Scientology—Percentage of Americans Who Consider It a "True Religion."
- World Religiosity.
  - ° Percentage of World Population by Religion.
  - ° Median Age of Adherents—Major Religions.

Renting or "Sharing" Economy—10 Examples of America's Increased Use of Renting (vs. Owning).

Social Media—Facebook—Active Members—Number Of.

Vacation Homes—Average Annual Income of Vacation-Home Buyers.

Vacation Time.
- Availability of Paid Vacations—U.S. Compared With Other Countries.
- Length of U.S. Vacations—Decline of Average Length.
- Number of Weeks Most Americans "Would Want."
- Relaxation From—Extent Of.

Violence
- Personal Protections Items—Items, If Any, Carried for Protection Outside the Home.
- Relationship Between Violence in Popular Culture and Violence in Society.

Women—Number and Percentage of U.S. Public Statues of Women Compared With Men.

Data

Abortion.

- **New State Laws Restricting Access to Abortion Services—Number and Type Enacted in 2011.** 92 new laws—"3 times the prior record of 34, in 2005." They vary considerably and include allocating funds "for services designed to discourage women from having abortions" (56 states), banning of all abortions after 20 weeks, banning doctors from prescribing certain abortion-related medications (three states), and requiring abortion clinics "to meet the same building, parking, and record-keeping requirements as hospitals (one state). *The Economist,* September 8–14, 2012, p. 29. See also, new Arkansas law, entitled the "Pain Capable Unborn Child Protection Act," which shortens the time period for the allowance of abortions from 25 weeks to 20 weeks (except in cases of rape, incest, or to save a mother's life). There are now ten states (increased from the seven as reported in this February 19, 2013 citation) which have adopted the 20-week ban based, in part, upon the "hotly debated" medical research which suggests that a fetus can start feeling pain at 20 weeks. *News.msn.com* (February. 19, 2013). In addition, North Dakota in Spring 2013 adopted three new laws severely restricting access to abortion (prohibition of abortion if fetal heartbeat can be detected which can be as early as six weeks); a ban on abortions motivated by genetic defects such as Down syndrome; and new hospital guidelines which may effectively close the state's only abortion clinic).

- **Number of Abortions, Abortion Rate and Ratio, Percentage at Under 13 Weeks Gestation and Percentage Medical Abortions.** In 2009, the last year for which reliable data is available, there were appr. 784,500 legally induced abortions reported to the CDC. The "abortion rate was 15.1 abortions per 1,000 women aged 15–44, and the abortion ratio was 227 abortions per 1,000 live births." A great majority (appr. 91.7%) were performed at under 13 weeks and appr. 16.5% of all abortions were medical abortions. CDC at *cdc.gov.* See also, *The Week,* December 7, 2012, p. 18, citing *Associated Press* (noting a 5% decline in the number of abortions in 2009 from the prior year).

- **"Pro-Choice"—Percentage of Americans Identifying Themselves as "Pro-Choice."** Appr. 49% of Americans have repeatedly in 15 years of surveying declared themselves to be "pro-choice." Polling from May 2012 recorded an all-time low percentage of only 41% of Americans "who now consider themselves pro-choice." *The Week,* June 8, 2012, p. 19, citing A. McGuire, *WashingtonPost.com.*

- **Prohibited—Only State.** It is expected that Mississippi will soon become the first—and only—state which will be "abortion-free," due to a state law that became effective as of July 1, 2012, whereby doctors performing abortions in the state must have "admitting privileges at a local hospital." Since such admitting privileges can be denied for any reason and despite the fact that a legal challenge to this circumvention law is likely, it is anticipated that Mississippi's sole remaining abortion clinic in Jackson, Mississippi, the state capital, may soon close. Abortion rights activities refer to these types of law and regulations as "TRAP" (targeted regulations of abortion provider) laws. *The Economist*, September 8–14, 2012, p. 29.
- **Time Limits On.**
  - **12-Week Arkansas Ban—Adopted 2013**. Overriding the veto of the state Democrat Gov. Mike Beebe, the Arkansas legislature adopted the "Human Heartbeat Prevention Act," which may be the most restrictive abortion law in the country. It bans "most terminations after 12 weeks of pregnancy." *The Week,* March 22, 2013, p. 5. See also, Radnofsky, L., *The Wall Street Journal*, March 7, 2013, noting that while eight states now have 20-week prohibitions, Arkansas now has "the most-stringent abortion restrictions in the nation.").
  - **Permissible Refusal to Perform—States With 20-Week Bans— Number Of.** Ten states, after a federal judge upheld Arizona's new 20-week ban, reducing it from the prior 24-week period. *The Week,* August 10, 2012, p. 5.
- **Waiting Periods.**
  - **Longest and "More Common" Mandatory Waiting Period in U.S.** Utah, after its 2012 enactment of a 72-hour post-consultation waiting period. In most of the 26 states, mandatory waiting periods are 24 hours. *The Week*, March 30, 2012, p. 9 (Note: The 2011 South Dakota 72-hour waiting period was "blocked by a federal judge").
  - **States With—Number Of.** 26 states—more than half of the states. Normally, such waiting periods are 24 hours. *The Week,* March 30, 2012, p. 9.

Absurdities.

Author's Note:

It is recognized that the very concept of what may or may not be an "absurdity" is highly subjective. In many instances, it is possible that some of the things hereinbelow listed as examples of "absurdities" in American life are merely the exuberant and sometimes harmless wildnesses, passions, obsessions, extravagances, and mere quirks of others. The list is not included to dismiss or even necessarily denigrate these items. Instead, the list is included solely as an attempt to help lighten the spirits (if not the load) of our commonly-shared American life and as selective examples of the many curious, mind-challenging aspects of American life which add, for some, awe and wonder and for others, pause, shock, and in some instances even disappointment or judgmental disapproval.

- **24-Mile Space Jump by Daredevil Felix Baumgartner.** This jump from the earth's stratosphere was made by Felix Baumgartner, the Austrian daredevil who at one point traveled at 833.9 mph—fast enough to become the first person to ever individually break the sound barrier.

- **Air Travel—TSA—Full-Body Pat-Down of 4-Year-Old.** Isabella Brademeyer, a Montana girl, was subjected to full-body pat-down after she hugged her grandmother while passing through security. *The Week*, May 4, 2012, p. 6.

- **Air Travel—TSA—Age at Which Passengers Are Subject to "Less Stringent Searching."** Passengers 75 and older, pursuant to TSA announcement in March 2012. *The Week,* March 30, 2012, p.8.

- **Amount of Money the Late Leona Helmsley Bequeathed to Her Dog, Trouble.** $12MM in 2007. The dog died in June 2012.

- **Anyone Going by the Name "The Situation" (aka Mike Sorentino) or "The Artist Formerly Known As…."** "The Situation" is, well, just a situation, but this absurdity could arguably apply to anyone who, even despite his talent and brilliance, changes his name to an un-tenable and un-pronounceable love symbol and who has to sign his checks "The Artist Formerly Known as Prince" (aka Prince Rogers Nelson). Possibly there is some name-changing custom in Minnesota of which many Americans are unaware. Prince was born in Minneapolis, Minnesota, and changed his name in 1993, at the appr. age of 35. Robert Allen Zimmerman was born in Duluth, Minnesota, nearly 17 years earlier, and he too changed his name. He is now known around the world as Bob Dylan.

- **Auction Prices—Art, Movies, Celebrity, and Sports Items.**
  - ○ **Art—Highest Amount Ever Paid for an Artwork at Auction.** In May 2012, after a "dramatic 12-minute sale," a then-unidentified buyer paid $120MM for one of four versions of *The Scream*, which was painted in about 1895 by Norwegian artist Edvard Munch. Crow, K., "An Art Mystery Solved: Mogul Is 'Scream' Buyer," *The Wall Street Journal*, July 12, 2012; and *The Week*, May 18, 2012, p. 19. In July 2012, New York financier Leon Black, who already has a "750 million [art] collection" was identified as the purchaser. See also, Crow, K.,

"'Scream' Brings Record $119.9 Million," *The Wall Street Journal*, May 3, 2012 (noting that this price "surpasses the $106.5(MM) spent two years ago for Pablo Picasso's 1932 portrait of his mistress, "Nude, Green Leaves and Bust...." However, it has also been reported that as least $250MM was recently paid "(o)utside the auction houses" when "Greek shipping magnate George Embiricos sold his Paul Cezanne painting, "Card Players" to an anonymous buyer.).

○ **Chewbacca Headpiece Used in Original *Star Wars* Trilogy.** $172,000. *Time,* August 13, 2012, p. 9.

○ **Diamonds—Recent Auction Prices.** Although the auction sales prices of paintings have garnered the most focus in recent years, the auction sales of diamonds are "quietly starting to shine"—$14.2MM for 75-carat white diamond (previously sold for $4.3MM in 2001), $46.2MM for 25-carat pink diamond (highest price diamond in 2010), and $39.3MM for 300-year old "Princie" diamond in 2013. Crow, K., "Hard Assets," *The Wall Street Journal*, May 10, 2013.

○ **Marilyn Monroe's Dress She Wore in Famous Scene in *The Seven Year Itch.*** $4.6MM for the dress she wore in the famous subway grate scene. *Time,* July 4, 2011, p. 11.

○ **Sports—Don Larsen's New York Yankee's Perfect Game Uniform.** $756,000 for the uniform worn by Yankees pitcher, Don Larsen, in 1956 when he pitched the only perfect game in World Series history and shut out the then Brooklyn Dodgers. There have only been 23 perfect games in all of major league baseball history. *Foxsports.com,* December 6, 2012.

• **Congressional Appropriations—Homeland Security Department— Underwater Robot, Hog Catcher, Fish Tank.** According to a Congressional Report, the department paid $98,000 for an "underwater robot in Columbus, Ohio, $24,000 for a hog catcher in Fort Worth, Texas, and (at least at a more reasonable price of $21) a fish tank in Seguin, Texas." *The Wall Street Journal*, December 6, 2012, citing The Associated Press.

• **Garage Sale 690 Miles Long.** A bargain hunter's paradise was created "after vendors set up 'The World's Longest Garage Sale' on a 690-mile stretch of U.S. Highway 127 from Alabama to Michigan." *The Week,* August 17, 2012, p.4.

• **Lady Gaga—Anything About.** While highly entertaining and successful, anything about Stefani Germanotta's "outrageous, avant-garde persona," could be deemed absurd, and her boyfriend has "asked her to be 'more ordinary.' " *The Week,* February 10, 2012, p. 12.

- **Lawsuit Regarding Claimed Free Speech Right to Yell Profanities At Football Game**. A game-ejected football fan has filed a lawsuit against the City of San Diego for "the right to yell profanities at sporting events," claiming the NFL's prohibition on fan cursing is unconstitutional. *The Week*, February 17, 2012, p. 6.

- **Mayan Apocalypse—December 21, 2012.** Conspiracy theorists and fringe historians have been making claims about the Mayan Apocalypse since "back to the 1960s, when various New Age authors predicted December 21, 2012, would usher in a new age of cosmic peace and understanding." Interest was reinforced and "hundreds of books … and tens of thousands of websites" were launched after the publication of Maurice Cottrell and Adrian Gilbert's *The Mayan Prophecies* in 1996. *The Week*, February 10, 2012, p. 11. If this book is being read, it would appear that the world survived.

- **Pet Obesity Center Opened in Massachusetts.** For $250 the pet receives medical assistance and the pets and their owners meet with a "pet nutritionist." *The Week*, October 5, 2012, p. 6.

- **Security Cameras—Police in Prince George's County, Maryland, Setting Up Security Cameras to Monitor Their Speeding Cameras.** This occurred after six of the speeding cameras were "vandalized, burned, and shot by angry motorists." In response, the police have installed security cameras to monitor the speeding cameras. *The Week*, September 28, 2012, p. 4.

- **Sports—Tennis—Decibels of Sharapova's "Screeches and Grunts."** The "screeches and grunts" in question have been measured at 101 decibels, "or roughly the loudness of a chain saw." *The Week*, October 12, 2012, p. 12, citing *CSMonitor.com*.

- **Whistleblower Award of $104MM to Convicted Felon.** This amount was awarded to Bradley Birkenfeld, an American banker, for his disclosure to the IRS and his cooperation with the IRS and various agencies which eventually led to the uncovering of UBS's massive scheme to identify and then to assist U.S. citizens in evading U.S. taxes. The inclusion of this item as an absurdity is not primarily with reference to the possible payment of some amount to Birkenfeld under the federal whistleblower statute but with respect to the size of the award, which was determined by the use of a percentage-of-recovery calculation.

Books.

- **Nonfiction—Best-Selling Nonfiction Books in U.S. History.** The Bible (No. 1) and *The Purpose Driven Life*, by Rick Warren (No. 2) "with 32 million in print worldwide and editions published in 97 languages." Kluger, J., Dias, E., "Does God Want You To Be Thin?," *Time*, June 11, 2012, p. 40.

- **Nonfiction—First Megaselling Personal-Organization Book**. *The 7 Habits of Highly Effective People*, written by Stephen Covey. The book, published in 1989, sold more than 20MM copies and was translated into 38 languages. Miller, S., "Remembrances—Author's '7 Habits' Fueled Business-Book Boom," *The Wall Street Journal*, July 17, 2012.

Caffeinated Society.

- **Amount of Mgs of Caffeine Dispensed by Aeroshot, an Inhalable Caffeine Dispenser.** 100 mg of caffeine powder—"about as much as there is in a cup of coffee." Already on the market in New York and Massachusetts, the FDA is considering whether "inhalable caffeine is safe or tempts teens to overdose," *Time*, March 5, 2012, p. 10.
- **Where Consumers Get Their Coffee—Home, Starbucks, McDonalds.** Appr. 29% of Americans get their coffee at home, but the rest of Americans get their coffee at Starbucks (25%), McDonald's (16%), Dunkin' Donuts (11%), or some other place (19%). Saporito, B., "Starbuck's Big Mug," *Time*, June 25, 2012, p. 52.

Celebrities, Heroes, and the Rich, Powerful, and Influential People.

- **Celebrities—American Obsession With.**
  - **Jessica Simpson's Baby.** Amount of money Jessica Simpson "could make through the sale of baby pictures, mommy-related fashion products, … and other marketing ploys" after the birth of her baby girl—$14,000,000. *The Week*, May 18, 2012, p. 8.
  - **Kim Kardashian's Frustration With People "Questioning Her Right to Be Famous."** *The Week*, October 12, 2012, p. 10, citing reporting by *The Guardian* (U.K.).
  - **Lady Gaga—Number of Twitter Users Who Follow.** 20MM—"7.2 million more than President Obama." *Time*, March 19, 2012, p. 5.
- **Heroes—Recipients of Carnegie Hero Fund Commission—Number Of.** 9,539 Hero Medals (44 so far in 2012 alone have been awarded by the Pittsburgh, PA–based Commission. The Commission was founded in 1904 by Andrew Carnegie. The purpose of awarding the Carnegie Hero Medals is to recognize persons who "perform acts of heroism in civilian life in the U.S. and Canada," and "about 20% of the medals are awarded posthumously." *carnegiehero.org*.
- **Rich, Powerful, and Influential People.**
  - **20 Most Powerful People in the World in 2012.** The 20 most powerful people in the world in 2012, according to the annual *Forbes Magazine* list, are as follows:

20 Most Powerful People in 2012

Ranking	Name	Title or Position	Age
1.	Barack Obama	President, U.S.	51
2.	Angela Merkel	Chancellor, Germany	58
3.	Vladimir Putin	President, Russia	60
4.	Bill Gates	Bill & Melinda Gates Foundation	57
5.	Pope Benedict XVI	Pope, Roman Catholic Church	85
6.	Ben Bernanke	Chairman, U.S. Federal Reserve	59
7.	Abdullah bin Abdulaziz Saud	King, Saudi Arabia	88
8.	Mario Draghi	Pres., European Central Bank	65
9.	Xi Jinping	Gen. Sec'y, Communist Party of China	59
10.	David Cameron	Prime Minister, United Kingdom	46
11.	Carlos Slim Helu	Chairman, Carlos Slim Foundation	72
12.	Sonia Gandhi	Pres., Indian National Congress	66
13.	Li Keqiang	VP, People's Rep. of China	57
14.	François Hollande	President, France	58
15.	Warren Buffett	CEO, Berkshire Hathaway	82
16.	Michael Bloomberg	Mayor, New York City	70
17.	Michael T. Duke	CEO, Walmart	63
18.	Dilma Rouseff	President, Brazil	65
19.	Manmohan Singh	Prime Minister, India	80
20.	Sergey Brin/ Larry Page	Co-Founders, Google	39

Analysis and Alternative Presentation

Age: Average Age: 64

Age:	Under 40:	1	60-69:	5
	40-49:	1	70-79:	2
	50-59:	7	80 or Older:	4

Youngest: No. 10, David Cameron, PM, United Kingdom   46
Oldest: No. 7, Abdullah bin Abdulaziz Saud, King, Saudi Arabia   88

Profession

Political Leaders:	12 (60%)
Business and Economics	6 (30%)
Other:	2 (10%)

Gender: Men—17 (85%); Women—3 (15%)
U.S. Citizens: 7 (35%)
Forbes.com, December 5, 2012.

○ **Listings and Trackings of the American Rich, Powerful, and Influential.** There are innumerable (usually annual) lists of the famous, rich, powerful, influential, and elite—fewer based upon mere talent. Examples of such lists (which sometimes include summary biographical information, achievements (or recent achievements), titles and positions, and even income and wealth information) include, for example, the following:

Vanity Fair—The 2012 New Establishment and The 2012 Powers To Be

Top 5—The 2012 New Establishment:

1.	Tim Cook and Jonathan Ive	Apple
2.	Larry Page and Sergey Brin	Google
3.	Jeff Bezos	Amazon
4.	Mark Zuckerberg	Facebook
5.	Jack Dorsey	Twitter, Square

Top 5—The 2012 Powers That Be:

1.	Michael Bloomberg	NYC Mayor
2.	Brian Roberts and Steve Burke	Comcast
3.	Rupert Murdoch	News Corporation
4.	Bob Iger	Walt Disney Co.
5.	Jeffrey Bewkes	Time Warner

Vanity Fair, October 2012, pp. 159. (Industry and Media Only).

○ **Person of the Year—Time Magazine—Modern America 1957–2012—Names and Categories.** In a sense, reflecting the fact that *Time* magazine "has always viewed history through the lens of personality, it may not be surprising that *Time* has named a 'Person of the Year' for the last 85 years ever since in 1927 it titled Charles Lindbergh 'The Man of the Year.'" (Note: In 1999 it changed "Man of the Year" to "Person of the Year"). The tradition of naming a Person of the Year has continued even though, as the *Time e*ditors correctly note, it has been "conducted under an oftentimes misunderstood title and sometimes (is) at its best when it violates its own rules" as, for example, in 1950 when the magazine named "The U.S. Fighting Man," in 1966 when it named "Twenty-Five and Under," or in 1969 when it named "The Middle Americans." At all times, however, it has been successful. It is surrounded with national interest, curiosity, involvement, and—after the naming—a number of weeks filled with "scorn and praise, ridicule and rebuttal."

The Persons of the Year
Modern America (1957-2012)

1957 Nikita Khrushchev	1986 Corazon Aquino
1958 Charles de Gaulle	1987 Mikhail Gorbachev
1959 Dwight Eisenhower	1988 Endangered Earth: Plant of the Year
1960 U.S. Scientists	1989 Mikhail Gorbachev: Man of the Decade
1961 John F. Kennedy	1990 George H.W. Bush
1962 Pope John XXIII	1991 Ted Turner
1963 Martin Luther King, Jr.	1992 Bill Clinton
1964 Lyndon Johnson	1993 The Peacemakers
1965 William Westmoreland	1994 Pope John Paul II
1966 Twenty-five and Under	1995 Newt Gingrich
1967 Lyndon Johnson	1996 Dr. David Ho
1968 William Anders, Frank Borman, and James Lovell	1997 Andy Grove
	1998 Bill Clinton & Kenneth Starr
1969 The Middle Americans	1999 Jeff Bezos
1970 Willy Brandt	2000 George W. Bush
1971 Richard Nixon	2001 Rudolph Giuliani
1972 Richard Nixon & Henry Kissinger	2002 The Whistleblowers
1973 John J. Sirica	2003 The American Soldier
1974 King Faisal	2004 George W. Bush
1975 U.S. Woman	2005 Bill Gates, Melinda Gates & Bono
1976 Jimmy Carter	2006 You
1977 Anwar Sadat	2007 Vladimir Putin
1978 Deng Xiaoping	2008 Barack Obama
1979 Ayatollah Khomeini	2009 Ben Bernanke
1980 Ronald Reagan	2010 Mark Zuckerberg
1981 Lech Walesa	2011 The Protester ("No one could have known that when a Tunisian fruit vendor set himself on himself on fire in a public square would incite protests that would topple dictators and start a wave of global dissent. In 2011, protestors didn't just voice their complaints; they changed the world."
1982 The Personal Computer: Machine of the Year	
1983 Ronald Reagan & Yuri Andropov	
1984 Peter Ueberroth	
1985 Deng Xiaoping	2012 Barack Obama

Time, Person of the Year: 75th Anniversary Celebration, 2002, and *time.com.* The six categories of such "persons of the year" have been (1) U.S. political and military leaders, (2) international leaders, (3) business and technology, (4) science and medicine, (5) religion and philanthropy, and (6) concepts (e.g., 1950, GI Joe; 1966, Young People; and 1982, The Computer).

○ **Person of the Year—2012—Top 5—Time Magazine.** While Barack Obama was named Person of the Year the following are the next four (4) runner-ups:

No. 2   Malala Yousafzai   Young, 17-year-old Pakistani schoolgirl, who became a honored world symbol in the struggle for women's rights after she was nearly killed by the Taliban.

No. 3   Tim Cook   The technologist who inherited the management of Apple Computer upon the passing of Steve Jobs.

No. 4   Mohamed Morsi   Egypt's new president, who has won both praise and severe criticism for his post-Mubarak leadership of Egypt.

No. 5   Fabiola Gianotti   One of the scientists at the European Organization for Nuclear Research (more commonly known as CERN) who discovered the tiny Higgs Boson—the "elusive particle that physicists had been seeking for the better part of a century."

Time, December 31, 2012, p. 96.

• **Twitter Accounts—Comparative Trackings Of—Top 15 Accounts.** All popularity contents are subjective and volatile, and the tracking of the number of persons following one's Twitter account is, at best, a crude measure of the public's curiosity, interest, or obsession. As of March 2013, the following is a list of the top 15 Twitter accounts by volume of followers.

Ranking Number	Name	Category	Number of Twitter Accounts
1.	Justin Bieber	Entertainment	35.9 MM
2.	Lady Gaga	Entertainment	35.0 MM
3.	Katy Perry	Entertainment	33.5 MM
4.	Rihanna	Entertainment	28.7 MM
5.	Barack Obama	Politics	28.3 MM
6.	Taylor Swift	Entertainment	24.9 MM

7.	Britney Spears	Entertainment	24.6 MM
8.	Shakira	Entertainment	20.0 MM
9.	Kim Kardashian	Celebritiness	17.5 MM
	(No 34 Paris Hilton—10MM)		
10.	Ellen DeGeneres	Entertainment/TV Talk Show	17.5 MM
11.	Justin Timberlake	Entertainment	17.3 MM
12.	Oprah Winfrey	Entertainment/TV Talk Show	17.2 MM
13.	Cristiano Tonasldo	Sports—Soccer Player	16.7 MM
14.	Nicki Minaj	Entertainment	16.0 MM
15.	Bruno Mars	Entertainment	15.7 MM
—			
28.	Snoop Dogg	Entertainment	10.5 MM
32.	Bill Gates	Business/Philanthropy	10.2 MM

MSN Entertainment News—Most Twitter Accounts, *msn.com*, March 21, 2013.

- **Trusted Celebrities—America's 50 Most.**

Ranking Name/Profession	Ranking Name/Profession
1. Tom Hanks, actor	26. Travis Stork, MD, Co -host
2. Sandra Bullock, actor	The Doctors
3. Denzel Washington, actor	27. Peyton Manning, NFL Football QB
4. Meryl Streep, actor	28. Judith Sheindlin, Judge Judy
5. Maya Angelou, poet	29. Brian Williams, Host, NBC
6. Steven Spielberg, director	Nightly News
7. Bill Gates, Microsoft founder	30. Nancy Snyderman, MD, TV
8. Alex Trebeck, Host, Jeopardy!	Correspondent, Today
9. Melinda Gates, Co-Chair,	31. Rachael Ray, R Ray Show
Bill & Melinda Gates Fnd	
10. Julia Roberts, actor	32. Colin Powell, Former Sec'y of State.
11. Robert Lefkowitz, Nobel-prize-	33. Nancy Brinker, founder, Susan G.
winning chemist	Komen for the Cure of breast Cancer
12. Robin Roberts, Host, Good	34. Barbara Walters, Co-Host, The View
Morning, America	
13. Clint Eastwood, actor/director	35. Johnny Depp, actor
14. Brian Kobilka, MD, Nobel	36. Ruth Bader Ginsberg, USSC Justice
prize-winning chemist	
15. Lloyd Shapely, Nobel prize-	37. Katie Couric, TV Host
winning chemist	
16. Mehmet Oz, The Dr. Oz Show	38. Alvin Roth, Nobel Prize-winning
	economist
17. Sanjay Gupta, MD, TV host	39. Joe Brown, Host, Judge Joe Brown

18. Ellen DeGeneres, comedienne
19. Michelle Obama, First Lady
20. Noam Chomsky , Linguistics Professor, MIT
21. Tony Dungy, football coach
22. Regina Benjamin, MD, U.S. Surgeon General
23. Madeleine Albright, former U.S. Secretary of State
24. Jimmy Carter, former U.S. President
25. Diane Sawyer, anchor, ABC World News

40. Tim Tebow, NFL Football QB
41. Muhammad Ali, former world champion boxer
42. George Lucas, Director
43. Stephen Breyer, USSC Justice
44. John Roberts, USSC Chief Justice
45. Ben Affleck, Director
46. Whoopi Goldberg, Co-host, The View
47. Richard Besser, MD, Correspondent Good Morning America
48. Rabbi Arthur Schneier, Recipient, Presidential Citizens Medal
49. Anthony Kennedy, USSC Justice
50. Anderson Cooper, Host, CNN

Even a brief analysis of the Top 100 Most Trusted Americans is revealing. This type of sampling poll is partly, if not largely, a name-recognition poll. However, in light of the commonly suggested disdain for the objectivity and reliability of the American media, a surprisingly high number of 26 journalists and news reporters are listed as the "most trusted" Americans. It is almost reassuring that all nine of the USSC Justices made the list (from No. 36 Ruth Bader Ginsberg to No. 88 Clarence Thomas), but there were no Members of Congress (from either the House of Representatives or the Senate). Only seven politicians and diplomats are listed (Michelle Obama (No. 19); Madeleine Albright (No. 23); former President Jimmy Carter (No. 24); Colin Powell (No. 32); Hillary Clinton (No. 51); Barack Obama (No. 65); and Condoleezza Rice (No. 68)). The following categorizations are tenuous at best since it is extremely difficult to characterize some of these individuals. For example, Colin Powell has been included in the category of "Political and Diplomacy," however the category of "Military" may be more accurate and preferred. Similarly, nearly all of the physicians are included on this list due to their TV show and not their medical practice. However, even accepting the difficulties attendant to such assignments, such analysis is revealing and shows as follows:

Profession

Television and Journalism	26
Actors/Directors/Film Industry	19

Medical (Incl. Physicians with Medical-Based TV Shows)	11
Business and Philanthropy	9
Justices of USSC	9
Political and Diplomacy	7
Sports	6
Academic and Professors	5
Economists and Science	4
Religious Leaders	2
Education	1
Military	1
Poet/Writer	1

Gender:

Male	65
Female	35

Race:

White	81
Black	18
Hispanic/Latino	1

Reader's Digest, 2013.

Charity and Philanthropy.

• **2004 South Asian Tsunami Relief Given by Americans and Comparison of Varying World Disaster-Relief Donations as Percentage of Total Incident Damages.** To assist in relief efforts after the 2004 South Asian tsunami, Americans donated $1.9BB with a median contribution of $50. Clinton, B., "The Case for Optimism," *Time,* October 1, 2012, p. 38, however, world charitable donations and reactions to various disasters vary radically, as shown below:

Disaster	Total Damage	Total World Donations	Total World Donations As Percentage of Total Damage
(Presented in Descending Order of Percentage of Needed Assistance)			
2004 Asian Tsunami	$15BB	$6,800MM	45.4%
2010 Haiti Earthquake	$14BB	$4,600MM	32.9%
2010 Pakistan Floods	$10BB	$2,800MM	28.0%
2005 Hurricane Katrina	$81BB	$3,400MM	4.2%
2011 Japan Earthquake And Tsunami	$235BB	$704MM	0.3%
1995 Kobe Japan Earthquake	$100BB	$14MM	0.1%
2010 Chile Earthquake	$30BB	$74MM	Negligible

Sanburn, J., "Donations to Japan Are Lagging Behind ...," *Time,* April 11, 2011, p. 17.

- **Charitable Giving as Percentage of Disposable Income and Correlation of Charitable Giving to Marginal Tax Rates.** The charitable giving percentage since 1971 has remained highly consistent at appr. 2% of disposable income, regardless of the marginal tax rates, which during that period have varied from a low of 28% in 1989 to a high of 70% in 1974. Similarly, the charitable giving has remained at a steady 2% (1.7% to 2.3%) as a percentage of GDP. Dennis, K., *The Wall Street Journal,* December 19, 2012, citing data from Giving USA.
- **Charitable Giving—Comparison of Giving by Low Income vs. High Income Individuals.** As of 2011, the lowest 20% of Americans donated appr. 3.2% of their income to charity as compared with 1.3% (appr. 60% less) of high income individuals. *The Week,* April 5, 2013, p. 16, citing *TheAtlantic.com.* This data is consistent with the Harper Index's reporting that Americans with annual incomes over $200,000 donated appr. 4.2% of their income while Americans with annual income between $50,000 and $100,000 gave a higher percentage—appr. 6%. Harper's Index, *Harper's Magazine,* June 2013, p. 15, citing Chronicle of Philanthropy, a Washington, DC,–based bi-weekly magazine that reports on matters of interest in and to nonprofit organizations and their leaders.
- **Charitable Giving in U.S. in 2011.** The total estimated charitable giving in the U.S. increased by 4% over 2010 to $298BB (Fowler, G., "More Billionaires Vow to Give Money Away," *The Wall Street Journal,* September 19, 2012, citing data of the Giving USA Foundation).
- **Giving Pledge—92 Billionaires Commit to Giving Away One-Half of Their Wealth.** The Giving Pledge was initiated by Bill Gates and Warren Buffett in 2010 "to try to kick-start a new era of American philanthropy in which tycoons start making donations earlier in their lives." While the pledge is merely a nonbinding promise and does not "impose any contractual requirements on how the money is distributed, or any penalties for failing to give it away," and while the Bill and Melinda Gates Foundation (which coordinates the Giving Pledge) does not track the signatories' donations, at least there are 92 billionaires as of September 2012 who have so committed to give away one-half of their wealth. Fowler, G., "More Billionaires Vow to Give Money Away," *The Wall Street Journal,* September 19, 2012.
- **Government Fees and Grants as Percentage of Nonprofits' Revenues.** In 2009, "nonprofits derived 32% of their revenues from government fees and grants." Dennis, K., *The Wall Street Journal,* December 19, 2012, citing the Urban Institute.

- **Massive Personal Donations.**
  - ○ **Central Park Conservancy—John Paulson—$100MM— Arguable Distinction Between Absolute and Relative Donations.** Although criticized by some as a low-impact use of funds, hedge fund manager John Paulson pledged $100MM to the Central Park Conservancy. *The Week*, November 2, 2012, p. 7. While this represents an amount equal to less than 1% (i.e., roughly 0.8%) of his net wealth, it was also "the largest monetary donation in the history of the New York City's park system." *Id.*
  - ○ **Polio Eradication—Michael Bloomberg—$100MM and Bill and Melinda Gates $1.5 BB Since 2008.** Bloomberg's contribution was announced to support Bill Gates's call to raise $5.5BB for the final worldwide eradication of polio. Only two cases of polio had been reported worldwide as of February 28, 2013, however nine vaccinators were killed in Nigeria, and the vaccination is still opposed in some Muslim countries. Nevertheless, polio eradication may be in the endgame. The global eradication program began in 1988—just 25 years ago. At that time polio was in 125 countries and "more than 350,000 children were paralyzed annually." In 2011 India declared itself polio-free, and in 2012 the worldwide number of new cases was down to 223, a 60% drop from the 2011 total. McKay, B., *The Wall Street Journal*, February 28, 2013; and Bloomberg, M., Gates, B., *The Wall Street Journal*, February 28, 2013.
- **Reported "Worst 10 Charities"—Lowest Percentage of Contributions Used for Intended Beneficiary Purpose.** Based upon a joint investigation by the *Tampa Bay Times* and the Center for Investigative Reporting, certain charities spend a massive percentage of their contribution receipts on further money-raising solicitation expenses and de minimus amounts for at least the cash benefit of the intended beneficiaries. The investigation, using federal and state records, "identified a list of what it called the 50 worst charities in America." According to that investigation and "ranked according to money spent on fundraising over a decade," the worst ten charities are set forth below:

Ranking As Worst	Name	Ranking As Worst	Name
1.	Kids Wish Network	6.	Breast Cancer Relief Foundation
2.	Cancer Fund of America	7.	Int'l Union of Police Assns, AFL-CIO
3.	Children's Wish Foundation Int'l	8.	Nat'l Veterans Service Fund.
4.	Am Breast Cancer Foundation	9.	Am Ass'n of State Troopers
5.	Firefighters Charitable Foundation	10.	Children's Cancer Fund of Am

Bhattacharjee, R., *news.msn.com*, June 13, 2013.

Civility of Discourse.
- **Cost of Civil Ticket for Swearing in Middleborough, Massachusetts.** $20, Levitz, J., "Dagnabit, This Town Is Fed Up With Cursing," *The Wall Street Journal*, June 11, 2012.
- **Harsh Words—The Growing List of Harsh Words and the Coarseness of American Political and Social Debate.** There is a growing list of harsh words in the American lexicon—the F-bomb, the L-word (Liar—"a potent and ugly word with a sleazy political pedigree"), and the N-word. See Henninger, D., "Obama and the L-Word," *The Wall Street Journal*, October 11, 2012. (Noting that "(e)xplicitly calling someone a 'liar' is—or used to be—a serious and rare charge, in or out of politics. It's a loaded word. It crosses a line. 'Liar' suggests bad faith and conscious duplicity—a total, cynical falsity.").
- **Profanity—Impact Upon Likelihood of Employee Promotion.** 57% of surveyed employers stated that "they'd be less likely to promote someone who curses." *The Week*, August 10, 2012, p. 4, citing *CareerBuilder.com*.
- **"Slut" Remark—Number of Advertisers Who Withdrew Sponsorship of Rush Limbaugh.** More than 30 advertisers. *Time*, March 19, 2012, p. 10. See also, *news.msn.com*, May 6, 2013 (Reporting that although Limbaugh remains "the most highly rated talk radio host in the country," Cumulus Network may sever its relations with Limbaugh at the end of 2013 because, Cumulas' CEO Lew Dickey still blames Limbaugh for causing the advertisers' boycotts in response to Limbaugh's remarks about Sandra Fluke and for thereby causing $5.5MM in lost advertising revenues to Cumulas' top three stations.).

Compassion—Willingness of Surveyed Americans to Donate a Kidney. 18% said that they were willing to donate a kidney "to anyone," and another 63% said they would donate a kidney to their spouse, child, or close friend or member of their extended family. "The 60 Minutes/Vanity Fair Poll," *Vanity Fair*, August 2012, p. 32.

Condition, Perception, and Popularity of Country.
- **"Best Days" for America Ahead or Behind—Perception of Americans.** 35% of Americans believe that "America's best days are behind it." *The Economist*, May 12–18, 2012, p. 40.
- **Best Place To Be Born—Worldwide—Ranking of Top 80 Best Places to Be Born in 2013.** Based on a serious ranking of the best opportunities for "a healthy, safe, and prosperous life" and incorporating 11 statistically significant indicators, the Economist Intelligence Unit made the following findings:

Where-To-Be-Born Index, 2013

Ranking	Country	Score	Ranking	Country	Score
1.	Switzerland	8.22	20.	Israel	7.23
2.	Australia	8.12	21.	Italy	7.21
3.	Norway	8.09	23.	Chile	7.10
4.	Sweden	8.02	25.	Japan	7.08
5.	Denmark	8.01	26.	France	7.04
9.	Canada	7.81	27.	Britain	7.01
12.	Ireland	7.74	37.	Brazil	6.52
16.	Germany	7.38	49.	China	5.99
16.	*United States*	*7.38*	66.	India	5.67

Kekic, L., "The Lottery of Life," *The Economist: The World in 2013*, p. 91.

- **Inter-Generational Expectation of Children's Jobs, Salaries, and Benefits—Negative Outlook**. Two out of three Americans believe that their children's jobs, salaries, and benefits will be "worse than their own." *The Economist*, May 12–18, 2012, p. 40.

- **Popularity of U.S. Compared with Other Countries.** Based upon a BBC worldwide poll, the following countries were rated "mainly positive:"

Ranking	Country	Percentage of Persons Identifying Perception Of Country as "Mainly Positive"
1.	Germany	59%
2.	*United States*	*45%*
3.	South Africa	35%
4.	Israel	21%
5.	Pakistan	15%

Time, June 10, 2013, p. 12.

- **Right Track/Wrong Track Surveys.** Wrong track—more than 60% of Americans. *The Economist*, September 1–7, 2012, p. 11. See also, *The Week*, May 4, 2012, p. 6, stating that 64% of Americans believe that the country is on "wrong track," and citing McGurn, W., *The Wall Street Journal*.

- **Satisfaction/Dissatisfaction Surveys—Perception of Condition of Country.** Only 28% of Americans are "satisfied with the condition of the country" and 70% were dissatisfied according to four separate surveys. *The Economist*, May 12–18, 2012, p. 40.

- **Year-End (2012) Surveys about U.S. Condition—Compilation Summary Of.** The following is based upon a compilation of numerous different year-end surveys by different polling organizations. See *The Week*, December 28–January 4, 2012, p. 20. The various surveys simultaneously evidence both optimism (i.e., the U.S. on "right track") and pessimism (U.S. civilization "in decline"). Furthermore, the various surveys evidence that even though there may be generalized agreements (e.g. necessity for political compromise), there is little agreement on the nature or even the subjects of such compromise. Lastly, the polls may underscore the bias and orientation of the polling body itself (e.g., compare the 61% America-in-recovery poll results of Pew Research Center with the polling results indicating that 7% believes the U.S. is "in decline" as reported by the *Fox News* poll).

Compilation of 2012 Year-End Polls

Poll Subject and Summary	Percentage	Source
General		
Right direction	42%	Note 2
Challenges to U.S. may be too great	31%	Note 4
U.S. "evolving into socialist state"	40%	Note 5
U.S. civilization "in decline"	57%	Note 6
Economy		
In recovery or would be soon	61%	Note 1
Strong economic recovery in Obama 2nd term	54%	Note 3
Unemployment Obama will reduce in 2nd term	56%	Note 3
Health Care System—Obama will improve in 2nd term	55%	Note 3
Fears and Perceived Problems		
Fears		
Global warming	66%	Note 12
Identity theft	59%	Note 14
Loss of privacy due to unmanned drones	35%	Note 13
Terrorism-Another 9/11-type attack	65%	Note 10
Partisan politics		
Obama makes "them feel angry"	21%	Note 1
Republicans—ACORN stole election	49%	Note 7
The 2 parties should compromise more	85%	Note 8
But compromise less acceptable in context of specific issues:		
On budget deficit	41%	Note 9
On immigration	34%	Note 9
On health-care reform	33%	Note 9
Society and Culture		
Drugs		
Support legalization of marijuana	58%	Note 11
U.S. losing war on drugs	82%	Note 10
End of world (12/21/12) will occur-Mayan prophesy	12%	Note 15

Gays and Lesbians:

More acceptance by their communities	91%	Note 16
Adoption of children by gay and lesbian couples	61%	Note 3
Same-Sex Marriage—Approval of	53%	Note 3

Note 1. *Pew Research Center*; Note 2. The highest number in 3 years. *ABC News/The Washington Post* (October 2012); Note 3. *USA Today/Gallup*; Note 4. *Allstate/National Journal*; Note 5. *Investors Business Daily/TIPP*; Note 6. *Fox News*; Note 7. Even though the organization, ACORN, closed in 2010. *Public Policy Polling*; Note 8. *The New York Times/CBS Poll*; Note 9. *Goldfarb Center/Survey USA*; Note 10. *Rasmussen*; Note 11. *Public Policy Polling*; Note 12. *Quinnipiac*; Note 13. *Associated Press*; Note 14. *Unisys*; Note 15. *Ipsos/Reuters*; Note 16. *USA Today/Gallup*. This reflects the response opinion of 91% of the gays and lesbians to whom this question was asked.

Consumerism.

• **Black Friday—Average Amount Spent per Shopper.** Although there have been some slight fluctuations, from 2005 to 2011 the average amount spent on Black Friday per shopper was $356 (Low: $303 in 2005; High: $399 in 2011). In 2012, the amount went up 6% to another all-time high of $423. Black Friday has commonly been known as the busiest shopping day of the year, accounting for as much as 10%–11% of all holiday sales. However, Black Friday actually ranked from the 5th to the 10th busiest shopping day until the 1990s, and it has only been ranked first since 1993 (excepting 2004, when it ranked 2nd). Black Friday must also compete with Cyber Monday (a phrase introduced in 2006 by *Shop.org* to recognize the increasing number of people who now shop on-line on the Monday following Thanksgiving) and Gray Thursday (a phrase introduced in 2012 to recognize those stores (most large retailers such as Walmart and Target) who began to advance their Black Friday midnight opening to as early as 8:00 PM on Thanksgiving Day itself to the disappointment of the stores' employees and their families and to the disappointment of many store employees and many traditionalists who believe that the holiday of Thanksgiving should remain inviolate). National Retail Federation.

• **Black Friday/Thanksgiving Holiday—Number of People Who Visited Stores or Shopped Online—Total Sales.** Appr. 247MM Americans (nearly 80% of the population) visited stores or shopped online in November 2012. Total spending "hit an estimated $59.1BB." In 2012, Cyber Monday sales increased 20%, over 2012 and set a record of $1.5BB. *The Week*, December 7, 2012, p. 5.

- **Children's Toys—Average Price of Items on Toys R Us 2012 Holiday Hot Toys List.** $83, including Furby, WiiU, and Doc McStuffin's Time for Your Checkup doll. *Time,* October 8, 2012, p. 59.
- **Holiday Spending Amounts and Percentages—Winter Holidays Compared with Other Holiday and Back-to-School Spending Periods.** The extent of the dominance of the Winter Holiday sales period is reflected in the following percentage allocations of holiday and back-to-school spending:

Holiday Spending Amounts and Percentages (2011–2012)

Category	Percentage of Holiday Spending Totals	Amount of Spending
Winter Holidays (Christmas)	77.2%	$586.1BB
Back to School /College	11.0%	$83.8BB
Mother's Day	2.5%	$18.6BB
Valentine's Day	2.3%	$17.6BB
Easter	2.2%	$16.8BB
Father's Day	1.7%	$12.7BB
Super Bowl	1.4%	$11.0BB
Halloween	1.1%	$8.0BB
St. Patrick's Day	0.6%	$4.6BB

National Retail Federation at *nrf.com.* See also, *Time,* November 5, 2012, p. 7. The amount spent in U.S. on Halloween costumes in 2012 was $1.4BB for adults and $1.1BB for children.
- **Restoration Hardware 2012 Catalogue—Size in Weight and Pages.** 5.5 pounds and 992 pages. *Time,* October 8, 2012, p. 11.
- **"Twelve Days of Christmas"—2012 Cost for the 364 Gifts Referenced in the Song.** $107,000, plus an additional $15,000 for shipping, *The Week,* December 7, 2012, p., 36, quoting N. Carbone, *Time.com.*

Curiosities and Americana.
- **Abraham Lincoln—One of America's First Historical Celebrities—16,000 Books and Counting.** There is an almost peculiar "national obsession" with Lincoln, the U.S.'s 16th President. There have now been "roughly 16,000" books written about him. In addition to historian David Von Drehle's new book, *Rise to Greatness,* Bill O'Reilly and Martin Dugard's popular *Killing Lincoln,* and Steven Spielberg's new movie, *Lincoln,* based on Doris Kearns Goodwin's 2005 biography of Lincoln entitled *Team of Rivals,* there are another "20 new books [about Lincoln] coming soon." Cohen, S., "Fourscore and 16,000 Books," *The Wall Street Journal,* October 12, 2012.
- **Aging—Average Age of Rolling Stones Exceeds Average Age of the Justices of the U.S. Supreme Court.** The average age of Mick Jagger, Keith

Richards, Charlie Watts, and Ronnie Woods is appr. 69. The current average age of the U.S. Supreme Court is appr. 67. *The Week*, December 7, 2012, p. 18, citing *Associated Press*. It is good to know that at least David Bowie is still a youngster. He is *only* 66. McAllester, M.,"Where Is He Now? David Bowie Is Back to His Mysterious Best," *Time,* March 18, 2013, p. 52.

- **Cost of a Piece of History—Selling Price for George Washington's Annotated Copy of U.S. Constitution and Bill of Rights.** $9.8MM. *Time,* July 9, 2012, p. 50.
- **Cost of "Triple Bypass (Pastrami) Sandwich" in New York City.** $34.95. *The Week*, July 20, 2012, p. 6.
- **Death and Dying—Number of Burials Compared with Cremations in U.S.** 80% of all Americans are now cremated as opposed to being buried. *The Week*, April 19, 2013, p. 18, citing *The Wall Street Journal.*
- **Highest Paid Public Employees by State—Dominance of Athletic Coaches**. The only states where an athletic coach (27 football coaches, 13 basketball coaches, and one hockey coach) is *not* the highest paid public employee are as follows:

Alaska	College President
Delaware	College President
Maine	Law School Dean
Massachusetts	Medical School Chancellor
Montana	College President
Nevada	Dean of Medical School
New Hampshire	College President
New York	Medical School—Department Chair
North Dakota	Dean of Medical School
Vermont	College President

Deadspin Report , news,msn,.com, May 10, 2013.
- **Major Life Changes—Frequency of in Current America.** On average and based upon "data collected by Intuit, which sells the tax-prep TurboTax," "every year about 40% of (Americans experience) a "major life event such as marriage, job loss, or retirement." (Emphasis added). Saunders, L, "Tax Tips for Life's Big Changes," *The Wall Street Journal*, March 16-17, 2013.
- **Tooth Fairy—Average Amount Left by per Tooth in U.S.** $3, according to a 2010 survey by Visa, however, the average "so far in 2011" has dropped to $2.60. Harper's Index, *Harper's Magazine,* October 2011, p. 15.

Dating.
- **High School Proms—Average Expected Prom Cost to Family of Teenager.** $1,078 in 2012. *The Week*, April 27, 2012 citing *USA Today*. See also, F. Sun. "Last Dance," *Time*, June 11, 2012, p. 32.

- **On-Line Introductions and Dating—Number of Subscribers to** *FarmersOnly.com.* 200,000. The website "features the tagline 'City folks just don't get it.'" *Time,* April 9, 2012, p.9.

Divorce and Alimony

- **Alimony—Total Alimony Received Annually in U.S.—Legislation Limiting Availability or Duration Of.** $8.2BB in alimony paid in 2011 according to reported alimony income to IRS. Now, for the first time since the alimony reforms in the 1970s (among other things, changing the awards of alimony to need-based rather than based upon a assumption of a woman's need), a number of states (e.g. Florida, Massachusetts, New Jersey, Connecticut, Colorado, and Oregon) are revising or considering revising their alimony laws to "end permanent alimony and create formulas to determine the amount and duration of awards" (e.g. cap alimony periods to one-half of the marriage period; cap alimony to X% for marriages of less than Y years). Campo-Flores, A., *The Wall Street Journal*, April 17, 2013.

- **Marital Fault as Relevant Factor in Awarding Alimony—Number of States.** Alimony is treated considerably different by the various states. 29 states (including D.C.) permit "marital fault" to be consider as a relevant factor in the awarding of divorce although some states limit alimony to a certain number of years (e.g., Kansas—no more than ten years; Utah—duration of divorce cannot exceed the length of the marriage). See generally, Luscombe, B., "The End of Alimony," *Time,* May 27, 2013, p. 44.

- **Number of Americans Currently Receiving Alimony.** Appr. 420,000 (or, less than 1/5th of 1% of the U.S. adult population) with an aggregate amount of $8.2 BB reported to the IRS in 2011). See generally, Luscombe, B., "The End of Alimony," *Time,* May 27, 2013, p. 44.

Entertainment, Music and Sports.

- **Burning Man Festival—Current Size of Festival and Number of Years Held.** 26 years. The festival was initially conceived and held among a small group of about 20 people in 1986 at Baker Beach in San Francisco. Since 1990, it has been held on a remote dry lake known as Black Rock Desert in Nevada—about 110 miles north of Reno. The attendance now exceeds 50,000 people. While there is still a focus upon "radical self-reliance" and "radical inclusion," the festival rules and organization have grown commensurate with the size of the gathering." Carlton, J., "Bad Days at Black Rock," *The Wall Street Journal*, September 1–2, 2012; *wikipedia.com*; and *burningman.com*.

- **Cruising—Number of Annual Cruise Passengers from North America.** 17.2 MM in 2012 despite the substantial level of adverse publicity due to various problems. Royal Caribbean and Carnival's 143 ships still "control about 70% of the (appr. 430,000) global berths." Sanburn, J., *Time,* June 10, 2013, p. 22.

- **Gambling Casinos—Number of States Which Allow**. 24 states, as of March, 2012. *The Economist,* March 17–23, 2012, p. 33.
- **Movies.**
    - ○ **Demographics of Selectors of Academy Awards**. The primary demographics of the selectors of the Academy Awards are as follows:

White	94%
Male	77%
Age 50 or Older	86%

        Time, March 5, 2012, p. 50.
    - ○ **Least Favorite Types of Movies.** The types of movies which polled viewers are least interested in watching are as follows:

Type of Movie	Percentage Indicating This Least Favorite Category
Foreign Films With Subtitles	46%
3-D Movies	21%
Musicals	17%
Animated Movies	11%

        The 60 Minutes/Vanity Fair Poll, *Vanity Fair,* p. 130, March, 2013.
    - ○ **Quintessential Leading-Male and Leading-Female Actors.** While these results vary dramatically based upon age and generational association, the "quintessential" leading actors according to one recent U.S. poll are as follows:

Leading Males Actors		Leading Female Actors	
Clint Eastwood	28%	Meryl Streep	31%
Denzel Washington	23%	Julia Roberts	24%
Cary Grant	12%	Elizabeth Taylor	11%
Jack Nicholson/George Clooney	9%	Halle Berry/Bette Davis	9%
Humphrey Bogart	8%	Sophia Loren	7%

        The 60 Minutes/Vanity Fair Poll, *Vanity Fair,* p. 130, March, 2013.
    - ○ **Types—U.S. Preference for Great Films vs. Documentaries**. While 54% of those Americans polled stated that they would prefer to watch a "great film," a surprising 42% indicated that they would prefer watching a powerful documentary. The 60 Minutes/Vanity Fair Poll, *Vanity Fair,* p. 130, March, 2013.
- **Music.**
    - ○ **Most Spending by Population on Music—By Nation and as Percentage of GDP.**

Country	Music Sales Sale in $US	Appr. Percentage of National GDP
Japan	$3,900MM	7.0%
United Kingdom	$1,300MM	5.5%
United States	*$4,100MM*	*2.5%*
China	$64MM	0.1%

The Economist, April 30–May 6, 2011, p. 102.

○ **Rolling Stone's 500 Greatest Album Hits—Percentage of Recorded in the 1960s and 1970s.** 60%. *The Week*, July 20, 2012, p. 6.

• **Sports.**

  ○ **Baseball.**

    – **Baseball History—Oldest Pitcher in Major League History to Win a Game.** Colorado Rockies pitcher Jamie Moyer, at the age of 49 years and 151 days. *Time*, May 7, 2012, p. 18. Just weeks earlier, he had pitched against 22-year-old Madison Bumgarner and almost set a record with one of the biggest age gaps (26.7 years) between starting pitchers.

    – **Ticket Prices—Escalation of MLB Tickets.** In constant dollars, adjusted for inflation, the average MLB ticket has increased 17% *per year* for 19 years. The ticket prices have increased from $8.30 in 1991 to $26.75 in 2010. *Time*, April 11, 2011, p. 69, citing Team Marketing Report.

  ○ **Basketball.**

    – **Colleges—U.S. Minimum Graduation Rate for NCAA Basketball Team Qualification.** 50% graduation requirement must be "fully phased in" by 2016. If the rule were in effect as of spring 2012, the University of Connecticut, Syracuse, Indiana, and Florida State, among others, would not have been permitted to participate in the NCAA Championships. Gregory, S., "Bench Bracket, *Time*, March 26, 2012, p. 54.

    – **Education—Number of University of Kentucky, National Championship Starters Who Quit College to Join the NBA Draft.** All five. They were all freshman and sophomore players. *The Week*, April 13, 2012, p. 6.

  ○ **Collegiate Conferences—Number of Teams in The Big Ten Conference.** 14 teams "now that Rutgers and the University of Maryland have joined." *Time*, December 3, 2012, p. 11.

○ **Golf and Golf Courses.**
  – **Americans Who Play Golf—Percentage Of.** 9.2% of Americans (or, appr. 28.7MM Americans in 2010 (down from 11.1% in 2000). Keates, N., "For Sale...Luxury Golf Communities," *The Wall Street Journal,* July 20, 2012.
  – **Net Number of Golf Courses Closed Since 2005.** A net number (i.e., newly closed less newly opened) of 350 golf courses have closed since 2005, and "(i)n 2011, more than 150 courses closed, outpacing the 19 courses that debuted last year." This can be compared with the 3,000 new courses which were built between 1990 and 2003. Keates, N., "For Sale...Luxury Golf Communities," *The Wall Street Journal,* July 20, 2012.
  – **Women—Augusta National Golf Club—Number of Women Admitted To.** Two women. The August National Golf Club was founded in the midst of the Depression in 1933. In August 2012, for the first time in its 79 years, Augusta National admitted two women—former U.S. Secretary of State Condoleezza Rice and South Carolina investment banker Darla Moore. Martin, T., Dawsey, J., and McKay, B., "The Gender Barrier Falls at Augusta," *The Wall Street Journal,* August 21, 2012.
○ **Hunting—Active Hunters in U.S.—Number Of.** Appr. 14MM or "about 1 in every 18 people." *The Week,* December 28, 2012–January 4, 2013, p. 16, citing *The Atlantic.com.*
○ **Olympics.**
  – **Actual "Gold Contained in Olympics' "Gold Medal."** 1.34% gold since "(a)t current prices, a solid gold medal would cost about $25,000." This is not a change. "The last time ... pure gold medals (were used) was (100 years ago) at the 1912 Stockholm Games." *The Week,* August 10, 2012, p. 16, citing *Forbes.com.*
  – **Medals Count—All-Time Medalist Michael Phelps—Number of Medals.** 22 medals (18 gold) by Michael Phelps, age 22, surpassing Soviet gymnast Larisa Latynina's records of 18 medals which she had held since 1964. *The Week,* August 17, 2012, p. 15.
  – **Medal Count—U.S. Vs Other Major Competitor Nations.** The nations with the top number of (but who's counting) Olympic medals are as follows:

Olympic Medals Count—By Country	
Country	Number of Medals
United States	*2,302*
Former USSR	1,122

United Kingdom	725.5 (UK)
Germany	658.5
France	633
—	
China	385

Time, July 30, 2012, p. 11 citing *NBC.com.*

- **Olympic 2012 U.S. Team—Size Of.** 530 athletes (269 women and 261 men). *The Week,* July 27, 2012, p. 16 citing *USA Today.*
- **Olympic Gold Medal—More Coveted Than Pulitzer Prize, Oscar, Grammy, and Tony Awards.** The most coveted awards of those polled were as follows:

Olympic Gold Medal	40%
Pulitzer Prize	36%
Oscar Academy Award	7%
Grammy	6%
Tony	2%

The 60 Minutes/Vanity Fair Poll, *Vanity Fair,* November 2012, p. 62.
- **Popularity—2012 Loss of U.S. Productivity Due to People Watching Olympics**. An estimated $650MM of business productivity. *Time,* August 13, 2012, p. 9.
- **Viewership—Olympics and Paralympics Opening Ceremonies—Number of Worldwide Viewers of 2012 Summer Olympics and Paralympic Opening Ceremonies.** 27MM at the Summer Olympics and 11MM at the Summer Paralympics. *The Economist,* September 8–14, 2012, p. 58.
- **Viewership—Number of U.S. Viewers of Olympics' Opening Ceremony.** 40.6MM which is an "all-time high"—appr. one out of every eight Americans. *Time,* August 13, 2012, p. 55.
- **Women—Olympic History—Number of Times More American Women Athletes Competing Than American Men.** Only once—2012. In this year, and for the first time ever, there were more American women athletes competing than American men: 269 women, 261 men. *The Week,* July 27, 2012, p. 16, citing *USA Today.*
- **Women—Olympic History—Track and Field—Number of Years Women Competing in Track and Field.** 84 years—since 1928—eight years after women obtained the right to vote by adoption of the 19th Amendment.

– **Women—Compared With Men—Speed in Running and Swimming Events.** Almost the same. "(T)heir times are now about 90% as fast (as men) in all such events." *The Week*, August 17, 2012, p. 14, citing *TheAtlantic.com*.

○ **Paralympic Games—2012—Size and History.** The events were sold out in London for the first time in the event's 52-year history. The event started with a group of British World War II veterans in 1948, and the first official Paralympic Games were held in Rome in 1960. This year, in London, a "record 2.5MM people will watch 4,200 athletes from 165 nations compete." *The Week*, August 24–31, 2012, p. 2.

○ **Professional Sports—Ticket Costs—Average Cost Of—Major League Baseball, NBA, and NFL.** The respective average ticket costs are as follows:

Major League Baseball	$27
NBA (Basketball)	$48
NFL (Football)	$113

The Week, April 13, 2012, p. 14, citing M. Kazin, *The New Republic*.

• **Theme Parks—Ticket Costs—Top New U.S. Thrills and Theme-Park Attractions.** Attendance in 2012 has been steadily increasing, despite increases in prices to, for example a one-day pass ticket price of $89 (Disney World) and $80 (Universal Studios). Some of the 135 new U.S. theme park attractions in 2012 offered by the U.S.'s 600,000 theme park employees are the X Flight at Six Flags, Gurnee, IL (3,000-ft winged roller coaster); Bonsai Pipeline at Six Flags, St. Louis (riders shoot through 290 clear tubes and 350-degree loops before splashing into the water); and Manta at SeaWorld (coaster is an interactive manta-ray experience). *Time,* June 18, 2012, p. 18.

• **YouTube—Most Watched Clip in 2012—Psy's Gangnam Style.** With more than 988MM viewers, Psy's "Gangnam style" video was the most watched YouTube video of the year. In 2011, it was Rebecca Black's "Friday."

Food Resources—Wasted or Thrown Out—Est. Percentage Annually in U.S. 40%, or an average of about $2,275 food per year per family of four. *The Week*, September 7, 2012, p. 16, citing the *Los Angeles Times*. See also, Park, A., "Waste Not," *Time*, September 10, 2012, p. 14, citing Natural Resources Defense Council.

Groups and Associations.

• **Boy Scouts.**

○ **Homosexuality.**

– **Acceptance of Openly Gay Scouts—Policy Change.** Starting in 2014 Boy Scouts will start accepting openly gay scouts—but not leaders. This change of policy was adopted in May 2013 with the approval of appr. 60% of scout leaders and, possibly more importantly, with two of the "largest sponsors of scouting—the Mormons and the United Methodists indicat(ing) that they would not obstruct the new policy." *The Economist,* June 1-7, 2013, p. 28. But see, *Time,* June 10, 2013 noting that despite the support of the Mormons (and the United Methodists), the Southern Baptist Convention and the Assemblies of God objected to the policy change. Dias, E., *Time,* June 10, 2013.

- **Years of Internal Study Until Boy Scouts Announced Decision to Retain Exclusion Policy Regarding Openly Gay Scouts and Troop Leaders.** Two years of confidential examination and review of subject. *The Week*, August 3, 2012, p. 17.

  ○ **Membership Size.** 2.7MM children (app. 44% less than the 4.8MM members 40 years ago in 1972). *The Week,* p. 17, citing S. Nielsen in *The Portland Oregonian.*

  ○ **Religious Sponsorship or Association—Extent Of.** Appr. 70% of all scout troops are sponsored by religious groups. *The Economist,* June 1-7, 2013, p. 28.

- **Militia and "Patriot Groups"—Number Of.** 1,274 militia and "patriot groups" in 2011 compared with 149 just three years earlier in 2008. *The Week*, March 23, 2012, citing *CSMonitor.com* and referencing data by the Southern Poverty Law Center.

- **National Rifle Association ("NRA")—Size and Growth Of.** As of 2012, appr. 4.3MM members which number equates to appr. 1.4% of the U.S. population and appr. 2.1% of the U.S. adult population. The NRA membership base has grown substantially in the last 30 years and has nearly doubled since the appr. 2.4MM membership base in 1982. Klein, J., "How the Gun Won," *Time,* August 6, 2012, p. 26. See also, *The Week*, December 28, 2012—January 4, 2013, p. 12, citing Weissman, J. in *TheAtlantic.com*. (Noting that in addition to representing the individual members, the NRA also represents gun manufacturers since the NRA has received "at least $39MM" in donations from Bushmaster, Browning, Smith & Wesson, and others in recent years.).

Guns and Second Amendment Rights.

- **College Campuses—States Varying Policies Regarding Permissibility Of.** State laws vary substantially. As of September 2012, the number and percentage of all states, by policy mandate, were as follows:

24 states (48% of states) allow each individual university to determine its own policy.

21 states (44% of states) ban the carrying of a concealed weapon on campuses.

5 states (10% of states) (Up from just one state in 2010) now allow students to carry guns on public campuses.

Palazzolo, J., Eder, S., "Push to Let College Students Carry Guns Picks Up Steam," *The Wall Street Journal*, September 22–23, 2012.

- **Concealed Weapons Laws.**
  - ○ **Concealed Weapons Permits Issued and Permits Issued Monthly in Florida.** Florida will soon be the first state to have issued more than 1MM concealed weapons permits. This number would represent appr. 1 in 5 of the appr. 19MM Floridians. In addition, Florida currently issues appr. 15,000 new concealed weapons permits per month. *The Week*, August 10, 2012, p. 16, citing the *South Florida Sun-Sentinel*.
  - ○ **First State to Permit Citizens to Carry Concealed Weapons in Public and Year of Enactment.** Florida, 1987.
  - ○ **States Which Have Considered Law Permitting Its Residents to Carry a Concealed Weapons Without Obtaining a Permit— Number Of.** 12 states. *Time*, March 19, 2012, at p. 10.
- **Deaths.**
  - ○ **Americans (Excluding Military Personnel) Killed in U.S. with Guns in 2009—Number Of.** 31,347 persons in 2009 (or appr. 1 person per 10,000 persons) compared with, for example, 51 persons in the United Kingdom in 2009 (or appr. 1 person per 1,250,000). *The Week*, August 3, 2012, p. 14. See also, *The Week*, December 28, 2012–January 4, 2013, p. 3. ("Every year, more than 30,000 people (the equivalent of ten 9/11s) die of gunshot wounds; 55% of these are suicides. Another 60,000 are wounded.").
  - ○ **Children—Age 14 and Under—Killed and Injured in U.S. in 2010 as Result of Gun Accidents**. 62 children (age 14 and under) were killed and appr. 15,500 were injured in 2010 as the result of gun accidents. *The Week*, May 17, 2013, p. 18.
- **Enforcement of Proposed Federal Gun-Control Legislation—Percentage of U.S. Sheriffs Who Have Vowed Not to Enforce**. 14% (or one in seven) according to the Constitutional Sheriffs and Peace Officers Association. Harper's Index, *Harper's Magazine*, June, 2013, p. 15. See also, Baum, D., "How to Make Your Own AR-15," *Harper's Magazine*, June, 2013, p. 37.

- **"Guns in Trunk"—"Safe Commute" Laws.** Tennessee is prepared to adopt a "guns in trunk" law whereby gun owners would be allowed to keep weapons in their vehicles "in parking lots at work, school or government offices." McWhirter, C., *The Wall Street Journal*, February. 28, 2013
- **Guns Ownership Rate.**
  - **Number of and in Civilian Circulation in U.S.** Appr. 300MM— or roughly "one for every person in the country." *The Economist*, December 22, 2012–January 4, 2013. p. 37. According to one writer, 92MM of these guns (appr. 31%) are handguns. Jenkins, H.W., *The Wall Street Journal*, December 19, 2012.
  - **U.S.—Compared with Other Countries.** The U.S. has the highest gun ownership rate in the world—appr. 89 guns for every 100 people. Yemen and Iraq, respectively, have the second and third highest rates with appr. 55 guns per 100 persons in Yemen and 34 guns per 100 persons in Iraq. *The Week*, December 28, 2012—January 4, 2013, p. 16, citing *The Washington Post*. See also, *The Economist*, December 22, 2012–January 4, 2013. p. 37 (Citing survey that "roughly a third of all (U.S.) households own firearms (and) (t)hree-quarters of those own more than one.").
  - **U.S.—Drop in Household Ownership Rate Since 1970.** The percentage of households which own a gun has dropped from about 50% in 1970 to 34% in 2012 according to General Social Survey, an organization which tracks key demographic, behavioral, and attitudinal data. The GSS attributes a considerable portion of this decline to the marked decrease in guns in households of persons under age 30. *The Week*, March 22, 2013, p. 18, citing *The New York Times*.
- **Guns and Annual Gun Purchases—Number of in U.S.** Appr. 300MM guns owned by private citizens in the U.S. The FBI conducted over 155,000 background checks for Black Friday gun purchases alone. *Time*, December 17, 2012, p. 9.
- **"Open Carry" Laws—States With—Number Of.** With the recent addition of Oklahoma, 15 states now have "open carry laws," whereby anyone who is licensed to carry a weapon (142,000 people in Oklahoma alone), can carry and display the weapon "in the open, in a belt, or shoulder holster, loaded or unloaded." *The Week*, November 9, 2012, p. 7.
- **Purchase Access To—Refusal Rate under Federal Background Check Law and Percentage of Guns Purchased Without Requirement of Federal Background Check.** The refusal rate of federal background checks, is a "very low, 0.6%%," and nearly 40%% of all guns are lawfully purchased

without the need of any background checks such as at gun shows or from private sellers. *The Economist,* December 22, 2012–January 4, 2013, p. 38.

- **"Stand Your Ground" Laws.**
  - ○ **First State to Enact and Year of Enactment.** Florida in 2005. But see, *The Week,* May 4, 2012, p. 13, identifying the year 2004 as the year of initial passage.
  - ○ **"Justifiable Homicides" per Year—Increase in States with "Stand Your Ground" Laws.** The number of "justifiable homicides" in Florida increased from 12 per year in 2005 to appr. 40 per year in 2007. Other states have had "similar spikes." A study of FBI Data by the Office of New York Mayor Michael Bloomberg, an admitted gun control advocate, shows an average of about a 53% increase in the number of "justifiable homicides" as opposed to a 4.3% increase in states without such stand your ground laws. *The Week,* May 4, 2012, p. 13.
  - ○ **States with "Stand Your Ground" Statutes as of 2012—Number Of.** 25 states. *The Week,* "The NRA: Fighting To Stay Relevant," April 27, 2012, citing E.J. Dionne, *The Washington Post.* See also, Cloud, J., "The Law Heard Round the World," *Time,* April 9, 2012, p. 36 and *The Week,* May 4, 2012, p. 13.

Language.

- **"English as Official Language" Statutes—Number of States.** 31 states (62%, or about three in five). *Proenglish.org.*
- **English Required for Obtaining Driver's License—Number of States.** nine states (18%, or about one in five states) *Proenglish.org.*

Memoriam—2012—A Listing in Honor of Those Who Died in 2012. Each year appr. 2.5MM Americans die—the good and the bad, the wonderful, the kind, the young and the old, mothers, fathers, wives, husbands, partners, sisters, brothers, friends, the well-fed and cared for and the homeless and lost and ... and sometimes, possibly most tragically, even the young. Any In Memoriam list is incomplete and any brief description of their lives is incomplete and inadequate. Such a list is not a matter of brevity since words are rarely—and, in fact, never—enough. But, with humility, the following is a brief list of some of those who died in 2012 and who may have, at one time or way, may have kept us safe or otherwise touched our live.

301 U. S. Troops killed in Afghanistan in 2012

123 U.S. Law Enforcement Officers killed in Line of Duty in 2012 (Note 1).

83 U.S. Firefighters who died in 2012 (Note 2) .

20 young school children, their principal, school psychologist, and two teachers killed in the ten-minute rampage in Newtown, Connecticut.

Armstrong, Neil, astronaut, first man on the moon, age 82.

Arnold, Eve, photojournalist, age 99.

Borgnine, Ernest, actor, age 95.

Bork, Robert, conservative jurist and activist, age 85.

Bradbury, Ray, writer, science-fiction, age 91.

Breitbart, Andrew, conservative political activist, age 43.

Brown, Helen Gurley, writer and editor (*Cosmopolitan*), age 90.

Brubeck, Dave, jazz pianist, age 91.

Camacho, Hector "Macho," boxer, age 50.

Carter, Gary, sports, baseball, 11-time All-Star catcher, age 57.

Clark, Dick, ageless TV host of *American Bandstand*, age 82.

Cornelius, Don, creator of TV's *Soul Train*, age 75.

Covey, Stephen, writer (*The 7 Habits of Highly Effective People*), age 79.

Crist, Judith, film critic, age 90.

David, Hal, lyricist ("What the World Needs Now Is Love"), age 91.

Dawson, Richard, actor, age 79.

Diller, Phyllis comedienne, age 95.

Dobrowolski, Antoni, the oldest known survivor of Auschwitz, age 108.

Dorman, Lee, musician, Iron Butterfly, age 70.

Duncan, Michael Clark, actor (*The Green Mile*), age 54.

Durning, Charles, actor, age 88.

Ephron, Nora, author and filmmaker, age 71.

Gazzara, Ben, actor, age 81.

Gibb, Robin, member of pop singing group the Bee Gees, age 62.

Griffith, Andy, actor and folksy star of *The Andy Griffith Show*, age 86)
    (also this year, George Lindsey, who played Goober on the show,
    passed away).

Hagman, Larry, actor and TV Star (J.R. Ewing), age 81.

Hamlisch, Marvin, Pulitzer prize-winning composer, age 68.

Helm, Levon, member of The Band, age 71.

Hemsley, Sherman, actor (*The Jefferson's*), age 74.

Houston, Whitney, singer, age 48.

Inouye, Daniel, politician, Senator from Hawaii for nearly one-half century,
    age 88.

James, Etta, blue singer ("At Last"), age 73.

Jones, Davy, lead singer, The Monkees, age 66.

Karras, Alex, sports, football, actor, age 77.

King, Rodney, beaten by LA police which instigated the 1992 Los Angeles
    riots, age 47.

Kinkade, Thomas, painter, age 54.

Klugman, Jack, actor (*The Odd Couple* and *Quincy*), age 90.

Lord, Jon, co-founder of rock group Deep Purple, 71.

McGovern, George, politician, Senator from South Dakota, Dem. Pres. Nominee, 1972, age 90.

Means, Russell, Native American activist and actor, age 72.

Moon, Rev. Sun Myung, founder Unification Church, age 92.

Murray, Joseph, physician who performed first human organ transplant, age 93.

Neiman, LeRoy, painter and sketcher, age 91.

Ostram, Elinor, economist who in 2009 became 1st women to win Nobel Prize in Economics, age 78.

Otis, Johnny, bandleader, age 90.

Paterno, Joe, sports, legendary, but disgraced, Penn State football coach, age 85.

Pesky, Johnny sports, baseball, Boston Red Sox shortstop and club icon, age 92.

Polley, Eugene, inventor of Flash-Matic, the first TV remote, age 96.

Raspberry, William, Pulitzer prize-winning columnist, age 76.

Reed, Herb, founding member of the R&B group The Platters, age 83.

Rivera, Jenni, singer, age 43.

Ride, Sally, astronaut, first American woman in space, age 61.

Rudman, Warren, former U.S. Senator from New Hampshire, age 82.

Sabol, Steve, sports and entertainment, co-founder NFL Films, age 69.

Sassoon, Vidal, hairdresser and entrepreneur, age 84.

Schwarzkopf, Norman, U.S. General and Commander of U.S.-led forces during Desert Storm, age 78.

Scruggs, Earl, bluegrass banjo player, age 88.

Seau, Junior, sports, football, linebacker, age 43.

Sendak, Maurice, writer and illustrator, *Where the Wild Things Are*, age 83.

Shadid, Anthony, Pulitzer Prize-winning journalist, Syria, age 43.

Shamir, Yitzhak, for Israeli Prime Minister, age 96.

Shankar, Ravi, sitar musician, age 92.

Specter, Arlen, politician and U.S. Senator from Pennsylvania, age 82.

Stevens, J. Christopher, U.S. Ambassador to Libya, age 52.

Stevenson, Teofilo, Cuban boxer who won Gold Medal in 1972, 1976, and 1980 Olympics, at age 60.

Sulzberger, Arthur Ochs, publisher (*The New York Times*), age 86.

Sugar, Bert, boxing writer, age 75.

Summer, Donna, singer and disco queen, age 63.

Vidal, Gore, writer, age 86.

Wallace, Mike, CBS Report—*60 Minutes*, age 93.

Watson, Doc, guitarist, age 89.

Welch, Bob, musician from Fleetwood Mac, age 66.

Williams, Andy, singer ("Moon River"), age 84.

Yauch, Adam, member of the Beastie Boys, age 47.

Zanuck, Richard, movie producer, age 77.

Note 1: Officer Down Memorial Page at odmp.com. The average age of those law enforcement officers killed in the Line of Duty was 41 years. Note 2: U.S. Fire Administration.

Mistakes in U.S.'s Public and Social History—Examples Of. While both the concept and the specific definition of "mistake" is to a degree subjective, remembering public and social mistakes (wholly in addition to our personal foibles, errors, and gaffes) is useful if for no other reason than as a tool to soften the adamancy, arrogance, and intransigence. Any listing will be inadequate and incomplete, but such a listing may be useful as merely a reminder of where we have been and what we have done—imperfectly. The listing of just a few of the more commonly recognized mistakes (and, in some cases, tragedies) in U.S. public and social history is set forth below (listed roughly chronologically):

1820 Missouri Compromise.

The Millerites of the early 19th Century who encapsulated their group's mistake within the concept of the aptly titled Great Disappointment.

Slavery.

Preclusion of Women's Right to Vote for the first 130 years of the Republic.

Prohibition and the 18th Amendment.

Internment of Japanese-Americans.

The Edsel.

Bay of Pigs.

Vietnam.

Allowing the word "gang" to become a four-letter word.

The book entitled *88 Reasons Why the Rapture Will Be in 1988.*

Hubble telescope mismeasurements.

The Y2K bug of 2000 that never materialized.

Color-Coded Security Threats.

Christian Broadcaster Harold Camping's failed apocalypse of May 2011.*

The Mayan Calendar end-of-time prophesy of December 21, 2012.*

* For a different, but related consideration of some of these subjects and a brief review of the anti-intellectualism of end-of-age literature, see Frank, T. "Easy Chair: Appetite for Destruction," *Harper's Magazine,* December 2012, p. 6.

Mobility in American Society—Geographic and Social.
- **Geographic Mobility.**
    - **Frequency of Change of Address.** About 50% of Americans change address every five years. Moretti, E, "What Workers Lose by Staying Put," *The Wall Street Journal*, May 26–27, 2012, citing his book *The New Geography of Jobs,* 2012. See also, Shah, N., *The Wall Street Journal*, March 14, 2013 (4% of Americans relocated to a different county in 2011 (the highest percentage since the 2008 recession) which means that even at that low rate one in five Americans will relocate to a different county each five years).
    - **Impacts of Income and Education Upon Geographic Mobility.** The likelihood that people will move from their birth states by age 30 is a function of education: 40% for college graduates, 27% for high school graduates, and 17% for those without a high school diploma. Moretti, E, "What Workers Lose by Staying Put," *The Wall Street Journal*, May 26-27, 2012, citing his book *The New Geography of Jobs.*
    - **Planned Relocations As Function of Age.** Surveyed adults responded as follows:

	Ages 50-64	Ages 65+
Plan To Move		
Within Next 2 Years	16%	10%
In Three + Years	27%	12%
Do Not Plan to Move	57%	78%

Tergesen, A., *The Wall Street Journal*, December 10, 2012.
    - **State to State Changes of Residence—Extent of California Exodus to Other States—Number Who Have Left in Last 20 Years.** 33% of Americans reside in the state where they were born. Moretti, E, "What Workers Lose by Staying Put," *The Wall Street Journal*, May 26–27, 2012. (Compared with just 20% who stayed in their state of birth in 1900.) However, due particularly to the cost of housing, nearly 3.4MM Californians (a "vast majority" of whom are low- and middle-income people) have left the state in the last 20 years. *The Week*, March 15, 2013, p. 16, citing *The Wall Street Journal.*
- **Social Mobility—Percentage Likelihood That One's "Social Status" Pre-determined by One's Birth.** "As much as 60%," regardless of whether one is born in "Chile, China, England, Japan, Sweden, or the U.S." *The Week,* November 2, 2012, p. 23, citing research conducted by economic historian Gregory Clark of the University of California, Davis, by analyzing surnames from various families over a 200-year period.

- **"Success" and Optimism—Percentage of Americans Who Believe Success Achievable—Compared With Russians.** The respective percentages of American and Russian who believe that "most people can succeed if they are willing to work hard" is as follow:

Americans	75%	3 out of 4
Russians	33%	1 out of 3

Harper's Index, *Harper's Magazine,* October 2012, p. 15, citing Pew Research Center.

Nanny State. (Writer's Note: This phrase is colloquially used to encompass governmental laws and regulations which are deemed by some to invade one's personal freedom. However, this phrase is used here solely as a reference category, and the phrase is *not* intended in a pejorative or derogatory sense.)

- **Disney Nutritional Standards.** Disney, possibly following the lead of NYC's recent attempted ban on sugar-sweetened beverages, has adopted "strict nutritional standards" for all foods advertised on its TV channels, radio stations, websites, and theme parks. *Time,* "New York City and Disney Are Cracking Down on Junk Food," June 18, 2012, p. 20.

- **New York City's Attempted Ban on Sale of Sugary Drinks in Containers Larger Than 16 oz. and Examples of Other Legislative Bans**. While limited to only those establishments which are graded by the health department (thus, not including supermarkets and convenience stores), this law was enacted in the hopes of countering the rise of obesity and in light of the fact that the City's health department currently estimates that 50% of all New Yorkers are now overweight or obese. *The Week,* September 28, 2012, p. 5. See also, *Time,* June 18, 2012, p. 14. However, in March 2013, pursuant to a decision by a New York State Supreme Justice, the ban was effectively halted because it was deemed "fraught with arbitrary and capricious consequences" since such large drinks were prohibited to be sold at certain sites (restaurants, movie theatres, and bodegas) but were still permitted to be sold, as noted above, at supermarkets and convenience stores). Other cities ban medical marijuana gardens (Pasco, WA), plastic bags at supermarkets (Los Angeles, CA), and the wearing of low-fit pants and the exposing of underwear (Chicago, IL).

- **Political Correctness—New York City's Sensitivity Guidelines.** New York City has established "sensitivity guidelines" for its standardized tests which included the banning of words such as "dancing," "dinosaurs," "birthdays," "Halloween," and "junk food." The reasoning is, for example, that some Fundamentalist Christians may be "upset" by dinosaurs and

dancing and that Jehovah's Witnesses don't celebrate birthdays. *The Week,*
April 6, 2012, p. 6.

- **Posting of Calorie Counts.** Following NYC's 2008 lead, federal laws now
require the posting of calories for all retailers with more than 20 locations.
"New York City and Disney Are Cracking Down on Junk Food," *Time,*
June 18, 2012, p. 20.

- **Trans Fats.** NYC required "restaurants and food vendors to phase out" the
use of these fats, and now Philadelphia and San Francisco have adopted
similar ordinances. "New York City and Disney Are Cracking Down on
Junk Food," *Time,* June 18, 2012, p. 20. But see, *The Economist,* November
17-23, 2012, p. 52 (after only one year Denmark repealed its "hated," albeit
health-conscious and well-intended, tax on saturated fats due to a multitude
of adverse consequences, unyielding imposition, and a soaring amount of
cross-border shopping by Danes.)

- **Outdoor Smoking Ban.** In NYC, it is illegal to smoke in public parks,
plazas, or beaches, and San Jose, California, and Boulder, Colorado, are
considering similar ordinances. "New York City and Disney Are Cracking
Down on Junk Food," *Time,* June 18, 2012, p. 20.

Pets—Monthly Cost of New TV Channel for Dogs. $4.99 a month for a
station dedicated to entertaining pet dogs while their owners are away.
Highlight shows are "dogs horsing (a seeming non-sequitur) around a pool
and dogs napping while New Age music plays." *Time,* May 7, 2012, p. 45.

Pornography vs. News Media Websites—Respective Page Views per Month.
"The largest porn site on the Web gets about 4.4BB page views per month,
or about triple the (web) traffic of CNN or ESPN." *The Week,* May 4, 2012,
p. 18, citing *ExtremeTech.com.*

Quality of Life.
- **Basic Conveniences.**
    - ○ **Air-Conditioning—U.S. Homes and Cars—Percentage of Homes
    and Cars With.** 86% of U.S. homes and 99% of U.S. cars now have
    air-conditioning. The Rivoli Theatre in New York was the first theatre
    in the U.S. with air-conditioning, and air-conditioning was installed
    in the House of Representatives in 1928 (followed shortly thereafter
    by the Senate and the White House). However, air-conditioning was
    not "commercially available" until after World War II when design
    changes allowed them to be small enough to fit in a window and cool
    just one room...." Gordon, J., "Air Conditioning, Blessed Invention,"
    The Wall Street Journal, July 11, 2012. See also, *The Week,* November
    30, 2012, p. 18. (While 13% of U.S. households as of 2009 still did
    not have any form of air-conditioning, of the homes which did have

household air-conditioning, the allocation by type was as of 2009 appr. 28% were window or wall units, and 72% central-air systems.)

o **Air-Conditioning, Dishwashers, and Microwaves—Availabilities and Disbursement Of.** The steady increases in the availability of these conveniences over the 15-year period from 1992 to 2005 are as follows:

Item	Percentage of Households With	
	1992	2005
Air-conditioning	50%	79%
Dishwashers	20%	37%
Microwaves	60%	91%

Schoenfeld, M., "Air Jordan and the 1%," *The Wall Street Journal*, July 11, 2012.

o **Internet—Percentage of Americans With Access to High-Speed Internet Service.** 94% of the U.S. population now has access to high-speed Internet service—leaving about 19MM Americans *without* such access. There was $7.2 BB in federal stimulus funds allocated to bringing high-speed Internet service to rural communities. Dugan, I., *The Wall Street Journal*, February 25, 2013.

• **Food and Dining Out—Percentage of Annual Income Spent On—As Function of Income Level.** The percentage of one's annual income spent on food is, unsurprisingly, a function of one's income level. Thus, the poorest Americans spend appr. 16% of their income on food compared with the wealthiest Americans who spend only about 11.6% on food—nearly 30% less of their annual income. Conversely, however, the wealthiest Americans spend nearly five times as much money "going out." *The Week*, March 22, 2013, p. 18, citing *Bloomberg Businessweek*.

• **Friendships and Confidants.**

o **Close Confidants—Number of for Average Americans.** As of 2004, the year Facebook was launched, most Americans had only two close confidants. This number is down from three as of about 20 years earlier in 1985, and it is possibly more disturbing is that one in four Americans has no close confidants. *The Week,* May 4, 2012, p. 18, citing J. Bercovici in *Forbes.com.*

o **Loneliness—Percentage of U.S. Adults Over Age 45 Who Are Chronically Lonely.** 35% per AARP study as opposed to 20% finding a decade earlier. *The Week*, May 4, 2012, p. 18.

• **Mail Delivery—Scheduled Elimination of Saturday Postal Delivery.** The U.S. Postal Service announced (and then retracted) that Saturday mail deliveries will cease in August 2013 in order to save nearly $1.9BB a year and as a component of the USPS's plan to eliminate annual losses which have recently "ballooned" to $15.9BB. This elimination of service "would have applied to all mail, including letters, bills, catalogues, advertising" but would not have applied to packages such as the premium-priced Express Mail, which would continue to be delivered on Saturdays. Levitz, J., Morath, E., *The Wall Street Journal,* February 7, 2013. Despite the constant ridicule of the USPS by some, its delivery costs are far less than postage costs in Europe, and the USPS recently did better than any other country in a delivery accuracy test. *The Week,* March 15, 2013, p. 11.

• **States—10 Happiest and 10 Most Miserable States** There are reasonable questions as to both (a) the importance and relevance of happiness and well-being, and (b) the capacity of such subjective criteria to be accurately measured. However, following the somewhat international trend of measuring and tracking happiness and well-being, Gallup started its Gallup-Healthways Well-Being Index in 2008. While there has not been a marked variation amidst the U.S. results since 2008, well-being is viewed as important "because happier, healthier citizens tend to have positive social and economic impacts on the places where they live." For example, in those states with higher well-being scores, the populations tended to smoke less, exercised more, tried new things more frequently, and had more energy and lower health problems such as blood pressure, diabetes, and heart attacks. The 24/7 website analysis of the Gallup Index also incorporated data from the U.S. Census Bureau, the U.S. Dept. of Labor's Bureau of Labor Statistics, the Henry J. Kaiser Foundation Health Reform Source, and the FBI Uniform Crime Reports. *Money.msn.com.* March 21, 2013 quoting Frank Newport, Gallup's Editor-in-Chief. According the 24/7's analysis of the Gallup Well-Being Index the following are the "happiest" and the "most miserable" states.

Happiest States

Ranking	State	Well-Being Index Score	Life Expectancy	Obesity Percentage	Median Household Income	Percentage Adult Population w/High School Diploma or Higher
States With Happiest/Greatest Sense of Well-Being						
1.	Hawaii	71.1	81.5 yrs	25.7%	$61,800	90.6%
2.	Colorado	69.7	79.9 yrs	18.7%	$55,400	90.2%
3.	Minnesota	68.9	80.9 yrs	24.7%	$57,000	92.0%
4.	Utah	68.8	80.1 yrs	23.9%	$55,900	90.3%
5.	Vermont	68.6	79.7 yrs	25.7%	$53,800	91.8%

46.	Arkansas	64.1	76.1 yrs	31.4%	$38,800	83.8%
47.	Tennessee	64.0	76.2 yrs	29.6%	$41,700	84.2%
48.	Mississippi	63.6	74.8 yrs	32.3%	$36,900	81.1%
49.	Kentucky	62.7	76.2 yrs	29.7%	$41,100	83.1%
50.	West Virginia	61.3	75.2 yrs	35.5%	$38,500	84.2%

States with Least Happy/Least Sense of Well-Being

Money.msn.com., March 21 2013

• **U.S. Happiness Compared With Other 36 OECD Nations.** Even though the U.S. once again had the highest disposable income of any of the 36 measured countries and a "high rate of self-reported good health," for the third year in a row, the U.S. in 2012 failed to make the top 10 happiest nations based upon the OECD's Better Life Index (the "BLI"). The BLI indices are comprised of eleven categories: housing, income, jobs, community, education, the environment, health, life satisfaction, safety, and work-life balance. The top ten happiest countries are as follows:

Ranking	Country	Life Satisfaction Score Health	Self-Reported Good	Employees Working Long Hrs	Disposable Income	Life Expectancy
1.	Switz.	7.8	81%	5.9%	$30,100	82.8 yrs
2.	Norway	7.7	73%	2.8%	$31,500	81.4 yrs
3.	Iceland	7.6	77%	13.5%	$21,200	82.4 yrs
4.	Sweden	7.6	80%	1.2%	$26,200	81.9 yrs
5.	Denmark	7.5	70%	2.0%	$24,700	79.9 yrs
6.	Netherlands	7.5	76%	0.7%	$25,500	81.3 yrs
7.	Austria	7.4	69%	8.8%	$28,900	81.1 yrs
8.	Canada	7.4	88%	3.9%	$28,200	81.0 yrs
9.	Finland	7.4	69%	3.9%	$25,700	80.6 yrs
10.	Mexico	7.3	66%	28.6%	$12,700	74.2 yrs
14.	*United States*			*11.0%*	*$38,000*	*79.0 yrs*
	OECD Country Average				$23,000	

Sauter, M., *24/7 Wall St,* June 1, 2013. But see, another reported index which ranked the world's happiest OECD countries as follows:

Ranking	Country	Ranking	Country
1.	Australia	*6.*	*United States*
2.	Sweden	7.	Denmark
3.	Canada	8.	Netherlands
4.	Norway	9.	Iceland
5.	Switzerland	10.	United Kingdom

oecdebetterlifeindex.org.

Lastly, the Social Progress Index, which measures 50 countries "selected as a representative sample of the world" ranked the following countries based upon "benchmarks such as nutrition, medical care and access to higher education. The top 10 countries in that survey were as follows:

Ranking	Country	Index Score	Ranking	Country	Index Score
1.	Sweden	64.81	*6.*	*United States*	*61.56*
2.	U.K.	63.41	7.	Australia	61.26
3.	Switzerland	63.28	8.	Japan	61.01
4.	Canada	62.63	9.	France	60.70
5.	Germany	62.47	10.	Spain	60.43

Cronin, B., The Wall Street Journal, April 11, 2013.

- **U.S. Quality of Life Compared with Other Nations—U.N. Human Development Index**. While GDP or per capita GDP is oftentimes used as a measure of how developed a nation is, it is deemed by some to focus too narrowly upon economic factors. The U.N. Development Program combines other data such as information relating to life expectancy and level and availability of education. The human development index (the "HDI") rates the country on a scale of 0 to 100. Countries which have a HDI above 80 are considered to have very high human development. As of 2010 the UN's HDI Index identified 38 countries with an HDI above 80. The U.S. was No. 4, with a 90.2 rating. The top five countries were as follows:

U.N. Human Development Index

Ranking	Country	HDI Rating
1.	Norway	93.8
2.	Australia	93.7
3.	New Zealand	90.7
4.	*United States*	*90.2*
5.	Ireland	89.5

The Economist: Pocket World in Figures, 2012 Edition. When adjusted for material inequality in the distribution of health, education and income, the IHDI (the "Inequality-Adjusted Human Development Index") generates considerably different ratings, and the U.S. falls below (albeit only slightly) the minimum 80 threshold for having "very high human development." The U.S. is, instead, rated as having only "high human development." The U.S. is ranked only 12th in the world on the IHDI with a rating of 79.9 (down from 90.2 on the non-adjusted HDI). The top five countries on the IHDI are as follows:

U.N. Inequality-Adjusted Human Development Index

Ranking	Country	IHDI Rating	
1.	Norway	87.6	(Down from 93.8 HDI)
2.	Australia	86.4	(Down from 93.7 HDI)
3.	Sweden	82.4	(Down from 88.5 HDI)
4.	Netherlands	81.8	(Down from 89.0 HDI)
5.	Germany	81.4	(Down from 88.5 HDI)

12. ***United States*** *79.9* ***(Down from 90.2 HDI)***

The Economist: Pocket World in Figures, 2012 Edition. Global happiness, contentment, and development surveys and analyses can be, however, notoriously subjective, depending on their purpose and their objectivity. Consider, for example, the North Korean self-serving index of global happiness announced in 2011 and in which China came in first, North Korea came in second, and the U.S. came in "dead last" at No. 203. *Time,* June 6, 2011, p. 14.

Race, Ethnicity, and Diversity.

- **College Education—Affirmative Action—Extent of Receipt of Admission Preferences.** "At selective schools, more than 80% of blacks and (66%) of Hispanics have received at least moderately large admissions preferences." The equivalence of such admissions preferences can be similar to a "100-point SAT boost, and often much more." Sander, R., Taylor, S., Jr., "The Unraveling of Affirmative Action," *The Wall Street Journal,* October 13–14, 2012, citing the authors' analysis of data from "several dozen selective schools."

- **Judiciary—Diversity Of Recent Appointments.** Of the 35 judicial nominations made by President Obama between January and March 2013, the diversity thereof was as follows:

Women	17
Ethnic Minorities	15
Openly Gay	5

  The Week, March 15, 2013, p. 16, citing *The Washington Post.*

- **Largest Minority Group in America.** Hispanics. Fields, G., "Hispanics Take a Page From '60s To Add Clout," *The Wall Street Journal,* July 21–22, 2012, citing recent U.S. Census data.

- **Misperceptions of Blacks—As Threat to Public Safety.** "15% of Americans believe blacks 'pose a greater threat to public safety than other groups.'" Toure, "Inside the Racist Mind," *Time,* May 7, 2012, p. 20, quoting the journal *Social Forces* (2007).

- **Newborn Children—Percentage Who Are Whites of European Ancestry.** For the first time in American history, between July 2010 and July 2011, less than 50% of newborn children born in the U.S. were white or of European ancestry. Fields, G., "Hispanics Take a Page From '60s To Add Clout," *The Wall Street Journal*, July 21–22, 2012, citing recent U.S. Census data.
- **Plight of Black Families and Males—School Drop-out Rates, Incarceration Rates, Fewer Two-Parent Families.** In addition to (or reflecting) growing up in an "'oppositional culture' that undermines achievement," more than 50% of urban males drop out of high school, more than 33% are incarcerated at some point in their lives, and "just 38% of black children (are) raised in two-parent families." *The Week*, December 28, 2012–January 4, 2013, p. 12, citing Gerson, M., *The Washington Post*.
- **Religion—Southern Baptist Convention (SBC)—Number of Times SBC Has Elected a Black Leader.** Only one. The SBC was founded in 1845 as a "breakaway sect from the anti-slavery Baptists of the north." Although about 15 years ago (in 1995), the SBC "formally apologized and promise(d) to make amends," it was not until June, 2012 that Fred Luter became the first black President of the SBC. *The Economist,* March 17–23, 2012, p. 36.
- **Segregation—Continuation Of—First Integrated High School Prom—Mt. Vernon, Georgia, High School.** The first integrated Montgomery County High School Prom was held just a few years ago (2010). F. Sun. "Last Dance," *Time*, June 11, 2012, p. 32. In a related instance of recent or continued segregation, see also, *The Week*, August 10, 2012, p. 4, noting that a black Mississippi couple was refused permission to conduct their marriage in a predominantly white Baptist church because the congregation decided that "no black could be married at the church."

Regional Disparities.
- **Alcohol Sales.**
  - **Bars Per Capita—Variance by States—Top 5 and Lowest 5 Numbers of Bars per Capita.** The number of bars per capita varies radically in the U.S. The Top 5 and Lowest 5 are as follows:

Most Bars Per Capita

Ranking	State	Number of Bars Per Capita
1.	North Dakota	1,621
2.	Montana	1,658
3.	Wisconsin	1,877
4.	South Dakota	2,258
5.	Nebraska	3,102

Fewest Bars Per Capita

46.	Arkansas	21,445
47.	Georgia	21,812
48.	Mississippi	27,326
49.	New Hampshire	34,689
50.	Virginia	64,773

Data assembled by INFORUM and based upon U.S. Census county business data. Sun, J., *eater.com.*, May 29, 2013.

○ **Government-Maintained Monopoly on Sale or Distribution of—Number of States**. 17 states—about 1/3rd of the states. *The Economist*, March 17–23, 2012, p. 33.

○ **Sales on Sunday—Counties in Georgia and Texas Where Still Illegal.** Effective as of March 2012, only three counties in Georgia and seven counties in Texas remain. Nine states have loosened liquor-selling laws since 2009 as "(t)he world is getting wetter" according to Frank Coleman of the Distilled Spirits Council of the United States. *The Economist*, March 17–23, 2012, p. 33.

• **Washington, DC Area—Unique Demographic Differences from Rest of Country.** The unique demographic differences between Washington, D.C. and the surrounding seven counties are as set forth below. (National comparative data indicted in parenthesis):

Category	District of Columbia And Surrounding Counties	National Average
Unemployment rate	5.5%	8.2%
Cost of office space	$50 per sq ft (similar to New York)	
Household Wealth	The "(r)ichest metropolitan area in the U S "	
Median household income	$84,523	$50,046

Other facts regarding District of Columbia and surrounding seven counties:
  Number of DC-Proximity Counties Which Are Among 15 Richest Counties in America: 9 ("including Nos. 1, 3, 4, and 5");
  Highest Percentage of 25-34-year-olds in national poverty rate (20% in DC vs. national average percentage of 15%).
Ferguson, A., "Bubble on the Potomac," *Time,* May 28, 2012, p. 46, citing S. Fuller, economist, George Mason University and Bloomberg News.

Religion.

• **Amish Population in America—Settlements—Number Of.** Doubling about every 22 years, there are now about 456 Amish settlements in the U.S. compared with 179 settlements in 1990. *The Week*, August 17, 2012, p., 14, citing *Columbus, Ohio Dispatch.*

- **Atheists, "Nones," and "Unaffiliated."**
  - ○ **"Nones" and "Unaffiliated" Percentage of Population in U.S. Who Self-Describe Themselves As.** Nones, those who declare themselves not to be associated with any organized or recognized religion—19%; Atheists—Between 1.4% and 4%. *The Week,* April 20, 2012, p. 11. See also, (i) *Time,* October 22, 2012, p. 9, citing Pew Study (Appr. 20% of the U.S. population—"up 5 percentage points in the past (5) years" self-describe themselves as being "unaffiliated" with any religion); and (ii) *pewforum.org* for Executive Summary or full Pew Study Report.
  - ○ **States Where Atheists Precluded from Holding Public Office— Number Of.** Seven states (Arkansas, Maryland, Mississippi, North Carolina, South Carolina, Tennessee, and Texas) and Pennsylvania (depending upon the interpretation and application of this statue law). Such seven state prohibitions are almost unquestionably unconstitutional, are never in practice enforced, and are never needed since appr. 40% of the U.S. adult population insist that they would never knowingly vote for an atheist. See *The Economist,* August 25–31, 2012, p. 23 and *www.americanhumanist.org.*
  - ○ **U.S. Congressmen As of 2012 Who Identify Themselves as Atheistic—Number Of.** None. The last such U.S. Congressman was the former Rep. Pete Stark (D-CA). At the time Congressman Stark left office in 2013, he was the 5th most senior Representative and the sixth most senior member of Congress. He had served in Congress from 1975 until his retirement in 2013.
- **Catholic Popes—Number from the New World—Number from Jesuit Order.** Only one. The March 2013 appointment of Jorge Bergoglio, the archbishop of Buenos Aires, as the 266th Catholic Pope, was the first time a priest has been appointed from the New World and was the first time a new pontiff has been selected from the Jesuit Order. He is also the first pope to select the name Francis, the saint devoted to the poor. *The Week,* March 22, 2013, p. 2.
- **Church Contributions—Amount Of—Aggregate and Average Per Capita Per Church Member.** Aggregate annual contributions in 2011 were appr. $29BB—which was appr. 4% lower than the prior year. The average per capita contribution in 2011 was appr. $763—which was appr. 2.2% less than the prior year. National Council of Churches 2012 Yearbook (Reporting on U.S. and Canadian Churches).

- **Heaven—Percentage of Americans Who Profess Belief In.** 85%, although there are many interpretations, meanings, and views of the concept of heaven. For example, for some it is the placed described and ordained in the Bible. For others, "(it) isn't just a place you go—heaven is how you live your life." Meacham, J., "Heaven Can't Wait," *Time*, April 16, 2012, p. 30, citing Gallup Poll and quoting John Blanchard, Executive Director of the 4,000-member Rock Church International in Virginia Beach, Virginia.
- **Largest Churches.**
  - ○ **By Membership—U.S. and Canada—Top 10 in Size.**

    Largest Churches—By Membership—U.S. and Canada

Ranking	Church	Number of Members
1.	Catholic Church	68.2MM
2.	Southern Baptist Convention	16.1MM
3.	United Methodist Church	7.7 MM
4.	Church of Jesus Christ of Latter-Day Saints (the Mormons)	6.2MM
5.	Church of God in Christ	5.5MM
6.	National Baptist Convention (USA)	5.2MM
7.	Evangelical Lutheran Church in Am.	4.3MM
8.	National Baptist Convention, USA, Inc.	3.5MM
9.	Assemblies of God	3.1MM
10.	Presbyterian Church (USA)	2.7MM

    National Council of Churches 2012 Yearbook (Reporting on U.S. and Canadian Churches unless otherwise noted). See also, *The Week*, May 18, 2012, p. 18, citing study by Association of Religion Data Archives and reporting that there are currently 58.9MM U.S. Catholics which number evidences a decline of 5% between 2000 and 2010. The same study reported that there are currently 6.1MM Mormons evidencing a growth of 45% between 2000 and 2010.
  - ○ **Fastest Five *Declining* (Largest Churches) Memberships.**

    Fastest *Declining* (Largest Churches) Membership

Ranking (In Order of Fastest Declining)	Church	Percentage Decline
1.	Evangelical Lutheran Church in America	Down 5.90%
2.	Presbyterian Church (USA)	Down 3.42%
3.	Episcopal Church	Down 2.71%
4.	United Church of Christ	Down 2.02%
5.	The Lutheran Church—Missouri Synod	Down 1.45%

Based upon reports of the sixteen Top 25 Churches reporting data. National Council of Churches 2012 Yearbook (Reporting on U.S. and Canadian Churches unless otherwise noted).

○ **Fastest Five *Growing* Memberships**.

Fastest *Growing* Church Memberships

Ranking (In Order of Fastest Growing)	Church	Percentage Growing
1.	Pentecostal Assemblies of the World	Up 20.00%
2.	Assemblies of God	Up 3.99%
3.	National Baptist Convention, USA, Inc.	Up 3.95%
4.	Jehovah's Witnesses	Up 1.85%
5.	Mormons and Seventh-Day Adventist (Statistical Tie)	Up 1.62 and 1.61%, respectively.

Based on reports of the sixteen Top 25 Churches reporting data. National Council of Churches 2012 Yearbook (reporting on U.S. and Canadian Churches).

○ **Top 25 Churches—Number Currently Growing in Membership Size**. Six of sixteen churches reported growing in membership. Ten churches reported a decline in membership. Nine churches did not provide updated data. National Council of Churches 2012 Yearbook (reporting on U.S. and Canadian Churches).

- **Reincarnation—Percentage of Americans Who Believe In**. 25%—and this percentage does not change as between those persons who self-identify themselves as "religious" and those who self-identify themselves as "nonreligious." Harper's Index, *Harper's Magazine,* June 2013, p. 15, citing The Pew Forum on Religion & Public Life.

- **"Religious"—Percentage of Americans Who Profess To Be**. 60% in 2011—which is a substantial 13% drop from 73% in 2005. *The Economist*, August 25–31, 2012, p. 23, citing WIN-Gallup International, an association of pollsters.

- **Scientology—Percentage of Americans Who Consider It a "True Religion.** Only 13%. 70% of those polled do not consider scientology a "true religion." The 60 Minutes/Vanity Fair Poll, *Vanity Fair,* November 2012, p. 62.

- **World Religiosity.**

  ○ **Percentage of World Population by Religion**. Appr. 84% of the world population "(has) some kind of religious affiliation." The breakdown by religion is as follows:

Religion or Association	Percentage of Total World Population
Christian	31.5%
Muslim	23.2%
Unaffiliated (Agnostic, atheist, no religion)	16.3%
Hindu	15.0%
Buddhist	7.1%
Folk/Traditional	5.9%
Other (Sikh, Shintoist, Taoist, Jainism, and others)	0.8%
Jewish	0.2%

The Economist, December 22, 2012–January 4, 2013, p. 102, citing Pew Research Center.

○ **Median Age of Adherents—Major Religions.** The median age by religions varies considerably from 22 years (Muslim) to 37 years (Jewish) and are as set forth below.

Religion or Association	Median Age of Religion or Association
Jewish	37 years
Unaffiliated (Agnostic, atheist, no religion)	34 years
Buddhist	33 years
Folk/Traditional	32 years
Other (Sikh, Shintoist, Taoist, Jainism, and others)	31 years
Christian	30 years
Global Median Age	***28 years***
Hindu	26 years
Muslim	22 years

The Economist, December 22, 2012–January 4, 2013, p. 102, citing Pew Research Center.

Renting or "Sharing" Economy—10 Examples of America's Increased Use of Renting (vs. Owning). Listed alphabetically, and *not* in any order, of dollar volume or priority, the following are ten examples evidencing the American consumer's seeming embrace of a rental or sharing economy as opposed to the traditional aspiration of ownership:

Art and Furnishings;

Automobiles (e.g., Zipcar car-sharing services with 4.4MM North American members);

Boats;

Chefs;

Children's Toys (BabyToys.com, a toy-rental company);

Dresses and Jewelry (Rent the Runway);

Housing and Housing Appliances;

Movies/Entertainment ("On-line movie consumption increased 160-fold—2007 to 2011");

Parking (On-line parking space services such as LAX's ParkatMyHome.com);

Tools and Electronics; and

Vacation Housing (e.g., VRBO.com and Airbnb.com).

See, Wolverson, R., "Welcome to the 'Sharing Economy,'" *Time,* September 24, 2012, p. 44.

Social Media—Facebook—Active Members—Number Of. More than 1BB as of September 14, 2012 —less than eight years after Mark Zuckerberg started the social network in his Harvard dorm in 2004. "If Facebook were a nation, it would have the third-largest population (behind only China and India). But if you compared its revenues to national GDPs, it would rank 156th." Fowler, G., "Facebook: One Billion and Counting," *The Wall Street Journal,* October 5, 2012, citing The World Bank (Economic and population data), Facebook (Monthly active users and revenue).

Vacation Homes—Average Annual Income of Vacation-Home Buyers. $88,600 in 2011 (down from $99,500 in 2010). Whelan, R., "Getting Away—But Not Too Far," *The Wall Street Journal,* May 2, 2012, citing survey by National Association of Realtors.

Vacation Time.

• **Availability of Paid Vacations—U.S. Compared With Other Countries.** The U.S. is the only highly developed country which does not require employers to offer paid vacation time. Except for the U.S., all other 21 developed countries mandated that employers grant vacation time of from 10 days (e.g., Japan and Canada) to 30 days (France). The following is a list of certain select countries and the average number of paid vacation days per year received by employees:

Country	Average Number of Paid Vacation Days
Italy	42 days
France	37 days
Germany	35 days
Brazil	34 days
United Kingdom	28 days
Canada	26 days
Korea	25 days
Japan	25 days
United States	*13 days*

Infoplease.com, Linn, A., CNBC.com, May 28, 2013.

- **Length of U.S. Vacations—Decline of Average Length.** The average length of U.S. vacation has been steadily declining for decades. The two-week vacation, "once the gold standard of family time," has been declined for decades due to double-income households and the "always-on business environment" which has become commonplace in the U.S. While the frequency of short vacations has increased, the average length of vacations has declined as follows:

Year	Average Length of Vacation
1975	More than one week
1985	5.4 days
2010	3.8 days

Copeland, L., *chicagobusiness.com,,* July 23, 2012, citing data from U.S. Travel Association.

- **Number of Weeks Most Americans "Would Want."**

Number of Desired Vacation Weeks Per Year	Percentage of Americans Preferring This Duration of Annual Vacation
2 weeks	18% (Appr.)
4 weeks	**43-48% (All age groups)**
6 weeks	20%%
8 weeks	16-18%% (For the dreamers)

Note: The Swiss recently voted *not* to increase their vacations from four weeks to six weeks. "The 60 Minutes/Vanity Fair Poll, *Vanity Fair*, June 2012, p. 56.

- **Relaxation From—Extent Of.** There appears to be *little correlation* between relaxation, the reduction or elimination of stress, and the taking of vacation. By U.S. workers.

Description	Percentage So Reporting
Achievement of Complete Relaxation	Less than 10%
No Stress Relief	58%
Greater Stress By End of Vacation	27%

The Week, June 7, 2013, p. 35, citing *CSMonitor.com.*

Violence.

- **Personal Protections Items—Items, If Any, Carried for Protection Outside the Home.** The following respective percentages of respondents indicated that they carried the following items for their own personal protection outside the home:

Carried Item of Protection, If Any	Percentage of Respondents
None	66%
Gun	12%
Pepper Spray	10%
Knife	7%
Whistle	2%

The 60 Minutes/Vanity Fair Poll, *Vanity Fair,* April, 2013, p. 68.

- **Relationship Between Violence in Popular Culture and Violence in Society.** A recent poll indicated that most Americans believe that there is a strong correlation between violence in our country's "popular culture" (e.g., movies and video games) and violence in our society. 80% of respondents believe that there is "a lot" (45%) or "some" (35%) such correlation whereas only 18%, less than 1 in 5, believed that there is "not much" or "not at all." The 60 Minutes/Vanity Fair Poll, *Vanity Fair,* April, 2013, p. 68.

Women—Number and Percentage of U.S. Public Statues of Women Compared With Men. Of the 5,193 public statues of individuals in the U.S., only 394 (or 7.6%) depict women. Harper's Index, *Harper's Magazine,* July, 2011, p. 17, citing Smithsonian American Art Museum.

APPENDIX A

Introduction To
THE CHANCE OF A LIFETIME

A Series of Books About
The Patient Remaking of American Life

For More Information about *The Chance of a Lifetime* Series of Books,
see www.mackwborgen.com.

Book Series
THE CHANCE OF A LIFETIME
A Series of Short Books About The Patient Remaking of American Life

Book One
THE RELEVANCE OF REASON – BUSINESS AND POLITICS
The Hard Facts and Real Data About the State of Current America

Book Two
THE RELEVANCE OF REASON – SOCIETY AND CULTURE
The Hard Facts and Real Data About the State of Current America

Book Three
DEAD SERIOUS AND LIGHT-HEARTED
How To Get America ~~Right~~ Fixed
(Scheduled Publication: Winter, 2013)

Book Four
> *GRADING ON THE CURVE*
> *Towards A More Objective Understanding of America*
> *(Projected Publication: Spring, 2014)*

Book Five
> *REASONED CASE FOR OPTIMISM*
> *America in the Early 21ˢᵗ Century*
> *(Projected Publication: Fall, 2014)*

Book Six
> *NO DOG IN THE FIGHT*
> *The 10 Changes Necessary for the Remaking of American Life*
> *(Projected Publication: Winter, 2014)*

Book Seven
> *THE BRILLIANCE OF MANY*
> *1,000 Ideas for Improving Life in America*
> *(Projected Publication: Spring, 2015)*

Synopsis Of
The Chance of a Lifetime Book Series
& Books One and Two

The Chance of a Lifetime is a series of books about the need and the means for the patient remaking of American life.

Drawing upon an analysis of the last 55 years from 1957 through 2012, these books will describe the current state of the American condition. They will identify what must be done to change the direction of our country and to improve the quality of American life.

The frequent references to America's recent history are intended to remind us of both our accomplishments and our failings. These books draw upon a wide range of writings—from the wisdom of Herbert Croly's *Promise of American Life*, the breadth of Durant's *History of Civilization*, the cultural narrative of William Manchester's *The Glory and the Dream*, the academic precision of James T. Patterson's *Restless Giant*, the period insights of Halberstam's *The Fifties* and *The Best and the Brightest*, the almost personal and touching historical writings of Michael Beschloss and David McCullough, the brilliant succinctness of Kurt Andersen's *Reset,* and the perspectives of a wide array of contemporary writers, essayists, columnists, and critics holding vastly differing perspectives.

Our American history has a particular relevance to this series of books because it is our history that can best grant us the perspective and the patience to change. And these are not idle companions. To the contrary, perspective and patience are two of the precursors to meaningful progress. The devolution of American life has occurred over many decades. Our solutions are going to take several more. In the meantime, we are going to have to learn to enjoy, or at least survive, the ride.

As suggested by the title of the third book, *Dead Serious and Light-Hearted*, these books address serious subjects, but they do so with a degree of humor and levity. They do not hesitate to also draw upon the balloon-boy, Lady Gaga, and Red Bull absurdities that have become a part of American life over the last few decades.

The reasons for the inclusion of humor, levity, and the absurd are far more than mere matters of style.

Americans have not taken a deep breath in two decades, and humor and levity can be humanizing. They may help us take the edge off of our conversations. They may be the best means to slowly change the scowling, go-figure, grumpy tone of our current American conversation. Americans have forgotten that we laugh better than we argue, and we have let the list of toxic subjects grow too long—guns and butter, war and peace, the role of the government, states' rights, church and state, and personal and civic responsibility. Each of these subjects summons a witch's brew of emotions. Frustration, disillusionment, and anger surface too often and too readily.

Our anger invokes hostility. It blinds our vision and tempts us into using hyperbole and generalizations about, for example, politicians, public servants, and the media. In our anger, we round the truth to make a point or win an argument. We dismiss all politicians as bad, despite knowing that there remain some decent and well-meaning politicians. We dismiss all government servants as "faceless bureaucrats" and exempt only soldiers to whom we still offer up deserved praise and thanks. We dismiss journalists, despite knowing that there remain some fine, thoughtful columnists who are deserving of our time. We dismiss television and radio media, despite knowing that there remain some shows that are informative and good. We dismiss newspapers and periodicals, despite knowing that some are far better and more accurate than others.

Although the frustration is understandable and the disillusionment is real, our anger must be constrained. Furthermore, anger is neither the only nor even the best voice of passion. More importantly, America needs precision as much as it needs passion. There is no easy or quick way to ebb the anger or redirect our passion. Our recovery is going to take a long time. But, in the interim, we can present a different sense of ourselves, and the reinfusion of humor and levity will help. Years ago, e.e. cummings said that we should laugh at everything but the circus. Possibly he was right.

In addition to the use of humor and levity, these books are kept short. Americans are tired of talking in paragraphs. We don't need another inch-thick book about defeatism and decline. Defeatism serves no purpose. Suggestions of declinism are misguided. The very words—defeatism and declinism—affront America's long traditions of ingenuity, self-reliance and success. While some would disagree, these books suggest that strains of denialism are too prevalent and that mere incantations of America's exceptionalism will not enough. Just like the tab on Facebook—"It's complicated."

But there are areas of broadening consensus, and these books build upon them.

There is a broadening consensus that America's problems are numerous, compounding, and inter-related. Except in the one instance relating to generational role and conduct of us baby-boomers, these books do not expend energy or words in honing criticism or assigning blame. Those subjects have been well-covered by a hundred other writers.

There is a broadening consensus that our political system is dysfunctional and that it is not going to correct itself by the electoral arrival of unifying political leader, by a crop of new faces, by the improved behaviors of our leaders, by the occurrence of some epiphanous enlightenment. Similarly, we can no longer await bursts of brilliance or accidental honesty. Instead, we must adjust to the reality that our electoral and legislative processes are not going to readily change or quickly improve.

There is a broadening consensus that our economic system has become too Darwinian. Many now believe that the disparate allocations of income, wealth, and opportunity may be counter-productive to the long-run success and safety of our country. These are fair matters of honest debate, but it is unlikely that our economic system is going to correct itself by the free run of market forces or by the application of either more or less regulation. In frustration and as a matter of strategy, many aspects of our economic system have become a mere part of the political grudge match currently in play.

Our society has changed in many other ways and for many other reasons. Many of our traditional behavioral restraints have been diminished. Many of our communities have been re-defined; others have been dangerously weakened. Anxiety, fear and pessimism have become pervasive forces. Good people fight for their jobs. Good parents fight for the good education of their children. Accurate information is terribly difficult to find despite the cascade of Google-Wiki data which keeps coming. More and more it seems as though America can color within the lines, but it is having trouble connecting the dots.

Our senses of personal and civic responsibilities have been affronted by the disappointing acts of some of our leaders and by the media's continuing obsession with ratings, celebrities, New Jersey housewives, ice road truckers, and pawn shop owners. Half of America knows Lindsey Lohan's next prison release date. That itself is a problem.

For these and other reasons, enough is enough. The patience of many Americans has expired. We must act.

Defining the direction and achieving the changes which are necessary to improve the security and quality of American life are up to us. It is time for America to change. Once again.

Through our words, actions, and example, it is now time *for us* to lead; to think; to restrain; and to encourage. We need to reign in our anxieties. We must contain our fears. We must stand together and stare down the face of crazy.

There are many things which we can do to improve our own lives and those of our families, friends, and communities. We do not need to wait for funding to come through; for coalitions to be built; for third-parties to be formed; or for another economy calamity to reach critical mass meltdown.

There is a path home, and we may be in a period of peculiar opportunity.

These books (gently) encourage the assertion of personal powers and the better acceptance of personal responsibilities. These books identify with specificity those things which we, *not they*, can do for our country and in our own self-interest. One by one, we must re-take the lead; we must re-direct the focus of our country from critique to effort; and we must apply our energies. And the place to begin is everywhere.

The breadth of these topics is, admittedly, terribly wide. Over the last several years I have, at times, feared that this entire effort may be nothing more than a fool's errand or what the historian, Will Durant, used to refer to as, more gently, a "brave stupidity." Nevertheless, I have chosen to continue my undertaking—my brave stupidity—with a certain stubborn diligence.

The methodology of these books is direct. The first two books *(The Relevance of Reason—The Hard Facts and Real Data About the State of Current America)* focus, respectively upon *Business and Politics* (Book One) and *Society and Culture* (Book Two). They present facts and data about Current America in the context of the period 1957-2012 which is introduced as Modern America. Book Three *(Dead Serious and Light-Hearted, How to Get America Right Fixed)* introduces the multiple objectives of these books, the nature and importance of the national community, and the necessity for patience. Because we live in an age of deep cynicism and cluttered agendas, the personal background of the author and the motivations behind these books are also presented. Conclusions about the current state of America are presented in Book Four *(Grading on the Curve—Towards a More Objective Understanding of America)* and the reasons why Americans should have and hold a strong sense of optimism is presented in Book Five (*A Reasoned Case for Optimism—America in the 21st Century*). Finally, ten specific changes are identified in Book Six *(No Dog in the Fight—The Ten Changes Necessary for the Remaking of American Life)* which we, as individuals, must make in order to patiently achieve the promise of American life.

Some of these changes, such as those relating to education and parenting, are based upon mistakes which we have made as a society over the last several decades. Some of the changes, such as our unfiltered acceptance of data, our undue deference to experts, the reach of America's compromised media, and our growing disdain for logic and reason, result partly from the challenges of adjusting to our new age of information and technology. Other changes, such as the need for a resurgence of personal ethics, for the restoration of accountability and civility, and for a better definition and stronger sense of community, will be recognized as recurrent themes in American history. These needed changes are humbly offered by the author as a possible template for the evolution of a consensus agenda for this country.

Lastly, these books reference the many things which remain steadfastly great about this country—our country's litany of good. This litany of good is highlighted and repeated in these books for at least two reasons. First, the good, just like the bad, is highly relevant to any accurate assessment of American life. Second, the good is far too easily forgotten and far too often under-reported.

The final book, Book Seven (*The Brilliance of Many—1,000 Ideas for Improving Life in America),* is entirely different. This book is a compilation of the many, sometimes brilliant, ideas about improving American life *which already exist.* These ideas have been assembled by the author, and they are presented without comment or recommendation. Some of them are already being implemented or tested either in America or elsewhere. However, due usually to under-funding and under-reporting, they are not well known and have not yet been widely considered.

On a personal note, it has taken nearly five years to write these books. I know that America does not need merely another perspective. That has already been done. In some cases, it has already been done brilliantly. But, now, it is time for a new approach.

I hope that you will find these books useful. Remembering the importance of humor and levity, I offer that these books were written with coffee. They should be read with beer.

Synopsis of Book Three
Dead Serious and Light-Hearted
How To Get America ~~Right~~ Fixed
(Scheduled Publication: Spring, 2014)

Dead Serious and Light-Hearted is the third book in *The Chance of a Lifetime* series. This book presents the objectives of the series and some of the author's threshold conclusions about contemporary American economic, political and social life. Book Three also introduces the concept of America's litany of good—those wonderful features of American life that are too often forgotten and too consistently under-reported.

The book starts by addressing the fragmentation of knowledge and the separateness of facts which characterize American life. The book analyzes how different groups of Americans are increasingly relying upon narrow and often incomplete senses of their own reality. All of us are burdened by our own biases and perspectives due to our varying ages, backgrounds, race, ethnicity, educational achievement, and the latitude and longitude of our birth, but the nature and extent of this fragmentation of knowledge is new. We are now burdened by the presentations of wholly differing truths. My facts vs. your facts. My Fox News vs. your MSNBC—or the other way around.

These problems distort our conversations. They undermine our ability to reach consensus. We now, almost routinely, talk pass one another. Tempers flare and in no time at all the square root of 9 is a rainbow. Believing our own sources and relying upon our own set of facts, we hold onto our perceived truths. We allow strong senses of political enemies and allies to creep into our lives. *Dead Serious and Light-Hearted* tries to assess the extent and reversibility of this fragmentation of knowledge and its resultant confusion and anger.

The book recognizes that other Americans have reacted differently. Disillusioned and exhausted, they have simply withdrawn from much of civic (or at least civil) society. However, this withdrawal is not a mere reflection of apathy. Other forces are at work. Different truths are in play.

In fact, America has much on which to build, and it obvious that many Americans still care deeply about this country. Many Americans try to keep well-informed. Many Americans appear willing to again become engaged, but changes need to be made in how we talk with one another. More importantly, Americans need both the sense and the reality of progress.

This book addresses the prevalence of anxiety and fear which has come to dominant the lives of many Americans. The rise of terrorism, the continuing economic chaos, and the inflammatory reporting of the American media keep some Americans bound together in their shared anxiety and fear. Almost through no fault of their own, they sit wide-eyed in the dark. However, our jittery apprehensions are neither the natural nor the historical state of our nation or its peoples. Book Two starts to lay the groundwork for regaining our confidence, for recovering our balance, and for rediscovering our senses of humor, levity, and perspective.

Dead Serious sets forth certain basic requisites for a new American conversation. It focuses upon the importance of civility, the need for caution, and need for discretion in relying upon the reporting of the media and the counsel of experts. The author argues that before meaningful conversations can re-commence, Americans must set aside (or at least contain) the more common weapons of our contemporary discourse— the bluster of anger, the twisting of words, the games of blame, and the sometimes baseless accusations of bias, ignorance, disinterest, or agenda. We Americans must also abandon our relentless demand for brevity, our obsession with techno-twitter speed, and our growing willingness to rely upon a mere sense of "gist" rather than understanding. Neither Cheney's head-tilting, gravitas nor Obama's power of oratory can be allowed to supplant our independent powers of common sense and reasoning. As implied in the subtitle of this series—the *patient* remaking of American life—there is a need to remember that there are no short-cuts. There are no quick fixes. It took us a long time to reach our current condition. It is going to take us a long time to correct and again remake American life.

The underlying reason for focusing upon the power and responsibilities of individuals is the conclusion that America's real problems are not going to be resolved by tinkering with public policies. These matters are important, and their wise resolution will help. But they are background noise compared to the importance of Americans, one by one, child by child, family by family, block by block, community by community taking action and changing our behaviors.

The author then digresses and takes the liberty of introducing himself. However, this is not a matter of self-indulgence. This introduction is included because contemporary America is encrusted with cynicism. Such cynicism has led to an expectation of self-interest and an assumption of agenda in all endeavors, and these books are not immune from such cynicism. The author introduces himself from his youth in the Pacific Northwest through his years in college; from his years at Harvard Law School through his four years of military service; from his time in Spain through his return to America and his professional life in the United States; from his life as a young man to, allow me this, a loving husband and an adoring father of a still young boy. Readily confessing, just like Hemingway said, that it all reads better than it lived, the author then addresses the fair questions of any thoughtful reader—why these books now and for what purpose.

The objectives, assumptions, and methodology which are used in this series of books are also addressed. Despite the possibly boring nature of the "ologies" and despite the fact that they are oftentimes seen as mere matters of process, they need to be explained. The clarity of objectives, the reasonableness of assumptions, and the methodologies of research are how any author, innocently or otherwise, tailors his arguments, controls the story, and reaches his conclusions. There is no misunderstanding by the author that brevity is important or that we live in a bottom-line, answer-insistent, culture, but some details are important and there is no time for secrets.

In the closing sections of Book Two, the importance of community and the unique importance of our national community are discussed.

These subjects remain surprisingly under-discussed in America. However, they are critical, and they are complicated. On the one hand, a sense of community is at the core of our social contract. It is the source of many of our expectations and our responsibilities with respect to our country. On the other hand, more and more Americans seem to be concluding that the reach of one's obligations extends only to one's own family and small circle of friends or one's self-defined sense of community. Furthermore, there appears to be a resurgent sense that the obligations to one's community, national or otherwise, can be conveniently subordinated to one's own sense and right of individualism.

The inclusion of this subject of community in this Book *Dead Serious and Light-Hearted* is because the state of, especially, our national community is fragile. It is at risk. It is challenged by numerous centrifugal forces of our modern culture. Especially over the last two decades there has been a rise in the sense of regionalism and political, social and religious associations. Our divisiveness has come to over-shadow our unity. This cannot safely continue, and especially our national community cannot be held together merely by the periodic occurrence of shared events, joys, calamities, fears, or even prayers.

We cannot stand side by side; coldly in isolation from one another. We cannot pretend to be bound together solidly as a nation by watching the same shows, sharing the same highways, or rooting for common favorites or even against common enemies. Conversely, it is not enough to be held together by our shared tragedies or fears. For example, neither our shared sadness of 9/11 nor our shared fears of terrorism are enough to keep this country together. We need deeper roots. We need stronger, better, and more long lasting mortar.

The last chapter starts the introduction of Book Four, *Grading on the Curve—Towards A More Objective Understanding of America*. It focuses upon the dichotomous importance and difficulty of getting a clear read on America. Only a part of the problem of "seeing" America is attendant to the count of our population and the size of our country. Clarity is also obscured because America is complex, heterogeneous, multi-generational, and constantly changing. In addition, few aspects of American life are easily or accurately measured, and each of our perspectives remains almost separate, distinct, and personal unto ourselves. They are built upon our own memories, histories, condition, and place of being. America looks a lot different in Beehive, Alabama (yes, there is one) than it does in New York City. The street corners of Compton don't resemble the roads of New England. There is little resemblance (and possibly little in common) between a country store and an urban mall. The gray cloverleafs of LA don't look anything like the green cloverleafs of the Great Plains.

Nevertheless, there is a threshold importance in trying to "see" the same America. Accurately and thoroughly understanding the true condition of our country is the best basis by which we can define our objectives, establish our priorities, and decide, together, what we must do. While difficult, we must try to see and know the same country. That is the subject of the next book— *Grading on the Curve—Towards A More Objective Understanding of America.*

Synopsis of Book Four
Grading on the Curve
Towards a More Objective Understanding of America
(Projected Publication: Summer, 2014)

Grading on the Curve is the fourth book in *The Chance of a Lifetime* series. It attempts to present a thorough and objective description of the contemporary American condition. The book's genesis lies in the fact that we Americans do not have an accurate understanding, a shared memory, or a shared perspective about our country. This contributes greatly to the very divergent beliefs held by Americans about our nation's strengths, weaknesses, and capabilities.

An understanding of our own country will not, by itself, calm our nerves or diminish our fears. But it will allow us to better evaluate the empty simplicities and hyperbole which frequently characterize our political campaigns, the buckets of data dumps thrown onto our American conversations by various experts—self-declared or otherwise, and the bounty of factoids which are served up by the media. Most importantly, understanding

America's true condition may also be a useful guide in determining where we should go and what we should do. It may serve as a common place from which to begin the resolution of America's issues. It may be another basis for improving the tone and the substance of our American conversation. Lastly, it may help us realize that America may be in a period of peculiar opportunity and that there is a basis for much optimism.

But descriptions of America are difficult. Accuracy, measurement and even truth are elusive. Reason can be easily replaced by ideology, twisted by hope, buried by anger, or otherwise lost amidst the myriad passions of the moment. Data, definitions, period selection, and statistical models are subject to easy manipulation. It does not help that new chapters of history are written and more data is assembled each day.

Similarly, any snap-shot of America is, by definition, "history" the moment the picture is taken. No matter how fast the shutter speed of our camera, the picture distorts that which it memorializes. It fails to show that which preceded or that which will follow. It fails to capture what is behind the camera, down the road, around the corner, or over the horizon. America is just damn hard to "see."

America is also hard to see because American society is subject to division in a hundred different ways—by our ages; by our place of birth or place of residence; by the extent and quality of our education; by our biases, predilections, curiosities, and even our dispositions; by the nature of our appearance and the condition of our health; by the structure and strength of our families and friends; by our race, ethnicity, and religion; and by the amount of our income or the type of our employment.

Partly because of the number and significance of such divisions, any attempt at a composite description of America is both difficult and dangerous. It is not surprising that Americans have difficulty sharing common agreement about the state of our own nation and our prospects for change. It is not surprising that we get all twisted in the mirror as we try to discuss our problems and resolve our differences. Worse yet, our unfamiliarity with one another and with other parts of our country makes all of us vulnerable to the mischief and mischaracterizations of others—especially social and political leaders.

Nevertheless, such description is the only place to begin. Any serious discussion about America and about our alternatives for change must begin with knowing, to even the limited extent possible, who we are and how we are.

This is the subject of Book Four, *Grading on the Curve*. In this book an attempt is made at the impossible: to summarily, objectively, accurately, and interestingly describe America. The book's title is intended to suggest both a comfort and a reminder.

The comfort portion of the title is that America, like all countries, deserves to be "graded on the curve." There are several reasons.

First, any description of America can become easily buried in data and bogged down in a cascade of numbers. But the meaning of that data and the importance of those numbers are oftentimes found only in the context of comparisons. Randomly dropped factoids about America are common. Sometimes they are even interesting. But, alone and without context, they are rarely useful. They rarely help. While comparing America with other countries is exponentially more difficult, it is far more meaningful. For example, it may be nice to know that the average life expectancy in America has been extended to 78.7 years, but this number has limited absolute meaning. It gains far more traction when compared to parallel data of other nations or in the context of trending patterns. It becomes far more meaningful number when we understand that America's life expectancy is not ranked first in the world. It is ranked 50th in the world—below Portugal, Jordon and even Bosnia. On a brighter note, American's life expectancy has roughly doubled in the last century and has increased by another roughly ten years since the 1970's.

Secondly, grading on the curve may be especially relevant in this age of globalism. The use of a comparison may help us to better understand our own country as we stand in contrast to our friends, our enemies, and our competitors. At least since the end of World War II, most Americans have accepted that we cannot meaningfully view ourselves as separate, apart, or distant from the world. Partly for that reason as well—comparisons, not absolutes, matter.

Consider a few examples. Pakistan possesses nuclear weapons. It is an important nation especially in the context of national security. Nevertheless, it is still somehow strangely relevant, if not strangely comforting, to know that Pakistan's economy is only slightly larger than that of the State of Oregon. Russia is another example. Russia remains a dominant player on the world stage. It possesses a seemingly impressive gross national product of approximately 2.2 Trillion (U.S.) dollars. However, like Pakistan, these facts seem to take on more much meaning and perspective in the context of comparison since this entire Russian economy is only about the size of the State of Texas and a few Midwestern states. American has some of the greatest health care facilities in the world, but the troublesome fact is that infant mortality rates in the Unites States are *comparatively* high. They are higher than Greece and Italy. They are nearly three times those of Singapore. This should give us pause, and in these ways, the use of *comparative* analyses may be far more useful isolated data. America should take great pride in the fact that our crime rate has been dropping for nearly two decades now. However, America remains, for better or worse, a nation of punishment and incarceration. Our incarceration rate is the highest in the world—more than twice that of Iran and seven times as high as the United Kingdom.

This book recognizes that there are limits to this type of analysis. Comparative analyses are terribly difficult to apply in certain contexts, such as assessing political and economic stability or evaluating the quality or state of aspirational goals, such as equality, opportunity, achievement, idealism, or perfection. Evaluating the level of our success in achieving these goals is critical to any full description of American life, but in these contexts the utility of grading on the curve is far more limited.

The reminder portion of Book Four's *Grading on the Curve* title is that the world is often the more correct standard.

Understanding America in comparison to its stated ideals is incredibly important. Evaluating ourselves in the context of our own past and against our own potential remains inevitable. In fact, America already is compared and evaluated every day in the flow of capital, the net migrations of peoples, and the evaluation and debates about the many alternative models of social, political and economic systems.

Nevertheless and however disquieting as it may be to some, *comparing* America to the rest of the world may help us understand ourselves better.

In some instances this book will give us more reasons to be proud and appreciative of our country. It may help us achieve some patience with ourselves—which we so desperately need. In other instances, we may find ourselves challenged, disappointed and even embarrassed for our country which, in turn, may help us embrace humility and contain arrogance.

In sum, considering ourselves in comparison with the rest of the world is an admittedly difficult and even clumsy task. But it is important.

While Book Four acknowledges, indeed highlights, some of the serious issues facing America, it also starts to present some of the reasoned bases why Americans should feel proud, energetic, and steadily confident and secure about itself.

All of these reasons combined, lead to the next book—Book Five— *A Reasoned Case for Optimism—America in the Early 21st Century.*

Synopsis of Book Five
A Reasoned Case For Optimism
America in the Early 21st Century
(Projected Publication: Winter, 2014)

A Reasoned Case for Optimism is the fifth book in *The Chance of a Lifetime* series. This book presents the many reasons for Americans to have and *to exercise* optimism in the resolution of the fundamental issues facing our country. This book further suggests that we may even be in a period of peculiar opportunity.

There are two reasons for addressing the subject of optimism. First, America is going to need a lot of it. Second, for many reasons optimism seems to be in short supply of late.

Americans are more and more understanding the nature and extent of our problems. Americans are slowly coming to the conclusion that our problems will not come from tinkering with public policy or from the election of a new crop of politicians. The problems are far deeper. They are more fundamental. The solutions will require a sustained effort by a wide swath of our population. The solutions will have to come first from changes in how we, *not they*, behave, think, and reason. The solutions will require a blend of focus, energy, patience and humility—the last two of which are not America's strong suit.

At first blush, there is a troublesome kumbaya ring to these suggestions—"fundamental changes" and "wide swath of our population." But these matters are not left vague. They are not left open for widely personalized interpretation. Instead, the next book, *No Dog in the Fight—The Ten Changes Necessary for the Remaking of American Life,* identifies the decisions which we must make and what we must do as a country. As tempting as it is to dive in, the issues of focus, resources, energy, patience, and humility—and ultimately optimism must first be addressed.

Book Four presents substantial evidence that America has the focus. We are a smart people. We know we have been—in some aspects of our social, political, and economic lives—aimless for several decades. We know there are changes which need to be addressed.

A Reasoned Case for Optimism presents substantial evidence that America has great resources and great energy—but our energy has, of late, been of the wrong type. It has been jumpy, caffeinated, agitated, and angry. It has stemmed too much from fear and anxiety rather than from hope and optimism. We will eventually regain our steady confidence, and our confidence will once again flow from our progress—but not at first. Initially, however, our energy must flow from a regained sense of optimism.

America has historically been an optimistic nation, but pessimism has crept deep into our thinking. Times have changed, and we know that fireside chats are not going to be enough. We know that we all have a lot more to fear than fear itself. The last decade neither began nor ended well. Our horizon is cloudy, and declinist books are everywhere. We carry around that Gibbon's *Rise and Fall of the ...* in our heads. Most of us never read it, but we know the theme.

Thus, the reason for this book. The subject is optimism. It is critical.

This book will explain how America can reclaim its sense of optimism. This book will explore how our optimism has become lost amidst our arguing. It has been buried under the headlines. Now, it is waiting to be reclaimed, and it is time to do so.

The reasons for optimism discussed in this book are not rooted in giddy hope, wishful thinking, or blind faith. They do not rest upon some kind of pathetic, we-are-all-in-it-together, lifeboat analogy. Data, far more than emotion, is used, and this book's conclusions are based upon America's traditional sense of resilience, our history, and our resources.

Pushing even further, this book concludes that America may be in a period of peculiar opportunity. There may be an opening for something different, but some changes will need to be made.

The television may need to be turned off and the radio may need to be turned down. The breaking news of the day may need to be received with less alarm and more perspective. We must stop the empty banter and slowly, even if begrudgingly at first, we must find ways to reach out to one another. Our leaders are not going to lead us to unification. It will have to come from us.

And we may be in a period of peculiar opportunity. Americans are coming to better understand that few of us are able to withdraw from the American community. The doors cannot be made thick enough. The community walls cannot be built high enough. The woods are not deep enough. Our stake in America's future is shared.

And precisely because we are in the foxhole together, looking over the edge and trying to sneak a peak at the future, there are signs of a growing commonality among us. More Americans are holding the growing sense of a common struggle. More Americans share feelings of loss, fear, failure, confusion, and frustration.

These feelings result partly from America's recent economic collapse and partly from the conspicuous dysfunction of our political system, but there are social dimensions as well. Some Americans actually miss the silence. They miss the calm, grace, and common courtesies of days gone by. Those days cannot be fully reclaimed, and it is important to remember that for some Americans, the good old days never were). However, even though we cannot go back, we can decide how we wish to go forward.

We have to relax and remember that, just like high school, there will always be the 2% who will remain balloon-boy crazy, stupid stubborn, or brain-locked by disposition or habit. But the noisy influence of 2% crazy needs to be contained. Their role (and their volume) in our national debates must be diminished. Instead, we have to literally build upon our common senses of frustration with the courser of our country. We have to force ourselves to be open to changing the way they think, behave, and converse. In this manner, almost curiously, it is these feelings of shared frustration and exhaustion that may unite us. Again. Our collective displeasure may finally work in our favor.

Some of the most challenging issues will at first be the subject of tough debate and divisive opinions, but there is growing evidence of consensus here as well. For example, most Americans, though certainly not all, believe that America's allocations of income, wealth, and opportunity do need to be improved. Most Americans believe that innovation needs to be encouraged and that honest effort and constructive ingenuity should be rewarded. For now, these can serve as places for starting-line consensus.

Optimism can be also be rooted in our better remembering the very nature of democracy. It is a god-love-it, imperfect and terribly inefficient system of governance. On our best, flag-waiving day, our government rests on the rough theory that, as Bertrand Russell said, 51% of the people are right 51% of the time. These are not good numbers, but they closely reflect the percentages of nearly all of our national elections over the last century. And so patience and a sense of optimism will be required. A lot of it. There is work to be done, and the place to begin is everywhere.

Optimism can also be drawn from the nature and proximities of our communities. Our national community is obviously important, but it siphons off too much of our attention. The place to begin may be closer to home. These are the issues which affect us the most, and these are the issues which can most readily and effectively be addressed.

The reasoning is that most Americans live, almost by definition, close to home. We live as a part of one or more distinguishable communities defined by family, friends, neighborhoods, religion, age, and interests. Our place of worship is down the road. Our favorite restaurant is around the corner. Our favorite stores are not far away. Our children's schools are close at hand. These aspects of our American life are close. They are within our reach.

It may be national political or economic matters which most often inflame our tempers, but it is the things closer to home affect us the most. We are more impacted by the obnoxious neighbor next door, by the litter along our roads, and by the graffiti in our parks. We are hurt more by the rudeness of surly clerk or the grumpy silence of the passerby than we do. We work longer due to the employee who doesn't show up or by the co-worker who doesn't carry his load. These things are close to home. These are the things which impact us the most. And these things *we* can change. Most of us would happily trade in another conversation about Romney's marginal tax rate for a waive from a friend—any day.

It will require a measure of optimism to improve our own lives and to re-define the American creed of behavior and social expectations. It will take optimism to stretch those expectations so that they are reflected in the operations of our economy and our politics, in the programming of our media, and in the education content of our schools. But it can be done.

The bases for such optimism are set forth in this Book Four, but we must also identify, with specificity and priority, the issues which we need to address and what must be done. That is the subject of the next book.

Book Five is entitled *No Dog In the Fight—The 10 Changes Necessary for the Remaking of American Life*. It identifies the issues we need to address, the decisions we need to make; and the things we must do.

Synopsis of Book Six
No Dog in the Fight
The 10 Changes Necessary for the Remaking of American Life
(Projected Publication: Spring, 2015)

No Dog in the Fight is the sixth book in *The Chance of a Lifetime* series. It addresses the need for America to once again embrace the need for "change"—an admittedly over-worked word. This book reminds us that change has been an integral and inevitable part of American history. Fortunately, America is good at it.

With a degree of much-needed humor and levity and by drawing heavily from contemporary American history, the ten changes which are needed to remake American life are identified.

This book builds upon an understanding of the American condition as set forth in Book Four (*Grading on the Curve*) and the many reasons for optimism as set forth in Book Five (A *Reasoned Case for Optimism*). As suggested by those books, America remains bountiful, but American life has changed and we are in trouble. Fortunately, we live in an age of opportunity.

I started writing these books over five years ago. In that time, many things have changed. Our economy has been battered by greed and incompetence. New crops of politicians have been elected, but our political system remains stubbornly dysfunctional. Discontentment has become widespread, and fears have multiplied. Our government is broke. Wars continue. BP leaked. Tempers flair. Tsunamis and twisters and superstorms seem to be everywhere. And just for somebody's good measure, there was a hurricane in Vermont and an earthquake in Ohio last year. We have all seen the physical condition of many of our communities deteriorate. Materialism and self-centrism remain powerful influences. Accurate information remains hard too find. Our allocations of income, wealth, and opportunity have become far too disparate, and our senses of reason, ethics, accountability, and community have diminished.

There has also been a calcification of American thought. Positions are taken. Alliances are forged. Do-or-die teams are chosen. Blind ideology is honored. Intolerance is rewarded. Compromise is seen as a sign of appeasement, concession or weakness. We too passively have allowed much, but not all, of our media to remain irresponsible, and we have even allowed it to color our states as red, blue or purple.

This is certainly not the first time that America has been in trouble but two aspects of the contemporary American situation are somewhat new in their extent and implications.

First, America's issues are numerous, complex, and inter-related. Many of our issues can be resolved only with the simultaneous resolution of other issues. For example, the issues of our educational system cannot be easily separated from matters of funding, priorities, curricula, parenting, community, and even culture. The issues of crime are closely entwined with the issues of race, education, employment opportunity, the administration of justice, and the containment of drugs. Personal accountability relates closely to our senses of personal and even situational ethics, and our legal code is far too frequently (and conveniently) used in place and substitution of a more honorable and broad-based sense of ethics and code of behavior. Legality does not make one's action ethical. Statutory compliance, by itself, cannot set the boundaries of our obligations to one another. They cannot be the cold parameters controlling our conduct.

Secondly, our economic system has become more closed and our political system has become gridlocked. While avenues for opportunity and reward still exist in our economic system, our political leaders have been compromised by money and favor, and our electoral process has been compromised, if not hijacked, by the deep entrenchment of advisors and consultants and by the heavy overlay of marketing, advertising, and public relations.

However, despite the long lead-in, this is not a declinist book. To the contrary, this is a book about restoring our national conversation so that people can once again listen. It is time and we are ready to move from critique to effort.

The good news is that America's real problems are neither inevitable nor intractable.

This book starts by distinguishing between "surface issues" and "fundamental issues." This distinction between these types of issues is important, but it is also a difficult for several reasons. First, hard delineations between the two are admittedly difficult to make, and there is a constant temptation to view them merely as distinctions between long-term vs. short-term issues. Secondly, societies routinely deal with them simultaneously even though at any given moment one set of issues tends to dominate. Nevertheless, the distinction between surface and fundamental issues are real, and they are substantial.

Preliminarily, it must be understood that the use of the word *surface* is not meant to be dismissive. To the contrary, surface issues include matters of great importance, and they deserve our constant and careful attention.

Regardless of their huge import, they remain largely matters of operation and response. They involve issues which are addressed routinely and in the ordinary course of our institutions. They may include matters of operation, such as the actions of our legislative bodies, the management of our nation's schools, the containment of our nation's debt, the administration of justice, the placement and protection of our armed forces, and even the election of our next president. They may include matters of response such as issues created by specific events or triggered by the actions of our enemies, the forces of nature or the stirrings of other nations—the horrifics of 9/11, the catastrophes of Hurricanes Katrina and Superstorm Sandy, and the occurrence and consequences of the Arab Spring.

But fundamental issues are wholly different. They lie at the bedrock of society. They affect our very ability to function well—or at least honorably and stably—as a nation. They relate directly to surface issues because they affect, and even control, our ability to better understand and intelligently respond to such issues, to wisely select our leaders, to improve the functioning of our society, and to more fairly allocate our nation's income, wealth, and opportunity. But they do far more.

By addressing our fundamental issues we will be more able to distinguish between truth and hyperbole. We will better parent and educate our children. We will be more restrained and cautious in our deference to experts. We will better contain our almost natural inclinations towards hedonism, materialism, and narcissism. Addressing certain fundamental issues can help us to better understand the importance of community; to exhibit and require a stronger sense of ethics, to demand more accountability in the actions of our economic and political leaders; to better understand both the uses and limitations of our history; and to possess confidence, practice, contain arrogance, and exercise grace.

The concept of addressing our fundamental issues is not offered as some variant self-help, back-to-basics, aspirational dream for a return to some by-gone day. Paraphrasing from the great title of David Satter's recent book, all of those things were a long time ago—and they never happened anyway. Resolution of our fundamental issues can no longer be seen as aspirational. Instead, steps must be taken and progress must be commenced.

Addressing our fundamental issues lies at the core—or at least the extent—of our success. It is in our own self-interests to address these fundamental issues if for no other reason than because they will rarely be addressed by our institutions and because they rarely create that sense of firestorm immediacy which is necessary to attract the true attention and efforts of our leaders. They remain—and will remain—merely the stuff of stump speeches. For example, three of our last four presidents vowed to be the Education President. None were. The issues of education, like the other fundamental issues in this book, were left to be addressed later; on another day; by another mayor; by another governor, by the next congress; or by some future president.

Now, however, things are different. The luxury of further deferral is no longer available. We can no longer fake it. Complaining will not be enough and screaming from our sofas will no longer do the trick. We know that our country needs our help. We know that denialism, incantations of exceptionalism, and prayers will not be enough. We know that allocating blame is a heck of a fine parlor game, but it is largely irrelevant to our finding of solutions.

Now, however, things are different. Addressing our fundamental issues has become a pre-condition to the safety and the re-making of American life. Addressing our fundamental issues *is* not just an idea—it is the path home.

Drawing heavily upon an examination of the last approximately 55 years of American history—1957 to 2011, this book identifies the ten fundamental changes which we must make. In some instances, the changes are necessary to correct specific actions which we, individually or as a society, have made over the last decades. In other instances, the changes are necessary to correct actions, habits, or patterns of behavior which have proven, upon reflection, to be simply erroneous, misguided, and wrong. The last set of changes is necessitated largely as the result of the growth, diversification, or technological evolution of our nation and the vast impacts of globalism.

In this book I will try to root out certain truths by squeezing them, methodically, from the writings and wisdom of others, from the data and information available to us, and from an analysis of recent American history—or, more precisely, from America's many recent histories—its social, cultural, political, economic, and military histories.

A brief explanation of the title, *No Dog in the Fight,* may be useful. As discussed in earlier books, I readily recognize that I remain tethered to my own past. I cannot claim to be without bias or, the more gentle word, perspective. I cannot claim—and do not claim to be—a distant observer,. However, the roots of those biases are the lingering remnants of my upbringing. They come from my life's experiences, but they are not used with the intention of advancing or concealing any subtle agenda.

My absence of agenda may be assured, in some small part, by the fact that I am no longer a young man. I have no parents to please. They are long deceased. I have no woman or family to impress. My wife and son, bless them, long ago decided to love me and to accept my many faults. I have no assets needing of protection; no scores still to settle; and no career to advance. Possibly most importantly, I understand (and begrudgingly accept) that the subjects, ideas and proposals discussed in these books will be adopted or rejected long after I am dead.

Thus, I have no dog in the fight. I hold no agenda other than, like you and so many others, caring for and still believing in this country. This book offers one path home; one possible beginning for the needed re-making of American life.

Synopsis Of Book Seven
The Brilliance of Many
1,000 Ideas for Improving Life in America
(Projected Publication: Summer, 2015)

The Brilliance of Many is the final book in *The Chance of a Lifetime* series. It is wholly different than the previous books. I had not originally intended it to be a part of this series of books. However, I came to realize that, in a sense, it had to be written.

In the course of my research over these last years, I have been surprised, indeed overwhelmed, by the number of creative ideas which have been already offered up by the American people. Many of these ideas are good. Some of them are very good. A few of them are brilliant.

I readily confess to the embarrassment of my own surprise. I should have known that despite the anger of our headlines and the widely-reported acrimonious nature of contemporary America, many Americans were still working together—oftentimes in small groups or within narrow communities—to address the problems of American life. However, as a nation, we can no longer afford to have good people with good ideas work in isolation. We can no longer permit these ideas remain to remain unknown or underreported due to a lack of funding or the too frequent disinterest of the media.

I have long suspected that some of the best, creative ideas had only the life-span of a good conversation. I have long feared that some of the best, creative ideas (and, admittedly, some of the stupidest) arrive at closing time. They are scribbled on cocktail napkins, shown to a few friends, and then left on the bar to be quickly discarded and soon forgotten.

Nevertheless, as I read more and more over these last years, I have come to better appreciate that many of the ideas which America needs are already "out there." They have not been discarded. They have not been forgotten. They just have not yet received the publicity which they deserve.

Some of the ideas are complicated and are fraught with the potential for unforeseen consequences. Others are disarmingly simple. Some have already being tried in locales all across America, but they are not receiving their just and needed presentation. They are worthy of broader consideration and application.

Most of the ideas presented in this book are culled from the books, speeches, articles, columns, research papers, books and blogs of others. Many of the best ideas seem to have been included almost as throwaway parts of books and articles written on various subjects. Too often that is where they seem to stay—left to die with the shelf life of the article or left buried deep within the books in which they have been placed.

This book also reminds us of the many potential sources of new ideas. Currently in the United States, there are about 312,000,000 Americans, 27,000,000 corporations and employers, 275,000 large cities, 13,500 school districts, and 3,100 counties, parishes, and boroughs. In addition, there are thousands of universities and colleges, legislative bodies, public and quasi-governmental agencies and departments, think tanks, interest groups, religious congregations, social clubs and organizations, charities, business trade groups and associations, commissions, and study groups. To all of the foregoing should be added the ideas and experiences of other countries. Some of their ideas and practices are amazingly creative. Some of their ideas are worthy of more consideration and wider adaptation.

It is hardly surprising that ideas abound, but other problems exist. Our large, diversified, and highly complex society creates numerous barriers to idea development, refinement, implementation, and publicity. These barriers themselves contribute to what is described in this book as "idea vaporization" which is alluded to above.

Some ideas get a bit further, but their implementation is too often frustrated by the interposition of legal barriers, by concerns about risks and liabilities, and by the relentless, project-deflecting search for reliable funding, As a result, good ideas are routinely forced to fall by the wayside. Good ideas are lost. Noble efforts are abandoned.

This book is presented, in part, because America no longer has the luxury of time. This book is presented, in part, to highlight the need for the development of formalized, expeditious, and widely-known policies for encouraging, preserving, and circulating new ideas.

These ideas must become more accessible and widely circulated. Their potential must be more widely appreciated. The success or failure of ideas cannot any longer be allowed to so routinely depend upon the fortuitous interest of the media or the findings of a moneyed benefactor. We cannot allow good ideas to remain confined within small groups or the private province of experts and subject professionals.

While these matters are discussed in this book, the core of this book is the compendium of some of the best ideas which this author came across in his research for this series of books. The ideas are presented without comment or recommendation. They are organized and indexed by subject and topic including, for example, business and economy, public debt and tax policy, education and literacy, environmental preservation, military and national security, political governance, political elections, social behavior, accountability, civility, crime, justice, and incarceration, health and health care delivery, and families and parenting.

You will find that a few of the ideas are large and grandiose such Kennedy's 1961 challenge to put a man on the moon or Reagan's 1987 challenged to Gorbachev to tear down the Berlin Wall. Big ideas; big results. But, with only a few exceptions, they are not what we need now.

Instead, most of the ideas are far smaller, but they are equally critical to the success of our country and to the remaking of American life. Most of the ideas relate to matters closer to home. Initially, some of them may seem narrow and possibly even community-tailored or community-specific such as Geoffrey Canada's ideas in the early 1990s about the creation of the Harlem Children's Zone or the ideas of that small group of citizens in Albert Lea, Minnesota who decided in 2009 to live healthier and longer lives by becoming the first pioneer town in the Blue Zone's Vitality Project.

Some of the ideas address arcane aspects of our nation's tax policy, securities regulation and insider trading rules. Other ideas relate to the matters of our judiciary—the misuse of our litigation system, the payment allocations of legal fees, and the various burdens of proof associated with criminal prosecutions and civil liabilities.

Some of the ideas relate to the media and our political processes. They address how we can make changes in order to encourage (and reward) a stronger sense of ethics and public responsibility in the media. Others creatively address the many problems inherent in our system of political elections or the methodologies of our campaign financing. Some of the ideas relate to our families, our children, and our communities such as ideas about teaching the meaning of education, the importance of life skills, and the tools and even skills of injecting more reason and civility into our American conversation.

The ideas are everywhere. They are merely in need of better organization, presentation, review and consideration. This book is offered merely the start of that process. This book will present 1,000 of the best ideas. It is humbly offered by the author as a compendium and a commendation. It is a compendium of ideas, and it is offered as a commendation to—*The Brilliance of Many—1,000 Ideas for Improving Life in America.*

APPENDIX B

---·•·---

Definitions, Abbreviations, and The New Words, Phrases, and Colloquialisms of Current America

3-G Campaigns. Political term for Republican political campaigns which have emphasized the subjects of "God, guns, and gays."

9/11. September 2001 attacks killing over 3,000 people (including 19 hijackers) by four hijacked planes on, respectively, the World Trade Center in New York City, the Pentagon, and an attempt on the White House (plane crashed in Pennsylvania field after interference by passengers and crew)

100-Year Storm. A storm that has a 1% chance of occurring in any given year.

Assisted living facilities. *See Nursing Homes.*

BB. Billion(s)

Belmont and Fishtown. Two fictitious, distinct communities used by Charles Murray in his book *Coming Apart: The State of White America, 1960-2001* to describe the "deeper (than simply income disparity) cultural cleavage, even among white Americans" that exists. "In Belmont (the "elite" community) natives perpetuate their advantages in our knowledge-based economy by sending their children to top-tier schools and seeing that they marry their own kind. In Fishtown, marriage, industriousness and religion are meanwhile in steep decline, depriving individuals of the traditional pillars of happy, successful lives." *The Week*, February 10, 2012, p. 20.

Binge Viewing. New manner of watching television in which tech-savvy viewers use new technologies such as on-demand TV, DVRs, or streaming websites to watch a whole season of a TV series in one sitting which often lasts a day or more and is interrupted only by brief breaks for meals and bathroom breaks.

Biometrics. The science of identifying individuals by their unique biological characteristics such as fingerprinting and, more recently, "their voices, the irises of their eyes (90–99% accuracy rate), the geometry of their faces, and the way they walk ("gait biometrics"), ... (and) the unique rhythm of a person's heartbeat." *The Week*, June 7, 2013, p. 11.

Broken Windows. Theory first advanced by James Q. Wilson in an article in *The Atlantic* which summarily proposed that "cracking down on small, but visible crimes—graffiti drawing, street-corner drug dealing—could prevent neighborhoods form fostering more serious (crimes)." *Time*, March 19, 2012, quoting Nate Rawlings writing in memory of James Q. Wilson, who died on March 2, 2012, at the age of 80.

Bucket List. Phrase derived from the mixed-reviews Rob Reiner movie by the same name and starring Jack Nicholson and Morgan Freeman, the "bucket list" is another wish list variant of the "10,000 Things To Do Before You Die" or the "1,000 Places To See Before You Die."

Bullycide. A word used to describe a suicide carried out by a victim of bullying. The word is believed to have derived from the 2010 suicide of 15-year-old Phoebe Prince which in part resulted from the bullying to which she was subjected. Six of her fellow Massachusetts high schoolers were later indicted in association with her death. Although the initial indictments includes a number of felonies, including statutory rape with respect to two of the defendants, all the charges were dropped in exchange for the entry of guilty pleas by five of the six defendants of minor charges and the imposition of probation and community service. (The charges against the sixth defendant were dropped at the request of the Prince family.)

C9 League. The colloquial name given to China's initiative, which began in 2009, to create an imitation of the Ivy League universities. "The objective is to attract the best graduates and faculty with an array of super-funded institutions." China has been offering $270MM governmental subsidies to these institutions and even relocation bonuses to attract "sea turtles"—Chinese PhDs from abroad). Silverstein, M., Singhi, A., "Can Universities Stay on Top?," *The Wall Street Journal*, September 29–30, 2012.

Cash Mob. A "group of consumers that supports a local retailer by showing up to shop at a store on a designated day." *Time,* July 16, 2012, p. 16. See also, (i) *The Week*, February 10, 2012, p. 2, describing the "cash mob" in (sadly named) Chagrin Falls, Ohio, making a statement against big-box retailers and in the process, expressing community support for an 1857-established local hardware store, (ii) *The Week,* November 30, 2012, p. 4, describing the "cashmob" organized in Tigard, Oregon, by local patrons of a popular coffee had been recently robbed twice in two weeks; and (iii) Steinmetz, K., "Buying-Local Advocates Are Rallying Mobs To Shop," *Time,* November 5, 2012, p. 56. The first cash-mob was in Buffalo, New York, in 2011, but since then after "going viral" hundreds of cash mobs have come up across the U.S. in all 50 states as well as in large European cities.

Castle Doctrine. Long-standing legal principle in which an individual is allowed to use reasonable force (including lethal force in some circumstances) to protect themselves from an assailant in or invader into their home. It is, in a sense, this principle that has been expanded by the state stand-your-ground statutes in which an individual no longer has a duty to retreat in other circumstances, and can, instead, use such force wholly apart from the protection of one's home.

Cattledrone. The flying surveillance device (a.k.a. cow spybot) used by the EPA to monitor ranging practices, to observe cattle, and to look for violations of Clean Water Act violations in Nebraska and Iowa. *Time*, June 18, 2012, p. 14.

CBO. U.S. Congressional Budget Office.

CDC. U.S. Center for Disease Control and Prevention.

Chain Migration. Legal immigration based upon the application of a broadly defined concept of family reunification and preferences extending not only to spouses and minor children but also to parents and siblings.

Choking Game. A dangerous "game" in which youths strangle or choke themselves or a friend with their hands, belt, or a rope until they feel light-headed. A study in Oregon found that 1 in 16 students claim to have tried the game. *The Week*, May 4, 2012, p. 21.

Competency-Based College Degrees. A relatively new type of university degree program whereby the students can (and are even encouraged) to complete their education independently through online courses. Degrees are then awarded to those students who pass assessment tests and related online courses.

Compstat. A policing technique which is used by police departments in some larger cities, such as Los Angeles and New York and which tracks the number of types of crimes within geographic areas of a police jurisdiction. Compstat is used in order to increase both the effectiveness and efficiency of allocating crime prevention resources and to facilitate accountability amongst police units. See, e.g., *The Economist*, August 25-31, 2012, p. 21.

Corruption. "The abuse of entrusted power for public gain," which is the definition used by Transparency International, a non-governmental organization headquartered in Berlin, Germany with operations and offices in 70 other countries. Founded in 1993, TI monitors and reports private and public corruption and since 1995 has published its Corruption Perceptions Index.

Creeping Disaster. Name given by meteorologists to droughts (unlike the "flash drought of 2012") which "unlike hurricanes and tornadoes, … normally unfold in slow motion, day after dry day." Walsh, B., "When the Rains Stop," *Time*, August 6, 2012, p. 34.

Crowdfunding. A potential alternative to personal funding, venture capital and other forms of start-up financing, "crowd-sourcing" is an Internet-/social-media-based method of asking a wide body (or "crowd") of people, groups, institutions, and funds to invest or donate a specified or unspecified amount of money for a specific cause or project as an investment and in return for equity, as a loan in exchange for evidence of debt and expectation of repayment, or donation in exchange for "tangible or non-monetary rewards such as an ecard, T-shirt, pre-released CD, or the finished product." *Dailycrowdsource.com.*

Crowdsourcing. A process that involves outsourcing tasks or data collection from or using a large group of undefined people as opposed to a specific body or population of individuals. For example, in the context of health care, experts and analysis may rely upon a *de facto* mass surveillance in order to monitor the outbreak of a single contagious disease or "doctors or patients, (when) stumped by symptoms (may, in effect, reach out to the users of) Facebook, Twitter, and medical networks (to) allow them to tap the wisdom of crowds." Park, A., "Web MDs—Social Media Are Changing How We Diagnose Disease," *Time,* August 6, 2012, p. 16.

CTE. Career and Technical Education (new name for vocational education programs).

DACA. The Deferred Action for Childhood Arrivals is an immigration enforcement policy which Homeland Security Secretary Janet Napolitano "delicately termed an 'exercise of prosecutorial discretion.' " Under this policy any (currently undocumented or illegal) immigrant (a) under the age of 30, (b) without criminal records (c) who came to (the U.S.) before they were 16, (d) have lived in (the U.S.) for at least five continuous years, and (e) are enrolled in or have graduated from school or university or have been dishonorably discharged form military service, may apply for DACA. While this policy "confers neither citizenship for permanent-resident status," it is an assurance from the U.S. government that no action will be taken to deport the applicant for a period of two years. The DACA application costs $465 and can be renewed each two years." *The Economist,* August 25-31, 2012, p. 24.

Disinhibition Effect or the "Internet's Disinhibition Effect." Term used by some psychologists describing the phenomenon that people "feel emboldened (especially when, for example, using the Internet) by the lack of real-time response and the sense that the things they do online are less serious than (their) actions in the real world." Steinmetz, K., "Unfriending the Enemy," *Time,* October 22, 2012, p. 15, citing John Suler's article in *CyberPsychology & Behavior.*

Diversity Index. A measure used by demographers to measure the racial and ethnic diversity of a given place. "The index weighs how even the place's population is spread across (5) groups"—whites, black, Hispanics, Asians, and Other. "A perfectly diverse place would have a population with 20% in each group" in which case the Diversity Index score would be 100. Dougherty, C., Jordan, M., "Stirring Up the Melting Pot," *The Wall Street Journal,* September 7, 2012, citing U.S. 2010 Project at Brown University.

DOD. U.S. Department of Defense.

DSM. Diagnostic and Statistical Manual of Mental Disorders.

Drunkorexia. A frightening trend among college students who choose to "diet all day so that they can drink at night without gaining weight." *The Week,* April 19, 2013, p. 21, citing *TheAtlantic.com.*

FDA. U.S. Food and Drug Administration.

Flipped Classroom. Phrase used by proponents of re-structuring the U.S. education model so that "the teacher shifts from being the sage on the stage to being the guide on the side, ... (and) (a)ll lecture time is converted to personalized attention." "Traditional Teaching Model: Daytime—Teacher delivers lecture to class; Nighttime—Students complete homework exercises. Model of Khan's Academy: Nighttime—Students receive instruction via videos; Daytime—Students do exercise while teacher helps those who are struggling." Webley, K., "Reboot School," *Time,* July 9, 2012, p. 36.

Flynn Effect. A pattern of intellectual development originally noted by psychologist James R. Flynn in the 1950s whereby a "nation's average measured intelligence (IQ') (rises) over time" Caplan, B., "The Intelligence Boom," *The Wall Street Journal,* October 10, 2012 reviewing

James R. Flynn's new book *Are We Getting Smarter? Rising IQ in the Twenty-First Century.*

GMO. Genetically modified organism.

GNI. Gross National Income.

Gray Thursday. A new phrase which came into some common usage in 2012. The phrase is intended to parallel the concept of the phrase Black Friday (first used in 1961) and Cyber Monday (first used in 2005). It used to designate the controversial advancing of Black Friday from Midnight on Thanksgiving Day to times such as 8:00 PM on Thursday. Such "early" openings were initiated in 2012 by some major retailers such as Walmart, Toys R Us, and Target in order to take earlier advantage of this busy shopping day, and led, unsurprisingly, to some employee walk-outs and on-line petitions not to be required to work on Thanksgiving Day. Continuing this possible trend towards extended customer "shopping hours," it was recently reported that in 2012 McDonald's urged all of its franchises to stay open on Christmas Day with McDonald's COO Jim Johannesen coldly writing that their "largest holiday opportunity as a system is Christmas Day." *The Week,* December 28–January 4, 2012, p. 46, citing *Advertising Age.* In a more charitable and possibly a more socially constructive manner, the commercialism of traditional Black Friday and Cyber Monday after Thanksgiving in 2012 was countered when appr. 2,000 nonprofit corporations and charities "inaugurated" the new holiday of Giving Tuesday and "launched their seasonal charity drives … to encourage Americans to consider spending money (or volunteering) on good causes as well as on discounted goods." *The Week*, December 7, 2012, p. 4.

"Guns in Trunk" or "Safe Commute" Laws. State laws authorizing gun owners to keep weapons in their vehicles in parking lots at work, school or government offices in order to, among other things say proponents, enable workers protect themselves while commuting to and from work. McWhirter, C., *The Wall Street Journal*, February 28, 2013.

HDI. The Human Development Index used by U.N. Development Program to measure the overall quality of life condition of a country.

This HDI is used in place of the economically-based GDP measures and other data such as that relating to life expectancy and level and availability of education within a measured nation. The HDI rates countries on a scale of 0 to 100. Countries which have a HDI above 80 are considered to have very high human development. See also the IDHI.

Hood Days. A colloquial reference to those dates "that correspond to numbered street (e.g., October 3rd or 10-3 for 103rd Street) (and on which) the gang within whose territory the street falls holds a big party." *The Economist,* August 25–31, 2012, p. 21.

House Flipping. The practice or business of purchasing a residence and reselling it (either as is or after making small, usually cosmetic, changes, improvements, or repairs) for a profit within appr. six months.

Internet Use Disorder. New psychiatric disorder being added in 2013 to the DSM.

LGBT. Lesbian, Gay, Bisexual, Transgendered community.

Life Expectancy at Birth. Indicates the number of years a newborn infant would live if prevailing patterns of mortality at the time for its birth were to stay the same throughout its life. *data.worldbank.org.*

Micropolitan. An demographic term used to describe small, but regionally important, population centers of 10,000 to 50,0000, such as Hilton Head, S.C., and Wooster, Ohio. *Time,* November 5, 2012, p. 13.

Middlessence. A phrase for that period in one's life between middle age and old age. It has also been referred to as the "third age" and by some academics as "midcourse."

MM. Million(s).

MOOCS. The shorthand for "massive open on-line courses" which are now available on-line from or through sites such as Udacity, Coursera, edX, and others.

Motivated Reasoning. The effort to rationalize one's belief and to distort, consciously or otherwise, the processes of reasoning and the evaluation and synthesis of new information in order to coincide with one's previously held beliefs or understandings.

NASA. U.S. National Aeronautics and Space Administration.

NCAA. National Collegiate Athletic Association.

NOAA. U.S. National Oceanic and Atmospheric Administration, an agency of the U.S. government.

Nominal Tax Rate. *See Tax Rate.*

Nones. Colloquial phrase used to refer to those persons who are "religiously unaffiliated."

NRA. National Rifle Association.

Nursing Homes vs. Assisted Living Facilities. Nursing homes can provide extensive, skilled medical care whereas assisted living facilities offer the ready availability of such care but are designed as more homelike living for more ambulatory, cognitive, and healthy seniors.

OECD. The Organization for Economic Cooperation and Development (the "OECD") is the successor international agency to the Organization for European Economic Cooperation (the "OEEC") which was formed in 1948 to assist in the administration of the post-World War II Marshall Plan. The OECD was formed in 1960 in order to "provide a forum in which (member) governments can work together to share experiences and seek solutions to common problems." *oecd. org.* The initial OECD members were the eighteen founder countries of the OEEC plus the U.S. and Canada. Since that time an additional fourteen countries have become members of the OECD. Most of the OECD countries are highly-developed, high-income economies with high HDI (Human Development Index) ratings, however some emerging countries such as Mexico are also members. The OECD is designed to provide a forum committed to democracy and market economies. It also publishes numerous books and reports, provides an ongoing stream of statistics about many key economic and market and other social performance indices, including, for example, the OECD Economic Outlook (published twice a year) and PISA (the Program for International Student Assessment), which compares the decisional performance of the respective member countries. *oecd.org.*

OMB. U.S. Office of Management and Budget.

Omerta. The principle and matter-of-pledged-faith which prohibits the divulging of secret information by any member of an organized crime syndicate or family that might incriminate other members of such syndicate or family.

"Open Carry" Laws. States laws pursuant to which any person who is licensed to own a weapon may carry and display their weapon, loaded or unloaded, in the open, in their belt, or in a shoulder holster.

Parent-Trigger Laws. The name given to a wide-variety of state laws which authorize parents and/or others upon, for example, a majority vote of the parents (a) to reform failing schools (i.e., schools which have been on some under-performing school list for a designated period of time), (b) close them, or (c) in some states, convert them into charter schools. The first parent-trigger law was adopted in 2010 in California, and they are the subject of the movie *Won't Back Down*. See, Manno, B., "Education Reform Gets a Hollywood Boost, "*The Wall Street Journal*, September 29–30, 2012.

Peak Car. Similar in concept to the most commonly used phrase, peak oil, peak car is a colloquial reference to the concept that car ownership and/or vehicle-miles driven may be reaching a point of saturation in any given area, country, or other target measure. See also *Saturating Trend* and the somewhat analogous concept of *Sprawl Wall*.

Peer-to-Peer Lending. An emerging business that matches individual lenders and borrowers via online platforms such as Lending Club and Prosper. Reflecting the growing "democratization of finance," banks, credit card companies, and other traditional lenders are "kept out of the picture." A "bulk of its lending is for debt consolidation by credit-card borrowers," but the interest rates are oftentimes at 14%, which is substantially lower than the "standard charge of 18%." *The Economist*, June 1-7, 2013, p. 74.

Population Density. The measure of the number of persons per unit area (e.g., per square mile or per kilometer or per acre) and is calculated by dividing the total area population by the total land area. Obviously because of the existence of urban area, it is, at best, only a rough gauge of the population's disbursement over an area.

Poverty Line. Government-defined poverty is about $11,000 per year annual income for an individual and appr. $23,000 for a family of four. See also, *Deep Poverty*.

PTSD. Post-traumatic stress disorder was referred to during the Civil War as a "soldier's heart," during World War I as "shell shock," and World War II as "battle fatigue." See, Morgenthau, R., "The Death of Peter Wielunski," *The Wall Street Journal*, September 24, 2012.

Saturating Trend. Similar in certain respects to "peak car" and analogous to the concept of the "sprawl wall," the phrase "saturating trend" is sometimes used to refer to the point at which individuals who, after years of travelling more and travelling farther each year, are no longer increasing such miles or distances. There are a number of different measures that can be used to measure and evidence such saturating trends, such as (a) the total miles driven by a given population, (b) the total miles driven per driver, or (c) total trips made by such population or per driver. See, e.g., *The Economist*, September 22–28, 2012, p. 29.

Sharing or Renting Economy. A non-acquisitive lifestyle (as opposed to America's traditional "ownership society") largely achievable as the result of technology whereby consumers, rather than purchasing goods and services for their own possession and use, "through online marketplaces … rent (and/or) exchange idle goods and services" such as "boats, cars, housekeepers, chefs, … tools and electronics, … designer dresses, haute tech gadgets (and) modern art" and jewelry. See, e.g., Wolverson, R., "Welcome to the 'Sharing Economy,'" *Time*, September 24, 2012, p. 44.

Smurfing. The term used by police to refer to the cigarette resale racket where cigarette are smuggled from low-tax states such as Virginia to high-tax states such as New York or New Jersey.

SNAP. Supplemental Nutrition Assistance Program, formerly known as food stamps.

Sprawl Wall. A concept in the study of urbanization pattern in which a city or metropolitan area grows and spreads via suburbanization until it eventually hits a point (the sprawl wall) in which the traveling and commuting time between one's residence and the city grow too far and a significant number of people start moving "back towards the city centre." See *The Economist*, September 22–28, 2012, pp. 30, 32. See also, *peak car* and *saturating trend*.

Status Dropout Rate. Represents the percentage of 16- through 24-year-olds who are not enrolled in school and have not earned a high school credential (either by diploma or an equivalency credential such as a General Education Development (GED) certificate).

STEM Classes or STEM Fields. Education classes or fields of study or employment relating to Science, Technology, Engineering or Math—i.e.,"STEM" classes or fields of study or employment.

Supercommuter. A person who travels long distances to and from work via any means or combination of means such as car, plane, train, etc.

SuperZIPs. In furtherance of his argument that "the wedge driving America apart isn't its economy but its culture," writer Charles Murray uses this term to describe the pockets of increasing isolation in which the elite live in the U.S. See Wallace-Wells, B., "Return of the Radical," *Time,* April 16, 2012, p. 38, which discusses Murray's 2012 book *Coming Apart: The State of White America, 1960–2010.* See also, *Belmont and Fishtown* above.

Textualists. Those scholars of the constitution and other canonical legal texts who "feel a strong loyalty, even a moral commitment" to the words themselves and the meanings they were intended to convey." Harshly and arguably over-stating, the contrast is to define non-textualists as scholars who "vest judges with the ability to 'adjust' the law in order to ensure a more 'progressive' direction, loosely interpreting the wording of statutes and the Constitution and sometimes disregarding the wording entirely." Rivkin, D., "The Triumph of the Text," *The Wall Street Journal*, August 29, 2012, reviewing *Reading Law* by Antonin Scalia and Bryan A. Garner (2012). In *Reading Law* the authors "argue forcefully for a textualist approach—for interpreting legal document, especially the Constitution, by focusing on written words in their original meaning." But see, Breyer, S. *Making Our Democracy Work: A Judge's View,"* (2010) in which he asks, "(w)hy would people want to live under the 'dead-hand' of an (18th Century) constitution that preserved not enduring values but specific (18th Century) thoughts about how those values then applied?"

Transhumanism. An intellectual and cultural movement that addresses the ethics and science of using advanced technologies (e.g., genetic engineering) to improve and enhance human intellectual, physical, and psychological capacities.

Twerking. A type of popular dance "which involves popping one's hips suggestively" and which was the reason a California high school suspended 33 students who had made a twerking video. In a possible instance of overkill and overreaction, the high school also banned the students from the forthcoming prom. *The Week,* May 17, 2013, p. 4.

TSA. U.S. Transportation Security Agency.

UNHCR. United Nations High Commissioner on Refugees.

USSC. United States Supreme Court.

Acknowledgements

It is with great humility and appreciation that I here offer my thanks to the many people who have encouraged and helped me in the writing and publishing of this book and its companion book *The Relevance of Reason—Business and Politics*. However, I confess that I have long believed that the very word "Acknowledgements" is too lame; too inadequate; too limited. In common parlance, it seems to suggest a mere head nod as a person "acknowledges" a friend on a crowded street or, in the world of thoughts and ideas, it seems to describe the cautioned recognition, the "acknowledgement," of another person's beliefs or the mere "acknowledgement" of the possibility as to the correctness of another person's thoughts or theories.

But here the acknowledgements are so much more. The first deserved acknowledgements are generalized and widely disbursed because the inspiration for this book comes from my observation of our people. The inspiration for these books derives from that broad swath of the American people who—despite the relentless challenges of our American, 21st Century life—still have honorable aspirations and decent hopes for themselves and their families; to those millions of Americans that work hard, day in and day out; to those veterans who are serving or who have served this country, oftentimes with great sacrifice to themselves and their families; to those families—however structured and composed, who try hard and pray for the safety and success of their children; to those millions of

Americans that start work or come home in the dark—sometimes "another day older and deeper in debt."

I am a student of history, but as with all of us, it is the America which I have seen and lived which has affected me the most. But the way that history is received and absorbed is also relevant, and I know that a special acknowledgement is owed—and is here willingly given—to my parents. They are both deceased now, but I think of them often, and it was they who helped instill a certain irrepressible sense of optimism in me which allows me to sometimes see through the heavy headlines of our contemporary America.

The second set of acknowledgements are also somewhat generalized, and amidst the somewhat coarse tone of America's conversation this round of acknowledgements could possibly be challenged and criticized, but I hope not. These acknowledgements are to the thousands of authors, writers, commentators, analysts, reporters, researchers, statisticians, investigators, and groups and associations who collectively have assembled and made available many of the facts and much of the data which are herein organized and presented. While it is here unnecessary for me to comment on their respective motives—political, social, monetary, self-serving or self-aggrandizing, their work is too often overlooked and too easily discounted. However, their writing, when carefully and broadly studied, allows us to understand our own country possible. Parts of the media deserve our severe criticism at times—and that too is included in these books, but there is a cadre of responsible media. They too deserve our thanks and here my acknowledgements.

I wish to thank my friends for having patience, for offering criticism—genuinely and gently given, and, when necessary, for encouraging me to keep writing. There is little doubt, at least in my mind, that most writers write because they can't sing. If I could have wrapped up this entire book into one great Guthrie ballad, I would have. I promise. But it was my friends who were honest enough to remind me that I couldn't sing worth a ... It was my friends who cared enough to keep me writing. To them, finally, thank you.

I offer my special thanks as well to that group of friends who have taken the time over the past several years to review, critique, and comment upon my initial drafts. I have taken the liberty at times to refer to them as my Board of Editors, and their contributions have been both thoughtful and greatly appreciated. While I alone am responsible for the words, thoughts, subject and excerpt selections, and certainly any errors or omissions contained in this book, I here most humbly thank Dr. Roger Acheatel, a brilliant cardiologist and attorney; Mark Adams, Partner, Jeffer, Mangels & Butler; Phillip Ashman, Partner, McQueen & Ashman; Wayne S. Bell, General Counsel of the California Department of Real Estate; Michael Christian, an engineer and entrepreneur; Keith Dawson, Partner, Dawson & Dawson; Nicholas Honchariw, a financier and entrepreneur; Scott King, Principal, Merit Commercial Group; Martha Lange, Program Manager, The Aspen Institute; Brigadier General (Ret) Dulaney O'Roark; Dr. Donna Ronzone, educator and school principal; and Scott Somers, Managing Partner, Windale Group.

However, even with the words assembled, this book could not have been finalized, organized, polished, and published without first the guidance of Ellen Reid, my book shepherd, whose talent and experience (and friendship) were invaluable and who was able to assemble and guide a team of wonderful people to see this book through to publication. My special thanks to Laren Bright, who gently and firmly helped me better articulate the visions and purposes of these books, and to Ghislain Viau, who designed my page layouts with an extraordinary blend of creativity, patience, and relentless commitment. I also wish to specially thank George Foster, one of America's great book cover artists, for encapsulating my thoughts and ideas into the cover design, and both Pamela Guerrieri and Gabriella West for their separate copyediting and for the literal feat of getting more wise editing comments onto an 8 ½ X 11 page than any persons I have ever met. I thank Jen Burton for her invaluable indexing—too often an under-appreciated talent and skill—no, science.

I wish to extend my special thanks and appreciation to Jolinda Pizzirani and Jerry Newton of Summerland Publishing for their skills, patience, efforts, and creativity in assisting me in the final release, marketing, and distribution of this book and its companion book, *The Relevance of Reason—Business and Culture.*

Lastly, I want to again thank my beautiful wife for continuing to allow me both the time and the freedom to write, and my son who when he was "oh so much younger than today," used to ask me when I was going to start reading some of my own books. As with my prior book, maybe now, little man. Maybe now.

Sources, Materials and Articles

(**Author's Note:** For the convenience of the reader, the following is a combined list of the Source Materials and Articles for both of the companion books: *The Relevance of Reason—Business and Politics*, and *The Relevance of Reason—Society and Culture*)

General Source Materials

Boyer, Paul S. (Editor in Chief), *The Oxford Companion to United States History*, Oxford University Press, New York, NY (2001).

Browne, Ray B.; Brown, Pat, *The Guide to United States Popular Culture*, Bowling Green State University Popular Press, Bowling Green, OH (2001).

Carruth, Gorton, *The Encyclopedia of American Facts and Dates, (10th Edition)*, HarperCollins Publishers, Inc., New York, NY (1997).

Evans, Harold, *The American Century*, Alfred A. Knopf, Inc., New York, NY (2000).

Grun, Bernard (Based Upon Werner Stein's Kulturfahrplan), *The Timetables of History: A Horizontal Linkage of People and Events*, Simon and Schuster, Inc., New York, 1982.

Hirsch, Jr., E.D.; Kett, Joseph F.; Trefil, James, *The Dictionary of Cultural Literacy— What Every American Needs to Know*, Houghton Mifflin Company, Boston, MA (1988).

Jennings, Peter; Brewster, Todd, *The Century*, Doubleday, New York, NY (1998).

Kirchon, John W. (Editor-in-Chief), *Chronicle of America*, Chronicle Publications, Inc. Mount Kisco, NY (1989) (Publication Undated).

Knauer, Kelly (Editor), *Time—Person of the Year—75th Anniversary Celebration*, Time, Inc., New York, NY. 2002.

Lewis, R.W.B.; Lewis, Nancy, *American Characters,* Yale University Press, New Haven, CT (1999).

Martin, Michael; Gelber, Leonard, *Dictionary of American History*, Rowan & Allanheld Publishers, Totowa, NY (1978).

Ravitch, Diane (Editor), *The American Reader: Words That Moved a Nation*, HarperCollins Publishers, Inc., New York, NY (1990).

Safire, William; Safir, Leonard, *Words of Wisdom: More Good Advice*, Simon & Schuster, Inc., New York, NY (1989).

Smith-Davies, *Speeches That Changed the World: The Stories and Transcripts of the Moments That Made History*, Smith-Davies Publishing, Ltd., London, U.K. (2005).

The Economist, Pocket World in Figures, 2012, Profile Books, Ltd., London, U.K. (2012).

The New York Times, Guide to Essential Knowledge, St Martin's Press, New York, NY (2007).

The World Almanac and Book of Facts—2009, Readers Digest Trade Publishing, Pleasantville, NY (2009).

Worth, Fred L., *The Trivia Encyclopedia*, Brooke House Publishers, Los Angeles, CA. (1974).

Secondary Background Sources

Boller, Jr., Paul E., *Presidential Anecdotes*, Penguin Books, New York, NY (1981).

Carlson, Elwood., "20th-Century U.S. Generations, Population Bulletin 64, No. 1 (2009).

Davis, Kenneth C., *Don't Know Much About Geography*, Avon Books, New York, NY (1992).

Korach, Myron, *Common Phrases and Where They Come From*, The Lyons Press, Guilford, CT, 2002.

Nelson, Rebecca (Editor), *The Handy History Answer Book ™*, Visible Ink Press, Canton, MI (1999).

Reay-Smith, John, *The Lawyer's Quotation Book: A Legal Companion*, Barnes & Noble Books, New York, NY (1991).

Robinson, Ray (Compiled By), *Famous Last World: Fond Farewells, Deathbed Diatribes, and Exclamations Upon Expiration*, Workman Publishing, New York, NY (2003).

Washington, Peter (Editor), *Comic Poems*, Albert A. Knopf, Inc., New York, NY (2001).

Webster III, Orville V., *The Book of Presidents*, Santa Monica Press LLC, Santa Monica, CA. (1998).

Webster III, Orville V., *The United States of America: Reference Book*, Santa Monica Press LLC, Santa Monica, CA. (1998).

Articles, Columnists, and Writers

Abramsky, S., "The Other America 2012, *The Nation*, May 14, 2012, p. 11.

Adamy, J., "U.S. Ties Hospital Payments To Making Patients Happy," *The Wall Street Journal,* October 15, 2012.

Adner, R., "Solving the Electric Car Puzzle," *The Wall Street Journal*, May 30, 2012.

Albergotti, R., O'Connell, V., "Drug Case Against Armstrong Detailed," *The Wall Street Journal*, October 11, 2012.

Alperovtiz, G., Hanna, T., "Not So Wild a Dream," *The Nation*, June 11, 2012, p. 18.

Alpert, L., Martson, J., *The Wall Street Journal*, February 26, 2013.

Alterman, E., "All the Media Money Can Buy," *The Nation*, June 11, 2012, p. 9.

Anapol, D. author of *Polyamory in the 21St Century,* Rowman & Littlefield, 2010.

Anderson, T., Johnson, D.B, *The Wall Street Journal*, December 28, 2012.

Andriotis, A., *SmartMoney.com*.

Angell, Marcia., "May Doctors Help You to Die?" *The New York Review of Books*, October 11, 2012, p. 39.

Audi, T., "School Districts Cut More Nurses," *The Wall Street Journal*, May 25, 2012.

Audi,. T., *The Wall Street Journal,* May 24, 2012.

Banchero, S., "Eight More States Receive Waiver from No-Child Law," *The Wall Street Journal,* May 30, 2012.

Banchero, S., "SAT Scores Fall as More Students Take Exam," *The Wall Street Journal*, September 25, 2012.

Banchero, S., *The Wall Street Journal*, March 7, 2013.

Banchero, S., "School-Test Backlash*," The Wall Street Journal,* May 16, 2012.

Banchero, S., *The Wall Street Journal*, December 11, 2012.

Banchero, S., *The Wall Street Journal*, December 13, 2012.

Banchero, S., Porter, C., *The Wall Street Journal*, April 16, 2013.

Bassetti, V., "In Search of the Right to Vote," excerpted from "Electoral Dysfunction," *Harper's Mag.* October 2012, p. 17.

Baum, D., "How to Make Your Own AR-15," *Harper's Magazine*, June, 2013, p. 37.

Beck, M., *The Wall Street Journal,* February 4, 2013.

Beck, M., *The Wall Street Journal*, March 14, 2013.

Beha, C., "Leveling the Playing Field," *Harper's Magazine*, October 2011, p. 52-53.

Belkin, D., *The Wall Street Journal*, March 14, 2013.

Belkin, D., Korn, M., *The Wall Street Journal*, March 12, 2013.

Bercovici, J., in *Forbes.com*.

Bhattacharjee, R., *news.msn.com*, June 13, 2013.

Bialik, C., *The Wall Street Journal,* December 8–9, 2012.

Bialik, C., "Border Delay Data Leave Fliers Up in the Air," *The Wall Street Journal*, May 5–6, 2012.

Bialik, C., "Don't Blame Sitting—Yet—for Shorter Lives of the Sedentary," *The Wall Street Journal*, July 21–22, 2012.

Bialik, C., "Voter Fraud: Hard to Identify?" *The Wall Street Journal*, September 1-2, 2012.

Biggs, A., "College Grads Need Jobs, Not a Lower Loan Rate," *The Wall Street Journal*, May 4, 2012.

Biggs, A., Richwine, J., "The Underworked Public Employee," *The Wall Street Journal*, December 5, 2012.

Birnbaum, J., "The Road to Riches Is Called K Street," *The Washington Post*, June 22, 2005.

Bloomberg, M., Gates, B., *The Wall Street Journal*, February 28, 2013.

Boston, W., Pangalos, P., *The Wall Street Journal*, December 6, 2012.

Bray, C., "Long Jail Term for Manager (Anthony Chiasson)," *The Wall Street Journal*, May 14, 2013.

Brooks, A., "A '47%' Solution for Romney, *The Wall Street Journal*, October 8, 2012.

Brooks, D. and DeParle, J. in *The New York Times*.

Browning, E.S., "New Wave of Workers Tries Novel Approach: Save More," *The Wall Street Journal*, September 25, 2012.

Browning, E. S., Russolillo, Vascellaro, J., "Apple Now Biggest Ever U.S. Company," *The Wall Street Journal*, August 21, 2012.

Burrough, B., "Remembrance of Wings Past," *Vanity Fair*, March, 2013, p. 254.

Bush, J., Bolick, C., *The Wall Street Journal*, January 25, 2013.

Byrce, R., *The Wall Street Journal*.

Bussey, J., "The Shale Revolution: What Could Go Wrong?" *The Wall Street Journal*, September 7, 2012.

Bustillo, M., *The Wall Street Journal*, February 7, 2013.

Bustillo, M., Millman, J., "Voters Weight Eased Pot Laws," *The Wall Street Journal*, September 24, 2012.

Calabresi, M., Crowley, M., "Homeland and Insecurity," *Time*, May 13, 2013.

Campo-Flores, A., *The Wall Street Journal*, December 28, 2012.

Campo-Flores, A., *The Wall Street Journal*, April 17, 2013.

Campoy, A., "Medical-Marijuana Vote in Arkansas to Go Ahead," *The Wall Street Journal*, September 28, 2012.

Cannato, V., *The Wall Street Journal*, March 12, 2013.

Carbone, N., *Time.com*.

Catan, T., Barrett, D., Martin, T., "Prescription for Addiction," *The Wall Street Journal*, October 6-7, 2012.

Catan, T., Perez, E., "A Pain-Drug Champion Has Second Thoughts," *The Wall Street Journal*, December 15–16, 2012.

Carlton, J., "Bad Days at Black Rock ...," *The Wall Street Journal*, September 1-2, 2012.

Carter, G., *Vanity Fair*, September 2012, p. 108.

Casselman, B., "Americans' Asset Shifts to Stocks from Homes," *The Wall Street Journal*, June 8, 2012.

Casselman, B., *The Wall Street Journal*, December 24, 2012.

Chafkin, M., "A Kickstart for Art," *Vanity Fair*, October 2012, p. 136.

Chandra, A., Jena, A., Seabury, S., *The Wall Street Journal*, February 8, 2013.

Chapman, S., *Chicago Tribune*.

Chasan, E., "Executive Pay Gets New Spin," *The Wall Street Journal*, September 25, 2012.

Christie, L., CNN Money, *money.cnn.com* (January 23, 2013).

Clark, D.; Worthen, B., "Larry Ellison to Buy Island in Hawaii," *The Wall Street Journal*, June 21, 2012.

Clinton, B., "The Case for Optimism," *Time,* October 1, 2012, p. 38.

Cloud, J., "The Law Heard Round the World," *Time,* April 9, 2012, p. 36.

Cloud, J., "Preventing Mass Murder—Can We Identify Dangerous Men Before They Kill?" *Time,* August 6, 2012, p. 33.

Cloud, J., *Time,* December 17, 2012, p. 18.

Cloud, J., "What Counts As Crazy?" *Time.* March 19, 2012.

Cohen, S., "Fourscore and 16,000 Books," *The Wall Street Journal*, October 12, 2012.

Coll, S. *NewYorker.com*.

Copeland, L., *chicagobusiness.com,* July 23, 2012.

Cordesman, A., Center for Strategic and International Studies.

Corcoran, T., *NationalPost.com*.

Corkery, M., "Pension Crisis Looms Despite Cuts,*"* *The Wall Street Journal*, September 22–23, 2012.

Cronin, B., *The Wall Street Journal*, April 11, 2013.

Crovitz, L.G., *The Wall Street Journal*, September 10, 2012.

Crow, K., "An Art Mystery Solved: Mogul Is 'Scream' Buyer," *The Wall Street Journal*, July 12, 2012.

Crow, K., "'Scream' Bring Record $119.9 Million," *The Wall Street Journal,* May 3, 2012.

Crow, K., "Hard Assets," *The Wall Street Journal*, May 10, 2013.

Crowley, M., "Return of the Architect," *Time,* August 13, 2012, p. 36.

Curry, T., "Lots of Litigating," July 19, 2012, *NBCPolitics.com*.

Dalmia, S., Snell, L., *The Wall Street Journal,* March 1, 2013.

Daniel, R., Hagey, K., *The Wall Street Journal*, December 26, 2012.

Davidson, A. in *The New York Times Magazine*.

DeMint, J., "No Internet Taxation Without Representation, *The Wall Street Journal*, August 1, 2012.

Dennis, K., *The Wall Street Journal*, December 19, 2012.

Dias, E., *Time,* June 10, 2013.

Dionne, E.J., *The Washington Post.*

Dockterman, E., *Time,* July 16, 2012, p. 16.

Dockterman, E., *Time,* July 23, 2012, p. 14 .

Doherty, B. in *Reason.com.*

Dolan, M., "Detroit on the Verge of Insolvency, Again," *The Wall Street Journal,* November 30, 2012.

Dougherty, C., Jordan, M., "Stirring Up the Melting Pot," *The Wall Street Journal,* September 7, 2012.

Dougherty, C., Mathews, A., "Household Income Sinks to '95 Level," *The Wall Street Journal,* September 13, 2012.

Douthat, R., *The New York Times.*

Drescher, J., *The (Raleigh, N.C.) News & Observer,* December 3, 2012.

Dugan, I., *The Wall Street Journal,* February 25, 2013.

Duhigg, C., Kocieniewski, D., *The New York Times.*

Eaglesham, J., Neumann, J., Perez, E., *The Wall Street Journal,* February 5, 2013.

Eaglesham, J., Neumann, J., Albergotti, R., "Clock Is Ticking on Crisis Charges," *The Wall Street Journal,* July 12, 2012.

Eavis, P., Craig, S., *The New York Times.*

Eberstadt, N. "Are Entitlements Corrupting Us?—American Character Is at Stake," *The Wall Street Journal,* September 1–2, 2012. (Part of a 2-Part Article With W. Galston).

Eisinger, J., *ProPublica.org.*

Emshwiller, J., "Lawyers Land in Hot Water—Criminal and Civil Mortgage-Fraud Cass Have Exploded Since Housing Crisis," *The Wall Street Journal,* September 19, 2012.

Engler, J., "Corporate Taxes, the Myths and Facts, *The Wall Street Journal,* October 12, 2012.

Ensign, R., Wealth Management—Journal Report, *The Wall Street Journal,* February 25, 2013.

Epstein, R., Review of *The Lawyer Bubble* by S. Harper, *The Wall Street Journal,* May 6, 2013.

Falk, A., *The Wall Street Journal,* August 29, 2012.

Falk, W., *The Week,* April 27, 2012, p. 5.

Falk, W., *The Week,* March 30, 2012, p. 7.

Ferguson, A., "Bubble on the Potomac," *Time,* May 28, 2012, p. 46.

Fields, G., "Hispanics Take a Page From '60s To Add Clout," *The Wall Street Journal,* July 21–22, 2012.

Fields, G., Jackson-Randall, M., *The Wall Street Journal,* September 12, 2012.

Fields, G., King, N., *The Wall Street Journal,* May 6, 2013.

Fields, G., McWhirter, C., *The Wall Street Journal,* December 8–9, 2012.

Fields, G., Emshwiller, J., "Federal Guilty Pleas Soar as Bargains Trump Trials," *The Wall Street Journal*, September 24, 2012.

Fishman, R., "The American Metropolis at Century's End: Past and Future Influences," Housing Facts and Findings, Winter, 1999.

Ford, A., "How the U.S. Is Losing the Infrastructure Race," *Time,* June 25, 2012, p. 18.

Ford, A., *Time,* April 9, 2012, p. 16.

Ford, A., Macsai, D., Wolverson, R., "Ready, Set, Disrupt," *Time,* October 15, 2012, p. 38.

Foroohar, R., "Digging Out of the Debt Hole." *Time,* July 16, 2012, p. 26.

Foroohar, R., "She's Feeling Lucky," *Time,* July 30, 2012, p. 17.

Foroohar, R., "The Case for Banking Regulation," *Time,* June 4, 2012, p. 22.

Foroohar, R., "The S&P Soars, the Economy Snores," *Time,* September 24, 2012, p. 24.

Foroohar, R, "These Schools Mean Business," *Time,* April 9, 2012, p. 26.

Foroohar, R., "Walmart's Discounted Ethics," *Time,* May 7, 2012, p. 19.

Foroohar, R., "Why the World Isn't Getting Smaller," *Time,* June 27, 2011, p. 20.

Foroohar, R., "Your Global Economic Mess Is Now Being Served," *Time,* June 18, 2012, p. 40.

Fowler, G., "Facebook: One Billion and Counting," *The Wall Street Journal*, October 5, 2012.

Fowler, G., "More Billionaires Vow to Give Money Away," *The Wall Street Journal,* September 19, 2012.

Fowler, T., "BP Blocked from Deals," *The Wall Street Journal*, November 28, 2012.

Fowler, T., "Experts Weigh Spill's Lasting Effects," *The Wall Street Journal*, April 13, 2012.

Fox, J., The Riddle of Kate Moss, *Vanity Fair*, December 2012, p. 156.

Frank, T., "Easy Chair—Social Studies," *Harper's Magazine*, October 2011, p. 11.

Frank, T. "Gold Faithful: Profiting from Paranoia With Precious Metals," *Harper's Magazine*, July, 2011, p. 9.

Freedland, J. "The Republicans: Behinds the Barricades," *The New York Review of Books*, October 11, 2012, p. 26.

Frey, W., Brookings Institute.

Friedman, B., "The Oligarchy in America Today," (Review of Smith, Hedrick, *Who Stole the American Dream*, (Random House, 2012), *The New York Review of Books*, October 11, 2012, p. 36.

Frost, T., "The Big Danger With Big Banks," *The Wall Street Journal*, May 16, 2012.

Frum, D., *TheDailyBeast.com.*

Fund, J., *NationalReview.com.*

Gandel, S., "Want to Make More Than a Banker? Become a Farmer?" *Time,* July 11, 2011, p. 38.

Galston, W., "Are Entitlements Corrupting Us? They're Part of the Civic Compact," *The Wall Street Journal*, September 1–2, 2012 (Part of a 2-part Article with N. Eberstadt).

Garber, M., *TheAtlantic.com.*

Gau, X., Ritter, J., Zhu, Z., "Where Have All the IPOs Gone?' (April 3, 2012) *bear.warringtn.ufl.edu* .

Gerson, M., *The Washington Post.*

Ghemawat, P. *World 3.0.*

Ghilarducci, T., *The New York Times.*

Ghosh, B., Dias, E., "Change Agent," *Time*, April 9, 2012, p. 40.

Gill, A., *Vanity Fair*, September 2012, p. 202.

Gold, R., "DeLay's Attorney Says Jury in Texas Misconstrued Money-Laundering Law," *The Wall Street Journal*, October 11, 2012.

Gold, R., "Judges to Hear Appeal of DeLay's Conviction, *The Wall Street Journal*, October 9, 2012.

Goldin, C., Cellini., S., National Bureau of Economic Research Working Paper.

Gordon, J., "Air Conditioning, Blessed Invention," *The Wall Street Journal*, July 11, 2012.

Gottlieb, S., Kleinke, J. D., "There's a Medical App for That—Or Not," *The Wall Street Journal*, May 30, 2012.

Greene, J., "The Imaginary Teacher Shortage," *The Wall Street Journal*, October 9, 2012.

Gregoire, C., Jewell, S., *The Wall Street Journal*, December 10, 2012.

Gregory, S., "Bench Bracket, *Time,* March 26, 2012, p. 54.

Gregory, S., "Can Roger Goodell Save Football," *Time,* December 17, 2012, p. 36.

Grind, K., *The Wall Street Journal,* May 4-5, 2013.

Gross, D., "Renting Prosperity," *The Wall Street Journal*, May 5–6, 2012.

Grunwald, M., "Back on Tracks," *Time,* July 9, 2012, p. 22.

Grunwald, M., "How the Voters Won," *Time,* October 29, 2012, p. 26.

Grunwald, M.," One Nation On Welfare. Living Your Life on the Dole," *Time,* September 17, 2012, p. 52.

Gunter, L., *Toronto Star.*

Hagerty, J., *The Wall Street Journal,* December 28, 2012.

Haidt, J., "The New Culture War Over Fairness," *Time,* October 22, 2012, p. 25.

Hamilton, A., *Time,* June 25, 2012, p. 20.

Hansegard, J., "For Paternity Lease, Sweden Asks If Two Months Is Enough," *The Wall Street Journal*, August 1, 2012.

Hanson, V., *NationalReview.com.*

Hanushek, E. (Senior Fellow at Hoover Institution of Stanford University), Luque, J., "Efficiency and Equity in Schools Around the World," April, 2002 (Data summarized at *nationmaster.com.*).

Hargreaves, S., *CNNMoney.com*.

Harper's Index, *Harper's Magazine (Multiple Issues)*.

Helferich, G., "The Ties That Bound," *The Wall Street Journal*, October 6–7, 2012.

Heilpern, J., "Silver Streak," *Vanity Fair*, November 2012, p. 70.

Henninger, D., "Obama and the L-Word," *The Wall Street Journal*, October 11, 2012.

Hertsgaard, M. "Save Earth Day," *The Nation*, May 7, 2012, p. 3.

Hess, F., "The Irrational Fear of For-Profit Education," *The Wall Street Journal*, December 18, 2012.

Howard, P., Sykes, R., "Medicaid Is Broken—Let the States Fix It," *The Wall Street Journal*, October 11, 2012.

Huddleston, C., *Kiplinger*.

Hudson, A., "Approval Rating for Congress Hits a Dismal Low," September 17, 2012 at *humanevents.com*.

Humes, E., "Grappling With a Garbage Glut," *The Wall Street Journal*, April 14–15, 2012.

Huntsman, J., "A GOP Opportunity on Immigration," *The Wall Street Journal*, August 27, 2012.

Hymnowitz, K., *The Wall Street Journal*.

Isserman, M. "What Would Michael Harrington Say," *The Nation*, May 14, 2012, p.18.

James, S., NBC News, *vitals.nbcnews.com*, May 9, 2013.

Jargon, J., *The Wall Street Journal*.

Jenkins, H.W., *The Wall Street Journal*, December 19, 2012.

Johnson, D., "Mothers Beware!," *The New York Review of Books*, June 21, 2012.

Johnson, D., "Who Really Gets Rich Off High Gas Prices?" *The Wall Street Journal*, August 3, 2012.

Johnston, I., Eng, J., NBC News, *nbcnews.com*, November 15, 2012.

Johnson, K.C., Taylor, S., "Penn State, Duke and Integrity," *The Wall Street Journal*, September 17, 2012.

Jones, A., *The Wall Street Journal*, March 7, 2013.

Jones, A., "New Death Sentences Fall to Lowest Level in 35 Years," *The Wall Street Journal*, December 15, 2011.

Jones, A., Eder, S.," Death Penalty Costs Get Close Look," *The Wall Street Journal*, October 6–7, 2012.

Jones, J. "Congress' Job Approval Rating Worst in Gallup History," December 15, 2010, at *gallup.com*.

Jonsson, P. in *CSMonitor.com*.

Jordon, M., "The Costs and Benefits of an Immigration Overhaul," *The Wall Street Journal*, February 4, 2013.

Jordan, M., *The Wall Street Journal*, February 8, 2013.

Jordan, M., *The Wall Street Journal,* November 30, 2012.

Juhasz, A., "Two Years Later: BP's Toxic Legacy—Special Investigation," *The Nation,* p.11, May 7, 2012.

Kadlec, D., *Time.com.*

Karl, J., "Where Were You in 1979," (A Review of C. Caryl Book), *The Wall Street Journal,* May 4-5, 2013.

Kazin, M., *The New Republic.*

Keates, N., "For Sale...Luxury Golf Communities..." *The Wall Street Journal,* July 20, 2012.

Keating, D., Fallis, D., Kindy, K., and Higham, S. of *The Washington Post.*

Keenan, T., *New York Post.*

Kekic, L., "The Lottery of Life," *The Economist—The World in 2013,* p. 91.

Kenny, C., *Bloomberg Businessweek.*

Kenny, D. "Why Charter Schools Work," *The Wall Street Journal,* June 25, 2012.

Khanna, A. and P., "Northern Star," *Time,* July 4, 2011, p. 70.

Kenneally, C., "How to Fix 911," *Time,* April 11, 2011, p. 36.

Klein, J., "How the Gun Won," *Time,* August 6, 2012, p. 26.

Klein, J. "Learning That Works," *Time,* May 14, 2012, p. 36.

Klein, J., "The 20% Solution," *Time,* July 9, 2012, p. 26.

Klein, Joe, "The Long Good-Bye," *Time,* June 11, 2012, p. 18.

Klein, J., *Time,* September 10, 2012, p. 23.

Klinenberg, E. *The New York Times.*

Kluger, J., Dias, E., "Does God Want You To Be Thin?," *Time,* June 11, 2012, p. 40.

Kopel, D., "Guns, Mental Illness and Newtown," *The Wall Street Journal,* December 18, 2012.

Koppel, N.; Belkin, D., "Texas Pushes $10,000 Degree," *The Wall Street Journal,* October 8, 2012.

Koppel, N., "Dispute Over College Tuition Roils Flagship Texas Campus," *The Wall Street Journal,* May 18, 2012.

Koppel, N., *The Wall Street Journal,* September 8–9, 2012.

Korn, M., *The Wall Street Journal,* February 7, 2013.

Kwoh, L., "Firms Resist New Pay-Equity Rules, *The Wall Street Journal,* June 27, 2012.

Kwoh, L. *The Wall Street Journal,* April 6-7, 2013.

Krugman, P., "Off and Out With Romney," *The New York Times,* July 5, 2012.

Landro, L., "Hospital Horrors," *The Wall Street Journal,* October 4, 2012, (Review of Dr. Marty Makary's 2012 book *Unaccountable*).

Landro, L., "Ten Ways Patients Get Treated Better," *The Wall Street Journal,* December 18, 2012.

Last, J., "America's Baby Bust—The Nation's Falling Fertility Rate ...," The *Wall Street Journal,* February 2-3, 2013.

Levitz, J., "Dagnabit, This Town Is Fed Up With Cursing," *The Wall Street Journal*, June 11, 2012.

Levitz, J., "Ivy League School to Pay City Millions," *The Wall Street Journal*, May 2, 2012.

Levitz, J., "Party Laws Put Hosts on Hook," *The Wall Street Journal*, September 12, 2012.

Levitz, J., Morath, E., *The Wall Street Journal*, February 7, 2013.

Levitz, J., *The Wall Street Journal*, March 11, 2013.

Linebaugh, K., *The Wall Street Journal*, December 4, 2012.

Linn, A., *CNBC.com*, May 28, 2013.

Lippman, D., "In Turnaround, Pentagon Marks Gay Pride Month, *The Wall Street Journal*, June 27, 2012.

Lomborg, B., "Feel-Good Environmentalism at the U.N.," *The Wall Street Journal*, June. 21, 2012.

Lowenstein, R., *The New York Times*.

Lowry, R., "Just Not the Marrying Kind," *Time*, March 5, 2012, p. 13 citing *The New York Times*.

Lublin, J., "Pink Quotas' Alter Europe's Boards, *The Wall Street Journal*, September 12, 2012.

Luscombe, B., "I Do, I Do, I Do, I Do," *Time*, August 6, 2012, p. 42.

Luscombe, B., "The End of Alimony," *Time*, May 27, 2013, p. 44.

Madrick, J., "Obama & Healthcare: The Straight Story," *The New York Review of Books*, June 21, 2012.

Madrick, J., "The Anti-Economist—Half-Empty" *Harper's Magazine*, December, 2012, p. 11.

Madrigal, A., *TheAtlantic.com*.

Mahr, K., "The Coconut Crazy," *Time*, December 17, 2012, p. 45.

Makary, M., "How to Stop Hospitals From Killing Us," *The Wall Street Journal*, September 22-23, 2012.

Malkiel, B., "Telling Lies from Statistics," *The Wall Street Journal*, September 25, 2012 (Review of Silver, Nate, *The Signal and the Noise*, 2012.

Maloy, Professor R., University of San Diego (*Journal of Behavioral Sciences & the Law*).

Manno, B., "Education Reform Gets a Hollywood Boost," *The Wall Street Journal*, September 29–30, 2012.

Marche, S., *Bloomberg.com*.

Martin, T., "Nurses Seek Expanded Role," *The Wall Street Journal*, October 3, 2012.

Martin, T., *The Wall Street Journal*, March 11, 2013.

Martin, T., *The Wall Street Journal*, May 3, 2013.

Martin, T., Dawsey, J., and McKay, B., "The Gender Barrier Falls at Augusta," *The Wall Street Journal*, August 21, 2012.

Mathews, C., "Trickling Down. Why the Corporate Tax Rate Is So Low," *Time*, February 20, 2012, p. 16.

McAllester, M.,"Where Is He Now? David Bowie Is Back to His Mysterious Best," *Time,* March 18, 2013, p. 52.

McCracken, H., *Time.com.*

McCracken, H., The Kickstarter Economy," *Time*, October 1, 2012, p. 32.

McCrank, J., Moon, A., in *Reuters.com.*

McGuire, A., *WashingtonPost.com.*

McGurn, W., *The Wall Street Journal* (Review of J. Last's book *What To Expect When No One's Expecting*), February 21, 2013.

McKay, B., *The Wall Street Journal,* February 28, 2013.

McKinnon, J., "For Most, Tax Rates Hit Lows in 2009, " *The Wall Street Journal*, July 11, 2012.

McKinnon, J., Thurm, S., "U.S. Firms Move Aboard," *The Wall Street Journal*, August 29, 2012.

McWhirter, C., Fields, G., "Crime Migrates to Suburbs," *The Wall Street Journal*, December 31, 2012.

McWhirter, C., *The Wall Street Journal*, February. 28, 2013.

Meacham, J., "Heaven Can't Wait," *Time*, April 16, 2012, p. 30.

Meacham, J., "Keeping the Dream Alive," *Time*, July 2, 2012, p. 26.

Mead, W., "Infostructure Is the New Infrastructure," *The Wall Street Journal,* October 16, 2012.

Meckler, L., *The Wall Street Journal*, December 12, 2012.

Melloan, G. "Government to the Rescue (Reviewing Bartlett, D., Steele, J.'s book *The Betrayal of the American Dream*), *The Wall Street Journal*, July 31, 2012.

Melnick, M., "New Cigarette Warning Labels," *Time*, July 4, 2011, p. 25.

Miller, M. *Reuters.com.*

Miller, S., "Remembrances—Author's '7 Habits' Fueled Business-Book Boom," *The Wall Street Journal,* July 17, 2012.

Millman, J., "Many Apples, Few Pickers," *The Wall Street Journal*, October 10, 2012.

Millman, J., *The Wall Street Journal,* December 7, 2012.

Mirchandani, R. in *BostonHerald.com.*

Mitchell, J., Ensign, R., "Student-Loan Defaults Mount Again," *The Wall Street Journal*, September 29-30, 2012.

Mitchell, J., "Federal Student Lending Swells," *The Wall Street Journal,* November 28, 2012.

Mitchell, J., "Income Fell or Stagnated in Most States Last Year," *The Wall Street Journal,* September 20, 2012.

Mitchell, J., "New Course in College Costs," *The Wall Street Journal*, June 11, 2012.

Mitchell, J., *The Wall Street Journal*, December 5, 2012.

Mitchell, J., "U.S. Chips Away at the Debt on Their Homes," *The Wall Street Journal*, August 30, 2012.

Mone, L., "How to Avoid Making the Energy Boom Go Bust," *The Wall Street Journal*, August 25–26, 2012.

Moore, S., "The Weekend Interview with Grover Norquist," *The Wall Street Journal*, November 24–25, 2012.

Morales, L., "U.S. Trust in Media Hits New High," September 21, 2012, *gallup.com*.

Moreno, P., "How Public Unions Became So Powerful," *The Wall Street Journal*, September 12, 2012.

Moretti, E., "What Workers Lose by Staying Put," *The Wall Street Journal*, May 26–27, 2012.

Morgenson, G., *The New York Times*.

Morgenthau, R., "The Death of Peter Wielunski," *The Wall Street Journal*, September 24, 2012.

Morris, M., "Special Report—Fracking: The Opposition," *The Week*, September 7, 2012, p. 22.

Mracek, K., *Kiplinger.com*.

Mundy, A., *The Wall Street Journal*, December 5, 2012.

Mundy, L., "Women, Money and Power," *Time*, March 26, 2012, p. 28.

Murray, S., Mullins, B., "Investors Bankrolls Big Romney Campaign," *The Wall Street Journal*, September 17, 2012.

Naik, G., "Big Calorie Cuts Don't Equal Longer Life, Study Suggests," *The Wall Street Journal*, August 30, 2012.

Nelson, L., "Two-Year Default Rates for Student Loans Increase Again, October 1, 2012 at *insidehighered.com*.

Neugebauer, R., "A $447 Million Consumer Alert," *The Wall Street Journal*, September 20, 2012.

Newcomb, T., "Silver Bullitt," *Time*, July 2. 2012, p. 60.

Newport, F., "Congress Ends 2011 With Record-Low 11% Approval," December 19, 2011 at *gallup.com*.

Nicas, J., *The Wall Street Journal*, February. 5, 2013.

Nicas, J., "North Dakota Tops Alaska in Oil Production," *The Wall Street Journal*, May 16, 2012.

Nielsen, S., *Portland Oregonian*.

Nocera, J., *The New York Times*.

Nolan, J., "Imagined Inventions," *The New Yorker*, May 20, 2013.

Nutting, R., *MarketWatch.com*.

Obama, M., *The Wall Street Journal*, February 28, 2013.

Ohlemacher, S., "41 Nations Top U.S. Life Expectancy," August 12, 2007, Associated Press.

Orwall, B., Bray, C., "Ex-Banker Tried to Settle Charges," *The Wall Street Journal*, September 28, 2012.

Padgett, T., "Mexico's Tragedy," *Time*, July 11, 2011, p. 24.

Palazzolo, J., *The Wall Street Journal*, February 15, 2013.

Palazzolo, J., Phipps, C., "Law Schools Apply the Brakes," *The Wall Street Journal*, June 11, 2012.

Palazzolo, J., Eder, S., "Push to Let College Students Carry Guns Picks Up Steam," *The Wall Street Journal*, September 22–23, 2012.

Paletta, D., "Disability-Benefits System Faces Review," *The Wall Street Journal*, December 15, 2011.

Pallarito, K., "Life Expectancy in U.S. Trails Top Nations," June 16, 2011, *Health.com*.

Park, A., "Crowdfunding a Cure," *Time*, December 3, 2012, p. 22.

Park, A., "CSI TV," *Time*, June 27, 2011, p. 18.

Park, A., "Waste Not," *Time*, September 10, 2012, p. 14.

Pearlstein, S. *The Washington Post*.

Penn, M., "In Search of the Changing American Voter," *Time*, July 2, 2012, p. 40.

Perez, E., "FBI Files Go Digital, After Years of Delays, *The Wall Street Journal*, August 1, 2012.

Perry, A., "Africa Rising," *Time*, December 3, 2012, p. 48.

Peters, G. "Presidential News Conferences," *The American Presidency Project*, ED, John T. Woolley and G. Peters, Santa Barbara, CA. Univ. of CA, 1999–2012.

Peters, M., *The Wall Street Journal*, May 14, 2013.

Phillips, M. "One Taliban Bullet, Two Lives Lost," *The Wall Street Journal*, May 26–27, 2012.

Pianin, E., *The Washington Post*.

Pickert, K., "What the Affordable Care Act Means to You," *Time*, July 16, 2012, p. 38.

Pipes, S., *The Wall Street Journal*, February 5, 2013.

Poniewozik, J., "Big Bird Is a Republican," *Time*, October 22, 2012, p. 58.

Poole, S., "Not So Fast There," *The Wall Street Journal*, March 14, 2013.

Porter, C., "Suits Challenge Classrooms That Segregate Boys, Girls," *The Wall Street Journal*, September 5, 2012.

Porter, C., "College Degree, No Class Time Required," *The Wall Street Journal*, January 25, 2013.

Prescott, E., Ohanian, L., "Taxes Are Much Higher Than You Think," *The Wall Street Journal*, December 12, 2012.

Proctor, R., "What's Really in Your Cigarette?" *The Wall Street Journal*, September 1–2, 2012.

Pulliam, S., Eaglesham, J., *The Wall Street Journal*, December 5, 2012.

Purdum, Todd, *Vanity Fair.*

Quinton, S., *National Journal.*

Radnofsky, L., *The Wall Street Journal*, April 9, 2013.

Randall, D., *Reuters.com.*

Ravitch, D., "Do Our Public Schools Threaten National Security?" *The New York Review of Books*, June 7, 2012, p. 45.

Rector, R., Sheffield, R, *The National Review.*

Reif, L. "What Campuses Can Learn From Online Teaching," *The Wall Street Journal*, October 3, 2012.

Reynolds, R., *The Wall Street Journal*, December 23, 2012.

Riley, J. "The Good News About Race in America," (Interview with Abigail Thernstrom), *The Wall Street Journal*, May 19-20, 2012.

Riley, N., "Dazed and Gifted,," *The Wall Street Journal*, October 15, 2012, reviewing Chester E. Finn and Jessica A. Hockett's book *Exam Schools: Inside America's Most Selective Public Schools.*

Ripley, A., Special Report, *Time*, October 29, 2012, p. 33.

Rivkin, D., Carnbey, J., *The Wall Street Journal*, March 15, 2013.

Rochman, B., "Please, Please Go To Sleep," *Time*, March 26, 2012, p. 47.

Romano, T., *local.msn.com*, March 20, 2013.

Rothfeld, M., Eaglesham, J., Bray, C., *The Wall Street Journal*, March 16-17, 2013.

Samuelson, R., *The Washington Post.*

Sanburn, J., "Economy—Cut It Out," *Time,* June 27, 2011, p. 17.

Sanburn, J., "Donations to Japan Are Lagging Behind" *Time,* April 11, 2011, p. 17.

Sanburn, J., "Recovery for Real? Six Surprising Signs…That Point to Yes," *Time,* April 9, 2012, p. 16.

Sanburn, J., *Time,* June 10, 2013, p. 22.

Sander, R., Taylor, S., Jr., "The Unraveling of Affirmative Action," *The Wall Street Journal*, October 13–14, 2012.

Saporito, B., "Hack Attack," *Time*, July 4, 2011, p. 52.

Saporito, B., "Shut Up and Pay Up, Please," *Time,* April 23, 2012 p. 58.

Saporito, B., "Sit Tight," *Time,* October 22, 2012, p. 16.

Saporito, B., "Skyway Robbery," *Time,* June 13, 2011, p. 90.

Saporito, B., "Starbuck's Big Mug," *Time,* June 25, 2012, p. 52.

Saporito, B., "Stumped at the Pump," *Time*, March 19, 2012, p.12.

Saundcrs, L., Sidel, R., *The Wall Street Journal*, September 12, 2012.

Saunders, L, "Tax Tips for Life's Big Changes," *The Wall Street Journal*, March 16-17, 2013.

Saunders, L., *The Wall Street Journal*, May 6, 2013.

Sauter, M., *24/7 Wall St*, June 1, 2013.

Scheiber, N. in *TNR.com.*

Scherer, M. "A Rich Man's Game," *Time,* August 13, 2012, p. 42.

Scherer, M. "Blue Truth—Red Truth," *Time,* October 15, 2012, p. 24.

Scherer, M., "Hot Pot," *Time,* May 14, 2012. p. 14.

Scherer, M., "Why Latino Voters Will Swing the 2012 Election," *Time,* March 5, 2012, p. 22.

Schoen, J., *economywatch.nbcnews.com,* August 9, 2012 citing Federal Reserve data.

Schoenfeld, M., "Air Jordan and the 1%, *The Wall Street Journal,* July 11, 2012.

Schultz, G., Hanushek, E., "Education Is the Key to a Healthy Economy," *The Wall Street Journal,* May 1, 2012.

Schuman, M., The Jobless Generation," *Time,* April 16, 2012, p. 44.

Seib, G., "Visa Plan Poses Bipartisan Test," *The Wall Street Journal,* May 1, 2012.

Schumpeter, "Bargain Bosses," *The Economist,* September 8–12, 2012, p. 67.

Shaheen, S., Cohen, A., "Worldwide Carsharing Growth: An International Comparison," California PATH, University of California, Berkeley, California.

Shah, N., Casselman, B., "Right-to-Work' Economics," *The Wall Street Journal,* December 15–16, 2012.

Shah, N., *The Wall Street Journal,* March 1, 2013.

Shah, N., *The Wall Street Journal,* March 5, 2013.

Shah, N., *The Wall Street Journal,* March 14, 2013.

Shane, T., *ABC.com.*

Shellenbarger, S., Women in the Economy Report, *The Wall Street Journal,* May 7, 2012.

Silverman, R., *The Wall Street Journal,* February 26, 2013.

Silverstein, M., Singhi, A., "Can Universities Stay on Top?" *The Wall Street Journal,* September 29–30, 2012.

Simon, R., *The Wall Street Journal,* March 6, 2013.

Simon, R., *The Wall Street Journal,* May 6, 2013.

Simon, R., Corkery, M., *The Wall Street Journal,* February 12, 2013.

Slaughter, M.J., "How Skilled Immigrants Create Jobs," *The Wall Street Journal,* June 21, 2012.

Smith, G., "How Wall Street Is Still Rigging the Game," *Time,* November 5, 2012, p. 18.

Smith, R.J., *The Washington Post,* January 10, 2011.

Smith, R., "The Rich, The Poor, and the Oval Office," *Time,* February 20, 2012, p. 32.

Solnit, R., "The Separating Sickness," *Harper's Magazine,* June, 2013, p. 50.

Solomita, A. "The Wound-Up Nerd Chronicle," *The Wall Street Journal,* July 14-15, 2012.

Soumerai, S., Koppel, R., "A Major Glitch For Digitalized Health-Care Records," *The Wall Street Journal,* September 18, 2012.

Spector, M., McGinty, T., Feintzeig, *The Wall Street Journal*, December 4, 2012.

Steinmetz, K., "How Chobani Spread Geek Yogurt Across America," *Time*, June 25, 2012, p. 70.

Steinmetz, K., "Unfriending the Enemy," *Time*, October 22, 2012, p. 15.

Stelter, B., *The New York Times*.

Stengel, R., "One Document, Under Siege," *Time*, July 4., 2011, p. 42.

Stengel, R., "Reinventing College," *Time*, October 29, 2012, p. 31.

Stephenson, R., "Spectrum and the Wireless Revolution," *The Wall Street Journal*, June 11, 2012.

Strumpf, D., "With Fewer to Lock Up, Prisons Shut Doors," *The Wall Street Journal*, February 11, 2013.

Sumner, A., Britain's Institute of Development Studies.

Sun, F., "Last Dance," *Time*, June 11, 2012, p. 32.

Sun, J., *eater.com.*, May 29, 2013.

Sun, F., "Baby Mamas—Teen Moms Are Reality TV's New Stars. Is This A Good Thing," *Time*, July 18, 2011, p. 59.

Taranto, J., in *WSJ.com*.

Tergesen, A., "Counting on an Inheritance? Count Again," *The Wall Street Journal*, June 11, 2012.

Tergesen, A, *The Wall Street Journal*, December 10, 2012.

Thau,B., *DailyFinance.com*.

"The 60 Minutes/Vanity Fair Poll," *Vanity Fair*, (Multiple Issues).

Thomas, S., "Are Dads the New Moms?," *The Wall Street Journal*, May 12–13, 2012.

Thompson, M., Gibbs, N., "Why Can't The Army Win the War on Suicide?," *Time*, July 23, 2012, p. 22.

Thurm, S., "CEO Pay Moves With Corporate Results," *The Wall Street Journal*, May 21, 2012.

Thurm, S., "Who Can Still Afford State U?" *The Wall Street Journal*, December 15–16, 2012.

Tomson, B. "ABC Sued for 'Pink Slime' Defamation, *The Wall Street Journal*, September 14, 2012.

Torrey, E.F., Fuller, D., "The Potential Killers We Let Loose," *The Wall Street Journal*," December 19, 2012.

Torrey, E.F., *The Wall Street Journal*, February 5, 2013.

Toure, "Inside the Racist Mind," *Time*, May 7, 2012, p. 20.

Tully, S., *Fortune Magazine*.

Tuttle, B., "Home, Cheap Home," *Time*, November 5, 2012, p. 16.

Vargas, J., "Not Legal—Lot Leaving," *Time*, June 25,. 2012, p.34.

Von Drehle, D., "His Kind of Town," *Time*, June 10, 2013, p. 36.

Walsh, B., "Pedal Push—Biking Is on the Rise," *Time*, July 16, 2012, p. 52.

Walsh, B., "The Future of Oil," *Time,* April 9, 2012, p. 28.

Walsh, B., *Time,* June 13, 2011, p. 18.

Walsh, B., "When the Rains Stop," *Time,* August 6, 2012, p. 34.

Wattenberg, B., "What's Really Behind the Entitlement Crisis," *The Wall Street Journal,* July 13, 2012.

Wattenberg, B., *The Wall Street Journal,* May 24, 2012.

Webley, K., "Reboot School," *Time,* July 9, 2012, p. 36.

Weingroff, R., "The Genie in the Bottle: The Interstate System and Urban Problems, 1939–1957, at *fhwa.dot.gov.*

Weintraub, J., "Paul Anka—A V.F. Portrtait," *Vanity Fair,* May, 2013, p. 184.

Weissman, J., *TheAtlantic.com.*

Wessel, D.,"Everything You Ever Wanted to Know About The Budget * * But Were Afraid to Ask," *The Wall Street Journal,* July 21–22, 2012.

Wessel, D., "The 'Eureka' Moments Happen Later," *The Wall Street Journal,* September 6, 2012.

Whelan, R., "Getting Away—but Not Too Far," *The Wall Street Journal,* May 2, 2012.

White, A., Review of J. H. Wilkinson's book *Cosmic Constitutional Theory, The Wall Street Journal,* April 16, 2012.

White, Bobby, "City in California Nears Bankruptcy," *The Wall Street Journal,* June 25, 2012.

Wieczner, J., *The Wall Street Journal,* April 9, 2013.

Will, G., *The Washington Post.*

Wolverson, R, "Now What?" *Time,* June 13, 2011, p. 34.

Wolverson, R., Walt, V., "Take the Money and Run," *Time,* July 30, 2012, p. 13.

Wolverson, R., "Welcome to the 'Sharing Economy," " *Time,* September 24, 2012, p. 44.

Wotapka, D., "Big Homes Are Back in Business," *The Wall Street Journal,* June 8, 2012.

Zakaria, F., "Broken and Obsolete—An Immigration Deadlock Makes the U.S. a Second-Rate Nation," *Time,* June 18, 2012, p. 24.

Zakaria, F., "Innovate Better," *Time,* June 13, 2011, p. 30.

Zakaria, F., "Tax and Spend," *Time,* July 23, 2012, p. 20.

Zakaria, F., "The GOP's Abstract Professors," *Time,* June 27, 2011, p. 23.

Zakaria, F., "The New Oil and Gas Boom," *Time,* October 29, 2012, p. 20.

Zakaria, F., "Why We Need Pension Reform," *Time,* June 25, 2012, p. 28.

Zimmerman, A, Mattioli, D., "Retail's New Odd Couple," *The Wall Street Journal,* July 11, 2012.

Zingales, L., "Crony Capitalism and the Crisis of the West," *The Wall Street Journal,* June 7, 2012.

Magazines and Newspapers

Financial Times
Forbes.com
Fortune Magazine
Harper's Magazine
Investor's Business Daily
Los Angeles Times
Mother Jones
TheAtlantic.com.
The Daily Mail (U.K.)
The Economist
The Nation
The National Journal
The New York Review of Books
The New York Times
The Times (U.K).
The Wall Street Journal
The Washington Examiner
The Washington Monthly
The Week
Time and Time.com
USA Today
Vanity Fair
The Washington Post and WashingtonPost.com.

Books, Governmental, Research, Foundation, Data Sites, and Internet References

24/7 Wall Street.
2011 World Wealth Report from Merrill Lynch and Capgemini.
About.com/geography.
Albonetti, C., "Judicial Discretion in Federal Sentencing," *Criminology & Public Policy*, Vol. 10, Issue 4 (2011).
American Assembly of Columbia University.
americanhumanist.org.
American Institute of Architects' Home Design Trends Survey.
American Journal of Preventive Medicine.
American Library Association.
American Society of Civil Engineers.
American Time Use Survey.
americasroof.com.

Amnesty International.

Associated Press.

Association of Magazine Media.

Association of Medical Colleges.

Association of Religion Data Archives.

Audit Bureau of Circulations.

Bernstein Research.

blogs.marketwatch.com.

Bloomberg (Businessweek; .com; and .news).

bottomline.nbcnews.com.

Boston Consulting Group.

Brokaw, Tom. *Boom* (2007).

Brookings Institute.

Bureau of Economic Analysis.

Bureau of Labor Statistics (*data.bls.org).*

burningman.com.

CABE (Commission for Architecture and the Built Environment).

CareerBuilder.com.

carnegiehero.org.

Caro, R., *The Years of Lyndon Johnson: The Path to Power* (1982); *Means of Ascent* (1990); *Master of the Senate* (2002); and *The Passage of Power* (2012).

Carroll, P. *It Seemed Like Nothing Happened: The Tragedy and Promise of America in the 1970s* (1982).

Caryl, C., *Strange Rebels—1979 and the Birth of the 21ˢᵗ Century* (2013).

Center for Disease Control and Prevention (*cdc.gov.*).

Center for College Affordability and Productivity.

Center for International Media Ethics (Public Trust Survey 2011).

Center for Labor Market Studies at Northeastern University.

Center for Public Integrity.

Center for Responsive Politics (*opensecrets.org.*).

Center for Retirement Research at Boston College.

Centers for Medicare & Medicaid Services.

Centre on Budget and Policy Priorities.

Chronicle of Higher Education *(chronicle.com).*

CIA World Factbook (2010).

CNN.com.

cnngo.com (CNN Travel).

CNNMoney.com.

Coalition for the Homeless.

coli.org. (Cost of Living).

College Board.

Columbia Law Review.

Congressional Research Service.

constitutionfacts.com.

Council for Economic Research.

CSMonitor.com.

Current Population Survey.

dailycrowdsource.com.

Deadspin Report, news,msn,.com.

Death Penalty Information Center.

Economywatch.msnbc.

eiu.com (Economist Intelligence Unit) Employee Benefit Research Institute.

ExtremeTech.com.

Families & Work Institute.

Federal Election Commission.

Food Research and Action Center.

Forum.nationstates.net.

Foxnews.com.

Foxsports.com.

Gallup.com.

ga.water.usgs.gov/edu.

geography.about.com.

Giving USA Foundation.

Goodwin, D., *Lyndon Johnson and the American Dream* (1991).

Googlemaps.com.

Global Solutions at *gfmag.com.*

Gopconvention2012.com

guardian.co.u.k.

Halberstam, D., *The Best and the Brightest* (1972).

Halberstam, D., *The Fifties* (1993).

Hamilton Project at the Brookings Institute.

Hay Group (Consulting Firm).

Health Care Cost Institute.

heritage.org.

Honore, Carl, *In Prasie of Sklowness: How A Worldwide Movement Is Challenging the Cult of Speed* (2004) and *The Slow Fix: Solve Problems, Work Smarter and Live Better in a Fast World* (2013).

HuffingtonPost.com.

Hunger and Homelessness Survey released by the U.S. Conference of Mayors.

Infoplease.com.

insidehighered.com.

Kauffman Foundation Study (2011).

Lawyers' Committee for Civil Rights Under Law.

magazine.org.

Manchester, W. *The Glory and the Dream: A Narrative History of America 1932–1972*
        (1974).

miseryindex.us.

money.cnn.com.

moneyland.time.com.

monticello.org.

msn.travel.com.

n9jig.com.

National Alliance to End Homelessness.

National Association of Realtors.

National Association of School Nurses.

National Center for Education and National Center for Education Statistics.

National Center for Educational Studies.

National Center for Health Statistics.

National Center on Addiction and Substance Abuse at Columbia University.

National Climate Data Center.

National Coalition for the Homeless Reports.

National Council of Churches 2012 Yearbook.

National Education Association (*nea.org*).

National Employment Law Project.

National Golf Foundation.

National Institute for Early Education Research.

National Institute of Mental Health.

National Retail Federation (*nrf.com.*).

National Sleep Foundation.

National Vital Statistics Reports.

Natural Resources Defense Council.

Nbcnews.com.

NBCNewYork.com.

nbcpolitics.com.

New America Foundation Energy Trap Report.

newsconferences.php.

Nielsen Netview.

NPD Group.

oecd.org.; oecdebetterlifeindex.org;..

Office of Management and Budget *(*OMB at *whitehouse.gov/omb).*

Pew Hispanic Center; Pew Research Center; *Pew Research Center's Internet and
        American life Project.;* Pew Research Centers Project for Excellence in
        Journalism (2011 Data); Pew Social Mobility Project.

pisa2009.acer.edu. (OECD Programme for International Student Assessment).

Policyexchange.

Population Reference Bureau (PRB, including the World Population Data Sheet) *prb.org.*

presidency.ucsb.edu/data.

Proenglish.org.

Progressive Policy Institute.

Reach Advisors of the American Community Survey.

Reader's Digest (2013).

realestate.msc.com.

Reason.com.

Reuters/Ipsos Poll, February 20, 2013.

Roper Center—Public Opinion Archives.

Salon.com.

Sba.gov.com.(Small Business Administration).

Schlesinger, A., *A Thousand Days* (1965).

Schlesinger, A., *The Imperial Presidency* (1973).

Smart Media Group.

Social Security Administration.

State.gov.

stateofmedia.org.

TheDailyBeast.com.

The Economist: Pocket World in Figures, 2012.

Trulia.com.

Silver, N., *The Signal and the Noise: Why So Many Predictions Fail—But Some Don't* (2012).

unalaska-ak.us.

U.N. Department of Economic and Social Affairs, Population Division (World Urbanization Prospects—The 2011 Revision).

UNHCR.

United Nations Human Development Programme.

Urban Institute.

U.S. 2010 Project at Brown University.

U.S. Bureau of Alcohol, Tobacco, Firearms and Explosives Database.

U.S. Bureau of Labor Statistics.

U.S. Census Bureau (2010 Census Summary).

U.S. Census Bureau, 2009–2011 ACS Three-Year Estimates.

U.S. Census ACS Survey.

U.S. Citizens and Immigration Services.

U.S. Department of Commerce, Bureau of Economic Analysis, News Release, September 18, 2012. *bea.gov.*

U.S. Department of Education.

U.S. Department of Energy.

U.S. Department of Health and Human Services.

U.S. Energy Information Administration.

U.S. General Accounting Office.

U.S. Geological Survey Fact Sheet.

usgovinfo.com.

usnews.nbcnews.com.

U.S. National Oceanic and Atmospheric Administration.

U.S. Surgeon General's Office.

usgovinfo.about.com.

WealthX.com.

WebMD.com.

White House Office of National Drug Control Policy.

Wikipedia.com.

World Economic Forum's Global Competitiveness Report, Executive Opinion Survey, 2011—2012; World Economic Forum's Global Competitiveness Report (2012–2013) at *weform.org.*

World Bank (Population Data) and *data.worldbank.org.*

YouGov.com.

Index and
Topical Cross-References

Information in footnotes is indicated by the letter *n* in parentheses,
followed by note number.

Maryland *(cont.)*
  security cameras for traffic cameras
    in, 270
Massachusetts
  alimony law in, 287
  bullycide in, 346–347
  charter schools in, 214
  civil ticket for swearing in, 281
  death penalty abolished in, 151
  highest paid public employee in, 286
  low obesity percentage in, 248
  pet obesity center in, 270
  scenic drive in, 129
  school year in, increase in, 215
  state per student funding of colleges
    in, 207
Massachusetts Institute of Technology
    (MIT), 194, 197, 199, 200, 201
Massive open online courses (MOOCs),
    200–201, 352
Mass shootings, 157, 296
  average age of mass killer, 157
  average number per year, 157
  deadliest incidents since 1976, 157
  definition of, 157
  random, increase in, 157
Mass transit, 72
Maternal leave policies, 117–118
Mathematics
  academic performance in, 211–212
  STEM classes or STEM fields, 356
Mayan Apocalypse, 270
McAllen (Texas), 178
McAllester, M., 286
McCabe, Douglas, 165
McCarthy, Joe, 65–66, 73
McCartney, Paul, 74
McDonald's, 73–74, 271, 351
McGovern, George, 298
McGuire, A., 266
McGurn, W., 116, 282
McKay, B., 280, 290
McKinley, Mount, 129
McKinney, Michael, 202
McWhirter, C., 153, 295, 351
Meacham, J., 87(n.2), 311

Means, Russell, 298
Meat consumption, 228
Meckler, L., 140
Media
  bias in, 90–91
  critical evaluation of, as source, 89–91
  history and, 89
  journalism, 30–31
  objectivity in, 85
  perspective and, 90–91
  selection of, as sources, 91–92
  sorting role of, 91
  state of, 90
Median age
  of religious adherents, 313
  states with highest and lowest, 113
  U.S. and international comparisons, 113
Medicaid
  federal spending on, 227
  fraud, waste, and abuse in, 238
  number of Americans using, 238
  physicians not accepting patients, 238
Medical marijuana
  dispensaries closed in Los Angeles, 243
  legalization of, 243
  reasons for use, 243
Medical/medical services technology
  correlation to health-care costs, 238–239
  innovations in, 237
  iPad and tablet use by physicians, 238
Medical mistakes
  as cause of death, ranking of, 244
  number of annual deaths from and
    percentage of hospitalized
    patients suffering, 244
Medical schools
  foreign, graduates of, 230
  number of new in U.S., 230
Medical-training robots, 237
Medicare
  denial-of-payment appeals in, 239
  federal spending on, 227
  patient satisfaction and procedural
    metrics in, 239
Megacities
  number in U.S. in1970 *vs.* 2011, 181

Proms
    cost of, 286
    integration of, 308
Psy, "Gangnam style" video of, 292
Psychiatric beds, public, decline in,
        244–245
PTSD. *See* Post-traumatic stress disorder
Public K-12 schools
    attendance/absenteeism in, 215
    budget cuts on, 214
    charter, 214
    employment in, 215
    four-day school week in, 215
    gender segregation in, 215
    number of teachers and teacher-to-
        student ratio in, 215–216
    parent-trigger laws in, 215, 354
    perceived quality of, 216
    percentage of U.S. children in, 215
    school year in, increase in, 215
    teacher evaluation–test score linkage
        in, 215
    voucher use and results in, 216
Public libraries
    all-digital, first ever, 216
    digital books and e-readers in, 216
    number in U.S., 217
Pueblo (Colorado), 178
Puerto Rico
    Puerto Ricans in, *vs.* Puerto Ricans in
        U.S., 140
    urbanization of, 181
Pulitzer Prize, 291
Putin, Vladimir, 251, 272, 274

Q

Qatar
    immigrant population of, 121
    life expectancy in, 241
    male:female ratio in, 141
    obesity in, 247
    urbanization of, 181
Quality of life, 302–307
    basic conveniences, 302–303
    food and dining out, 303
    friendships and confidants, 303–304

Quality of life *(cont.)*
    happiest/most miserable states, 304–305
    mail delivery on Saturday, 304
    U.S. happiness, *vs.* other OECD
        nations, 305–306
    U.S., *vs.* other countries, 306–307
Quebec (Canada), assisted suicide/dying
        in, 249
Quinlan, Karen Ann, 249

R

Race and ethnicity, 117, 139–140,
        307–308
    admission preferences in colleges, 307
    arrests for violent crimes by, perceptions
        vs. reality, 148–149
    childbirths by, 117
    diversity in, 139–140
    Diversity Index of, 350
    diversity in judicial appointments, 307
    high school dropout rates by, 210, 308
    of homeless persons, 131
    incarceration rates of African
        Americans, 308
    largest minority group in U.S., 307
    in marriage, 136
    misperceptions of African Americans, 307
    of mother, and childbirths outside of
        marriage, 115
    newborns of white or European
        ancestry, 308
    places lacking diversity, 140
    prison sentencing by, 159
    and religion, 308
    in 1950s, 79–80, 80(n.54)
    segregation by, 308
    of shooting and murder victims in New
        York City, 159
    U.S. population by, 140
Radicalization, 60
Radnofsky, L., 227, 248, 267
Rajaratnam, Raj, 156
Raleigh (North Carolina), 177
Rancho Sante Fe (California), 183
Randomized, controlled studies, 99
Rankin, Jeannette, 51(n.3)